OUR FATHERS' FIELDS

A Southern Story

OUR FATHERS' FIELDS

A Southern Story

James Everett Kibler

When once thou shalt be able now to read the
glories of heroes and thy father's deeds, and to
know virtue as she is, slowly the plain shall grow
golden with the soft corn-spike, and the
reddening grape trail from the wild briar, and
hard oaks drip dew of honey.

—Virgil, *Eclogue 4*

UNIVERSITY OF SOUTH CAROLINA PRESS

Library of Congress Cataloging-in-Publication Data

Kibler, James E.
    Our fathers' fields : a southern story / James Everett Kibler.
      p. cm.
    Includes bibliographical references and index.
    ISBN 1–57003–214–9
    1. Hardy family.   2. Newberry County (S.C.)—Biography.
  3. Newberry County (S.C.)—Social life and customs.   I. Title.
CT274.H36K53   1998
929'.2'0973—dc21   97–50376

To the Memory of My Father
(1918–1996)

and to the People of Tyger

CONTENTS

Contents

ILLUSTRATIONS

Here, traveler, scholar, poet, take your stand
When all those rooms and passages are gone.

—Yeats, "Coole Park, 1929"

PROLOGUE

One of the first questions readers of this chronicle have asked is how I "relate" to the members of the families that are the main characters here. My relationship is neither by blood nor, sadly to say, more than casual acquaintance. I do, however, live in their family home; and dwelling in a place with such long history of impress of lives upon it, does serve to provide its own kind of kinship and bond. While the current descendants of these families have provided cordial encouragement through the gracious granting of interviews and the providing of letters, ledgers, and other documents, the volume before you was suggested not by them, but instead on the occasion of one of those violent summer tempests and spectacular electrical displays that only the Southern landscape can stage for dwellers on her hill and mountain tops. As I sat awed by the sight of the storm from an upstairs room, I watched the trees bending to the point of breaking, and wind-driven sheets of rain across the Tyger Valley and its blue folds of hills. During one of the worst heaves of storm, the old house shuddered on its foundations, and seemed to tense and brace itself. Lightning struck close by and a particularly fierce gust of wind brought brick and mortar dust whispering down the great chimney. A more terrific gust followed, and the wind dislodged an object from behind the high mantel to fall onto the hearth and roll slowly but surely across the room to the foot of my chair. Even in the grey-green light of the storm, I could clearly make out what the object was.

It was an antique stylus, a black-shanked pen with a still sharpened steel point, still shiny as if used only the day before. Some of its blue-black ink remained clotted on it—so well-preserved it had been after falling and lodging behind the mantel there in the last century. As is strangely often the case with those in such an odd circumstance, I made

1

little of the occasion, thinking to myself, "Well what about that!" Off-handedly, I tossed the pen on the nearest table and put it out of sight and mind as the skies cleared and a slender silver ribbon of mist began to rise from the river in the valley below. In the light of that bright late summer afternoon, I went on with my task of picking the tomatoes and okra for the family gumbo.

The pen remained for a time on the table, and then at the inkwell of the open secretary. For an author trained to see the symbolism of events, it took a remarkably long time to fathom the significance of both that moment and the pen the storm bore to my feet, and of whose pen it likely was, and of how it came to me, there in my first year of occupancy of the old house. Several months after that stormy summer afternoon in 1989, I first dipped the stylus and wrote a few jottings of my reactions to the place and some intuitions I was having about it—also some measurements of ceiling heights, room sizes, and the like . . . jottings that sounded right, thus accompanied by the scratchings of the sharp stylus-point against paper. Nothing fits the hand so comfortably as an old pen, admirably shaped to the human curve. Nothing better punctuates the act of writing with the proper rhythms, than a measured dipping into its well. I must admit, however, that the old pen soon gave way to its modern cartridged counterpart in the unfolding of this narrative. But the story's first words were in a sense penned by the summer storm; and five years of subsequent penning have led to this completion and fruition, like the bearing of a successful crop, carefully planned, planted, nurtured, harvested, and hopefully now to be of use. No good crop can be grown without good soil, carefully prepared by others gone before and in partnership with nature, then augmented and cared for by one's own. I have had very fertile soil bequeathed to me in this place I live, and in many more ways than one. The old lush and overgrown boxwood garden attracted me here and fixed me to the place when the house and land were in danger of destruction. The regular circling visitation of a particular large red tailed hawk and its cries high in the valley sky overhead drew me back and pinned me to its doorsteps. The deep loam of the place succeeded in convincing a mind that did not really want to take on such a dubious big project of house restoration. But I was strengthening my ties with the county of my birth, and of both my parents and our German and Irish forebears going back six generations there, and of my native state, where Huguenot ancestors Jacques Varin of Rouen and his wife Susanne Horry of Neufchâtel had first set foot on the continent in 1680 as part of a farming venture to help establish the infant Carolina colony by the planting of vineyards and the making of olive oil, silk, and wine. So the choice was not an idle one, nor one done on a whim, but instead a necessary and fitting coming home.

I have always been the quiet but enthusiastic champion of the silent, of those who do not have the confidence or gift of articulation, of those who are filled with the great treasure-hoard of feelings and responses which yet cannot find their way into words, and, most particularly, of those long dead, whose stories have not been told and whose tales can only be communicated *to* the living *by* the living. That, then, was the message of the storm's pen, falling, loosened and released from behind the high mantel where it had lain quiet until its time had come. It had converged most literally with my path and destiny. What does one do with such a pen? Does one put it in a display case as an artifact from a former century to be looked at through glass, make of it a neat curiosity to place among the antiques? Or does one let it speak the voices of the silent? The fate of the storm's pen has been to do the latter. In providing tongue to those of this particular family, long since in the dust, it has also given voice to many families of this place and region whose stories shadow theirs. In short, the story chronicled here *had* to be told. It unfolded itself as surely, naturally, and steadily as pen rolled to my feet. In the doing, both pen and its holder have been only the instruments of time.

My relationship to this particular family then? Well, they *are* my family after all, as they may also prove to be the reader's; and their story and that of this place is a long one whose ending is yet to be.

Hardy Plantation
Maybinton, South Carolina
24 June 1997

1

A Land Called Amoy-és-chek

To view a new-arising Land
A Land, whose fertile Plains,
And peaceful shady woods
May well demand your loftiest Strains.
  —John Markland, Virginia, 1730

Before the white man came, the Cherokee called the River Tyger *Amoy-és-chek*, from a fable about a bear and a panther that fought to the death on its steep banks. The panther killed the stronger animal but was so weakened in the fierce struggle that it also perished. Such was the Indian legend pointing a moral. Then the new race gave *Amoy-és-chek* a simpler European name, possibly after the Tygart family who settled early along its banks; but this name was itself soon altered owing to the large number of "tygers" (or panthers) that still stalked their prey in the rich valley, a name that harkened back to the Indian original.

The hilly dark lands of Tyger were formed from an ancient plateau carved slowly over the centuries by the swift *Amoy-és-chek*, the *Es-waw-púd-dee-neh* (Broad), and the gentle but deep *Eń-o-rée*. The Cherokee nation, whose territory this was, had also named these watercourses. *Es-waw-púd-dee-neh* signified "line"—the boundary separating Cherokee and Catawba hunting grounds to the east. *Eń-o-rée* meant "river of muscadines," a stream along whose banks this grape still flourishes luxuriantly.

The aboriginal forest through which these waters flowed was ancient indeed, being part of the area protected from destruction by the great mountains during the Glacial Age, and thus a remnant of the original pre–Ice Age wood. As such, it was a section of the oldest forest in America, in its pristine splendor comprised of huge hardwoods and intermittent giant pines so thick that no underbrush could grow beneath them, and yet spaced so far apart that a herd of deer or flock of turkeys could be seen from afar as in an open park. Its trees and flowers were so richly diverse that they surpassed in number the total existing in the whole of Europe. Only along the open waterways was there sufficient light to allow such vines as the muscadine, fox grape, and scuppernong. The rich river and creek bottomlands were often filled with evergreen cane thickets that sometimes reached thirty feet in height. In places, prairies made open vistas that relieved the sameness of wood, these covered waist-high in the pink wild flowering pea that sustained herds of buffalo. Game abounded. The Cherokee, and ancient tribes long before them, used these fertile forest and prairie lands for hunting grounds; and judging from the great number of spear and arrowheads still to be found over them, one must conclude that they were indeed well hunted. The game included deer, elk, buffalo, wolf, black bear, "tyger," bobcat, raccoon, turkey, opossum, beaver, mink, and muskrat. The streams abounded in sturgeon, rockfish, shad, herring, trout, perch, cat, and pike, while the air teemed with flocks of parakeets and herons. Wild pigeons were so numerous that they broke giant oak limbs from the pressure of their weight. Ducks and geese fed by the thousands in the lowlands. Red tailed hawks took their occasional rabbit and field mouse; but reigning over all was the majestic bald eagle, which in 1820 could be remembered by the oldest inhabitants of the valley as once a common sight—and awesome in size, measuring "eight feet from wing tip to wing tip." The large raven was often seen, as were its cousins the rain crows, the former long since disappeared, the latter still sounding their melancholy cries as harbingers of spring or summer showers. All in all, but for the violent summer tempests, this was a silent, unchanging land, where time touched the hills gently and the sun brooded alternately on a misty landscape of morning river fogs or bright and crystal-clear noons.

With the coming of Europeans in the 1750s, however, the stage was set for a startlingly new chapter in the chronicles of this land. In this saga, the red man would depart, the final eagle be killed for destroying the white man's pigs and sheep, all the parakeets slain for ruining his peaches, and the pigeons hunted to extinction. Finally, the very last of the tygers that had inspired red and white men alike to name their river after them, would itself, according to the white man's written history, be killed on Indian Creek, a stream so named after a Cherokee village upon its banks, and now too vanished like the river mists of the valley burned away by the rising sun. After 1780 red hunter and his tyger prey, in the language of the old poem, were both become "shades," and their memories only remained in the placenames and legends of the white race.

In November of 1786, a tract along the branch already known as Peters Creek, a southern tributary of the Tyger—the land that was eventually to become the nucleus of the Hardy family plantation—passed from the hands of Thomas and Elizabeth Gordon into the ownership of Thomas and Phoebe Hardy. The original plot consisted of 204 acres, being part of a larger parcel granted by King George III of England to George Robinson on 13 October 1756, one year after Governor James Glen's treaty with the Cherokee Nation opened this part of the back-country to serious settlement. From 1759 to 1761, however, the Cherokee launched raids upon the valley in which pioneers of both sexes and all ages were killed; and a time of lawlessness then followed the new peace of 1761. It was a most unstable period. Robinson conveyed his land to John Mitchel Sr., whose children (John Jr. and Elizabeth Mitchel Campbell) sold it in turn to the Gordons just after Christmas 1785. The Gordons, while only keeping this particular tract for less than a year, were permanent settlers across the Tyger from the Hardys; and one of them eventually married into the family. Although they have since moved away in our time, their name is still remembered through nearby Gordon's Bridge, built shortly after 1800 on the lower Tyger, a place-name that had become a landmark, significant by 1860 as the spot for Sunday evening "Pick-Nick" gatherings. The deed to the 204–acre tract in 1786 also mentioned the conveyance to the Hardys of "Peters old Cabbin." Who this Peters was is a mystery, but he was doubtless an early pioneer settler of the mid–eighteenth century whose name has dropped from the records. The creek, however, happily, still bears his name, as does the road that crosses it. Already when the Hardys purchased the land in 1786, it was called a Plantation and consisted of both hardwood forest and land in tillage. It cost in that year 191 pounds, 9 shillings.

Unlike the three families before them in the short span of white ownership, the Hardy family was to remain on the soil for two centuries and become prosperous stewards of it. Theirs was not the New England Puritan ideal of John Winthrop's City on a Hill, but instead the Southern dream of a fertile, pleasant valley. In this, the Hardys realized their aim, for the land of Tyger was in many ways a perfect rendering of the agrarian ideal. By the year 1860, after seventy years under their good and steady management, the plantation would grow from 204 to 2,035 acres, eventually to stretch to the banks of the Tyger and number among the most valuable farm acreage in the South. It was a green land blessed with the fertility of field and forest.

What the first Hardys found, however, was a scorched and sparsely settled community not yet recovered from the late war with Britain that had ended but five years before. The nineteenth-century chronicler John Belton O'Neall described their Tyger valley in the 1780s as anything but pleasant. It lay "wasted; families were in poverty and want." Nine heads of families had died in various ways from the war: two imprisoned by the British at Ninety-Six, one on a prison ship in Charleston, and one of smallpox and exposure. No doubt the 191 pounds that the Hardys brought to the Gordons helped relieve what was a dire situation.

Who were these pioneer Hardys that took up and tilled the war-torn land? Both their deed to the original tract as well as family tradition tell us that they came from Lunenburg County in southern Virginia. There they may have known the Gordons, for a branch of that family was also prominent in Lunenburg. One can conjecture that it was through this contact that the Hardys learned of this new land in the first place. More significantly, however, the eldest daughter of the family, Elizabeth, had married her cousin Samuel Hardy in 1782 and moved to Union District just across the Tyger from where they bought their land. With their migration to Carolina, the family would again be reunited.

The original settlers in Newberry County were Thomas Hardy Sr. and his wife, Phoebe Jeter. In 1932 their ninety-one-year-old great-grandson, William Dixon Hardy, could sit on the porch of the Hardy home and say that these first settlers came with eight children, "the youngest on a sidesaddle with her mother," riding on horseback from Lunenburg County down through the woods of the Carolinas to Newberry County, where they "built a log cabin on a beautiful knoll several hundred yards from the Old Columbia Road," near its intersection with the main highway between Pennsylvania and Georgia—that is, the Great Philadelphia Wagon Road of the eighteenth century. Captain

Dick, as the old gentleman was then called, also stated that it was in this cabin on the old coach road that this "first generation grew to manhood." The entourage included wagons of personal belongings, farm tools, livestock, and eleven or more slaves.

In Virginia the Hardys had been part of a very large and moderately prosperous family with some just claim to illustrious parentage. They traced their ancestry to the Norman knight le Hardi, who was the first of their name to come across the channel from France to "the greater pastures of England for their cattle and horses," arriving with William the Conqueror in 1066. As the French Hardys chronicle it, a Hardy rode "next to William at Hastings." In England the family became notable as farmers, horsemen, and landed gentry in Dorset and Westmorland beginning in the eleventh century, and were later known for naval service, with portraits of several of their distinguished line hanging in the Greenwich Naval Gallery. It was in the arms of Sir Thomas Hardy, flag captain on board the *Victory* at Trafalgar, that Admiral Nelson spoke his last words and died, a story well known to English schoolchildren. Earlier, in the mid-1500s, Sir John de Hardy was Lord Mayor of London. Sir John was descended from Sir John de Hardy of Bedfordshire and Lady Margaret, daughter of Michael de la Pole, a younger son of the Earl of Suffolk. Sir John, Lord Mayor, married Lady Mary de Stanley, whose ancestry included lords, ladies, the Dukes of Earl and of Westmorland, princes, barons, and seven kings of Scotland (from the years 942 to 1214). One of these sovereigns was King Duncan I MacCrinin, murdered by Macbeth on 14 August 1040. Other of Lady Mary's ancestors were John de Lacie, Magna Carta Baron, and William Malet, twenty-fourth in descent from Clovis, Sheriff of Somerset and Dorset, and also a Magna Carta Baron. Yet another of her family was Henry de Bohun, Earl of Hereford and Magna Carta Baron, fifth in line of descent from King Malcolm III of Scotland, and who died on pilgrimage to the Holy Land in 1220. Lady Mary was also lineally descended from Humphrey de Bohun VIII, Earl of Hereford and of Essex, Constable of England, born 1276 and slain 1332, and who married Isabel Plantagenet, daughter of King Edward I of England and Eleanor of Castile. Through their parentage on the distaff side, the Hardys could thus trace their lineage to King Edward. Through her descent from Lady Joan, daughter of John of Gaunt (son of King Edward III), they were likewise doubly lineal descendants of that monarch. Sir John de Hardy, Lord Mayor of London, by his marriage alliance to the de Stanleys, thus gave the future

Hardys of this union claim to royal blood, no matter how distant and diluted, for the seven Scottish sovereigns and the two King Edwards were no mean ancestral boasts.

The founder of the Hardy family in America was another John Hardy, who was born in Yorkshire, England, in 1613 and immigrated from Bedfordshire with his wife, Olive Council, whom he had married in England in 1632. He was settled in Isle of Wight, Virginia, by the year 1666. His sons had preceded him to the colony, where two of them played important roles in shaping its government and thereby in founding republican government in the New World. His children numbered six: (1) Col. John Hardy Jr. (1637–1677), a member of the Virginia House of Burgesses; (2) Olive; (3) Capt. George Hardy Sr. (died 1655), who came to Virginia as a shipwright, was a member of the House of Burgesses and a staunch supporter of the Anglican Church, and whose descendant Samuel Hardy was a member of the Continental Congress; (4) Richard Hardy Sr. (1640–1734), who married Mary Vincent of Virginia in 1694, and from whom the Hardys of Tyger River trace their lineage; (5) Lucy, who married Hodges Council; and (6) Deborah.

The first ancestor of the Hardy family of Tyger River to be born in Virginia was Richard Jr., son of Richard and Mary Vincent Hardy, who was born in 1699 in Isle of Wight, and thence removed to Lunenburg. He married Mary Covington of Amelia County, Virginia, and they had nine children. The eldest was Thomas Hardy Sr. (1732–1814), the progenitor of this branch of the family on Tyger River in South Carolina. At the age of forty-four, Thomas served in the Revolution with General Washington. His wife, Phoebe Jeter, was also born in Lunenburg and was nine years his junior. Many of her Anglo-Norman Jeter family likewise migrated to nearby Union District, South Carolina, where her patronym continues to be prominent. In 1768 Thomas and Phoebe lived in Nottoway Parish, Amelia County. When they sold 200 acres in Nottoway in that year, Thomas signed, but Phoebe "made her mark." Their first child had been born in 1762 and by 1782 they had nine more. Of their ten offspring, eight survived to come to Carolina, seven with their parents, as the great-grandson recalled a century and a half later. As we have seen, another, their eldest, Elizabeth, was already living on the Tyger with her new husband, Sam Hardy, the son of Thomas's brother William, when the rest of her family made the move. Thomas's eldest son, David, born in 1764, was said to have died young in Virginia.

Thomas Jr. (1767–1823), the third child, was one of the heirs to the Hardy land on the Tyger and a progenitor of the line. In 1810 he married Anna Powell Dixon, who like himself had been born in Lunenburg. She was then living in Person County, North Carolina, just over the state line from Lunenburg, and where the marriage took place. In Virginia, in fact, the Hardys and Dixons had been neighbors; and now they were once again, for some of the Dixons had also immigrated to South Carolina by way of Person County. When they took up land to the east of the Hardys, the old Virginia neighborhood appeared to be resurrecting itself beside a different river, with customs and ties holding firm, a distillation and remembrance of old Virginia times long gone.

The fourth child, James, was born in 1769, and eventually moved to Anderson County, South Carolina, some time after 1814. He became a minister. The fifth child, Freeman, was born in 1771, married Sara Rutherford, moved to Georgia around 1815, and died in 1848 in Dallas County, Alabama, where his two sons had numerous progeny. Mary, the sixth child, was born in 1773 and married her Tyger River neighbor Jesse Gordon. They also moved to Alabama. The seventh child, John Wesley (1776–1806), married Nancy Eppes of Newberry County. He was also an heir to the land in Carolina, and with his brother Thomas Jr., became co-progenitors of the line, for one of his sons in 1828 married his first cousin, Thomas Jr.'s heiress daughter, thus uniting the two branches of the family into single ownership of the Hardy lands and plantation. The eighth child, Nancy, was born in 1778 and married the Reverend George Clarke of Enoree River, to whom she bore six children, one of whom married back into the Hardy family. The ninth child, Susannah, born in 1780, married a neighboring Tyger River Crenshaw and moved to Alabama. The youngest, Phoebe, born in 1782, married a Reynolds and moved to Georgia. She was the infant who rode to Carolina on horseback with her mother.

But the story is getting ahead of itself; we must first return to Virginia, the previous century, and the Carolina pioneer Thomas Hardy Sr., in order to consider the Virginia "begats" of his ancestry. Of the younger siblings of this Thomas, the first was John Sr. (c. 1740–1799) born in Isle of Wight, Virginia, and married in 1773 to Ann Williams. The couple and their seven children were living in Edgefield District, South Carolina, by 1785. The second was Covington. The third, William (who died in 1790), was also a Revolutionary War soldier like his brother Thomas. He entered service in February 1779 and returned from battle to Lunenburg. One of his four children was the aforementioned Samuel, who had married his uncle Thomas's daughter Elizabeth and had come to Tyger River in 1782. Another of William's sons, Thomas, born in 1748, went to Kentucky with his wife Mary Isham. His third son, Covington, remained in Lunenburg, and it is from him that the current Hardys of Lunenburg descend. Pioneer Thomas Hardy Sr.'s other brothers and sisters were Samuel, Stith, Mary, Benjamin, (who moved to North Carolina), and Richard III, who remained in Isle of Wight. Little is known of them. The name of another sibling has not come down to us.

Like so many Virginia families of their day, the Hardys were scattered across a quarter of the new continent by 1800 and by 1850 would be spread to Mississippi, Louisiana, Arkansas, and Texas. The family had moved from France to England in the eleventh century and then across the Atlantic to another new world in the seventeenth. Moving and starting over "for greater pastures" for their cattle, sheep, and horses was in their blood, a pattern handed down to them by family. Such a venture a few hundred miles southward into Carolina may have given the eighteenth-century Hardys some momentary pause, but the idea did not frighten them. Picking up and striking out for new land and on new adventures almost seemed more natural to them than staying put. It had now been a part of the family's history and heritage for seven centuries. Le Hardi and Hardy, they could no doubt have faced one another with understanding across the centuries, and likely far better than the urban twentieth-century family could comprehend its agrarian forebears of less than a century ago. But that is another story.

2

The Sweet Fields of Eden

The branch cannot bear fruit of itself,
except it abide in the vine.
—St. John, XV

Thomas Hardy Sr. had seen the Revolution end and the colonies break their ties with Britain. He was forty-four when the great war began and had immediately volunteered his services that first year in Jonett's Seventh Virginia Regiment commanded by Colonel McClenachan. He survived his war service, was discharged in 1778 owing to age, and now at fifty-three was beginning a new life by pulling up and moving south to live near his eldest child, who had gone several years before. He had a family of eight children, some full-grown in their teens and twenties. It was for them and the younger ones that he was striking out for richer soil that could be had more abundantly in these new pioneering regions. And these lands bounded by the Tyger, Broad, and Enoree, although torn by the late war, were an island of richness: the game superabundant, the deep rivers full of fish, the topsoil mostly a dark deep woodsy loam, the subsoil mixed, red-clay in places, a tawny gold clay and silty clay loam in others, the hardwood forests full of oaks—the red, black, white, Spanish, upland, swamp, post, and overcup—abundant with black and white walnut, black gum and sweet gum, birch, elm, alder, and ash. The autumn hills blazed with maple, sourwood, tulip poplar, hickory (big-bud, pignut, scalybark, and white), the cucumber tree, chestnut, spicewood, sassafras, dogwood, and haw. Among holly, cedar, redbud, buckeye, pawpaw, cottonwood, styrax, tripetala magnolia, service, cherry, and witch hazel, grew intermittent scatterings of both long and shortleaf pines, the forest running down to riverbottoms covered with tall canebreaks. The woods floor was brightened by gentian, wild ginger, trillium, cardinal flower, snakeroot, wintergreen, ginseng, coltsfoot, spikenard, sweet annies, wild azalea, sweetshrub, and dozens of other wildflowers, some of which the Hardys knew from Virginia, but many new and strange which they did not. It was truly a beautiful land, and virgin.

When they started their journey south in 1785, Thomas's wife Phoebe was forty-four years old. Thomas Jr. was eighteen; James, fourteen; Mary, twelve; John Wesley, nine, and born in the year the war began; Nancy, seven; and Susannah, five. The least child was three. Down the Great Wagon Road, they made their long trek through the tall forests of the Carolinas, passing new hamlets on the build, Salem and Salisbury, Charlotte, Rock Hill, and Chester. It took their caravan over a month, traveling as they did ten miles a day in good weather. From beneath their broad Virginia bonnets, the women of the family peered with wide eyes. Behind the family followed the livestock and several wagons full of household goods, farm tools, and belongings. These were in the keeping of eleven or more Hardy slaves who had no choice but to start this venture and new lives with the white family. The fortunes and destiny of both master and bondsman were inextricably bound from the start. These shared experiences were yet another common bond that intertwined their lives.

The Gordon tract that Thomas had just purchased was not a howling wilderness or raw with the tygers that gave the river its name. The Hardys arrived on it the year Newberry County was divided from the old Ninety-Six District and its seat of government was being established some twenty miles distant. Their daughter Elizabeth already lived less than four miles away. The Lisles family had a two-story dwelling a quarter of a mile from where Thomas and his family were to build their own. The Lisleses had been there since before the Revolution, so there would already be neighbors to lend them a helping hand and to call on in times of need. These hearty Lisleses were also of Virginian stock and had been true pioneers in every sense of the word during the days of Indian scalpings and real hardships. Like the Hardys, they had sent fathers and sons (two of them called "Big Ephraim" and "Big Bill") into the fray for American independence. They were the pioneering tall men who first greeted the raw country, who took the rifle from the chimney crotch to defend liberty, hearth, and home—stalwart, robust souls who had perhaps never heard the name Runneymede, but who understood its principles well and, like the Hardys, put their lives on the line to defend them. "Little Eph" Lisles had been at Cowpens to give the British a licking. These strong men would indeed be comforting to have as close neighbors. There was a trading post run by Irish immigrants, the Maybins, about two miles off, and the famous Bishop Francis Asbury himself had promised a Methodist meetinghouse for the neighborhood. Even on their own Hardy lands, as we have seen, there was already a rude dwelling called "Peters old Cabbin," and some of the land was already cleared and tilled, so Thomas and his family were only in a limited sense pioneers, and would not be starting life completely fresh. He could not really afford to at his age. He well knew that pioneering was best suited for the young. Two hundred and four acres would provide a goodly beginning; and with energy, wise management, and thrift, he and his sons could add to their holdings. Yes, he and Phoebe would be founding a family seat for their children. This was now home. And life would not be solitary. Besides the Lisleses to his north, were the Crenshaws to his west, the Maybins to his south, and the Gordons to his northeast; many Hardy cousins were even now far flung in Carolina from Union to Edgefield or else planning their moves to settle there.

The enterprise on Tyger was essentially a family venture like most of these Virginian migrations. The Hardys of the Old Dominion had equipped, supplied, and given moral support and encouragement for their move; and the ties to Lunenburg would remain strong. Thomas and his brood were merely colonizing extenders of the family name into more fertile southern grounds; and in that way the family would grow and increase its sphere while peopling this new land with Christian values. "Be fruitful and multiply" was the Good Book's command.

Indeed, the old ties with the Lunenburg Hardys and their Virginia community would hold, and the family within two decades reach west into the rich Georgia and Alabama frontiers. And everywhere they went they would stamp the new land with Virginian ways as interpreted by their own particular family customs and rituals. They were not Scots-Irish, as were most of the settlers taking up land with and around them. They descended from English landed gentry and the Lord Mayor. They knew their ties to King Edward. In the American new world, their family customs had consistently been Church of England and their political principles those of Runneymede and Magna Carta. Their personal values were Christian chivalric. In his own day, the pioneering French knight le Hardi had not conquered in vain, and it was no accident that one of their ancestors had died on a knight's pilgrimage to the Holy Land in the year 1220. Questing had always been in their blood; new ventures exhilarated and brought them to life. They were more or less aware of all this in their stalwart way; and it was good to have that same family blood nearby in nephew and son-in-law Samuel. Thomas would have been truly gratified if he could have looked into the future and seen Samuel and his Elizabeth the parents of four daughters, two of whom (Mary and Henrietta) would in turn marry the Eppes brothers, Daniel and William, and whose sister Nancy Eppes would eventually also marry one of his (Thomas's) own sons. The Eppeses were a family of Welsh ancestry who had likewise come to Carolina from Lunenburg, where they had also been neighbors of the Hardys in that close-knit society. In fact, even before leaving the Old Dominion, the two families had intermarried. It was this same son-in-law Samuel Hardy whom the old pioneer would choose as executor of his estate in 1814 as he approached death at the goodly age of eighty-two, and after twenty-eight years in Carolina.

Like Thomas, Samuel's father had served in Virginia in the Revolution, and Thomas knew the mettle of both father and son, a knowledge that gave comfort and a feeling of security to his mind here among strangers in an unknown land, a mind which in its fifty-third year was getting more set in its ways, and he too old to undertake such rigorous new adventures as this, no matter how good they would be for the children. Yes, this would be his last move. He was sure of that. He would die and be buried by the Tyger. The music of its cold deep waters out of the mountains and hills of Carolina was already sweet to him, a home at last, past the disruptions of war and horseback moves. He and Phoebe, God willing, would not have to pick up and strike out again.

Here the good soil would sustain them. The growing seasons were so long they could sometimes get in two crops to the one they were used to in Virginia. Along the rich bottomlands of Peters Creek and the alluvial floodplains of Tyger, the dense canebrakes were perfect for the foraging cattle, which soon learned to walk down the thirty-foot-tall stalks to feed upon them. Neither fence nor sheltering barn was necessary here, for the thick evergreen brakes and cedar thickets provided excellent winter protection from wind and freezing rain; and unlike

Virginia, it was a gentler climate and did not often sleet and snow. The livestock were thus as free as the people to roam at will. Thomas's cows numbered forty or more by the time of his death in 1814.

When some of these canebrakes were cleared, they yielded a fertile soil that grew excellent tall corn with great bulging ears. And the Hardys did this clearing, planting not only corn but also all the other crops that would make them self-sufficient: wheat, oats, cane, and cotton. Precisely when the family first came to grow cotton is unknown; but when they did, they planted it on the uplands, while still reserving the moist bottomlands for grain crops, as was the case generally in upcountry Carolina—the custom of their new home.

The Hardys, both black and white, soon went to work side by side with broadax and crosscut saw and raised a new, larger cabin of square-hewn logs on a pleasant high knoll that looked out over hilly lands to the three river valleys. The line of blue-green hills to the north across the Tyger and into the District of Union had a haze on them, and the ribbon of mists rising from the river allowed the eye to follow its deep track for several miles in the distance to where it flowed into the Broad. It was a breezy, healthy, high spot for a house and several yards from the main Granby-Charleston Road, which they could see through the homespun curtains of their front window. This was also a major road from Charleston to the mountains; and nearby, it intersected with a major migration route from Pennsylvania and Virginia to Augusta, Georgia, and points west. This route passed through the raw new county-seat hamlets of Chester and Newberry and was the route the Hardys themselves had used to get to their new home. Before the white man came, these roads had been Indian peltry trails, and even before that, deer paths. Now they, like the Tyger (on which the boatmen poled their flats to the Broad and hence to market), were major arteries for people and commerce. The Tyger was navigable to a five-foot fall some eight miles from its confluence with the Broad, well upriver from their plantation and its landing. The Broad itself was navigable for boats carrying fifty to sixty 400-pound bales of cotton. They were blessed to have such fine avenues to the world. On the road to the Hardy cabin, traders traveled from the mountain districts in covered wagons loaded with pelts, apples, and chestnuts—headed for Charleston. By their cabin's doorsteps, farmers drove their flocks of turkeys or rolled their hogsheads of tobacco for shipping from the busy port, and would then return, climbing toward their mountain home with bright cones of sugar, salt, crockery, and tinware. Like the Hardys, other settlers were using the road to go south and west. Every year brought more wagon traffic as the ruts cut deeper into the impressionable soil. All this they witnessed from their front windows, the pageant of the settling of a continent. The Upcountry was filling up and out and bustling. Fortunes were being made as the land was being settled and tilled, and the Hardys would play their part in the drama.

The men of the family, now in the prime of life, lent their sweat and muscle to bring the land into cultivation. They and their black bondsmen worked side by side to erect great barns of broadax smoothed timber which they felled in the great virgin hardwood forest. These they roofed with froh-cut oak and cedar shingles. They got everything they needed from the bountiful land itself and began to live the life of the self-sufficient Southern pioneer, making their own furniture, baskets, barrels, soap, and candles, blacksmithing their own tools, spinning their own cloth, tanning their own leather, raising livestock, hunting in an area in which it was said that one could "stand in his own door and kill more game" than was sufficient to feed two families, living off the good land.

Two documents from 1806 and 1814 that have come down to us suggest much about what the plantation household's activities must have been at the close of the 1700s. These are the inventories of appraisement and sale of the estates of Thomas Sr., the old pioneer, and of his youngest son John Wesley, who until his death in 1806, had lived with his young family on the Hardy land which his father had divided for him.

The inventory of John Wesley's estate, made 23 August 1806, when he was thirty years old, lists eight head of cattle, fifty-two hogs, one horse, two "cotton spinning wheels," two pairs of "cotton cards," fourteen geese, and three beehives. The presence of cotton cards and wheels shows that by 1806 the Hardys were already growing this crop. The geese, no doubt, existed for the purpose of filling the three feather beds also listed in the appraisement. (This is no small matter, for some pioneer settlers slept on straw or cornshuck mattresses.) There was "a parcel of books," thus suggesting the family's literacy. Their little luxuries included coffee, tea, and sugar. They owned two trunks, seven chairs, "cupboard ware" of iron, wood, and copper, a wire sifter, two candlesticks, candle snuffers, and candle chisels, a parcel of knives and forks, a table, the aforementioned feather beds, two bedsteads and a cot for the little one, jugs, a tin bucket and a bandbox, four saddles, four bridles, a set of razors, and a "smooth-bore gun" for hunting. The young family was obviously just making a good start, but had already achieved some modest substance in their world.

The estate also included eight slaves: Amey and her two children Anderson and Henry, Moriah and her son Tom, Rachael (who by 1809 had borne a son named Jack), a boy named Matt and a girl named Holley.

The 28 December 1814 list of the old pioneer's belongings runs to four pages. It is an important document for the early plantation history of the upcountry seaboard South in general, but most particularly tells us what must have been the major farm emphases before the new generation took over at the beginning of the nineteenth century. There are one mare, four colts, eight steers, four heifers, two bulls, and four yearlings, 4,331 pounds of cured pork, forty-nine hogs and nine pigs, eight sheep and a set of sheep shears, twenty-one geese, and three portions of tanned leather. There are 6,000 pounds of green-seed cotton, a parcel of cotton "still in the patch" estimated at 1,500 pounds, thirty bushels of wheat, forty barrels of corn, six stacks of fodder, six stacks of oats, a "Grits mill," 18.5 pounds of goose feathers, a still, and a spinning wheel and cards.

The combined lists of John Wesley and Thomas therefore show self-sufficiency and diversity, with a large number of hogs in both households, a moderate number of cattle, some geese, sheep, horses, and bee skeps and hives. Although corn, oats, and wheat were also staples, the plantation was raising much cotton by 1814—7,500 pounds on Thomas's land alone. Thus the Hardys followed the general pattern for Newberry County, in which after the introduction of Colonel Robert Rutherford's new Whitney cotton gin in 1796, Newberry farmers realized the potential of growing the upland green-seed, or short-staple, cotton, which rapidly became the chief crop of the district. By 1820 cotton was "indeed king in Newberry District," as its modern historian has recorded. The Whitney gin, coupled with the Hardys' early ownership of both slaves and some of the richest land in the county, made it natural that they would prosper. Their white gold found its way to Charleston and eventually into the holds of tall ships bound to Liverpool, where in northern England it was made into cloth that would clothe the people of many continents.

Judging from the 7,500-pound yield in 1814, and using Robert Mills's 1826 estimate that an average of from 150 to 250 pounds of ginned green-seed cotton is raised on one acre, we can assume that the old pioneer in the year of his death had a minimum of 10 to 17 acres of his plantation in cotton culture, yielding approximately six and a quarter 400-pound bales. Although cotton had become his staple crop and a significant proportion of his cultivated acreage was planted in it, it was far from monopolizing his operation. Mills noted in 1826 that peas, corn, and oats were extensively raised in the county for domestic consumption of man and beast; and this was true of the Hardy plantation, only here wheat replaced peas.

But the old pioneer's large emphasis on swine (with 4,331 pounds curing and another forty-nine live hogs) was out of the ordinary and equalled cotton's importance in providing both food for his family and slaves, and cash in sale. This was to become traditional for this particular plantation into the second and third generations, for the old pioneer's grandson, William Eppes Hardy, continued to raise pork both as a means to self-sufficiency and as a significant cash venture—though in the case of the latter, not in a manner equal to cotton. Yet one could not eat cotton, however, and was forced to sell the majority of it, in other words, that which the family did not weave into cloth for its own use; whereas a large plantation population consumed a great quantity of the pork it produced. Although more cotton found its way to market, the energy to get it there came from pork.

The cards and spinning wheels in both inventories prove activity in making cloth. The sheep and sheep shears do the same. There is no mention of flax, flax breakers, or flax hackles; and from this conspicuous absence we assume linen was not made on the place, although it was a popular product among the German pioneers of the lower county at this same time. At the son's house, his two wheels are specified as *cotton* wheels; his cards, *cotton* cards. (His father's are listed simply as "wheels and cards" and may have been for either cotton or wool.) The still reflects masculine taste for spiritous liquors. The Hardys, self-sufficient and apparently not teetotalers, made their own. Pioneer Thomas's estate listed nine slaves: two females (Dillar and Rose) and seven males (Manuel, Isham, Ben, James, Sirus, Sirus Jr., and Ephraim). It is likely that some of these men and women had come from Virginia with Thomas twenty-eight years ago.

The instruments of pioneer land clearing and log construction also show clearly in the list: several lots of axes (for cutting the timber and notching the logs), two hooks and chains (for rolling and dragging logs

already ranked in the middle of the economic scale in his planting community, but Thomas (only four years after his arrival there) was at the top, for Thomas, as we have seen, was not beginning from scratch, but rather out of the accumulated labor of four decades.

In the 1800 census, Thomas owned nine slaves, and his youngest son John Wesley had four. His family thus entered the plantation system in backcountry Carolina in much better than typical fashion, fielding from the outset a relatively greater number of black laborers, but still closely sharing the tasks of everyday life with their bondsmen, eating largely the same diet, dressing in the same homespun.

By 1850 the plantation would grow ten-fold to 2,035 acres operated by forty-six slaves, an overseer, and a white tenant family, with a total of fifty-nine mouths to feed. The master's family and slaves would no longer work and eat and dress the same. But this was in a later time when cotton had indeed become king. The eighteenth-century Hardy plantation was at this point only at the stage of feeling its way and learning what it was capable of, a time of sinking its roots deep, and of attempting to establish stability for all its people, whose lives depended directly upon the rich dark soil that made all possible.

3

A Brave New Century

The year 1800 found the plantation less than two decades old but, as a result of the introduction into the county of the cotton gin in 1796, with great prosperity on the horizon. Steady hard work and excellent management had begun to pay off as the Hardy sons and daughters came of age. By 1800 a canal, the first of its kind in the new world, was cut from the Santee River to the Cooper, facilitating getting goods from the Upcountry to the Charleston market. As the *Charleston Times* of 29 May 1801 could relate:

> We are happy to announce that Mr. William Buford who lives on the banks of the Broad near Pinckney Courthouse (92 miles above Columbia) arrived in this city on the 26th with his own boat built on his own land and loaded with his own crop. With further improvements to the tributaries of the Santee, the superabounding products of the upper country will flow into Charleston in such full tides and with so much expedition and so little expense, as will lower our market, and at the same time fill the pockets of our remote fellow citizens.

And such was the case with the Hardys. Their surplus crops now found their way down the Tyger and Broad to Charleston on flatboats, the cotton to be loaded at the docks for Liverpool. In 1748 the first American cotton had been shipped to England from Charleston; and now in 1820 South Carolina produced more cotton than any other state. In 1830 Hardy cotton bales were on one of the seventeen hundred flatboats that brought eight thousand bales to the city that year via the Santee Canal. The family was indeed "making it." They would survive, and from the promising look of things, with the new green-seed cotton, might even flourish. In 1800 the father was sixty-eight; his wife, fifty-nine. His eldest child, Elizabeth, now thirty-eight, was still living nearby. Two of his daughters still lived at home but were soon to marry. His eldest son Thomas Jr., thirty-three and as yet unmarried, lived at home; he would marry in 1810 and then play his part at age forty-five in the War of 1812, shadowing his father's own volunteering at forty-four for the first war with Britain. The pattern of family life through the generations repeated itself with a satisfying and stabilizing rhythm. Like his father, Thomas Jr. whipped the British, survived the war, and came home to farm and raise a family.

In 1800, James, thirty-one, and Freeman, twenty-nine, were no longer living at the plantation, having established homesteads of their own. At their father's estate sale in 1814, they purchased some slaves and livestock and would soon move westward, repeating the pattern of pioneer settlement once again. The youngest son, John Wesley, was twenty-four now, the father of an infant son, and living nearby. This child soon died, however, for their eldest living son in 1806, named Hamlin, was born in 1801. John Wesley's wife was Nancy Eppes, as we have seen, also from a Lunenburg family that had been neighbors of the Hardys in Virginia and already intermarried with them in the Old Dominion. Nancy, in fact, was related to the illustrious Thomas Jefferson, whose wife's mother was an Eppes and whose daughter Martha married an Eppes. Nancy's family had come to Carolina some time after the Hardys. She was a Methodist from the Mt. Tabor Methodist section of the Enoree (south of the present town of Whitmire) and was a close neighbor to the Finch and Shell families who had founded the famous Mt. Bethel Academy in the last century. Yes, the Hardys and the Eppeses had been neighbors and kin in Lunenburg, and here they were again together, again marrying, establishing the old comfortable cadences that provided a necessary stability to life in a new place. Now that their old Virginia neighbors, the Dixons, lived near the Hardys just a few miles across the Tyger and their own Hardy relations Samuel and Thomas were just a few miles away, they were all indeed succeeding in recreating their old world and making it possible to hold this society together into the future by means of complex family ties and complicated allegiances. Because of his recent marriage and the birth of an only heir bearing the family name, John Wesley, even though he was the youngest son, was favored by the father, a fact clearly indicated by his will.

In 1800 the census for Thomas Sr.'s household also lists two unnamed white females under ten years of age, and one between ten and sixteen. In addition, one of the daughters (between sixteen and twenty-six) was still in residence. So the family circle was indeed full, comprising father, mother, unmarried eldest son, two unmarried daughters, two children, and a young woman under sixteen. The cabin, although undoubtedly added onto in the usual ways with shed rooms, must have been bursting at the notches in sheltering five adults and three children.

So on the land, about a hundred yards from the old log house, as William Dixon Hardy recalled in 1932, the family began to build a new dwelling nearer the Charleston Road. This in around 1803 when the old pioneer was seventy-one. It was a two-story frame house of large, heavy, broadax-hewn pine timbers completed in 1804. The date brick, bearing the white numerals "18004" (presumably reflecting the way the builder said 1800 and 4), was saved from the old building when a section of it was removed in 1951, thus verifying Hardy's testimony in 1932 that the house was completed in that year. The old pioneer enjoyed his home for only ten years, for he died in 1814. He had accomplished much in his eighty-two years and his nearly three decades by the Tyger. The house was itself a symbol of this accomplishment and thus tells its own story.

The 1804 structure faced north toward the Tyger. It was sheathed in clapboard and had a single massive interior chimney of a mixture of brick types, some red, some highly-glazed dark gray. The bricks, if not made on the place itself, were likely fired at the kiln at nearby Orange Hall plantation. The footing base of this chimney is still to be seen beneath the remaining section of the 1804 house. In the late 1950s its bricks and those of the piers of the demolished section of the house were used by Mrs. John Frost Hardy Sr. and her grandson John Hardy III to construct the central walkway to the front portico of the house's 1825 section. In 1990 the remnants of the fallen chimney pile were used for the piers of the reconstructed back porch. These piers had been torn away in 1951, but their footings buried in the soil became the foundations for the new ones. The 1804 house is built on brick piers that elevate the structure approximately two and a half feet from the ground.

The 1804 dwelling had two rooms over two rooms backed by a shed room and rear porch that faced south. The house was a single room deep. Its stairwell was "narrow" and "turned twice," as recollected by Haywood Hardy Henderson. It was not elaborate but nicely made and "pleasant to look at." The rear shed room was for sleeping, and there were two upstairs bedrooms, thus making it a three-bedroom house. The large room downstairs was the central gathering place for the family. It was dominated by a central interior chimney. The floor plan can be recreated in this fashion:

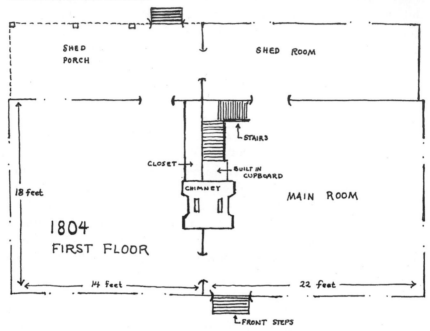

The two left (east) rooms still exist in the present structure and form its ell. In 1804, what William Dixon Hardy called the Columbia Road ran one or two hundred yards to the front of the house, thus beyond the present mule shed and harness barn on the north side of the house and across Pucpuggy Branch. Peters Creek Road was created only in the present century and skirts the south side of the garden.

From the evidence of the remaining upstairs room, one finds that this 1804 structure had hand-planed wooden ceilings. Around the walls under the ceiling ran a beaded board on which was surmounted a simple, deep crown molding painted buff. The walls were smooth-polished hard plaster over lathe, suggesting that the building was constructed at least partly by master builders, perhaps with the assistance of the Hardys. There were square wooden panels of wainscoting beneath each window.

This upstairs room, according to family tradition, was used in the early nineteenth century as a "traveler's room" for domiciling visitors. In true Southern fashion, the Hardys' doors were never closed to strangers. From all accounts they took hospitality seriously as a pleasant responsibility.

Today this room is unaltered and virtually intact. It has its original plaster, heart-pine flooring, black-stained baseboards, beaded crown molding, and buff paint on all moldings, wainscoting, and ceiling. Its pegged window sashes contain much of the original window glass (of eighteen window lights per window). The cavity where the central chimney ran into the attic is still visible. Around 1950, when the other rooms of the 1804 house had badly deteriorated, John Frost Hardy Sr. had them removed. The house thus began to shrink, quite graphically illustrating the reduced fortunes of the agricultural South in general and of this area in particular, and lending credence to the old Italian saying that "an old house is not a house, but a story." This one speaks volumes.

An interesting fact about the traveler's room is that Francis Asbury, America's first Methodist bishop, stayed here while preaching at nearby Ebenezer Methodist Church, which he helped bring into existence in the 1780s shortly after the Hardys arrived. The Hardy family was also instrumental in founding this early frontier church, and most of the family lie in its cemetery. Family tradition relates that Methodist meetings were held at the Hardy house before the first church building was built. In the 1960s John Frost Hardy Sr. still had the old metal lanterns said to have been used to light these meetings. In fact, Asbury was also a friend of the Hardys of Lunenburg, Virginia, for the first Methodist church in that area met in the granary of Covington Hardy's dwelling; and Covington, though an Episcopalian, donated the land to build Asbury's first church there. That Covington was pioneer Thomas Hardy Sr.'s nephew might be the reason this first Methodist church in upcountry South Carolina and the earliest in that southern part of Virginia were both established in these particular places—both within the shadow of Hardy family domiciles.

In his *Journal*, the good Bishop specifically reports staying with the Thomas Hardy family of Tyger River on at least two occasions. He likely continued to do so until his last trip to South Carolina in 1814. Asbury, traveling the circuit as strenuously as he did, must have provided welcome communication between the Virginia and Carolina branches of the family. What letters he must have carried back and forth! And what long fireside stories of family sayings and doings.

It is fortunate that the one room from the early house whose interior has been saved largely untouched, and even unrepainted, is this traveler's room where the bishop is likely to have slept. This chamber is now being restored as a library and guest room, thus bringing it back once again to its traditional use.

From the extant evidence, the 1804 dwelling measured 36 feet long by 18 feet deep, exactly twice as long as wide. The interior chimney provided heat for all four rooms and was capacious. Still to be seen on the front (north) side are the base stones for the steps to the front door. The door opened toward the Charleston Road and Tyger River.

It is easy to discern from looking at the floor joists exactly where the 1804 part of the dwelling ends and the 1825 section begins. In the 1804, the floor and ceiling joists run north-south; they run east-west in the 1825. The timbers are also larger in the 1804 section and are held together by 6- to 8-inch hand-carved wooden spikes fitted into auger holes. The brick foundation piers are massive throughout both sections and, along with the huge heart-pine timbers, are responsible for the house's remarkable solidity. Visitors remark that the floors never give or creak, nor does the great staircase; and this is owing to both the superior quality of the early building material and the expert building practices and craftsmanship of the time and place. The house demonstrates skill of a high level. The work done on it was obviously performed well and with pride and taste. Who its builders were must remain a mystery, although two possibilities are the neighboring Lisleses (some of whom had taken up the carpentry profession in the early century) and Nathaniel Henderson, a close neighbor on the Tyger from 1790 to 1804. Henderson is listed as a carpenter in his deed of land purchase in 1790. Obviously there was no lack of professional builders in the Tyger valley at the turn of the century; and it is clear that the area had now recovered from the scourge of the late war with Britain.

4

More Gold Than Grace

I cannot record great things upon religion in this quarter; but cotton sells high. *I fear there is more gold than grace—more of silver than of "that wisdom that cometh from above."* . . . *We lodged at Mr. Hardy's.*
                                    —Bishop Asbury, *Journal*, October 1801

It was also in 1804 that to the Hardy plantation was born its future plantation master, the man who more than any other, would establish its fortunes in the new century and be the paterfamilias during its flush antebellum years, who would live through those years, witness a tremendous war and the virtual destruction of the plantation way of life, see his sons go off to that conflict, bury one of them as a result of it, witness the plunder of his house and lands, and survive into the dark violent days of Federal occupation and outrage. This man was William Eppes Hardy, grandson of the old pioneer, the son of John Wesley and Nancy Eppes Hardy, who came into the world on the first of September, when his father's fields within view and hearing of the Tyger were white with cotton. At the early death of his older brother Hamlin in 1829, he was indeed to become *the* Hardy, the male heir to the estate and fortunes of the family; and with his marriage in 1828 to his first cousin Catharine Hardy (eldest of his uncle Thomas Jr.'s three children, all daughters), he would thus unite the two lines of the family into one—forging a real dynasty that would before his death boast as its base over two thousand of the richest acres in the South and a veritable plantation village of some sixty occupants. Perhaps more accurately, his world might be described as a small kingdom, with himself as its feudal overlord, with his vassals, loyal retainers, and bondsmen, much as his ancestor, the old Norman knight le Hardi, had envisioned life in his own century.

Two years after William's birth, his grandfather sold half of the family lands to his father and willed the other half to him as well. This was undoubtedly because his eldest, Thomas Jr., had not yet married at age thirty-nine. But John Wesley suddenly died later that year, throwing the line once again in doubt and possibly bringing the two-year-old William, his brothers, and their widowed mother into the newly built house.

If so, the widow Hardy and her children did not stay there long, for by December 1809, when William was five, she had married Lemmon Shell, himself a well-to-do widower, designated in his will as "Planter." Like all the Eppeses and Hardys, he was a staunch Methodist. Both the Eppeses and Shells were members of Mt. Tabor Church on Enoree, and it was likely through this means that the two widowers knew one another. The year before his marriage to Nancy, Lemmon, who was a well-educated man, was made a trustee of the famous Mt. Bethel Academy off the Old State Road south of the Enoree. This important school was begun in 1793 and formally opened in 1795 by Bishop Asbury and the Methodists of the area. It educated all the original students of South Carolina College, whose first graduate was Anderson Crenshaw in 1806, a son of the Hardys' Crenshaw neighbors along Tyger River. With Moses Waddel's Willington Academy, Mt. Bethel shared the distinction of being the only two schools in the Carolina Upcountry during the day. In Mt. Bethel's prime, the contemporary historian David Ramsay noted that there were from seventy to eighty students at the school, situated in a "wealthy neighborhood." In 1812 the *Charleston City Gazette* described its curriculum as consisting of Greek, Latin, geography, arithmetic, composition (two classes), writing, and oratory. Among the school's graduates were Chancellor William Harper, Richard Manning (governor of the state from 1820 to 1824), and Bishop Ellison Capers.

When Lemmon Shell died in 1814, six years after his marriage to the widow Hardy, he left a large inventory of books, whose purchasers included Daniel Eppes (Nancy's brother and guardian of William Eppes Hardy) and Elisha Hammond, principal at Mt. Bethel from 1802 to 1805 and from 1807 to 1820, and father of future governor and senator James Henry Hammond. (Elisha had left Mt. Bethel in 1806 to become the first chair of languages at the new South Carolina College but returned in January of the following year, as he said, "to save the school.") In 1826 Robert Mills noted that the Mt. Bethel United Fraternity was a library society whose purpose was to pool books for its members. When Lemmon's brother Stephen Shell Sr. died in 1822, he also left an impressive inventory of volumes. Although the Methodists ceased to support Mt. Bethel in 1820, the school continued for several decades in various sites around the original academy buildings in order to accommodate the changing population.

Nancy Eppes Hardy Shell bore her second husband a son, Charles Wesley Shell, who was thus William's half-brother. The father stipulated in his will that first priority be given to providing his children a "proper English Education." Such was his commitment to learning. Lemmon's son by his first marriage was Thomas Shell Sr., educated at Mt. Bethel. He was one of the tutors of his three Hardy stepbrothers and then went on to study medicine with Dr. Burr Johnstone of Newberry village. Thomas married Precious Schoppert in 1816. She was also a Methodist and, like himself, had well-known and respected master builders and carpenters in her family. The original Schoppert in the county, George, a German from Virginia, had been the supervising carpenter for the second Newberry courthouse from 1799 to 1801. His son Phillip was in 1842 master builder of Chancellor Job Johnstone's Coateswood, the finest house in Newberry village, and of many other early houses of the town. It is interesting to surmise that it was through the link of carpentering that the young Shell and his future wife may have met. Perhaps their relatives had even worked together at their trade, a fact which may have borne directly on the building of the new addition to the Hardy plantation in 1825, of which more later.

Thomas Shell attended medical lectures in Philadelphia and returned to Newberry to practice, first as a partner to Dr. Joseph Waldo in 1817. He attained popularity in the community but became addicted to drink before his death in 1826. His widow Precious died in 1836, leaving a daughter Frances and a son Thomas ("little Tom"), who also became a doctor in the village before moving west. The executor of Precious Shell's estate was her relative, the carpenter Phillip Schoppert. The appraisement of the contents of her home in Newberry reveals especially fine furnishings and the specific titles of an impressive library: medical, historical, and belletristic.

But to return to William Eppes Hardy and his brothers. From the time of their father's death in 1806, the children's guardians had been

Samuel Hardy (their father's brother-in-law) and Daniel Eppes (their mother's brother and Samuel Hardy's son-in-law). They had begun receiving "schooling" by the time of their mother's marriage to Lemmon Shell in 1809, and probably at Mt. Bethel Academy, where their stepfather and his brother Stephen Shell had been serving as trustees since 1808. The Shells, as we have seen, believed strongly in education. In 1809 the bills for "schooling," for four quires of paper, and for schoolbooks were paid from their father John Wesley's estate. In 1810 Arthur McCrackin of nearby Goshen Hill was given $6.00, and Lemmon's son Thomas $19.50 for "schooling three Children." Thus William began his formal education when he was no older than five. Expenditures for 1812 included money for "paper for the boys," and in 1813, $43.25, again for stepbrother Thomas's services in teaching them. There is no record for schooling in 1814, the year their stepfather died, or in the next, although there may have been. Their training had definitely resumed by 1816, when slate pencils, nine quires of paper, "3 school books," a *Gough's Arithmetic*, and other school items, all "for the boys," were charged against the estate. In addition, in that year there are three entries of pay for "Schooling Children": to James Blackburn for $21.00, to Arthur McCrackin for $2.00, and to Thomas Shell for $3.00. 1816 was the year of Thomas Shell's marriage, thus likely explaining Blackburn's and McCrackin's service rather than his own; but too, the children were now getting to the age at which they were needing tutors proficient in particular subjects. There is no mention of Thomas's teaching after 1816, no doubt owing to his studies in Philadelphia and his setting up medical practice in Newberry in 1817.

In 1818 the Hardy children were orphaned by the death of their mother. Only sketchy details are known about young William Eppes Hardy from this time until his marriage ten years later. He had been two when his father died, and now was fourteen when he lost his mother. With her demise, he added to his patrimony of slaves and land, a servant named Ben and (like his brothers) a modest sum of cash amounting to approximately $10,000 in today's currency. His seventeen-year-old brother Hamlin was willed slaves James and George; sixteen-year-old brother James received Delphy (sometimes called Delph) and her child Wesley, born in 1822. Half-brother Charles Wesley Shell received Fanny. Their mother's personal maidservant, named Guinea, to whom the Hardy sons also had some attachment, was given the choice either to go with whichever son she chose or to be free. Nancy Shell was thus anticipating by several years her distant kinsman Thomas Jefferson's manner of emancipation at his death. Rather than be free, however, Guinea chose to go with the youngest child, Charles Wesley, probably about seven or eight years old at the time, and to whom she would now act the part of the only mother he would have. Her choice likely reflects both her love and the fact that she was not ill-treated. In 1819 half-brother Dr. Thomas Shell would become young Charles Wesley's guardian, and Guinea would have probably gone into his and his wife Precious's household in Newberry.

In 1819 purchases for the three Hardy orphans were made by their guardians Sam Hardy and Dan Eppes at William Maybin's store in nearby Maybinton village, suggesting that they were often with Uncle Samuel at his home near the Tyger and the Hardy plantation. These expenditures were for paper, pocketknives, pantaloons, shirts, shoes, stockings, suspenders, handkerchiefs, black coats, and hats. By the end of this year, the orphans were eighteen, seventeen, and fifteen and were beginning to need to look the part of young gentlemen, for indeed they were. From the age of wee lads, they had owned in common a total of eight slaves from their father's estate alone, whom their guardians would not sell but instead had hired out since 1806 among family and neighbors. The revenue accrued thereby was paying the slaves' keep, and any surplus was returning to the estate. These slaves were cared for by both doctors and midwives, who presented their bills for services to the estate. For example, a midwife attended Delphy at the birth of her son Wesley in 1822, and several were treated for "sickness" throughout the period. Their blankets, clothing, and shoes were paid for in like manner with drafts on the estate.

John Wesley Hardy's will had stated that in the event his widow Nancy remarried, the family retainers would be divided into four lots. The children would have three lots, the mother one. This was carried out in 1809 at her remarriage to Shell. In 1819, the year after her death, stepson James Shell (later to become Dr. Shell) was paid $50 for boarding fifteen-year-old William for six months; and Eppes and Shell's store was paid $59 for mercantile accounts on behalf of the boys. In 1820, expenses for a *Murray's Grammar*, gumpaper, and buckskin shoes were paid for eighteen-year-old James Hardy to William Maybin & Co. of Maybinton; and for sixteen year-old William, sums for pantaloons and both "fine" and "coarse" shoes. Other items such as paper, ink, and textbooks prove that their schooling was continuing. In 1821 James, who was now nineteen, a young blade, and a gifted student, paid $10 for "tayloring" and $20 for "books bought at Charleston of W. P. Bason." He incurred expenses for a pair of boots and two pairs of shoes, a summer coat, shirts, and seven yards of linen (all items bought at Shell & Hatton and at Harrington & Dugan stores), and paid $82.50 to Robert R. Pearson "for boarding and Tuition." Pearson himself made purchases at the Orange Hall store, some four miles from the Hardy plantation, in 1821 and thus probably lived in the vicinity. He was no doubt operating a school in the area, a fact that explains James's dual expenses of "boarding and Tuition." About this time, James's guardian uncles had apprenticed him to a tailor to learn the trade; but as family tradition records, James would have none of it, possessing as he did "higher aspirations."

On 19 December 1821 we find him purchasing from the Orange Hall store buckskin suspenders (.75), 5½ yards of corduroy ($6.87), linings (.18¾), a jacket "shape" or pattern (.37), 6 buttons (.12), a pint of cordial (.37), and a pipe (.18¾); on 20 December, a knife ($1.25), cordial, another jacket pattern (1.50), one yard of linings (.50), a quire of paper (.50), a schoolbook (.50), and two sets of china ($4.50). On Christmas Eve he bought another pint of cordial; on Christmas Day, two half-pints of whiskey and a half-pint of cordial, and for Christmas gifts, a pitcher, "a fine shawl for Negroe named Grief" ($1.50), and two pounds of sugar for her (.40). On 29 December he purchased three yards of "Teap," another knife, and the inevitable pint of cordial. On 30 December he made an intriguing purchase of "2 birds." These must have been a fashionable present for the young ladies in these parts, for a belle at The Oaks, near Orange Hall, would later write a favorite male cousin that she would not turn one down if offered as a gift.

In 1821 seventeen-year-old William, like his brother, also purchased from Harrington & Dugan, Eppes & Shell, Shell & Hatton, and William Maybin & Co. a pocketknife, shoes, pantaloons, shirts, a trunk, a wool hat, and various other merchandise. His tuition, board, and "schooling" with Robert R. Pearson cost $82.50, the same amount James paid in this year. From these figures we learn that the two younger boys were still together and studying with the same teacher. Hamlin, who was now twenty, was apparently on his own.

William's two older brothers were Hamlin Eppes Hardy (1801–27 January 1829) and James Freeman Eppes Hardy (1802–1882). Little is known of Hamlin except that he died near Tyger River at the age of twenty-eight and is buried at Ebenezer Cemetery. About 1825 he had married his first cousin Mary Clarke, daughter of his aunt Nancy Hardy Clarke and her husband, the Reverend George Clarke of Enoree River. Clarke was described by a contemporary as "esteemed, social, and pleasant, . . . plain in his dress, but a man of considerable wealth." Hamlin and Mary had two sons, John Wesley (1827–1900) and H. Epps. At Christmas 1828, about a month before his death, Hamlin was buying household furnishings for his wife from the Orange Hall store: six large Blue Willow plates, cups and saucers, bowls, a sugar dish, a teapot, gilt tumblers, and milk pots. For himself, or perhaps for gifts, he bought a quart and three pint containers of whiskey. A few weeks before his death he purchased five pounds of sugar. His unexpected demise left yet another Hardy widow, like John Wesley's own mother before him, with little babes to tend. A strong pattern of fatherless children developed in the family. Were it not for the closeness of the extended family, this might have been destructive of stability. The relatives, bound by complex blood ties and close bonds of affection, pulled together, however, and saw the family members through. It was to the protecting Angel of the Hearth that the family always clung and to which they did sincerest homage. So deep in their psyches was she, in fact, that she was said to materialize before more than one of them on the stairs of the house, clad in shining silks of green and silver.

Much more is known of Hamlin's brother James—enough in fact to be an interesting story in itself. As a young man James suffered from ill health; and in 1821, at the age of nineteen, he relocated from Maybinton and Charleston to Asheville, North Carolina, in order to strengthen his lungs with "the health giving properties of the mountain ozone." By this time one of his lungs had completely failed him and the other was weakened. The mountain air proved salubrious and he became strong and vigorous during his six decades of life there. By January 1822 he was enrolled at the Asheville Academy, whose principal was Francis Porter, a Presbyterian clergyman. There he learned Latin and Greek, reading Virgil's *Aeneid* and *Bucolics*, Horace, Cicero, Caesar, and parts of the Bible in Greek. In May 1822 Hardy traveled back home for a visit in the company of Benjamin F. Perry, a fellow student at the Academy, who would become a life-long friend, and governor of South Carolina. Hardy procured a horse for them, and he and Perry rode and walked alternately until Hardy left him behind in Greenville District, South Carolina. Hardy's early friendship with Perry was no doubt strengthened through the years by both men's political allegiance to Unionism. At

Asheville Academy, Hardy also made friends with his fellow student Montraville Patton.

Hardy likely came to Asheville on the advice of Dr. George Phillips, who had practiced in Newberry and Union before moving to Asheville in the early 1820s. Phillips married Elizabeth Patton in 1823. The next year, on 23 December 1824, James betrothed Elizabeth's sister, Jane Shaw Patton, daughter of Colonel James Patton of Swannanoa River, one of Asheville's wealthiest and most prominent early citizens. Hardy, whose intelligence and smooth manners always stood him in good stead, thus made an auspicious marriage into the pioneering family of the town. The young couple resided in what was termed the town's "finest residence." In 1914 an Asheville historian described it as a "stylish wooden dwelling embowered in green vines and fragrant flowers." Around the time of his betrothal, Hardy began the study of medicine with Dr. Phillips, thus following in the footsteps of his old tutor and stepbrother from Newberry, Dr. Thomas Shell Sr., and of Shell's own son, Thomas Jr. The young couple then moved to Charleston while he studied at the medical college there. In 1825 they had their first child, James Patton, who would later die in the Siege of Puebla in the Mexican War at the age of twenty-two. In 1828 they had their first daughter, Emma.

James graduated from medical college in Charleston in the year 1831 at the age of twenty-eight and immediately began his career in Asheville. There he wrote his brother William in February 1832 that he had "a fine practice" that reached as far as Charlotte and had "made an arrangement to extend my Surgical Theatre, as I am becoming somewhat notorious in that Branch." In 1906 he was still remembered as "a fearless and skillful surgeon." As Ashevillians in the early century described him, he was "one of the most popular physicians this County has ever known and for many years, the acknowledged leader of the profession in Western North Carolina." His practice also finally "embraced the Flat Rock section of Henderson County," North Carolina, begun as a summer resort settlement of Charlestonians and lowcountry South Carolina planters. His sphere also spread "at times, as far as upper South Carolina." He was "the first physician to advertise the North Carolina mountains as a health resort—this he did in thankfulness for his own restoration to perfect health." Hardy was thus a pioneer in establishing the region as a tourist mecca. In 1935 he was said to have been more than a popular doctor; he was "one of the most universally beloved men that ever lived in this county."

Hardy's second son, John Geddings, was born 25 June 1830. Geddings would carry on the family tradition and become a well-respected physician-surgeon in Asheville until his death in 1884. The doctor and his wife were eager for a fourth child in February 1832; but Jane was not pregnant, as the would-be father reported back home to his brother: "Tell Catharine my wife is as slim as a may pole yet." This is more than he can say of his three very pregnant sisters-in-law; and he predicts "a world of grannying to do next summer, for [sister-in-law] Rose [Morrison] will be here, and she is as fat as a tick, yes even a dog tick." Jane became pregnant very shortly, however, and bore their third son, Charles Wesley on 20 November 1832. Their last child, George Phillips, was named for Dr. Hardy's mentor. In all, Jane would bear six children before her death in 1838.

By January 1833 James had become involved in gold-mining ventures in Georgia, an activity that had netted him $2,000 profit, sufficient revenue (coupled with the $1,000 he received for caring for his wife's uncle Joseph Patton, now recently deceased) to purchase 333 acres about a mile and a half from Asheville on the Swannanoa River, land, as he reported to brother William, comprised of "about 70 acres of river bottom, the remaining 263 acres upland, some very good." The goodness of the land would have not been lost on his farmer brother. By 1833 he had indeed established himself as among the thriving young town's most respected and influential citizens.

Politically at this time James was a staunch Unionist and an opinionated supporter of President Andrew Jackson. To his brother in 1832 and 1833, he wrote several strident letters respecting Nullification. Brother William was just as devoted to the cause of States' Rights and local autonomy. Their letters do not mince words on politics, and James writes that owing to the political stand of his brother and native community, "I have no idea of ever visiting Newberry again, until some sense gets in the heads of people, unless I go as a volunteer [soldier] under the President" to crush the Nullifiers. In September 1832 he declares to William:

> I am truly sorry to find you in the ranks of dissension. I would as soon see the names of my venerated forefathers on the pages of Toryism as to see any of their offspring favoring a party to destroy the tree of Liberty which was planted by

their muskets and nourished by their blood. . . . You & I stand on ground which is truly lamentable, for if I am called out to defend the general government, I shall most assuredly obey her commands. Not that I love So Ca less but I love [the] Union more.

Brother William countered with a well-reasoned defense of local sovereignty against the growth of "distant and overweening centralising power that serves one regional interest at the expense of another" and which thus "proves destructive of all the basic principles on which Union is founded." He invokes two illustrious names from English history to make his point that the Hardy family tradition is older than the American Revolution: "More important than any 'Union' are the principles it stands for. For such, did our Magna Carta ancestors make their stand on the plains of Runneymede."

But unlike his brother William, James was at heart neither a "stay-at-home" nor a quiet man of the soil. His interests ran more toward the flamboyant, of the cosmopolitanism of trips to Charleston, Washington, New York, and the West, of the big-business venture, of gold mines, land speculations, banking, and creating railroad lines and health resorts. For him, bigger was better. He thus fit well enough into the Hamiltonian scheme of a strong central government that would aid banking, business, and industry and would force, at public expense, the internal improvements that would encourage and promote them, even when these programs were carried out by virtue of taxes levied on the agrarians of the South, most specifically his brother William. So James continued his entrepreneurial interests in Georgia and Burke County, North Carolina, into the next decade. He and Jane often visited Flat Rock and the Warm Sulphur Springs four miles west of Asheville owned by her family. Here at the springs they erected a hotel and health spa. In 1835 James was planning a business trip to the West and was encouraging brother William and their cousin Samuel Clarke to go with him. William thanked him for the invitation but declined in order to "superintend the planting" and "pitch in where needed in the unglamorous activity of properly manuring the soil with hog and horse compost." William was always the practical, uncomplaining farmer satisfied with life in his "small" sphere even when attending to the homeliest everyday details of planting, work which an expansive spirit like "Dr. Jim" would have found tedious. So it was that brother James dreamed his big "progressive" dreams, and brother William stayed home and manured his fields.

In early 1836 the good doctor was "having a fine house built for Professor [Samuel Henry] Dickson [one of his old instructors at the Medical College] to spend the summer in." This dwelling, named Swannanoa Hill, was located near Hardy's own land. Here, as remembered in 1906, Dickson "entertained large parties of guests in the lavish style of the antebellum days." Dickson was among the most famous physicians of his day in America, an excellent essayist, poet, and public speaker. Hardy valued his company and they became close friends. When the Hardys moved to their Swannanoa estate in 1840, they became close neighbors as well. It was Dickson who had attended Hardy's son Charles during his illness and death in October 1833, while his father was away on business.

In March 1836 Hardy traveled with James W. Patton to Washington and New York. (Patton was Mrs. Hardy's thirty-three-year-old brother.) Dr. Hardy's letter dated from Washington on 17 March 1836, is worth quoting in full:

> Dear Wm:
> I have no doubt that you will be glad to hear from me, on my tour to the North. I have been here nearly a week, & have had introductions to many of the first men of the United States. I have heard the first orators, both in the Senate & House. I have allways been a Clay man, & am moreso since I have been introduced to him, & heard him make a speech in the Senate.
> Mr Calhoun speaks finely. I was pleased with him, Webster, Clay, Ewing. The city is crowded with company. Many flashy ladies but no handsome ones. I called on old Jackson yesterday. The old man looks feeble and worn out. I have no doubt he would be glad if he was in Tennessee. I spent an evening with Judge White. He is a clever old man.
> I think if I were situated as you are, I would come here some winter during the Session of Congress & see how the business of this mighty Nation is carried on. Tell Sam Clarke it would afford me a great deal of pleasure if I had him with me. Give my love to all—I shall write from New York—I hope you will be in our village this summer.
> Your brother
> J. F. E. Hardy

Over and above his important, far-flung, and lucrative medical practice, James thus became an early prominent landowner, civic leader, and "booster" of Asheville—something of a New South businessman fifty years before the term had been invented. He always had an eye to the profits, and of promoting the economy of his area—not so much for the sake of the money itself but for the "grand" style of life it made possible. With brother-in-law James Patton, he served as a member of the town's first board of commissioners. He was for a time the cashier of the town's first bank. In 1836 he was elected a commissioner to form the Charleston-Cincinnati Railroad. True Hamiltonian that he was, internal improvements were high on his list of economic priorities. He was also a religious leader; he helped build Asheville's first Methodist church and often served as a delegate to the state Methodist Conference. Despite his youthful purchases of cordial and brandy at Orange Hall, he became president of the Asheville Temperance Society and delivered its second annual address in 1832. His temperance activities no doubt came in response to the alcoholism that had ruined the career of his mentor, Tom Shell, and led to his premature death.

By 1840 Dr. Hardy, with his tremendous energy and expansive personality, had thus grown to be both the busiest, most respected man of medicine in western North Carolina and one of her most active entrepreneurs and business and civic leaders. To these endeavors, he added a significant career of medical instruction in Asheville, a position he held throughout the antebellum era.

With all its triumphs, his life was not without sadness. Jane, who had borne him six children, was never of very strong constitution; she died in Charleston in the winter of 1838. James, who had taken her there for the best medical treatment possible, accepted this loss in stride, returned to work in Asheville, and fulfilled his responsibilities without faltering. His children were soon to have a new mother in October of the following year, when Hardy married Cordelia (Delia) Haywood Erwin, daughter of William Willoughby and Matilda Sharp Erwin, of Morganton, Burke County, North Carolina. The Erwins, originally from Virginia, were a prominent pioneering family of that county, where Hardy had interests in gold mines and traveled often in their management. Hardy thus made a second auspicious match, but this time brought as much prominence to it as the family into which he had married.

During his second marriage he built a splendid new country seat in

1840 near his friend Dickson, a fine structure on Swannanoa Hill (at Biltmore Road, at the Swannanoa River), a home that commanded a beautiful view of the river and countryside. In choosing this site, perhaps he recalled the high ancestral home of the Hardys of Tyger, with its broad vistas. The place became a local landmark and showplace, described as having "approaches lined with white pines, cedars, and other trees and shrubbery [that] still make this one of the prettiest places in this section." This description of Dr. Hardy's house, given in 1914 by historian J. P. Arthur, concludes: "When he first improved it, it was far in advance of anything theretofore seen in these parts. It commands a fine view." Arthur calls Hardy "Asheville's First Landscape Architect." In fact, all four of Hardy's dwellings in Asheville were noted for their "commanding" views and the beauty of their flowers, vines, and trees. Hence, as we shall see, the Hardy plantation's formal gardens, with their non-native mountain hemlocks, are likely his work, for in 1932, Dr. Hardy's ninety-one-year-old nephew stated that the Hardy boxwood gardens were designed "by a landscape architect from Asheville."

The good doctor obviously had an eye to natural beauty in choosing "commanding sites and . . . augmenting them with the most beautiful productions of nature." Some of these plants, he purchased from Pomaria Nurseries, one of the best in America, conveniently located in Newberry County less than twenty miles down the State Road from the Hardy plantation. In October 1859 an entry in the nursery ledger reveals that he bought thirty grapevines. Hardy was no doubt trying to expand the agricultural base of his mountain community with this experiment, for grape culture on a large scale was in its beginnings in the South at this time and greatly encouraged by Pomaria Nurseries itself. The nursery catalogue for 1861–1862, which advertised the Catawba grape, noted: "There are many varieties of this Grape, the best of which is *Hardy*, a seedling of Asheville, N.C." Thus Dr. Jim must obviously have been involved more than casually in viticulture to have either introduced a variety or had one named for him.

At his new family seat on the Swannanoa, Hardy, like his friend and neighbor Dickson, dispensed a lavish hospitality of legendary proportion, a largesse that was still remembered in 1935 as being of "the old-fashioned antebellum Southern style, a broad hospitality to friends and visitors alike." Hardy was remembered as being "one of the most universally beloved men that has ever lived in this County." Again, he and his brother William had much in common as gentlemen of the old school: they were hospitable, high-toned, lively, fun-loving, witty, and possessed of a cultivated aesthetic sense. Another who knew the doctor well, described him in 1914 as having "commanding presence, with the manner of a lord." It was true that "at his home was dispensed much of the hospitality for which this section was noted, distinguished strangers finding there entertainment and intelligence at least equal to that of larger places." One such "ornament" often at his table was professor-orator-poet-essayist Sam Dickson; others were Dr. John Dickson and Dr. Charles Edward Tennent and his wife Julia Fripp, who had moved to Asheville from their plantations near Charleston. Hardy's daughter, Emma, in fact, married into the Tennent family in 1848.

In 1860 Hardy bought and moved to Belleview, on the eastern side of present-day South Main Street, one-half mile south of Patton and Lexington Avenues, and situated on yet "another commanding hill with a splendid view and approaches bordered and landscaped with pines and cedars." This home had been built in the early fifties as a summer retreat by son-in-law Gilbert B. Tennent of Charleston. Here he lived until after the great war, at which time he withdrew from medical practice and built Millwood, the brick house on the west side of the Hendersonville Road beyond the present Biltmore Estate, a Hardy home that afforded yet another fine view. As an indication of his standing at this time, we note that the peak which Arnold Guyot called "the culminating point of the Blue Ridge" was named Mt. Hardy in his honor.

It is interesting to record in passing that Asheville's Buck Hotel, a small frame building near Hardy's first residence in the village, built and run by his friend and in-law Colonel John Patton, had the same name as the famous hostelry in Maybinton village, some few miles from the Hardy plantation. Whether or not there is a connection between the two is unknown.

James Hardy and family never forgot their South Carolina ties. The children visited their cousins frequently. It is recorded that brother William, his wife, and their four children spent the "fever season" in Asheville with James and his family in 1836, returning to the plantation only in September. This, in fact, became a yearly ritual. The Hardys of Tyger River often visited the hotel at Warm Sulphur Springs owned by the Pattons. James, too, kept involved in the affairs of his native state and was often in Charleston. As we have seen, it was in that city that his first wife died in the winter of 1838, and it was there that both he and his son John Geddings were educated in medicine. His son James Patton was killed in the Battle of Puebla fighting as a member of the Fairfield South Carolina Company of the Palmetto Regiment. In his honor, Colonel A. H. Gladden, commander of the regiment, had a walking cane cut from the flagstaff that bore the regimental flag over the Palace of Mexico, and mounted with a head made from the metal of guns captured in Mexico City in 1847. This he inscribed as a gift to Dr. Hardy in memory of his dead son. Dr. Hardy's son William Henry, the first war casualty from Asheville in 1861, fought for the Confederacy as a member of the Second Regiment of South Carolina Volunteers, having joined at Morris Island while staying in nearby Charleston.

Because the Tyger River Hardys lived near the State (Buncombe) Road that ran from Charleston to Asheville, it was natural for Dr. Hardy to move to the mountains, and that such easy congress between the two places should exist for the brothers and their families. Further, Dr. Hardy's presence in Asheville after 1821 serves to explain the many connections between the Hardy plantation and that mountain town. As we have seen, it was likely Dr. Jim himself who laid out brother William's garden in the mid-1830s. It was also James who brought his young nephews, William's sons Charles Wesley, Haywood, and William Dixon Hardy, to Asheville to be educated at Stephen Lee's Academy in the 1850s. While at school, the nephews were often at their uncle James's home. Headmaster Lee, in June 1851, for example, reported Wesley's "spending a few days" with Dr. Hardy during vacation, and Charles Wesley commented to his father in 1857 that Uncle James "won't let us off until after a long visit." The Asheville family often visited by the Tyger as well, particularly on trips to and from Charleston and Columbia. Members of the two families swapped plants and seeds back and forth across the states, and wrote often.

During and after the war, the two families remained close and did what they could across the miles to aid one another. The Hardys of Asheville were particularly hard-pressed for food in 1864 and 1865 and had to rely on the help of their farming kin in Newberry to see them through. A letter from Delia Hardy to brother-in-law William in 1864 clearly reveals both their pathetic situation and the strength of the tie that still bound the family despite the distance, the contrasting personalities of the brothers, and the acute turmoil of war. This letter appears in full in chapter 12.

As for William Eppes Hardy, he grew to manhood in close touch with the Hardy lands because he owned some of its acreage and possessed faithful and dutiful blacks who were tied to it, and for whom he was responsible. He was also in touch with his grandmother Phoebe Hardy (until her death in 1810) and his grandfather Thomas Sr., the old pioneer (until his death in 1814). William was ten when the latter occurred; and from that period onward, the male authority figure for him was Uncle Thomas Hardy Jr., a veteran of the War of 1812 and now plantation master at the age of forty-seven after Thomas Sr.'s death. His closest bonds, however, were to his guardians, Uncle Samuel Hardy and Uncle Dan Eppes, and to Dr. Tom Shell Sr., his stepbrother and tutor.

In 1810, the same year that his mother Phoebe died, and at the age of forty-three, Uncle Thomas, eldest son of the old pioneer, took a wife. She was Anna Powell Dixon, a twenty-seven-year-old native of Lunenburg, Virginia, who was then living in Person County, North Carolina, and some of whose family had acquired lands a few miles across Tyger River from the Hardys. (When the Dixon family moved west to the new lands of Missouri and Mississippi, the family continued to keep in close touch with their Carolina kin through correspondence and occasional visits.) Uncle Thomas married Anna in Person County on 20 May 1811. The year after her marriage, the new Mrs. Hardy bore Thomas a daughter Catharine, named for her mother, Catharine Warren Dixon (1757–1838), and who was to become her first cousin William Eppes Hardy's young bride and eventual mistress of the plantation; then two years later, another daughter, Frances Jeter Hardy, named for Anna's sister, Frances Jeter Dixon Trotter; and finally her last child, Elmira, or Mira as the family called her, born in December 1814 and who died in 1830 at the age of sixteen.

The Dixons of Williamsville in Person County, North Carolina, and then later in Cole County, Missouri, remained in remarkably close touch with their Tyger River cousins, as proved by existing family correspondence. One such letter from Person County is worth quoting in full to give an idea of the social milieu of this branch of the extended family and of the tenor of the times. Uncle Jeremiah Dixon (1795–1860), Anna Dixon Hardy's younger brother, is addressing his nephew William Eppes Hardy:

Nov. 17th 1832

Dear Nephew William

After my respects to you and all the family, I herewith undertake to answer some of the inquiries in your letter.

Brothers Warren & Henry started to Missouri the 29th day of September last. I went with them about 60 miles. They went on well, and have had no intelligence from them since. Mr. Thomas L. Price went on the same time, for the same state. We have had no very late account from the friends in Missouri, but when we had last heard from them, they were injoying good health with a few exceptions. Sister Mary Carnal had been afflicted with the fever & ague, but was convalescent. Sister Martha and her son John Henry had been somewhat afflicted—both of them on the recovery. There had been some sickness among their slaves and one death in [brother-in-law] Waller Bolton's family (a man called Anderson). He was working at the Iron Works and thought to have been neglected. All of the Boltons appear to be pleased with the country except John, and that is not to be wondered at as he is a man particularly fond of company, and the section that they live in is but thinly inhabited. Dr. William Bolton has located himself in a town called Jefferson City, the seat of government, and is following his profession, gets an extensive practice. The balance of his connections are settling on the Osage River a few miles up the country from the city, and they say their land is equal to any perhaps in the world, and affords as good spring water as any in N. C. both in quantity and quality.

Father received a letter from Hubbard and Elizabeth Carnal some time this spring at which time they and all the children were injoying a tolerable portion of health. Hubbard was in the worst condition, having been afflicted by the rheumatism. Sister [Frances Jeter] Trotter is at this time in a low state and has been for several weeks. The first attack upon her was of a bilious nature, and secondly the Piles. She had a great Charge all the summer; her negro woman Harriet was taken sick in the spring and lingered a long while before she died, and then her oldest was taken and pined away and died. Then several more of the Blacks were taken sick, and about the time they recovered, the youngest of her children called F. I. Amanda was taken with the scarlet fever or St. Anthony's Fire, and settled in one of its legs and had to be opened in 3 places, and the last time but a few weeks ago. The child is reduced to a mere skeleton, and I think it doubtful whether it will recover. [Brother-in-law] Mr. [Thomas] Trotter has been somewhat unwell. The health of Father is as usual. Mother has been more afflicted this summer than for many years, but at this time is much better than any time during the summer.

Brother Edmund's wife has been somewhat more sickly than usual. She had the misfortune to miscarry and did not take that care of herself which she should, and she suffered for her imprudence. Brother Levi's family is not entirely clear from sickness though not very bad. His second daughter has had a slight touch of jaundice. The balance of your friends and relatives are all in good health. The crop of corn, considering the drauth, has come in better than was expected. What tobacco was made this year is of superior quality though a short crop.

You will have the goodness to write after the receipt of this as we should like to hear from you. When I say we, I mean Father, Mother, Sister & Brother together with myself. You accept my best wish for you and yours, and give my love to all.

Jeremiah Dixon

P.S. Edmund D. Bolton has a fine son called William Currie.

The Dixon letters reveal that the family were educated cultivators of corn and tobacco. Young nephew William's close knowledge of his aunt (and new mother-in-law's) family is remarkable for both its range and specificity. When Jeremiah writes him that "the balance of your friends and relatives are all in good health," the number with whom William was familiar included a considerable gathering. This same Jeremiah visited the Hardy plantation on at least one occasion. In the Hardy plantation ledger, an entry for 15 August 1845 notes his purchase of a sorrel horse from his nephew, this before his eventual migration to Cole County, Missouri, where he died in 1860. Anna's own father died in Person County in 1834; her widowed mother then migrated west and also died in Missouri in 1838 with her children.

During Thomas and Anna Dixon Hardy's management of the plantation occurred the two best crop years ever witnessed in the Upcountry: the years 1819 and 1823. Robert Mills's *Statistics* called these years "extraordinary." Then Uncle Thomas died in 1823, in the year of the great harvest, leaving a household of three young girls (aged nine, ten, and twelve) and their forty-year-old mother, who never remarried. In this year William's guardians were the only male family members left of his blood older than his brothers. Luckily, this was a period of good crops, and the plantation prospered despite the loss of its master. The Widow Hardy was herself a capable manager and planter, and she had the aid of good family servants who had many years of experience.

Hamlin (age twenty-two at the time of his uncle Thomas's death), James (twenty-one), and William (nineteen) may have taken some share of responsibility at the Hardy plantation as the eldest male Hardys in the extended household; but in 1823 Hamlin was courting his first cousin on Enoree River some six miles away and preparing to have a family of his own; James, who had already moved to Asheville, was at Asheville Academy and getting ready for medical school in Charleston; and William, sometime between 1822 and 1828, was studying law. Their own pursuits must have prevented any major involvement in plantation life. The family lands, therefore, must have had excellent management at the hands of the Widow Hardy and the Hardy slaves. This was indeed likely the case because into her seventy-eighth year, at yet another plantation at nearby Goshen Hill (itself the biblical name for "the land of plenty, the land of milk and honey"), she was still supervising without the assistance of an overseer, and with success, her own independent realm of 705 acres and thirty-one slaves. In fact, between the years 1850 and 1860, she more than tripled her holdings there and produced corn, oats, cotton, wheat, molasses, honey, cows, beef cattle, butter, and hogs in abundance. She was thus another of those strong Carolina ladies who grew from self-reliant pioneering stock. The portrait of Anna painted in her mid-sixties reveals great strength of character as well as gentleness. Her will of 1859 left bequests for the furthering of Christianity, a demonstration of her faith.

From the time they were old enough to toddle about, her daughters Catharine, Frances, and Mira had been playmates of the three Hardy orphans. In the dirt-swept yard of the Hardy house, they had created the usual child's play together, the older male cousins behaving more or less as little gentlemen. These childhood ties strengthened with age in the case of Catharine and William, and the childhood past they shared forged tender affections that grew to love. William was often present at the plantation as Catharine blossomed into a beautiful young woman.

At the age of nineteen, he comforted his twelve-year-old cousin at her father's death. He too had lost a parent when he was about the same age and knew the feeling. She never forgot his kindness and how "he played the young protector, so gentle quiet and manly." By the time she was sixteen, he had asked for her hand in marriage.

Family tradition relates that the imposing front portion of the Hardy plantation house was built in 1825. The bounty from the excellent crops of 1819 and 1823 no doubt provided the substance with which to do so. This great wing was attached at right angles to the 1804 structure, creating an L-shaped dwelling and thus altering its north-south orientation to east-west. The addition was begun perhaps as early as 1824, for it would have taken at least a year to complete. The construction date of around 1825 is corroborated by both its classical revival style and the existence of a near-duplicate in Pomaria plantation, which is said to have been built for Squire John Summer (1778–1855) in 1826 and 1827. Most features of both houses—their mantels, woodwork, walnut staircases, pine staircases running into the attic across a hall window, wainscoting, stairtread bud-and-scroll ornamentation, stair newels and spindles, doorknobs, hinges, locks and keys, and double-doored entrances with trabiated window lights and transoms on both floors—are all precisely the same. Also precisely alike are the exterior wooden pilasters at the house corners and the two-story projecting porticos complete with the same turned balusters and carved handrails. But for the variation in floor plans, the houses would be identical.

Another construction possibility is that the Widow Hardy, planning her eldest daughter Catharine's approaching marriage in 1828, had the house enlarged for her daughter and son-in-law's new home so that they all could remain in the same dwelling and the new groom could oversee the planting. Despite some vagueness in the details, then, and the uncertainty of whether it was Anna or Catharine and William who oversaw the building, one can be certain that the addition was made some time in the flush decade of the 1820s. Whether this was before or after Pomaria's 1826–1827 construction is therefore also debatable. In light of its architectural style and since there is no reason to question family tradition, I thus assign its date as 1825, as William Dixon Hardy said in 1932.

The 1804 house and its 1825 addition had no upstairs access between them. The dwelling was in modern terms a duplex and was thus especially convenient for the newlyweds. They could have their privacy from the mother and young sisters, but the family could all still live together under the same roof. From the beginning, there were always two front doors to the house, one facing north, the other east.

Performed by their relative the Reverend John Jennings (husband of Uncle Samuel and Aunt Elizabeth Hardy's daughter, Cousin Susannah), the grand event took place in the new drawing room of the Great House on 6 November 1828, when the twenty-four-year-old lawyer and heir to John Wesley's estate married his beautiful seventeen-year-old cousin Catharine, heiress to Thomas Jr.'s patrimony. Thus began the brief golden years of the plantation. The bride and groom were both grandchildren of the old pioneer Thomas Hardy Sr. and were well known in the community. Accordingly, the occasion was much celebrated and talked of throughout the countryside in Big House and Quarters alike. There was much merrymaking, feasting, and dancing, and fiddle and banjo playing in abundance. The twenty-foot-square drawing room with its big double doors that opened wide into the hall now proved a timely addition, for here in the space of the combined rooms was ample floor for the popular dances of the day, including the Virginia reel, always the traditional favorite of the Hardys.

The celebrating lasted for three days, with the bride's tall, slender, and beautiful black-haired sisters Frances and Mira, and their two male cousins—the groom's brothers James and Hamlin (with their new wives and babes)—much in the forefront of things. James and his young family came from Asheville to spend the week. The bride then moved to her new bedroom in the upstairs front of the new Palladian wing and settled in as the young mistress of the place by the side of "Ole Missus"—Miss Anna, who was rapidly becoming alike dowager matron, grand matriarch, and very symbol of the plantation itself. She, in fact, kept all in the control of her skilled and gentle hands. Perhaps learning her lesson well from Lear, though she had long since moved to another plantation by the time of her death in 1861, she kept title to the property, only willing it to Catharine at her demise. Younger sister Frances provided Catharine good company as usual, as they talked and confided for peaceful hours over their needlework. Not much had changed in Catharine's outer world. She still lived in the house where she was born, and the familiar fields greeted her eyes with each waking. She felt contentment and peace as she watched her new husband through the columns of the portico that framed her view from her high room—William as he mounted his bay to ride the Hardy fields of their ancestors, with the backdrop of blue-green hills and their silver ribbon of river. How natural their marriage was; they had always been close from as long as she could remember. Strangely, his face "was among the earliest and dearest" of her memories, even before father's, mother's, or that of her kindly old nurse. Her girlhood image of his blue eyes framed by the thick black locks of his hair kept coming to her as she awoke to the appropriateness of the old family ballad she was humming, one she had learned as a child at her mother's knee: *Black, black, black is the color of my truelove's hair; his face, his face is wondrous fair. I love the ground on which he stands.* His blue eyes so much like her own; his black locks so like her own dark curls. No wonder everyone recognized their kinship—"almost like brother and sister," some even said. As she sang her secret ballad softly to herself, she returned her attention from the window to her needlework, while the tall, straight figure on the bay remained firmly in her sight.

With Miss Anna's excellent guidance, the groom learned the ropes; Anna had grown up on a farm and was a good teacher. Planting was in her blood and she loved it. Because the cotton was being harvested at the time of the young couple's marriage, William set quickly to managing the process. "No better time to learn than the present," he said. They had had plenty of rain this summer, and at just the right times and not too much, so it was another good year for the crops, and all were in high spirits. Even the old mules were said "to walk with a jaunty air." The young squire took quickly to farming and to this life on the land. His heart brimmed to bursting with joy. The crisp autumn air with a hint of winter in it, and the bright clear sunlight provided his happiest time of the year, his favorite season. From across the soft white terraces, he occasionally glanced to the high windows by the portico where he could see barely revealed the silk-clad outline of his new bride at her needlework: Catharine, for so long the dearest desire of his life, "her smile like the spring rain to new-ploughed fields." She raised her gaze to him and each knew what the other felt. No need to doff hat, nod, or bow. My thoughts are with you. Indeed, they had been from the first day after his nineteenth birthday when he looked up from the supper table and saw the firelight reflected in her eyes. This he had finally managed the courage to write her, pouring out his love in an effusion that somewhat shocked even himself but did not surprise his young lady at all, for Catharine had already guessed his secret and was only waiting for the declaration. How small and fragile was her figure, so unlike his own square, tall build. He loved the smallness and fragileness of her. No lady in Carolina could be more beautiful, and no man any happier.

With the cotton all safely in, ginned, and at market, the fall butcherings began, and a bright, joyous Christmas celebration lasted longer than the usual. It was the newlyweds' first Christmas together on the bountiful land.

One month into the new year 1829, however, found the Great House saddened by the death of William's brother Hamlin, for the two boys had been especially close in the absence of parents. As he had on James's removal to Asheville seven years before, William felt the old grief of loss tug at him and return in earnest, a pain not new to him. He had felt it with both a lost father and mother and no home to call his own. Catharine, too, had felt it with her lost father, and she could console him as he had her. Now they had each other; and were it not for Catharine and her family, as he wrote his brother James, the sorrow would have been "too hard to bear."

Later that year, however, occurred an event that relieved some of the household's grief over Hamlin: the birth in October of a son. There was much rejoicing over the new young master, little Thomas Powell, named in homage both to his maternal grandmother Anna Powell and his grandfather Thomas. At last, after tenuous times occasioned by the deaths of so many male Hardys, there was a tiny heir to the Hardy lands that would carry the name into a new generation. His first name, going back to the old pioneer, itself would forge links to four generations. As the midwife spanked him into a new world, his infant cries gave added life to the land as they sounded down the cotton fields in full autumn blow, a year of still another incredibly rich harvest. At the sound, the field hands relaxed their busy fingers from their picking for a long pause to credit the occasion in witness to the renewal of life in the pageant of family continuity. The father, waiting outside the birthing room, was beside himself with pleasure at the announcement of the good health of mother and son, a prayer of thanks on his lips. To his brother, he wrote:

> James,
>   Today I am the happiest of men. This morning Catharine was delivered safely of a healthy boy. God be thanked. I know you share my joy. Though the busiest time of the year for us, the whole place has now come to a standstill, the clack of wagon wheels given way to the clack of female tongues. Every woman on the Plantation has had to hold him, the older the longer. I can scarcely get my turn. If you come up,

> I cant be better pleasd and what renders me more happy is Mrs Willey is delited with her plase and the cuntry. . . . I am truly sorry to see in the letter you say that yourself and Dr Douglass will not come to Florady, for sir I have a plase pickt out for you and the Docter ajoining each other, as Mrs Douglass wanted each residense a half mile apart. . . . There is some verry clever fellows hear—but I want yourself and Dr Douglass to make out the sosiety.

Knowing Douglass's and Hardy's strong stand in favor of States' Rights, Willey adds as even more tempting inducement: "We are all States Rites men here." The Jackson men are "in the minority" and have been labeled "the malign influence." Of reports from Georgia and Alabama belittling the Florida country, Willey cautions his friend not to believe a word because these folks only want more settlers in their states. As for "Florady," Willey concludes, "Never was cuntry more belied than this."

Cousin Sam Gordon's case for settling in "Ole Alabam" is even more eloquent. He wrote to Squire William from near Clinton, Greene County, Alabama, on 29 November 1836:

> Dear Wm.
>
> I received yours of the 27th Oct which gave me pleasure to hear that you and family were all well and likewise making a fine crop. This year has been manure for your old country, but take care for a dry year. These lines leave us all well and in high spirits. I have made what I call a tolerable crop. I shall make with four hands labor several lbs cotton more than Eig Volly and me both made with ten last year and made about five hunder bushels corn and there is no telling how many peas. Such a site you never saw. A plenty to make all my horses and hogs & cows fat and I cant tell the number of blackbirds, and I just completed the best gin house and screw that I have seen in Alabam and shall get my cotton out by Christmas with hiring two months' work. Well I will quit braggin but it is very *near* all true. You wished me to write to you wheather I thought that you had better sell out and move out hear. I will give you my candid opinion on the subject with many respectable men—I think a man may have his land give to him thare, say as much as he can well cultivate

and some to keep up his farm. Another with the same force and industry and economy will come hear, give twenty dollars per acre and in four years pay for his land and have the most cash. I speak of common places, not the choicest places—for you could not buy choice places hear for that price. Now, I will have you to judge what I think of this country. You will have no travling to the springs of summer if it remain healthy evry year as it has bin this year. Wee have not had a case of fever since we come hear. Give Doct. Douglass and Coz Frances our best love and tell them that wee are glad to hear of their increasing ther family, but tell them they should not run ahead of us so. Wee come to Alabama where it was said it was all sorts of a place for children, but the Doctor and Cozen Frances appears to go two to our one, but perhaps wee may creap up after awhile. Give Coz. Anna our love and accept for yourselves our warmest love— and write personly to me. You must excuse the letter for it was wrote in a hurry. If any person enquires about Sammy, tell them I was offered thirty dollars per acre for my land today and refused to take it.

Saml O. Gordon

NB. You may look for me when the Railroad gets so I can come on it.

All these enticing descriptions and even more testimony from friends and ex-Newberrians like William and John Wesley Ragsdale and a Mr. Aughtrey formerly of the Tyger valley did not succeed in uprooting them, although William and Catharine appear at least to have given it some thought once again in 1836.

For all that, under the benign influence of the Angel of the House, they remained on their ancestral soil, with which they decided to cast their lot. The excellent crop year of 1836 seemed to decide the issue forever; bountiful harvests (despite the freshets of 1833) allowed William to increase his plantation acreage throughout the 1830s and 1840s. He began buying land in earnest adjacent to his holdings during these decades. For example, he purchased 127.5 acres from Gideon Nelson in December 1831, 50 acres from Jim Hogg in May 1835, 138 acres on Tyger River from the estate of David G. Sims in November 1835, and 486 acres from Dr. Thomas Lyles in 1845. These facts do not show a man who is seriously contemplating selling out. His large purchases of 1835 came just in time to take advantage of the great banner crop year of 1836; and this fact further strengthened the likelihood that he would become a very successful planter indeed, and here in the place of his birth. The plantation was prospering as it was growing in size, so much so that he was calling on family members for aid in supplying necessaries like wagons. James Hardy Jr. of Anderson, South Carolina, son of the old pioneer's third son, wrote his reply touching the matter to William Eppes Hardy on 27 October 1835:

> Anderson District
> Dear Cousin. I have just received your letter and hasten to answer it. I can inform you there is a waggon here finished, but not exactly after your liking, but I will do this with you. It is worth $130 here; and as you are in a pinch, you can come immediately and get it (if you think you can sell it for me) and use it untill I can have one done according to your description, as I have the woodwork of one now which will suit you and shall be ironed as soon as possible. If therefore this plan will suit you, you come as soon as you receive this, as I will keep the one on hand until I hear from you; but if you would rather wait till I can iron you one, write me word immediately, as I may know how to proceed with the one I have now on hand. But whether you come on or not, I intend to iron the woodwork I have as soon as I can, as you know it is my interest to have all the work done possible. So that there will be no mistake, I will keep the one I have for you and iron the other as soon as selfinterest, industry, and desire to please you will allow. As to bringing it to you, it is beyond my power. I have not time to come by no means.
>
> We are all well and I hope these lines may find you all so accordingly. Give my love to all.
> James Hardy

William Eppes Hardy was also making substantial purchases of slaves during this decade, so as to double his plantation work force. His family circle grew in like proportion. By 1839 the couple had five children.

And so too was their family increasing its sphere with valued in-laws who would become and remain integral parts of their lives. Only three years after Catharine and William's marriage, Catharine's eighteen-year-old sister Frances married Dr. George Douglass of nearby Fish Dam (present-day Carlisle) on 12 January 1832, in another much-celebrated and festive ceremony at the Hardy Great House. The Douglasses of The Oaks would thus become William and Catharine's closest friends; there would be constant visiting between households, and the children of both families were to be affectionate and inseparable cousins. For over three decades the two families would spend weeks together, travel in tandem on the cars to the springs, mountains, or pinewoods for their health, would school their children at the same academies, throw big country dances and barbecues, go off to war together, write a barrage of letters when they had to be apart, and complain that one or another of them had not written or visited often enough.

Like Catharine's, the wedding of Frances and George was a grand occasion at the plantation. Once again, their kinsman the Reverend Jennings officiated; and the ceremony was followed by a three-day round of music, reel-dancing, and feasting. As one Carolinian noted, here in the country, balls differed from those in the city by being more "lively and less governed by restraint." Dances were more often characterized by "abandon," where "the heels fairly took possession of the head." The people of this upcountry land indeed took their music seriously—whether in church or on the dance floor. Singin' Billy Walker, who had only just a few years ago composed and collected his famous *Southern Harmony*, after all, was their close contemporary, born on Tyger River near Cross Keys not twenty miles away. Singin' Billy would have relished this great occasion with the men and women of his valley home, and would have appreciated their aims, accomplishments, and values, for now in their Great House by the river, the Hardys had established the harmonious rhythms of their life on the land. There was harmony between human beings, Nature, and God, all of which were closely bound; they were living in literal harmony with the seasons. Music had itself become a metaphor of their life.

The men and women of the Quarters, now into their slower midwinter work phase, were buzzing with their own excitement at all the wedding merriment. The corn and cotton harvests were in and the butcherings accomplished. The hams were curing, and sausages decorated the smokehouse in spicy garlands and festoons that smelled of sage, onion, and coriander. Sweet potatoes were mounded high in their pine-straw-covered banks for the winter. There was indeed food aplenty for both white and black alike; and Dan, the black fiddler, stood on a chair as he provided lively music for the Virginia reel, or neighbor Eppes played the slow and mystic strains of an ancient serpentine dance remembered out of a rural English past, when winter dancers would don antlers and pay reverence to the creatures of nature in sacramental salute. The antlers were gone, but the tune remained.

As they had at the marriage of William and Catharine, the big double doors of the candlelit drawing room once again swung wide into the bright hall to give room for the intricate mazes of the dance. The banjo was also much in evidence in the Quarters, where slaves of the visiting families from neighboring plantations had a good time seeing one another again, saying their "howdies," and catching up on the doings of the area. For all, there was "good gay abandon and happy rejoicing." At times, a group from the Quarters would break away to gather before the tall drawing-room windows bright with candles to watch and listen in the quiet dark, then walk their peaceful way home over the frozen fields in a night bright with constellations. Late into the night, as one recalled of the time, those in the Big House "could hear the mellow tones of black musicians sounding to them across ice-crusted fields and the ragged skeletons of the bare-picked cotton terraces." The far-off deep-chested baying of hounds in the forest as they chased the deer among the river sallows came to them as solemn, choral accompaniment on the clear and frosty air. Inside the hall, one, then another, would quit the dance to steal away alone to the window to listen. Hushed, they would stand for a time, their flushed faces feeling the cold through the window panes, for the night sounds on the land had their own lonely beauty and enchantment.

The darker and colder the night outside, the warmer and closer the guests and family circle within, while the higher and more cheerful burned the hearth fire. Even when most vibrantly engaged, however, those gathered inside had the peaceful images of the outer world in their deepest mind's eye: of the rack-heavy deer drawn from their coverts by the night to roam the dim country of the darkness, or yet of the sleeping winter fields that lay just outside the fall of light from the high windows, visions that never fully left their consciousness—always the unspoken yet deeply felt presence of the land, the dormant fields waiting through their rind of ice unconcernedly, placidly, for spring, and that would not be rushed. Perhaps this was the slow secret of the charm.

Strangely, like a seed kernel in its hard husk, the smell of new-turned spring soil itself lay sleeping and implied in the cold air. There were no fragrances like these to be bought in bottles and vials from the city shops. The nose-tingling winter air, the fresh musky smell of spring earth, like no other fragrances in the world, and on this January night, magically intertwined. All felt it, but none spoke it. Only one, many years later was to write of it. Instead, now, beneath the glowing candles and before the high-burning hearthfires, the dancers turned and doubled, doubled and turned, weaving their spell. In the children's beds in the high house, the little ones also fell under the spell and partook of the charm of the music, for through their sleep they still heard the mellow fiddle and the rhythmical pad and shuffle of the feet below, and in flitting dreams saw the same rack-heavy buck and smelled the same rich fields. Through closed eyelids, they too watched the wheeling constellations as the stars mirrored the dancers below with their own cosmic rhythms, turning wide and circling as if the tall, sturdy chimneys of the house themselves made the fixed axis point of the universe.

These were indeed enchanted times. It was this life on the timeless Southern land that magically gentled the manners of its people, softened the harsh edges of personality, even the sounds of the voice, making it slow and musical as well, that charmed one to be more generous, warmer to all. It knew little discord of machinery and none of factory. Instead, it was the blended harmonies of wagon, plough, field-song, fiddle, harp, and harpsichord, and of life slowed by and resigned to the unhurryable music of the seasons so that it could be relished in full. "Every time you hurry to get somewhere or do something," said many a wise old Colonel, "You run the risk of missing more than you gain by the speed, and get out of step with the music. How can life be rich and harmonious if you flail and dash through it?" Like the crops, the hours could not be the least pushed and speeded; why, above all, should the people? or the land? Surely not for the narrow purpose of getting and spending. The slow dance-procession of the stars in this winter sky would be their guide and model. Their wide paths could be rushed or altered not a whit. No chance of hurry here on the slow land, for the seasons that ordered and patterned their lives could not be hurried and the very hours themselves passed by enchanted, each a silk-clad daughter of slow time. Here one learned to accept, not alter and dominate, to fall into step with the easy rhythm. Here could be no shove and jangle of competition. That was for the new-building cities and their discordant clatter of machines, the grinding of steel on steel.

No, in their dance within their charmed realm, the wedding guests continued to weave their way in the spells of old and intricate patterns to the ancient mirrored motion of the stars, slowing their steps as within a dream, waiting only for the stroke of a clock that would end it all and make the dreamer awake; only the clock did not strike and the dreamers would wake only to find that this was, after all, no dream.

Golden times. As it has come down to us, the dashing young bachelor-doctor's courtship of the beautiful and accomplished young lady of the house was the talk of an even wider area than was Catharine and William's, for the hand of the tall, dark-eyed Frances "was being sought far and wide." There were during these days flesh and blood lords and ladies enough at Hardy House, the former riding their dappled bays, the latter clad in their iridescent silks; but for many years now a newly-throned king had held indisputable sway over the land and its inhabitants. This sovereign was King Cotton, and his devotees were being richly rewarded with white gold, translated for the humble field hands as denim, homespun, and "hog and hominy," and for the white family as a candlelit drawing room big enough for reel and serpentine dances, fine appointments of silver, mahogany, rich carpeting, books, and porcelain, and, above all, the domicile's imposing new Palladian portico that reflected life in some serene, reposeful, and idyllic Italian villa, its design a conscious link to the highest ideals of Classicism: graciousness, hospitality, harmony, order, balance, beauty, proportion—mirroring thus also the rural ideals of Southern character and personality—μηδὲν λίαν, "Nothing to extreme," the Horatian mean—to which William and Catharine themselves aspired, and would in turn endeavor to pass to their children. Indeed, all these boons were but trifles to His Majesty Cotton, who bestowed them on all the faithful subjects in his realm, where even in the dry, granulated blaze of late August the plantation rows themselves seemed to be hushed, magically sheltered, and asleep under their soft-blanketed "snow of Southern summers."

Now with this wedding, the solstice was past, the sun was returned, the days lengthening. The coldest days of winter were behind them for another year and thoughts were already turning to new beginnings, to a new family within the old, to births, and to the new tilling of the soil of their fathers' fields that gave their life its rhythm and abiding continuity.

5

Paterfamilias

Remember that a farm is like a man—however great the income, if there is extravagance, but little is left. . . . In his youth, the owner should devote his attention to planting. He should think a long time about building, but planting is a thing not to be thought about, but done.

—Marcus Cato, *De Agri Cultura*

If I had to say which was telling the truth about society, a speech by a Minister-of-Housing or the actual buildings put up in his time, I should believe the buildings.

—Lord Kenneth Clark

William Eppes Hardy was a remarkable man: intelligent, well-educated, public-spirited, and sensitive, an admirable gentleman whose manners and behavior were rather more typical of his era, class, and upcountry community than not. Preeminently, however, he was a man of realism and horse sense. His brother James noted "sensus communis"—common sense—as his "strong forte" even while William was a young squire in his twenties. As dignified and respected as he was, he balanced this serious side of his personality with wit, humor, and a gift for teasing. He always foreswore the popular Southern title "Colonel," for as he said, he was not one. He was simply, after all, as he called himself, "a countryman, minding my concerns and doing the best I can in the sphere in which God has placed me." His family circle was a warm one. In their letters, his children as often addressed him with the familiar "Pa" as with the formal "Father." The community called him Squire Hardy from respect and the understanding that he was one of the true landed gentry, whose model lay in that seventeenth- and eighteenth-century world in Britain, a way of life so quickly passing there to the onslaught of urbanity and the industrial revolution, and that the Hardys and their fellow planters of Tyger were trying in their modest but effective way to preserve on a new continent. To his black bondsmen he was Squire Willem, Squire Hardy, de Squire, and Marse Billy. To his many young nieces and nephews in both Carolinas, he was just good, plain Uncle Billy, his wife their Aunt Kate or Katie. "Uncle Billy," wrote his young niece at The Oaks in 1859, "came to see us yesterday. He is as great a tease as ever." Yes, all could see clearly that he relished life and that at the same time he was living a very deliberate and useful one. He passed both his sense of duty and his fun-loving and joking nature to his sons, grandsons, and great-grandsons. Still discernable in the family line is what must have been his own piquant wit, playfulness, and wry sense of the comic in a somewhat terse English rather than an exaggerated and prolix Southern frontier way. The latter was much more the manner of brother James, as often demonstrated in his letters, with his broad "fat as a tick, yes, even a dog tick" humor.

The squire was also reputed to have some skill as a writer, but other than letters and plantation ledgers, nothing has come down to us. The letters show a forceful, straightforward, realistic style, usually rather more spare than lyrical. At times, however, he can communicate effectively with a single striking image. A family member in 1965 recalled a book he wrote "more than a hundred years ago" and published in New York. He could not recollect its title but remembered that William's grandson John Frost Hardy Sr. had the only copy of it he had ever seen. Diligent searches have not discovered it; and perhaps one day it will surface, and the fabric of our chronicle can be enriched with William's own warp and woof.

His mother named him after her brother William Eppes, whose wife Henrietta was the daughter of William's own Aunt Elizabeth Hardy, and thus both his uncle and his first cousin. His namesake was a lawyer, magistrate, and justice of the peace; and William was likewise to receive legal training and eventually to become a magistrate himself. The Eppes and Hardy families were intricately entwined. A lifelong friend of Hardy's was his cousin Dr. James Monroe Eppes, whose mother was Polly Hardy Eppes, Henrietta Hardy Eppes's sister and thus William Eppes's sister-in-law. She was both William's and Catharine's first cousin. Polly lived with her son James Monroe Eppes ten miles from the Hardy plantation. While still at college in 1835, Eppes wrote his cousin William this interesting letter revealing much about the writer's personality and the social milieu of this branch of the family:

Randolph Macon College
April 13th, 1835

Friend and Relative,

I received your kind communication of the 15th ult, day before yesterday, and was glad to find that I had not been entirely forgotten. As it respects the weather, spring is now making its long wished for appearance. The weather had been very rigorous, indeed, and I have seen more snow this winter than I ever saw before. For the intensity of the cold, I cannot account. You, in your advising me to be economical as much so as possible, I approve; but if you will call to mind a verse which I will here insert, you will be compelled to draw the conclusion that I am not:

I know the right, and approve it too;
I know the wrong, and yet the wrong pursue.

So you see, without an open declaration from me that I am not as economical as old Jos. Hill. However, I will try to bear in mind your friendly admonition, and, at the same time, remind you that he who enjoys to-day, will not, on the morrow, *wish* he had enjoyed it. The next thing is, this here fashion of writing you have all got into down east (south). I think it smells of the Rev. B. Smith's hand. I rather think that your hand has been injured by it. As for my part, I do not believe in it, unless it will learn me to write straight, for you see I am getting quite crooked, but I will try to straighten them directly. The next thing in order is Doctor Clarke's Rabbit scrape. One hundred caught by one little Doctor! Surprising! I thought that overseers had no time for such sport, except Sundays; and I do not believe that Sam would violate the mandates of him whom he professes to adore. Tell Sam he had better been writing to me than selling Rabbit skins to Pedlars. You mention several deaths occasioned by the measles. I was sorry to hear it. The Small Pox is about ten miles of the College, and is progressing rapidly. I am very well pleased, and, although I wish to see my friends and Relations, I do not wish to go home until June 1837, if I shall live that long, when I shall be in the Senior Class. At that time, I wish to return, and not before. When I do come, I am going right straight to see some "gal," and not that often, but I intend to pop the question to her. To think about the "gals" is my chief employment. From this declaration you may reasonably suppose that I study very little. My determination is to marry soon as I can get from this place of confinement. These Brick walls hold many bodies but very few minds. Some lean to their textbook as they would to a plate of Peas, but for my part, I am not so fond of them at all. That my health is better, I believe, than it ever was in the winter. George's [his brother George Eppes, who graduated from Randolph Macon] is very good, and so is Clough's. I gave your respects to Clough. He in return wishes you good luck. Tell Doctor Douglass' boy Dick, that I wish his master would send me a letter. Tell Doctor Clarke to submit something to my consideration. Now for their respects to them kinfolks of mine. Oh! their names are too many to mention, so bulk them all together and tell 'em that I respect 'em very much, and would be very glad to hear from any of them, at any time. I forgot to offer an excuse for not writing to you before this time, but let it go, and write punctually for the future, and I will the same.

Yours with due respect,
J. M. C. Eppes

Randolph Macon was a Methodist College founded in Virginia in 1830. The George Eppes mentioned in the letter became a lawyer in 1842 and died in 1846. William Eppes Hardy named his son born in the following year George Eppes Hardy in his memory, so the ties between the families remained close and affectionate.

William Eppes Hardy kept abreast of political developments and was very much involved in States' Rights movements from 1830 to 1835. He supported Nullification wholeheartedly and, as we have seen, had strong differences of opinion on the subject with his brother James. He accused James of taking his stand out of "prejudice and not principle." For himself, his political philosophy "derived from the old Republic and Magna Carta," "proscribed Federal power," and the right of a people to self-government. In 1832 he agreed with the provision of the Ordinance of Nullification that if Washington used force against South Carolina, the state would consider itself separate and would organize an independent government, "whose base would be closer to the governed." Lawyer-planter, magistrate, political activist, writer, family man, hospitable and generous friend and neighbor, supporter of the church, a man of wealth and some influence, avid sportsman, and a gentleman respected in the community, he was the worthy inheritor of the blood of Magna Carta barons and of the old Hardy feudal claims to landed patrician caste and privilege. Indeed, his nickname the Young Squire was not an idle choice.

When he became plantation master at the age of twenty-four, he was already an independent man of substance. And he and the family he bore were soon to have a reputation for style, mirrored in part by their love of fine blooded horses with names like *Lady Albion*, *Black Knight*, *John Gidiron*, *Sir Tonson Archy*, *Flora*, and *Venus*. In a plantation ledger, the squire's jottings from 1838 to 1840 record his breeding of blooded mares and stallions. "Put Flora to John Gidiron the 29th of May 1839," he wrote. "Put Sall to Sir Tonson Archy the 15th of May 1839. . . . Sall mare foaled by Tonson Archy the 15th of April" "Put the Murat mare by Tonson Archy the 30th of April 1840. . . . My Flora mare took Bill Austin the 19th of May 1838. . . . Flora mare foaled by Bill Austin the 13th of May 1839." The name *Sir Tonson Archy* is interestingly close to the famous racehorse *Sir Archy, Jr.*, whose dam *Transport* was painted by Edward Troye in 1833. Troye was employed as painter at various important stud farms in the South. Colonel Wade Hampton, of neighboring Richland County, used Troye extensively; and Hampton no doubt knew and participated in the Maybinton, Goshen Hill, and Santuc races. Hampton himself owned a racetrack on an island in the Broad River in Newberry County. Whether or not Hampton and Hardy knew one another through the turf, Hardy shared his love with the wealthiest and most respected horseman in America. My surmise is that they were acquainted.

In 1860 there were nineteen horses on the Hardy plantation. While the master was cutting down on the number of other livestock, he was adding to his stable. Horses were his and his sons' hobby and a minor passion—as well as yet another practical means of diversifying his planta-tion bounty. His horses were well enough known for him to receive some impressive stud fees. And the men of the county recognized him as an authority on horses, for in the Newberry Agricultural Society, already boasting three hundred members in its second year of existence, Hardy was chosen as chairman of the committee to judge and award prizes for horses at the Agricultural Fair of July 1853. He did his duty and presented silver cups to three Newberry planters. Significantly, Hardy himself won a silver cup at the fair, but not for a horse. He took first prize for the best "sucking colt Mule," a fact that coincides well with what we know about him: that though he raised the aristocratic animal and was even an acknowledged connoisseur of it, he himself chose to exhibit the mule—the homely, practical work animal, "ex-tremely patient and faithful in labour," the symbol itself of common sense, endurance, and an even and stubborn patience. As he well knew, "A mule, unlike a horse is far too intelligent to break its heart for glory running around the rim of a mile long saucer." Here again is an indica-tion of "Marse Billy's" value system, and that of so many upcountry Carolinians: a foreswearing of ostentation—the high and flashy rejected for the down-to-earth and simple familiar. It was, after all, his pioneering heritage. Again, then, the good squire demonstrated balance and an easy aristocracy, marked by the highest elegance—that which forbears crying attention to itself by display. It is this sense of style that led Frederick Law Olmsted, a Northern critic of the South who begrudged her any praise, to write in 1856: "There is less vulgar display, and more intrinsic elegance, and habitual mental refinement in the best society of South Carolina, than in any distinct class anywhere among us" in America. Hardy was rightful heir to the tradition of healthy outdoorsmen, of Anglo-Norman squirearchy, complete with its ideas of understated style, manner, and decorum. So Hardy judged horses and himself exhibited mules; how perfectly appropriate. Interspersed rather casually with his jottings of breeding and foaling blooded animals is his record in the plantation ledgers of breeding mules, and such facts as the "Brindle Heifer Took the Bull 17 Feb. 1841."

Although William was a serious planter and a respected and respon-sible citizen, his life was by no means all work and no play. The closet below-stairs was well-stocked with wine. And besides using some of his horses on the autumn and winter hunts for which their Maybinton area was famous, he and the young Hardys entered their fastest in the local races at the track behind the Maybin house, at the Goshen Hill racetrack adjacent to the Orange Hall store three miles distant, and at Jeter's track in Santuc, some thirteen miles away. Goshen Hill, as its biblical name suggests, was a place of good farm land, the land of plenty, where the soil was said to be a "deep woodsy loam that was very easily tilled." Both Goshen Hill and Santuc were famous for wealthy planters whose chief sporting enthusiasm was fast horseflesh. These three tracks were much celebrated for this sport before the war; and silver trophy cups given to the winners are still to be found in the homes of at least two Newberry County descendants of these equestrians, one a descendant of George and Frances Hardy Douglass of The Oaks of Goshen Hill. The Jeters who owned the Santuc track were distant Hardy relatives. True to their Virginia heritage, they gave rather elaborate "fox chases" to which the Hardys were invited. A Jeter descendant recalls that her family so loved the sport that they imported red foxes to the countryside to "improve the quality of their hunts." Often these events were held on race day as an added attraction, and were always topped off with a large barbecue and lively dancing and frolics for the slaves. Into the twentieth century, the Jeters of Woodland Home plantation in Santuc were devoted to the formal hunt, and their hunter's horns are still to be seen hanging at the plantation.

At the Goshen Hill track, as remembered by former slave Gus Feaster in 1937, there was heavy imbibing of whiskey from a long row of barrels in front of the Orange Hall store, "for the rich men that carried on at the racetrack." At all three spots, on race days, as another account has it, "barrels of spirits were placed at intervals along the road and the celebrating sportsmen were regaled with handled drinking gourds full of liquor." A Caldwell descendant recalls that her ancestors (nearby neighbors of the Hardys), before they had raised a roof over their heads, had already laid out a racetrack. All this was the Caldwells' Scots-Irish Celtic tradition, and to which the Anglo-Norman Hardys and Jeters took readily. The Maybins of the Maybinton track were also Scots-Irish. In the old country, the Irishmen of the present day are still noted for their passion for horseracing. It is there at the rail, says one current Irish author, that the ghosts of the departed may be most readily found leaning against the palings.

By the 1850s a Hardy neighbor born at Pomaria plantation could write that in their neighborhood the horse had become "the Southron's cherished amusement" even to the extent that the "modern reared boy

. . . will *walk two* miles, to catch a horse to enable him to *ride one.*" The Hardy youths no doubt belonged to this class. They learned early as very little children to "play horse," one riding the other, then graduating to the real thing. Former slave George Briggs of a nearby Cross Keys plantation remembered that the master's son "was our play hoss . . . I was de mule. Henry was little and he rid our backs sometimes. Henry rid old man Sam, sometimes; and old man Sam jes' holler and haw-haw at us chilluns . . . from dis we rid de gentle hosses and mules." Pieces of two early-nineteenth-century children's toys have been found on the Hardy plantation grounds; significantly, one is a handsome porcelain horse.

All the young Hardy sons thus became much more than competent horsemen. Son Haywood was always reminding his father that he was preeminently a "Horse man." Bills for foxing boots, riding whips, riding gloves, fancy saddle blankets, riding reins, horse rasps, and currycombs appear among the accounts of purchases made by the squire's teenage sons in the 1850s. Some of the young Hardys rode their blooded "chargers" in the popular "jousts" held some twenty miles distant on a field a half-mile from the Great House at Cross Keys plantation, a plot that had been set aside expressly for this purpose. Here the "knights" in good medieval costume showed their skill before the gallery of finely dressed ladies in the hopes of receiving their favors of wreaths of laurel bay, and the winner's privilege of choosing one of them "Queen of the Tournament" and of crowning her with a chaplet of roses. The young especially found the occasion congenial to courtship. It was an old and well-established tradition throughout the plantation country of South Carolina, Lowcountry as well as Upcountry, and one that had been passed down intact and unbroken from the squires of Britain. It was decidedly not, as some detractors would have it, a faddish romantic reaction to the vogue of Sir Walter Scott's medieval novels, but instead a custom they were practicing in Carolina long before Scott began to write, and intrinsic to a traditional rural culture that valued so strongly both the horse and the deep ancestral past. Over and above the pageantry and romance was the frank reality that the horseman needed the most consummate skill to pass his lance at full gallop through a series of small, hanging rings that comprised the challenge. Two of these jousting lances and the "plated" stirrups used in these antebellum games were still to be seen in the attic at Cross Keys plantation as late as the 1950s. One of these lances now hangs on a wall of the Hardy plantation.

Hardy's blooded horses also cut a good figure when they pulled the family's buggy and carriage. As the family's fanciest mode of transportation, the carriage contributed significantly to its style. The buggy was used by the master when he rode out alone, but the carriage was reserved for family outings: to church, reel dances, picnics, the frequent July barbecues, and (before the advent in 1850 of the Columbia and Greenville rail line that stopped near them at Shelton on the Broad) to the springs in September, to take their sons and daughters to and from their academies and colleges, to witness their commencements, to do their shopping in Charleston and Columbia, and to make their many visits to their numerous relations. The closed vehicle was especially dear to milady Kate herself, who had fine silk and satin dresses to protect from dust and rain.

Despite his love of the sporting and social life and his penchant for annual visits to the springs, Squire Billy did not neglect his planting with long absences. He was aware of the old Southern adage that a planter's footsteps are like manure to his land. The soil indeed blossomed under the tread of its master. Hardy kept good, steady, and close control of his planting responsibilities and thus balanced his work with his play in a healthy golden mean, a wholeness that was engendered by his life on the land, and yet another ideal imbibed from the classical tradition to which he successfully aspired. Even as the young master, Squire William took to heart as his personal motto the inscription on the Apollo Temple at Delphi: $\mu\eta\delta\grave{\epsilon}\nu$ $\lambda\acute{\iota}\alpha\nu$, "Nothing to Excess," a basis of Greek wisdom. In the plantation ledgers of the 1830s and 1840s, his fine and disciplined hand kept daily records of sales from the plantation bounty.

William's love of his sons and daughters, while warm and genuine, did not allow him to dote. He was very careful to supervise his children's finances and expenditures while they were away at college and academy. He often cautioned them and their headmasters not to allow "extravagances." In no way might one call Hardy a wastrel and a spendthrift, and he made certain he would do all he could to prevent his children from acquiring these vices. The family had no hint of decadence in its makeup. It lived in quiet elegance, but never to excess.

As a newly married gentleman in 1829, young William's first plantation purchases were indicative of his practicality and seriousness in developing his stock of swine and expanding the plantation's scope. One early bill of 1829 recorded payment for a spotted sow and pigs at $3.00, a banded sow and pigs at $2.00, and a red spotted sow and brood at $2.62. Also purchased were forty fowl at 7¢ a head. These were for

Catharine and her cooks, whose province was the poultry yard. New agricultural implements included two harrows, two dagons, two plow-stocks, and three colters at $1.25; nine weeding hoes at $6^1/_4$¢; two sickles at 25¢; one lot of plow hoes at $43^3/_4$¢; and four plow-stocks and single-trees at $1.50. For the house, he bought a pair of candle molds at $37^1/_2$¢. Finally, he did not fail to remember Catharine, for whom he purchased "1 Blue Pitcher."

Hardy's early interest in swine accorded well with agriculturist-neighbor A. G. Summer's recommendation in the 1850s that Southern-ers raise their own bacon, not merely to provide rich, nutritious fare for the plantation community but also to supply the "richest compost so that many acres of sterile soil might be speedily reclaimed." Swine became a very practical solution for Hardy, who continued to live on his familial land rather than move west to virgin soil. By means of composting and other wise agricultural practices, he would not exhaust his land, but would leave it the richer each year he farmed it. Without the modern aid of chemicals, Hardy practiced what today is called sustainable agri-culture.

The most joyous time of the year for the plantation was after the cotton had been picked, ginned, and sold. This occurred in December, in time for Christmas and the new year. At this season, William had more time to hunt in his forest with his sons, and pocket money aplenty to buy presents. This was the season that he and Catharine usually pur-chased the household necessaries and nice extras, and most of the fine and common cloth that the ladies made into clothing throughout the year. Thus there was a flurry of shopping in Columbia. Often, as the plantation ledgers reveal, brother-in-law George Douglass accompanied the squire on these forays. (For example, to George, he records lending cash "for balance of things bought in Columbia" on 20 December 1842.)

Then too, at this season the plantation's black community had less to do and could celebrate as well. With the great abundance of swine on the place, hog butcherings provided much-relished pork for the families of both races, and everybody ate well in this richest and most abundant season for the plantation's three M's: Meat, Meal, and Molasses. Hardy found pork to be a perfect plantation food, "easily prepared and entirely congenial" to his people's "constitutions and natures." One Carolina planter aptly put it that Christmas on the Southern plantation was "em-phatically the sausage season. Then it is that every Negro is heard to whistle, and every mouth looks oily." The large hog butcherings in the cold weather were fondly anticipated by the entire plantation community.

Winter was also the time of fiddles, banjos, reel dancing, juba dancing, and the buck-and-pigeon-wing. Marse Billy did not forget his own or his black plantation families on Christmas morn, and the slaves loved surprising him and the "Mistis" with the exclamation "Christmas Gif!"—which, according to the strict rules of the game and ritual, meant the master and mistress must provide a present. These were shawls, handkerchiefs (the bright ones were preferred), caps, scissors, knives, razors, tobacco, pipes, and needles, as the records of Christmas purchases at the store at nearby Orange Hall so clearly provide the evidence.

For the menfolk, slave and master alike, Christmas day on the plantation was itself preeminently the day of the hunt, when father, sons, kin, and neighbors would take to the woods. Then came the Christmas supper for which the womenfolk had prepared all week, and served in a room freshly garlanded by the children with the aromatic cedar, holly, and smilax from the forest, in the good old country English way of their Anglo-Norman ancestors. Occasionally, as in 1848, even a boar's head "in procession" became the centerpiece of the evening feast, which was relished by all, but particularly by the hunters, whose exercise had built fierce winter appetites. In they came, stomping in their great heavy riding boots, spirits high, and a little rough, their cheeks red from the cold and a dram of Christmas brandy, bringing the smell of woods with them on their clothes, their hounds and setters boiling around their feet into the dining room, to the ladies' chagrin and the black cook Auntie Rachael's vociferous exclamations, accompanied by swift thrashes of the kitchen broom. A few of the more venerable and better mannered of these flop-eared and big-eyed veterans of the hunt were allowed to remain inside about the postprandial fire, while all the men and womenfolk gathered together in cirque before it to tell stories of the day, of the kitchen, the cousins, the children, the fields, the hunt. Then the children were off to their quilt-covered beds. The hounds and setters dozed, their noses wrinkling and tails and feet sometimes moving in their dreams as they rehearsed the day's events, momentous in their dog memories. The spaces of silence punctuating the talking grew longer and longer. The talk became cadenced like a fine old ballad in its regular rhythms of comment, silence, and reply: the special music of good conversation. The older folks began to nod off, as the fire glowed red into ashes. Then the comfortable rhythms of yet another deep Christmas night, when over the plantation, the constellations once again wheeled, the wind occasionally whistled about the house corners or down the chimneys, and the old, well-loved serenity of joyous peace descended—the familiar peace of hearts at rest with themselves in another Christmas on the land.

In our day when we are accustomed to monthly or weekly paychecks, it is perhaps difficult to realize how the cotton sale that came only once annually and provided the master with the means to pay bills and most of what cash there would be to live on for the next year, was a major event on his calendar providing, in times of good harvest, a real sense of satisfaction and completion to the year. That the harvest coincided in the South with holy and happy Christmas, the birth of the real Master above, made that holiday all the more festive. The new year marked a true beginning—the old crop was realized, and in January the mortal master looked to preparing his fields to begin anew with the help of the newly born divine one. His life was truly perfectly in tune with nature, the seasons, and the calendar of his own religion, all of which clearly held the proper symbolic meanings for him of fulfillments, completions, new beginnings, resurrections, and eternity, reinforced as they were by the days of his own life. Satisfying, yes indeed, this life on the good land, and nourishing to more than the physical body of the man.

Perhaps Robert Stokes, a planter from the adjacent county of Laurens, best described the life for the plantation master of this area at year's end:

> *December.* Settle up all your farm accounts, pay what you have borrowed from your neighbor, and require him to do the same—'short settlements make long friends.' Sell your cotton, pay off your debts, mend your fences, shut up all your slip gaps, fill up your stockyards and stables with leaves, see that your wheat fields are all free from water, repair harness, plowstocks, wagons, carts, and all farm implements; during wet days, thresh out peas, gin and pack cotton, haul plenty of wood into the back yard and about the quarters; make up your mind to be at peace with everybody, to enjoy a happy Christmas, and be ready to set out with us on the New Year in better spirits—a more cheerful heart—and a determination to do as little harm and as much good as possible.

So it was in the man's world in upcountry Carolina.

Less has come down to us of Squire Billy's lady. She was literate and wrote a beautiful hand. She dressed stylishly. From a December 1831 receipt from John I. Gracey & Co. of Columbia, one of the preferred mercantile establishments of the Hardys, of their Douglass kin at The Oaks, and of the Renwicks at Orange Hall, we find the new mistress of the plantation purchasing gloves, a pair of "side combs" for her long hair, cambric handkerchiefs, linen, white flannel, bobinet, a reticule, two lady's cloaks at $21 (approximately $400 in today's currency), and enough yards of cloth to make silk dresses, three chemises of "white figured satin," a dress of very expensive black "grosinap," and a dress of white muslin and cambric (a light summer dress popular in the South at the time). Milady also purchased a black bobinet veil at $5 (over $100 in today's currency) and a cap and belt "ribleands" (ribbons). Her purchases totaled $107 (over $2,000 today). Evidence of such finery presupposes at least a moderately fancy social life beyond churchgoing at Ebenezer. Squire William and his family traveled to Charleston, Columbia, and Spartanburg, South Carolina, and Salem, Flat Rock, and Asheville, North Carolina, as letters and purchase receipts tell us, and made frequent forays to the springs and watering spas each September, as we have seen. Like most Carolinians of their class, they were very sociable, and were frequently picking up trunks and portable furniture to "go a-visiting," particularly with their brothers, children, and their many cousins. The popular Southern tale of the maiden aunt who came for a visit and stayed for a lifetime was oft-repeated in this part of Carolina. It was not uncommon for some of the Hardys and Douglasses to spend a summer on a visit.

As was also the case with most planters' wives, the ladies of the house—that is, Catharine and her mother Anna, now forty-eight years old in 1831—spent much time in their rooms or sunny sewing closets, making clothing for themselves, their families, and the slaves. They were assisted by the ladies' waiting maids and other house servants when not otherwise occupied. Later on, when there were daughters, they helped as well. The presence at the plantation of at least five spinning wheels and a loom during antebellum days also suggests they worked many hours making homespun, a skill which sister Frances Hardy Douglass put to particularly good use in the 1860s making gray cloth for her son's uniforms while he was fighting in Virginia. This activity helped clothe the blacks and provided everyday raiment for the white family. The sheep on the Hardy place and the production of fifty pounds of wool in 1850 also point to the making of woolen cloth for clothing, coverlets, and blankets. Sheep had been listed in the Hardy plantation inventories since 1814 and were probably present from the start. There were 25 sheep on the place in 1850. At the Douglasses', there were 33 in 1850 and 76 in 1860. The 30¾ yards of "bleached shirting" purchased by Catharine Hardy from Gracey & Co. in 1831 likely went into shirts for the menfolk, including the squire. The 56½ yards of calico probably made everyday dresses for the mistress and/or clothing for the house servants.

The Gracey receipt is unfortunately the only one extant for this particular year and can thus give but a small idea of the style the family exhibited in 1831. Doubtless, however, there were other such purchases, and judging from this one alone, we know the squire's wife must have dressed fashionably. As befitted a newly married twenty-year-old from a family of considerable and rising substance, the plantation mistress's wardrobe included "figured" satin and silk. It is good to see cap ribbons and colors in her wardrobe, telling us that hers was not a too-sober life of severe blacks and somber hues. Her pious Methodist tradition would have prevented too much lavishness, however; and thus again a golden mean is suggested in wife as well as husband, for whom their "Nothing to Excess" motto reflected both classical and Christian precepts.

Recently come to light is the Hardys' account for the year 1835 with R. C. Anderson & Co., a fashionable gentleman's clothier on Richardson (Main) Street in Columbia. Catharine now had three boys in the household, and this bill reveals what their parents were purchasing for them. Little Thomas was five and Adolphus four. They received "Boy's pants" ($2.50), "Boy's Cass pants" (5.00), "Boy's Vest" (2.50), "Boy's Overcoat" (5.00), "Boy's Cloth Sack [coat]" (5.00), "Brown Hat" (2.00), "Drab Hat" (1.50), drawers (2.00), socks (1.50), and, named as being specifically for Adolphus, "1 Pair Cass Pants" (7.00). The list also has two items initialed for little Charles Wesley, then three years old: a "Blue coat (11.00) and "1 pair Drap D'Ete pants" (5.00). Likely the young squire purchased some of the following items for himself: a blue frock coat (12.00), a linen coat (3.50), an Alpaca frock coat (5.00), an Alpaca sack coat (3.00), three vests (10.00), a plaid vest (3.00), two pairs of linen pants (8.00), tweed pants (4.00), four shirts (8.00), six collars (1.00), and a black cravat (2.50).

Catharine helped to supervise the cooking and feeding on the plantation. In this capacity she also tended the poultry for eggs and fryers and oversaw the dairy yard with butter and milk preparation. She likewise had some part in growing things other than the major crops. Her present of gourds to her sister-in-law Delia Hardy in 1852 points up this truth. The family kitchen garden was at least partly in her care, as was the rather extensive ornamental garden about the Great House, as will be seen in the following chapter.

From extant furniture passed down to Hardy descendants, corroborated and augmented by bills for purchases and inventories of the period, one can recreate something of the physical environment and material culture of the Hardy household from the late 1820s onward. By the 1860s the dining room contained much silver. One piece, a handsome large compote decorated with grapevine, leaves, and grape clusters, and used to serve fruit, still belongs to a family member, as does a large matching bowl decorated with the same grape designs. There were silver trays, one with the initial "H" in its center, and a set of sterling spoons made by John Veal, a fine silversmith in Columbia, a few pieces of which still exist in the family. One bears the initials of Anna Hardy. There were a butter knife and fluted spoon engraved "W. E. Hardy" with the dates 1859 and 1860. These were made by William Gale of New York for John Veal's silver shop in Columbia. Since they bear dates, they were likely agricultural prizes. There were also sterling cups and candlesticks, as shown in the inventories. An extant bill of purchase reveals that Hardy purchased one pair of these candlesticks from the excellent Columbia silversmiths Glaze & Radcliffe on 20 December 1847 at a cost of $7.00. Also listed in the bill for this date were a set of dinner silver (25.00), tongs (2.50), a fireplace fender (3.50), castors (presumably for bed, table, or chair legs, 12.00), a cheap pair of brass candlesticks (.75), and a costly pair of "Looking Glasses" with "Rings & cord" (40.00). The 20 December date of these purchases indicates that the items may have been intended to brighten Christmas in the year 1847.

The dining room had a drop-leaf banquet table with semicircular detachable banquet ends in the Sheraton style, and said to have been bought in Charleston. This table was presented by the family to the Hardy plantation in 1994. For the bedrooms, there were at least two blanket chests made on the place of native walnut. The one survivor is dovetailed and has bracket feet and double drawers with wooden knob pulls at its base. It exhibits excellent plantation artistry and craftsmanship. At least one of the beds was a four-poster of mahogany, with slender posts, canopy, and bed curtains. In the drawing room there was a mahogany secretary with glass-paned doors. It still bears the hand-written note: "Bought by Wm. Eppes Hardy in Columbia in 1847 for $65.00." In 1925 it sat on the western wall between the windows and, according to a great-grandchild of William Eppes Hardy, was filled to overflowing with leather-bound volumes. A family member in Spartanburg still has the piece, but the books have since disappeared. Also in the drawing room was a slant-front walnut plantation desk with delicately made pigeonhole compartments and bracket feet. This was made on the place and likely by the same artisans who built the walnut blanket chests, as their wood, workmanship, proportion, and design are similar. This well-proportioned desk, still with a descendant, is an important example of excellent American furniture making and design. The Hardy baby cradle, also said to be made from walnut trees cut on the place, is still owned by the family. In one room hung an exceptional portrait of matriarch Anna Powell Dixon Hardy done in 1858 at a cost of $226 (nearly $5,000 in today's currency) by the talented artist William Harrison Scarborough (1812–1871), a favorite portrait painter with the wealthy planters of upcountry Carolina and particularly of the Columbia area. Such was his reputation that he was commissioned to paint the famous John C. Calhoun in 1847 and Governor James Henry Hammond in 1849. In fact, Scarborough made two identical portraits of the widow Hardy, one for each of her daughters Catharine and Frances. Today both of these are in the possession of the two lines of her descendants. Scarborough's account book lists them as done in 1858 and on 1 August 1859.

Family tradition states that by 1860 there was a pianoforte in the drawing room. This is corroborated by the fact that pianoforte wire was used to suspend silver in the well during Sherman's bummers' looting of the home in 1865. The pianoforte had provided entertainment, usually at the hands of daughter Mira and her several cousins from The Oaks, all of whom had musical training at Salem Academy in North Carolina, which, founded in 1772, was among the most venerable and best respected women's schools in the South.

The inventory of William Eppes Hardy's estate in 1870 adds other strokes to our picture of domestic life at the plantation in the previous decade. It shows that the drawing room did indeed contain its secretary and "library" just as the great-granddaughter remembered them in 1925, two "parlor tables," one "lot of parlor chairs," a sofa, two rocking chairs, three candlesticks, two silver candlesticks (the pair likely bought from Glaze & Radcliffe in 1847), two silver cups (at least one of these an agricultural prize), a pair of china vases, a firescreen (and fender bought from Glaze & Radcliffe in 1847), a set of andirons, and a hearth-dusting broom. The six windows were hung with "6 parlor shades." The floor had a "fine carpet." The walls had "pictures," some noted as bearing "glass frames." National portraits and portraits of "Generals" hung in the hall, possibly up the stairwell. These last would have been particularly appropriate to Federal period decor. No doubt one of them was of General Washington, with whom their Hardy ancestors had fought in Virginia. There was a carpet in the hall.

The other downstairs front room was used as an informal parlor and bedroom. It had "chairs," four curtains for its four windows, a rug, several spinning wheels (occasioned by the making of homespun during the war and its aftermath), two tables, a spittoon, a bed, a trundle bed for a child, "bed furniture," a safe, surgical and medical chests (probably the son, Dr. Charles Wesley's), a pair of andirons, firescreen, and fire-place trivet.

Beyond this room was a pantry, well equipped with crockery, silver plate, saucepans, candle molds, soap molds, coffee urn, coffee mill, two coffeepots, pitchers, alkaline glaze stoneware jugs, cake boxes and cake pans, tin boxes, and glassware. The dining room had the Sheraton banquet table and banquet ends, two pine tables (possibly hunt boards), a crumb brush, a grater, and three demi johns. There was a passage lamp in the 1804 stairwell. As both Haywood Hardy Henderson and William Dixon Hardy recall from their childhood, this stairway was always dark, there being no window; and the passage lamp was indeed a necessity.

Upstairs in the 1825 section were two bedrooms furnished with "bed furniture," five blankets, two quilts, two bedspreads, three coun-terpanes, eight linen sheets, and four linen pillowcases, a carpet, cane-bottom chairs, washstands, and washbowls. The bedding inventory taken in 1870 looks sparse considering the rest of the house furnishings and may have been the result of the immediate family's having had three sons and several body servants in service with the Confederacy, where blankets and sheeting for bandages were in desperately short supply by war's end. Upstairs in the 1804 section, one room was used as a "loom room," for a loom is listed at this point in the inventory. Another room, as stated earlier, was the traveler's room.

These surviving details from extant furniture, receipts of purchase, and the appraisal list of 1870 show that the family was interested in the aesthetic texture of day-to-day life. They had educated good taste and the means to cultivate it. They lived in an environment which that taste created. Most of the plantation's furnishings were acquired during the period when Catharine and William were mistress and master of the plantation, hence from 1828 onward—and they were bought to fit out the new imposing front of the house. The 1804 section kept its pewter and turn-of-the-century "country" furniture.

From this picture emerges the fact that the house was appointed with a restrained and elegant taste. The furnishings were both simple and understated. More often than not, discretion was the better part of good taste for them. Less was better. Larger was not necessarily desirable. There was absolutely no ostentation. The richness of mahogany and walnut and the cleanness of the Georgian and Sheraton styles perfectly suited their classical revival architectural surroundings. Neither is there evidence of heavy Victorian carved furniture introduced at a later date. The furniture was not updated in a more flamboyant era, either of the heavy Empire style of the prewar period or during the so-called Gilded Age of postbellum America, but instead remained of the elegant simplicity of the 1820s and '30s. After 1865 the South's ruined fortunes may perhaps have prevented the latter; but before the war, when the family was at its height of wealth and had the wherewithal to purchase items of late Empire or early Victorian excess and ostentation, it did not. Empire was, after all, the "style" in the 1850s when the family was the most prosperous and when they even had a young daughter who would be married in the house in 1861, a very good excuse to update. Thus we have solid evidence that their tastes dictated what they used, not their purses or the current fashions. They made no attempt to impress or to redecorate because it was "the thing to do" in the America of their era. In the upcountry Carolina of their day, to be ostentatious with wealth was decidedly *not* the thing to do.

The architecture of the 1825 section itself demonstrates an elegant taste compatible with its furnishings. Its double-tiered portico is a model of harmonious good proportion in the classical style. It is Palladian, inspired most closely by Palladio's villa for Giorgio Cornara constructed at Piombino, in the Italian countryside, in 1554. The Villa Cornara was pictured in Palladio's *Four Books of Architecture*, published in London in 1738, the primary source by which those in both England and America knew Palladio. When the Carolina planters of the colonial era built their great country houses, the style of this particular rural villa became one of their favorites. It served them both with a functional design for their hot climate and as a strong and satisfying link to the classical tradition. The first such Palladian portico in the New World appeared on Carolina soil at Drayton Hall near Charleston, a Great House built about 1740 as the seat of the English Drayton family of Ashley River. It also became one of the best-loved styles in the 1820s and '30s in upcountry South Carolina, a design so popular that one observer, himself born in one of these houses, could describe these "white, be-porticoed attempts at Villas" as veritably "*lining* the public roads" of this section of the Upcountry in 1852. Indeed, this observer must not have been exaggerating too much, for a number of good similar examples still exist within a twenty-mile radius of the Hardy plantation. One is Hillside plantation at Carlisle, twelve miles to the north; another is Pomaria, some eighteen miles to the south. All three were built in the 1820s. The fact that, in the words of the observer, these structures were "attempts at Villas" suggests the conscious desire to make the connection and is proof of an awareness of both their symbolism and the planter's recognition of the values such villas represent—in other words, the Great House tradition itself.

The Palladian style of the new Hardy home suited well the family who dwelled within it. Its young master, who was heir to the traditions of Magna Carta, of landed English gentry, and of the high principles of classicism as defined by his own Greek motto taken from Delphi, was, as well, direct heir to the ideals of the high Renaissance. The Palladian front of his "Villa" Great House on its hill by the deep-flowing river clearly reflected this fact. Significantly and appropriately, its design was derived specifically from Palladio's country rather than his city architecture. Squire Hardy and Palladio would have seen eye-to-eye across three centuries on the merits of the rural life. For Hardy, there would have been no dated, foreign, or distant sound to the great architect's syllables in his treatise on villas. The words are Palladio's, from Venice in 1570; but the sentiments are precisely Hardy's own:

> The city houses are certainly of great splendour and conveniency to a gentleman. . . . But perhaps he will not reap much less utility and consolation from the country house; where the time will be passed in seeing and adorning his own possessions, and by industry, and the art of agriculture, improving his estate; where also by the exercise which in a villa is commonly taken, on foot and on horseback, the body

will the more easily preserve its strength and health; and, finally, where the mind, fatigued by the agitations of the city,
will be greatly restor'd and comforted, and be able quietly to
attend the studies of letters, and contemplation. Hence it was
that the antient sages commonly used to retire to such like
places; where being oftentimes visited by their virtuous
friends and relations, having houses, gardens, fountains, and
such like pleasant places, and above all, their virtue, they
could easily attain to as much happiness as can be attained
here below.

The new young master and mistress were now living this rural ideal, not
philosophizing in the abstract about it. The daily and routine matter of
exercise "on foot and on horseback" was already proving beneficial, and
would provide their sons the stamina to get through a great war some
decades later. Indeed, one son would credit his survival to a healthy
constitution formed by a vigorous life on the land. Their "virtuous
friends and relations" were already about them in full abundance in an
ever-growing family circle of wide, close, and complex allegiances. The
family's "industry" and "the art of agriculture" which they practiced
had already mightily "improved their estate," as Palladio had predicted.
Under the guidance of brother James and Mistress Catharine, as we shall
see in the next chapter, Palladio's "garden" would soon spread its ordered paths about the house to create a setting in harmony and proportion with the structure itself. Indeed, as we move still further into this
chronicle, we discover just how truly and completely Palladio's words
apply to the story before us.

    With such an agrarian philosophy as this behind his art, it is little
wonder that the Palladian style was the most popular architectural form
for the Great Houses of Carolina planters like Drayton in his century
and William Eppes Hardy in his own, for these gentlemen were all
building in sympathy with a tradition that expressed perfectly their own
ideals of life on the land, a classicism to whose highest ideal they felt
themselves the legitimate heirs: of harmony between people, state, Nature, and God—of man living in musical relation to his world around
him. It was life set in an ordered garden, both metaphorical and literal,
and tended by good stewards. Here, on terra firma, the abstract ideal
would become concrete reality. Above all, their garden world would
prove a setting in which the "virtue" of the "antient sages" could take

root and find fit and nourishing soil in which to produce a new flowering, and where might be achieved "as much happiness as can be attained here below." This was indeed a Jeffersonian agrarian ideal, a philosophy that grew out of that great thinker's own Southern life on the land. The sage of Monticello himself raised his own Palladian villa on its high and fruitful hill in Virginia to seal the covenant and compact between the ages and make the word flesh.

As stated earlier, the Palladian house at "Pomaria" is too precisely the same in its workmanship and the little details of both its interior and exterior ornamentation and design not to have been planned and constructed by the same architect-builders as the Hardy plantation. These were the brothers Shell. From Pomaria plantation history, it is known that when they built the Big House there in 1826–1827, they quarreled and had to complete the structure by communicating through notes. It is perhaps significant that the Hardy and Shell families were connected by marriage; William's mother, Nancy Eppes Hardy, married Lemmon Shell in 1809 after William's father died; and this may have been how the builder was known and chosen. As we have already seen, her sons Hamlin, James, and William were in fact tutored by Thomas Shell, who later married into the Schoppert family, famous carpenters in Newberry village; and their guardian Daniel Eppes purchased merchandise for the boys at Eppes & Shell. Family ties to the Shell clan (who, like the Hardys, were all Methodists) were thus complex and close, and again provide further evidence that the architect-builders for the new section were the same Shell brothers who constructed Pomaria.

An Absalom D. Shell is listed as a carpenter in the 1850 census for Newberry County. He was born in 1813, had a wife Harriet, and was living among the Hattons, Abramses, and Shells in the Mt. Tabor Methodist community along the Enoree, the community in which Nancy Eppes Hardy was born. Absalom and his neighbor John A. Abrams (1809–1882), whose mother was also a Shell before her marriage, are known to have built Mt. Tabor Methodist Church in 1843 on land given by Allen Shell. (Mt. Tabor was organized by William Shell and David and John Eppes in 1820 and was attended by both Eppeses and Shells throughout its history.) Absalom died in 1874, leaving carpenter's tools to his son James H. Shell (1849–1901) of Peak, near the village of Pomaria. Absalom himself would likely have been too young for working on the Hardy house in 1825; but as professions were often passed from father to son, perhaps it was his father and uncle who did the building

81

at Hardy plantation and Pomaria. At any rate, the presence of several Shell carpenters in the county in two generations lends even more validity to the surmise that in the 1820s the Shells built both homes. It is likely that Absalom was responsible for some of the fine plantations in the Whitmire area during the 1850s, including both the renovation of Colonel Benjamin Herndon's plantation, Mollohon, which has some resemblance to the Hardy house, and the plantation of Hardy's friend and kinsman, Dr. James Monroe Eppes, son of Mary Hardy Eppes, built in 1857 when Absalom was forty-four years old.

Likely candidates for the Shell builders of Pomaria and the Hardy plantation are the brothers Edmund and Isham M. Shell, sons of John E. Shell Sr., and/or Allen S. Shell (1797–1863). All three were conspicuous buyers of "plank," "carpenter's tools," "cooper's tools," nails, hardware, and handsaws at the estate sales of John E. Shell Sr. (died 1818) and Amy Shell (died 1830), whose husband William had died in 1822 and thus could not have been one of the builders. Edmund and Isham were no longer in Newberry County in 1850, and little is known of them. Allen, however, according to the 1850 census, was still living in the Mt. Tabor Methodist community next to carpenters Absalom Shell and John A. Abrams, but is listed as a farmer. However, carpenter Abrams, his closest neighbor, is also given as a farmer, so this designation does not rule out the second occupation. As was often the case in the South of their day, both men had two occupations and planting was always considered the more prestigious of the two.

In the Hardy plantation ledger and account book (1842–1846) are entries for debts from Messrs. Absalom D. Shell and Jacob H. Shell, "carpenters." These debts involve William Eppes Hardy's hauling of many loads of shingles, plank, and lumber from Boyd's Mill and Maybin's Mill and from Gordon's Bridge on the Tyger (likely of materials poled up the Broad from Columbia or the vicinity). In fact, much hauling for them is noted in 1843 and 1844. Likewise, the ledger records the Hardy blacksmith's repairs of their carpenters' tools. Jacob had apparently either died or left the county by 1845, for in that year Absalom is listed alone in the accounts, and Jacob does not appear in the 1850 census for Newberry, whereas Absalom does. Jacob, perhaps older than Absalom, may have been a builder at the Hardy plantation and Pomaria. These Shell partners often boarded at the Hardys during 1842, 1844, and early 1845. They sometimes had with them slaves Jack and Turner, likely their apprentices. Whether or not they were working on the

Hardy place in some capacity, they were obviously building somewhere in this Tyger River–Maybinton area during the 1842–1845 period. From among the large number of Great Houses built in the vicinity during this era, one good candidate is the dwelling at the nearby Chick Place, called Rose Cottage, and said to have been built about this time. There are close similarities between the sidelights at the house's front entrance and those at the Hardy house, a fact that adds to the likelihood of Jacob Shell's involvement with the construction of both.

The 1825 section of the Hardy plantation house, like the original 1804 structure, has two rooms over two rooms with a central staircase between, only now the rooms have nearly doubled in size to 20 × 20 feet on the south and 17 × 20 feet on the north. The drawing room is 20 × 20 and thus follows the dictum of the famous Thomas Sheraton in 1803 that "The proportion of a good drawing room should be in length, at least equal to its width." The staircase is opened and widened. Its grand feature is a walnut hand rail (in four unspliced pieces, the longest measuring 13 feet 2 inches). The lathe-turned spindles are also of walnut. The trees from which these were made were said to be cut off the land; and this is likely so because today, despite over a century and a half of cotton cultivation, there are still many large walnut trees in the new forests surrounding the house. The hand railing is pegged and is richly colored. Its high polish, according to family tradition, "comes from the pants seats of generations of little Hardy children" as they performed one of their favorite pastimes while visiting grandparents. The newel posts, spindles, railings, and wainscoting somewhat resemble those of the mahogany staircase at Drayton Hall near Charleston.

The ends of the stair treads and risers are decorated with bud-and-scroll brackets carved from pine. These are pictured in Owen Biddle's *The Young Carpenter's Apprentice*, a work published in 1805 as a popular pattern book of the most current Federal design and fashion. Beneath the staircase is the "wine-closet," a common enough feature of the Great Houses of the area.

The baseboards of the hall today exhibit their original black opaque stain, after careful removal of modern coats of paint from 1989 to 1991. The heart-pine doors have been stripped to reveal the original opaque stain that resembles walnut. In refinishing these doors, I found no evidence of graining or faux painting techniques such as those used at sister plantations Pomaria, The Oaks, and Hillside. All the mantels in the house are opaque black-stained like the baseboards throughout the house; and most of the stain now seen on them is the original, revealed by careful heat stripping in 1990 and 1991. The panels beneath the windows in the drawing room are stained a rich cinnamon color, also revealed by stripping in 1991. The marks of hand planing on the doors and woodwork are a noticeable feature.

The plaster ceilings of all the rooms in the 1825 section were replaced in the 1950s, thus destroying the circular ceiling medallions in both front downstairs rooms and in both upstairs and downstairs halls. Hardy descendant Mary Ella Finlay, who lived in the house from 1926 to 1930, recalls the parlor medallions as being "a circle within a circle." The inner circle had at its center a large medallion of acanthus leaves. Filling in that circle were "raised delicate scallops that ran in a circle but did not quite touch each other." The medallions in these two sitting rooms were "the same or at the least very similar." Mrs. Finlay's sketch, made from memory in 1991, appears thus:

Haywood Hardy Henderson also remembers the medallions and estimates their size as about "four feet or better across." The ceiling medallions in the hall were smaller and had a simple concentric circle pattern with no leaf or scallop decorations. These descriptions recreate medallion patterns appropriate to the neoclassical era.

The decorative plasterwork was done by the artist John Finger. This was remembered in a 1937 interview with Fannie Epps, in which narrative she goes on to identify him as the creator as well of plasterwork ceiling designs in the home of her own grandfather, Dr. James M. Eppes: "A plasterer, Mr. Finger, did the plaster paris work in grandfather's house, and the Hardy home, in Maybinton. He also did the beautiful work in the Ben Sims home over in Fish Dam Township, and the same Mr. Finger worked on other houses in Newberry, Laurens, and Union County about that time." This is a very important identification because the plaster decorative work of this period in this part of the South Carolina Upcountry was exceptionally good. In Newberry County, the Peter Moon plantation house near Chappells has superb plasterwork, as does the Eppes house that Miss Epps described in 1937, located some twelve miles from the Hardy plantation. The Tom Suber Great House, eight miles distant from the Hardys, also has fine plaster detailing. Even closer, both Rose Cottage and the Ben Sims plantation, the latter also named by Miss Epps as decorated by Finger, had some of the finest plasterwork in America. Although the Sims plantation no longer stands, examples of its acanthus, egg-and-dart, and scroll bracket plaster ornamentation are displayed at the Hardy plantation.

William Heffernan was another craftsman who created ornate plaster ceilings in the Broad River area of Newberry County. He was an Irish immigrant who was reputed to have decorated Hollywood plantation near the Hardys on the Broad. He came from Dublin in 1828 and is said to have made the "art plasterwork" in many of Robert Mills's houses in South Carolina, the Job Johnstone house Coateswood in Newberry, and work for the antebellum architect Osborne Wells of Newberry. He was killed by Federal troops in 1864. Across the Broad in Fairfield County there was exceptionally fine and elaborate plaster ceiling decoration at Fair View plantation, now in ruins, and Albion, still standing. Their artisans are unknown.

For Finger, however, the Hardy plantation ledgers give us much significant information. He boarded off and on at the Hardy place from

1841 to 1845; and the plantation blacksmith repaired his trowel and stone hammer in 1842, 1843, and 1846. The ledgers also show that he had with him his two slave apprentices named Jes and Nick. He had a white assistant, J. Murphy, in 1842. The Murphy family was numerous in Maybinton at the time and owned at least one plantation there. It is interesting to note that both Heffernan and Murphy, like the Maybins who founded Maybinton, were Irish.

John Finger bought bushels of lime from the Hardy commissary in 1845–1846, likely as the prime component for the plaster he was making for use in the houses of the area. He also purchased from Hardy "2 negro blankets" for his slave helpers in December 1843. Hardy butchered one of Finger's hogs for him on 23 December 1843. These records prove his ties to the plantation and professional activity in the area during this decade. Because his name is also associated with the Shells in the ledgers, Finger often probably worked with them, as he did at the Hardy home. Thus the Shells built and he plastered and did the stone work. Finger was still in the area in the 1860s, for Garrie Douglass of The Oaks in a letter of December 1862 mentions that "Mr. Finger is about to leave" on a visit to Spartanburg, so she is sending things with him to be delivered to her correspondent. He must have become a trusted familiar neighbor by 1862, for he was elected a Methodist elder for Goshen Hill District from Ebenezer Church in both 1862 and 1863 and thus most certainly had settled in the Goshen Hill area near The Oaks. As we recall, both the Hardy and Douglass families attended Ebenezer and so were fellow church members with Finger.

Union County, outside the Tyger area, also has several extant examples of fine plaster ceiling decorations from the antebellum era. Finger, as Miss Epps stated in 1937, was no doubt responsible for many of these. Because medallions in the Jeter house (in the town of Union) are identical with the one in the Eppes house and the remnants of those in the Ben Sims plantation, both of which were created by Finger, we may now conclude that all three of these were his handiwork. The Hardy Plantation was therefore a part of this tradition of excellent ceiling art in upcountry South Carolina.

The plaster crown moldings at the Hardy plantation have also been lost. They were approximately 6 to 8 inches tall, and as Mary Ella Finlay recalls, "were similar in feel to the single wooden crown moldings" still to be seen in the traveler's room of the 1804 section. No one recalls egg-and-dart or fancy ornamental design used for the moldings, as was the case at both the Ben Sims Great House and Rose Cottage. When the ceilings in the two downstairs rooms that had decorations were lowered in 1951, the crown plasterwork was removed. The ceilings are now being restored to their original height and crown molding reinstalled.

The 5-inch heart-pine flooring throughout the house is all original and is unpieced for the twenty-foot length of the rooms. The flight of steps into the attic was a part of the original design because into the attic the stairwell is finished with the same hard plaster and hand-planed black-stained baseboard as the rest of the stairwell. The small section of the garret ceiling that can be seen from below through the stairwell opening was also plastered. This structural design produces a strong uprush of air three stories high into the garret as a very effective means of ventilation. As a result, no modern air-conditioning is necessary. At Pomaria plantation, precisely the same attic stair rail and design were used. The stairs at both houses thus led all the way into the garret even though this final flight partially obscures the window that lights the top of the stairwell. Here, form has been sacrificed to function. The attic garret has wide hand-planed heart-pine flooring and small windows to either side of the end chimneys, again providing additional ventilation, but is otherwise unfinished. Owing to the high location of the house, the views from its small third-story garret windows are among the most impressive on the place.

Both the bedrooms of the Palladian addition have eastern exposures to the morning sun, and are thus situated in accord with Thomas Sheraton's admonition to architects in 1803: "As the eastern sun ought to regulate our time of rising in general, bedrooms are properly on that side of the house. In this situation, a bedroom has early light without heat, which can be offensive to none but sluggards." The Hardys, living a sun-regulated life on the land, would no doubt find wisdom in Sheraton's words. True agrarians, they were certainly no sluggards.

The massive end chimneys are laid in "common" or American bond, repeating every sixth row. They have stepped bases, a fact partly responsible for their never having pulled away as much as an inch from the structure—even after the 1886 earthquake that cracked plaster and broke windows this far inland (notably at Pomaria plantation). The chimneys are stuccoed with a mortar made from the local golden-colored creek sand and are scored to resemble giant blocks of sandstone. The time when the stuccoing was done cannot be ascertained. The chimneys were probably unstuccoed in 1825. The work, however, still looks quite old, much like that at nearby Rose Hill plantation, which was done around 1850.

Another important Palladian house that was similar to the Hardy plantation was The Oaks of Goshen Hill, located five miles to the west. It was begun in 1838 and completed in 1840 by Dr. George Douglass so that his wife Frances Hardy Douglass could have a dwelling similar to her family home, now her sister Catharine's. Although The Oaks burned in 1977, there are many photographs of it. Its projecting Palladian portico and proportions and some of its interior details were strikingly similar to those at the Hardy plantation. In both houses hung the aforementioned Scarborough portraits of the family matriarch, Anna Powell Dixon Hardy, mother of Catharine Hardy and Frances Douglass, now in their turn mistresses of both the Hardy plantation and The Oaks.

6

In Tune with the Music of the Universe
A Southern Countryman's Villa Garden

To tend the soil is to make one love it. To possess himself of a chosen spot—to make of it a garden—to multiply its fruits around him—to live well and hospitably,—decently and reverently, should be one's leading objects.
—W. G. Simms, Woodlands Plantation (1843)

Decorate your homes with flowering shrubs, roses, and evergreens. Those who love and appreciate the beautiful, make these their study, and the communings of the mind open new stores of pleasure and instruction, and we become not merely dwellers on earth's surface, but wiser and better, living as we do with all the beauties of God and of Nature for our neighbors.
—William Summer, Pomaria Plantation (1860)

According to William Dixon Hardy in 1932, the extensive formal garden surrounding the house was designed and laid out in the decade after the Palladian front was added in 1825. It was thus done in the period in which his father and mother had charge of the plantation after their marriage in 1828. Hardy also stated in 1932 that "a landscape gardener was brought from Asheville to plan the formal garden and to plant the boxwood borders." As we learned earlier, this gardener was most likely Dr. James Hardy of Asheville, brother of Squire William. In 1932 the original borders were described as being "borders no longer; they almost touch in a solid mass of luxuriant boxwood. There is no room for but a single passageway down the main walk to the gate." William Dixon's granddaughter Mary Ella Finlay, who lived in the house from 1925 to 1930, recalls that at this time "the boxwood paths were well over head high."

The type of boxwood is the English variety *Buxus sempervirens suffruticosa* (or dwarf box) which is said to grow on average about an inch per year. It was very common in the gardens of this area of upcountry South Carolina, as will be shown. The conditions at the plantation are apparently ideal for it, with cool misty mornings in summer, good drainage and rich soil, high filtered shade, and excellent air circulation. The box are free of leaf miners and other pests. Mrs. Finlay remembers the beads of mist and dew caught in elaborate spiderweb tents early every morning. These natural pest controls are likely the reason there is no infestation. Morning still finds these tents sparkling as they did sixty years ago in her remembrance.

According to family tradition, the original start of this boxwood came from Mount Vernon as a gift from the Washingtons, for two Hardy brothers, Thomas and William, were Revolutionary patriots under his command, and it was Thomas who built the first house here in 1786. I am inclined to accept this tradition both because Washington himself is known to have planted the boxwood at Mount Vernon and valued it highly, and because other such family tales have been proved accurate by documentation.

That the landscape gardener hailed from Asheville also rings true for two reasons. One is the aforementioned family ties with Asheville through Dr. James Hardy, brother of William Eppes Hardy, master of the place when the garden was designed. Dr. Hardy, a founder and early prominent citizen of that town, called by its historian "her first landscape architect," designed the grounds of his own four dwellings there in similar manner. The second reason is the presence in the formal garden of a mountain conifer not native to Newberry County. This giant Eastern hemlock (*Tsuga canadensis*) is a part of the original planting. In 1997 the tree measured 6 feet, $11\frac{1}{2}$ inches in circumference at a height of $4\frac{1}{2}$ feet from the base. Its spire rises far above all the trees in the vicinity. It is one of the largest in the state, even among those in their native districts. Seedlings of this hemlock have come up along the adjacent road banks and as far as 120 yards to east and south and 400 yards to the northeast. A seedling over 30 feet tall grows 400 yards to the north in a wooded ravine leading to the spring, and is now itself bearing cones.

In 1932 Mr. Hardy stated that he had often been urged to sell the boxwood "but would never set a price until recently when a communication from a Virginia buyer has caused him to consider it." This was the period when Colonial Williamsburg was buying boxwood from old plantation gardens throughout a destitute upcountry South Carolina; and it may have been they who contacted him. The price offered was said to be $1,000, a significant sum for the Hardys at a time when land in the area was selling for only $3 an acre. This amount was probably accurately remembered. Boxwood from another sale to Colonial Williamsburg from lower Spartanburg County at this same time brought $1,500, as recorded by garden historian Ann Leighton. Luckily, Hardy did not sell, even when hard-pressed by the economic situation of the day; and as a result, this authentic garden was not destroyed to create a new, conjectural, less than authentic one in a distant state.

The central boxwood parterres were originally flanked to north and south by a large number of symmetrical flower plots in elaborate geometric design. One descendant recalls that her mother told her they had been edged in dwarf box and patterned "in an English [that is, formally elaborate] style." At The Oaks, the homeplace of Hardy kin, the geometric designs laid out in the 1840s were specifically named as hearts and diamonds. These were located to each side of a central box-edged path, just as they were at the Hardy plantation. In Colonel Robert Beaty's garden, fourteen miles up the State Road, the flower beds, "bordered with dwarf box," were "laid off in the shape of hearts, diamonds, and crescents." There the central brick walk was edged in larger box, "while in the corners of the yard, there were tree box." The original extant garden from the 1820s at Mountain Shoals plantation, about twenty-five miles to the northwest, also has heart and diamond stone-edged beds. These may thus have been the geometric patterns used in the Hardy garden as well, for they were obviously quite popular in the area at this time. Whatever their configuration, these "numerous and elaborate" designs, grown so luxuriant by the late 1800s, were removed around 1900 "for fear that one of the grandchildren would suffer a snakebite among them." The central parterred walk and one of the perpendicular side walks, however, were retained; and as the 1932 interview states, paths and borders had "grown together" into one "luxuriant mass." In photographs made in April 1932, roses in full bloom peep over the overgrown parterre hedges.

In 1989 I also found evidence of elaborate curved fieldstone borders

6 inches below the soil's surface to the north side of the 1804 section of the house. In this side yard, the soil has grown higher over the last century so as completely to cover the stones. Without disturbing these borders, I have planted a box-lined garden of old roses similar to the one at Rose Hill, also located along the Tyger about sixteen miles to the northwest.

Thus the extant boxwood consists of a central east-west walk with bordering parterres, and a perpendicular box-lined path leading north. These are all edged with fieldstone in the manner of most upcountry gardens of the day. The central walk measures 82½ feet long and 7¼ feet wide from trunk to trunk of the boxwood. Each bordering parterre is 8 feet wide from trunk to trunk, and the space in between was originally massed with flowers. The north boxwood walk that runs at right angles to the central path was said in 1932 to lead to the kitchen garden. It measures 36 feet long and 7 feet across. Although grown together today, it was originally a wide walk leading to a gate that opened onto a straight dirt path. This path paralleled the north side of the house and ran east-west to the dependencies, most notably (to the east) the smokehouse, corncrib, harness shed, barn, blacksmith's shop, and men's privy; and (to the west) the cook's house, women's privy, and several other small outbuildings whose uses are unknown today. There was likely also such a walk on the south side of the dwelling to balance the pattern, for it was obviously symmetrical, and the foundation stones of at least one structure exist there.

It is worth repeating that the extant historical garden design at Mountain Shoals is very close to the Hardy plan. Although about half the length and single lined, the same box-edged central walk leads to the front steps and has the same perpendicular box-lined paths extending left and right from these steps. The major difference in the geometric design is that in the Hardy garden, the central lane is curved outward at the ends to soften the corners and complement the projecting portico. It is a particularly graceful design. Because the Hardy house is larger and has the imposing double portico, the scale of its garden is larger than that at Mountain Shoals. Both gardens are properly proportioned to suit their dwellings.

From extant evidence, the Hardy plantation grounds appeared as follows:

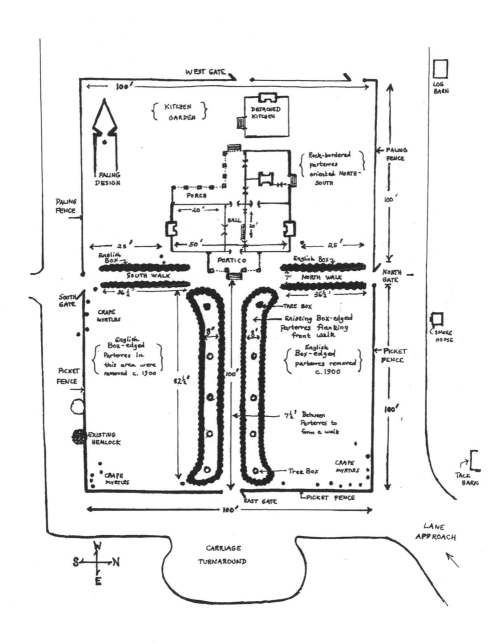

The sketch reveals that the width of the garden was precisely twice the width of the dwelling. The length of the front garden is the same as its width and thus forms a square, 100×100 feet. The rear garden, including the house space, is the same size as the front garden. The two perpendicular paths running north-south perfectly bisect the whole, which thus forms a rectangle twice as long as it is wide. The two front side gardens (50×100 feet) are therefore of the same proportion as the entire garden (100×200 feet). Harmony, symmetry, order, and geometric regularity were thus philosophically important to the landscaper of this garden and reflected the ideals of the men and women of this era who tended it. Even more so perhaps, the complicated symmetry of the pattern bespoke their belief in an orderly universe. The classicism revived by Palladio had its primary grounding in this same symmetry and harmony. It is no wonder that the interiors of Palladio's country homes were decorated with frescoes of gods, angels, and mortals playing musical instruments and that the primary ceiling fresco in one of his villas was on the theme of "Cosmic Harmony." A musical harmony was both the metaphor for life and its high aim, reflected in the design of both house and garden alike.

As at The Oaks, the Colonel Beaty house, the Reuben Sims Rice house, Hillside, the James Eppes house, Juxa at Santuc, and Mountain Shoals, either a white picket or paling fence completely surrounded the formal area around the Great House. This was a rule for the gardens of the area. Such a fence kept farm animals out and provided a necessary order and framework for the garden. At the Hardy plantation, its front gate had an iron ball-and-chain closing mechanism similar to that seen at Colonial Williamsburg today. The ball was discovered buried at the site of the front gate's north post in 1989. An excellent photograph of the house made in 1907 reveals a badly deteriorated white wooden fence and gate at the head of the boxwood walk. It appears to have been from 4 to 5 feet high, and had pointed square pickets over a solid wooden stringer-course base. The corner posts were square. This was removed some time after 1932, the date of the last photograph to show it. Two flat wooden palings in the design shown at the top left of the garden sketch were also discovered beneath the house in 1989. Their pattern was used for variety in the rear kitchen or side garden. The garden historian Ann Leighton notes that an interesting variety of fencing was used at Mountain Shoals, and at the Hardy garden this was also true.

It was near the front garden gate that the carriage drive terminated about 110 feet from the front steps. This had disappeared by 1980, after the new, wider loop around the house was created. Originally carriages left the main road to the east of the house in an approach through terraced fields. There was likely a carriage mounting block at this spot and some way of hitching the horses. In the 1930s a very large black walnut tree was said to grow about 30 feet to the south of the front gate outside the garden proper. Field hands of that day repaired farm implements on an anvil fixed beneath it. Several of William Dixon Hardy's grandchildren recall this scene from the 1920s and '30s, when cotton cultivation was still in high swing. The present pecan trees (originally two to each side flanking the front walk) already appear large on the 1907 photograph, as does the black walnut at the rear of the house. None of these trees, however, were a part of the original design; they were probably planted in the 1890s about the time the geometric box-edged flower beds were removed. The hemlock and possibly the giant elm at the front are the only trees remaining from the original landscape.

The large, old-fashioned lilac-pink crape myrtles were also a part of the nineteenth-century garden; but whether they belonged to the original conception cannot be ascertained. Owing to their popularity in South Carolina since André Michaux brought them to Charleston in the 1700s, it is very possible. They appear to have been planted along the front fence and to have formed a walkway just outside the north and south fence lines. They may have edged both sides of the perpendicular box lanes. Like the garden design in general, the crape myrtle planting is symmetrical; the extant ones show this clearly. As Ann Leighton accurately comments, for gardens like this, there are "few obvious rules," but one of them is that "symmetry is paramount." Of Mountain Shoals, she writes: "Crape myrtles at the sides balance each other. Each bed of sufficient size is centered with an ornamental shrub. Roses mass behind the box hedges that lead to the front door." As a descendant of the creator of the Mountain Shoals garden recalled, where her mother "had lilac crape myrtle on one side you would find some to balance on the other. . . . [The garden was] thoughtfully and rather symmetrically arranged—at least with a sense of balance."

The front flower parterres that run along either side of the front walk from the house steps to the front gate were anchored at both ends and on both sides by tree box, *Buxus sempervirens* (*arborescens*), which was kept pruned into cones. There were at least four originals and likely others spaced at equal distances down these central parterres. Of these, only one remains, grown now to 25 feet. Photographs from 1907 and 1932 show an even taller one flanking it across the walk in the adjacent flower parterre. It had been removed by 1970 and replaced by a pole covered by yellow jessamine. The current garden surrounding Palladio's

Villa Cornara, from which, as we have seen, the 1825 portico derives its inspiration, has exactly the same garden walk configuration anchored by cone-shaped standards. For both structures, this planting produces a pleasing design, with green "columns" in the garden in harmony with the portico's columns. In fact, the one remaining tree box in the Hardy garden is placed squarely in line with the portico's outside column and was obviously intended to function in relation to the architectural element. The natural column and the man-made one thus mirror each other and are directly tied. The symbolism is obvious. These tree box formed a natural colonnade down which one walked to the front steps of the house and thence into the porch's colonnade. These house columns ran north-south and thus stood in line with the box-edged paths that ran perpendicular to the front central walk and parterres. When both front and rear double doors of the house were opened, an unobstructed view through the dwelling (there were of course no screen doors in those days) led to and along a rear porch colonnade running westward in direct line with the tree box standards at the front. The dwelling thus stood as an elegant and elevated center at the crossing of the garden, whose four axes followed the points of the compass. Today, even with its screen doors and altered rear porch, the house seems very open to the outside. With its many tall windows, double doors, and trabiated sidelights and transoms, it gives the impression of a substantial and elaborate summerhouse set at the heart of a garden.

Tree box was used almost as extensively as dwarf box in upcountry South Carolina during this period. The remaining 7-acre garden at Rosemont plantation in Laurens County has luxuriant 30-foot tall cirques, lanes, and crossings of tree box. Photographs of The Oaks in the 1970s show a few huge remaining tree box at the front. The Colonel Robert Beaty house also used them symmetrically in the garden's corners to anchor the design. At the Reuben Sims Rice plantation (1836), again along the State (Buncombe) Road, the extant old garden has some tree box and extensive elaborate geometric flower parterres of circles and squares edged by now overgrown dwarf box.

All the original paths at the Hardy plantation were of swept sand and edged with the native fieldstone. The sand was brought from the nearby branch and was replenished when needed. Its color was soft tawny yellow, as is the stucco on the chimneys made from it. It contrasted nicely with the dark green of the box and the pastels of roses. The central brick path of today was laid by Mrs. John Frost Hardy Sr. in the 1950s, using bricks from the piers and central chimney of the section of the 1804 house that was torn away around 1950–1951. On the subject of sand, a pertinent description of an upcountry South Carolina garden appeared in 1942 in Ben Robertson's classic *Red Hills and Cotton*:

> All of our houses . . . had bare sanded yards surrounded by gardens of flowers. We did not care for green grass in our yards, as our country was a Southern country, and white sand to us was more restful and quieter-looking than grass. Besides, there was greenness all about us—the groves were green and so were the cottonfields and the valleys themselves. The white of the sand, shaded by the thick trees, formed an oasis, a solemn thing of contrast. Every Saturday morning, with corn-shuck brooms, we carefully swept the yard.

At the front parlor windows, a banana shrub (*Michelia*), like the large one that existed in antebellum days at Rose Cottage, is about 20 feet tall. It does not appear in a 1907 photograph but shows as a 6-foot shrub in 1929. Despite its size, this particular plant is thus not of antebellum origin but is very possibly a descendant of the old banana shrub at Rose Cottage, where its seedlings have naturalized.

In the plantation yard within the space of the old fenced garden are scatterings of red spider lilies, tiger lilies, orange daylilies, single-colored magenta four-o'clocks, variegated peach-colored hawthorne, red hawthorne, Jacob's ladder, rose of Sharon, eleagnus, white iris ("flags"), jonquils, snowdrops (*Leucojum vernum*), daffodils, butter-and-eggs, purple phlox, and narcissus. Adjacent to the central walk are late-flowering daffodils. The most common bulb, however, is the grape hyacinth, so extensive as to be naturalized around the house on all sides and even into the fields. One of the commonest bulbs at Mountain Shoals is a close relative, the feathered hyacinth (*Muscari comosum monstrosum*), which grows in profusion in the beds. There are purple violets in the south side yard that bloom freely from December through spring, even in the coldest winters and through the snow. At the north slave cabin sites are yellow jonquils, cream-white jonquils with yellow corollas, and yellow daffodils with red-orange corollas. Across Peters Creek Road at the south cabin sites is a profusion of late-flowering white daffodils identified as Twin Sisters. All these no doubt were divisions from the old plantation garden, which apparently had a great number and variety of bulbs. Only a few stray examples of these are now found in the plantation yard itself. The modern practice of lawn mowing has taken its toll.

But sturdy survivors are butter-and-eggs, jonquils (*Jonquilla simplex*), and both the daffodils with yellow and red-orange corollas.

Only three old garden roses were found on the place in 1989. One is an unidentified pink cluster rose. It blooms throughout the summer and is likely of the noisette class. It is a climber of vigorous habit, found originally within the central walk flower parterres, where others were shown blooming freely in a picture made in April 1932. It may possibly even be the original noisette, created by the Charleston rice planter John Champneys: the Champney's Pink Cluster. Its climbing habit and South Carolina origin give it better claim than the Champney's Pink Cluster being sold on the market today, a rose found in Virginia that does not climb. Contemporary descriptions of Champney's Pink Cluster said it did—vigorously and abundantly.

Roses, underplanted with bulbs and perennials, and punctuated by shaped tree box, may have been the original plantings within these parterres. At Mountain Shoals roses still rise over the central walk's box hedge. In the Hardy garden, a small, spring-blooming cluster rose of pale pink, with light green leaves and low spreading habit, is in the south garden area. The other rose found in 1989 is L'Évêque, sometimes called The Bishop, a tough old bright-purple gallica illustrated by Redouté in 1820. This rose was found on the front north corner of the old garden beneath crape myrtles. These roses are being propagated for distribution about the garden. In the 1970s Mrs. John Frost Hardy Sr. took a shrub rose from the plantation garden when she had to move to Union. Her grandson's wife was cautioned to dig this at her death and care for it, which she did. In Spartanburg this rose is now being propagated for its return to the plantation. It is a small-leaved plant that blooms in pink clusters throughout the summer and into the winter. It is an unidentified antique rose, likely a tea, china, or noisette. Descendants recall a spring-blooming white rose that climbed along the north fence in the 1920s. This may have been of antebellum origin, but it is unfortunately lost. Our three old survivors represent only a fraction of what was likely a very large collection grown in the boxwood-edged flower parterres and scattered throughout the garden.

At this point, certain generalizations can be made about the Hardy garden. Its unifying feature was (and is) box, both dwarf and tree; and its defining decorative frame was a fence that enclosed the whole. Crape myrtle lanes adjacent to the fence strengthened the sense of enclosure. Hemlocks likely used as a row of standards outside the fence on the north and south sides of the house provided more demarcation. Parallel to these hemlock rows were paths that ran to the utilitarian outbuildings that surrounded the Great House. Its paramount rule was symmetry. It was divided by a number of walks through and among geometric flower parterres edged with dwarf box and highlighted by shaped tree box. Its paths were of swept yellow sand and edged with fieldstone. As at Mountain Shoals (to use Ann Leighton's words), "This was obviously a garden designed to be enjoyed." Its patterned parterres were enjoyable at two levels: from the ground and from the high second story portico and windows of the upstairs bedrooms, where in the summer, there is always a breeze that brings in fragrance from the garden, particularly of boxwood and roses. The house is a lofty, tall house, very much open to the outside, and thus a natural for a parterred setting, which is always best viewed from a raised terrace, upper rooms, or the second stories of porticoes. It is from this vantage that the design can be most clearly articulated and thus best appreciated. Blooming crape myrtles are also quite effective seen from above because they have a rounded canopy of color.

For all its elaborate patterning and formal design, the Hardy garden was an intimate rural place, created to please family and friends, those who lived on the land rather than busy travelers passing by. Thus it was designed for relishing from the inside, and not to impress those outside. Its color was varied and seasonal, and not created from mass plantings of annuals—most assuredly not the dull Epcot Center style and philosophy of gardening. It relied on personality, harmony, balance, detail, and variety, on mild surprises and personal touches. Preeminently it was a garden of memories, owing to the associations summoned up by the love of the kinsman who planned its original design, by those who tended it through the years, by passalong plants given by friends, neighbors, and relations, by the particular flower best loved by particular kin, by remembering when a plant was put there and by whom. In some ways the garden of memories became like a calendar of their lives. "Such and such was planted the day so and so was born," one would remember.

Above all, the garden highlighted the progression of the seasons. As at Mountain Shoals, here "the Spring was a lovely, long, slow affair, full of fragrance and bright with bulbs, early blooming shrubs, and violets." The snowdrop, narcissus, grape hyacinth, and jonquil announced the season's approach. Then followed in procession the Jacob's ladder, white flag, Easter lily, and Twin Sisters daffodil. With May came roses— noisettes, chinas, bourbons, damasks, and old teas—that bloomed until frost and sometimes til Christmas. Fragrant magnolias and gardenias (called Cape jasmines and Cape jessamines), both traditional plants in the area during antebellum days, put on their most lavish displays in June; tiger lilies brightened July, and Naked Ladies amaryllis in early August. The abiding pink of crape myrtle showed elegantly throughout the deep summer. Ann Leighton's description of the end of the garden year at Mountain Shoals could serve for the Hardy garden as well: "The end of summer showed the late lilies and members of the amaryllis family; and the little fruits of the gay red hips of roses" came on among the occasional flush of noisettes, teas, and chinas. "And that was that. With ground-covers like periwinkle, borders of thrift and pinks, and edgings of box, the plan of the garden was secure throughout the year. Its effects were to be awaited annually—like early strawberries and asparagus before canning enabled us to eat things out of season." The garden thus defined the seasons in harmony with the seasonal activities of plowing, planting, and harvesting that went on busily outside its gates. The fields that stretched across hills in all directions from the Great House were themselves extensions of the garden, integral with it, and fitting complements to it. Like the green tree box columns planted in direct line with the architectural ones of the portico, the ordered fields existed in close and mirrored rhythm to the parterres and paths of the garden,—the man and his creations yoked to the land's and nature's own creative processes. The Hardy plantation garden was thus tied to that which went on about it, a microcosm of the tilled lands surrounding, and, as such, a realization of the pastoral ideal of a country environment. Unlike an urban garden, the countryman's plantation garden could exist in natural harmony with the tilled lands and, above all, be at peace with its environs, not in violent contrast to them. It was, however, more planned than the typical country cottage garden of loosely haphazard charm. Its formality was reminiscent of Italian country villas, but softened to its Southern plantation landscape and reflecting the Southern planter's innate love of simple elegance and the personal, intimate, and familiar.

In 1932 William Dixon Hardy, then ninety-one, stated that despite his advanced age, he had always been and still is "fond of gardening." Until his death later that year, he maintained the tradition of clean, broom-swept paths and dirt yards, in which no sprig of grass was allowed to grow. Mrs. Sarah Stokes, who lived on a neighboring plantation at that time, recalls that in his old age, he would walk around in his black coat and bow tie and point his cane at a sprig of grass for one of his sons to root up. She also remembers the largest native American holly she had ever seen to have been on the southwest side of the house just outside the garden fence, "a tree that people throughout the community would come to for Christmas greenery every year." Perhaps significantly, another such holly grew at the west side of the Covington Hardy house in Lunenburg, Virginia. A popular folk belief in Old England was that such a holly on the western side of a house whose shade fell on the yard would protect the place from evil influence. The Hardys may have brought some such custom with them from the mother country. Today, large native hollies grow commonly in the woods around the plantation.

The last plantation mistress, Miss Alice (Mrs. John Frost Hardy Sr.), also enjoyed gardening, both kitchen and flower. She was particularly fond of ginger lilies and old roses. In the 1950s and '60s, her vegetable garden was on the rich terraced slope to the west (rear) of the dwelling. Thad (Mrs. Clarence Hodges), a tenant who resided on the place, helped her tend this garden and the grounds around the house. In the summers during the late 1950s and early '60s, so did her grandson John Frost Hardy III. As he recalls it, his duty was weeding and grass cutting in the side yards.

Of some passing note today is the giant persimmon tree near the house, which in 1997 was 100 feet high, had a 40-foot spread, and was 9 feet in circumference at its base. These statistics make it close to the largest persimmon in the state, if not the champion big tree.

The remnant of a tree stump some 40 feet from the southeast corner of the house is probably from a black walnut shown in a photograph in 1953. A 45-foot-tall *magnolia grandiflora* now grows near this stump and will be maintained. Joseph Simpson recalls that before Peters Creek Road was paved in the 1950s, many magnolias grew along it. Since 1989 I have planted 42 *Magnolia grandifloras* outside the original fenced garden and along Peters Creek Road. These are accompanied on the grounds by extensive new plantings of native deciduous magnolias (*tripetala, ashei,* and *macrophyla*), several white-flowering oriental *Magnolia kobus, Magnolia soulangiana,* and *Magnolia stellata.* Other plants set on the grounds since 1989 and still living in 1997 are:

★Gingko (*Gingko biloba*) (6)
★California incense cedar (*Libocedrus decurrens,* an upcountry
    favorite in the antebellum era) (2)
★*Cryptomeria japonica* (another upcountry favorite) (2)

Chinese Cryptomeria (*Cryptomeria fortunei*) (2)

Taiwania cryptonoides

Torreya mucifera

*Funebral cypress (*Cupressus funebris*)

*Bald cypress (*Taxodium distichum*) (2)

*Italian cypress (*Cupressus sempervirens*)

*California redwood (*Sequoia sempervirens*) (2)

Dawn redwood (*Metasequoia glyptostroboides*)

*Cunninghamia (*Cunninghamia lanceolata*) (3)

*Deodar cedar (*Cedrus deodara*, a favorite tree in antebellum South
     Carolina) (4)

*Golden raintree (*Koelreuteria paniculata*) (2)

Swamp chestnut oak (*Quercus michauxii*) (2)

Burr oak (*Quercus macrocarpa*) (4)

*Live oak (*Quercus virginiana*) (2)

*Cork oak (*Quercus suber*)

Sawtooth oak (*Quercus acutissima*) (8)

*Carolina silver bell (*Halesia carolina*) (4)

Two-winged silver bell (*Halesia diptera*)

Carolina buckthorn (*Rhamnus caroliniana*) (2)

*Yellowwood (*Cladrastis lutea*) (4, with 10 more in the woods)

*Tea olive (*Olea fragrans*) (3)

Windmill palm (*Trachycarpus fortunei*) (3)

*Bay (*Laurus nobilis*) (2)

Pearlbush (*Exochorda giraldii*)

Breath of spring (*Lonicera fragrantissima*) (3)

*Strawberry tree (*Arbutus unedo*)

Pineapple guava (*Feijoa*)

*Aucuba (*Aucuba japonica*)

Winter daphne (*Daphne odora*)

Vitex rotunda

Loropetalum (*Loropetalum chinensis*, an antebellum favorite) (3)

*American fringe tree (*Chionanthus virginicus*) (2)

Chinese fringe tree (*Chionanthus retusus*)

*Japanese (luster-leaf) holly, or Big-leaf holly (*Ilex latifolia*, an
     upcountry favorite)

Chinese holly (*Ilex purpurea*)

Henry's anise (*Illicium henryi*)

Viburnum tinus (another South Carolina antebellum favorite)

These, along with the ornamental white-flowering peach, a Washington cherry, and six types of Japanese maple (including the amur, Siebold, *truncatum*, and trident), native maples, and several seedling Eastern hemlocks (*Tsuga canadensis*) from their parent in the old garden, round out a seven-year planting program aimed at creating a setting for the historical garden in informal English style, much as the Hardys of the eighteenth century were doing on country estates in England.

The majority of the plants in the preceding list (those starred with asterisks) were popularly ordered by planters in upcountry South Carolina during the 1850s from nearby Pomaria Nursery. I have used the extant Pomaria Nursery ledgers that record their antebellum sales in selecting most of the plants to place on the grounds. My planting philosophy has been to create a garden more or less compatible with historical possibilities in this part of South Carolina, to create a good aesthetic design to surround and complement the existing historical garden without tampering with it, and to assemble a collection of interesting and unusual plants on this one site.

Although William and Catharine Hardy are not listed as customers in the extant Pomaria ledgers of 1859 to 1862, odds are that they were in the two decades preceding, for Dr. James Hardy, the original architect of this garden, was in fact a patron, as proved by his orders in 1859. The Hardys, like so many sophisticated gardeners of upcountry Carolina, including nearby Colonel Robert Beaty and the Cunninghams of Rosemont in Laurens County, who are shown in the ledgers for these few years, thus had a convenient source for the rarer plants. For example, the Chick family at Rose Cottage, the Hardys' near neighbor, bought *Cryptomeria japonica* from Pomaria before today's standard authorities on plant introductions say that it was brought to this country. Its date of introduction is listed as 1860 and 1861, but Pomaria had been advertising it for sale as early as 1853. Pomaria's *Cupressus funebris* is even more interesting. It is listed for sale in 1853, though it came to Britain only in 1850. Pomaria was already selling it three years later, and upcountry gardeners may have had it at the same time or earlier than their English counterparts.

With a nursery selling plants like *Cupressus funebris*, *Torreya taxifolia*, redwood, giant sequoia, *Stewartia malachodendron*, Brazil pine, Chili pine, native and oriental azaleas, and the plants marked with an asterisk in the preceding list (to name only a fraction)—and five hundred varieties of roses chosen expressly for the Southern climate—it is obvious that Carolina gardeners of the antebellum era had a convenient local plant source from which they could create as sophisticated a garden as America could offer. The Reverend John Drayton of the famous Magnolia Gardens near Charleston used Pomaria as one source in the antebellum era to create a garden known internationally today as one of the world's finest.

In 1989 and 1990 I planted 26 *Camellia japonicas* in a double-lined 42-foot walk to the north side of the house to provide a complement to the new garden of antique roses and to be in rhythm with the boxwood lanes. My most ambitious undertaking on the grounds is a planting of *Magnolia grandifloras* that will make a frame for the house and fan out and down the old cotton terraces to a small meadow, beyond which will be forest. This is an attempt to restore as far as practical the formal appearance of the approach to the house that was originally the carriage lane through fields of cotton. From the house and front formal gardens, the lane should provide an excellent prospect. Landscape architect Dr. Hardy would likely have approved this picturesque style with formal axes and vistas.

To the rear of the dwelling are the scuppernong arbor (extended in 1989 and 1992), figs, pears, apricots, apples, pineapple guava, pomegranates, and other fruit trees. I planted a small cork oak (*Quercus suber*) here in 1990 that by 1994 had grown to 10 feet. This was also a tree sold commonly through Pomaria Nurseries in the 1850s. In general, this area will be a high orchard, essentially of utilitarian trees, rather more open than not, because through it there is a particularly fine view to the west from the Great House windows.

Ann Leighton writes that at Mountain Shoals the boxwood parterres have increased in size so as to form hedges "to walk between or to see over, as far as the river in the valley below and on to the far hills." This is also a perfect summary description of the Hardy garden. One of its most picturesque views is of sunset over the north boxwood walk, as seen from the front garden. Today the forested hills to the west form a distant prospect across the formal green of box. When the garden was young, the summer hills of this vista provided a patchwork of cotton, corn, sugarcane, and wheat fields, of orchard, vineyard, pasture land, lot, and woodland, and thus in their own way created an ordered picturesque garden as well.

Such a picturesque view does not happen by accident. We have only to recall that when he laid out the gardens at each of his own four dwellings in Asheville, Dr. Hardy gave special attention and consideration to the surrounding landscape in providing scenic views and prospects. Belleview, the name he chose for one of his estates, proves the point. He was thus obviously a devotee of the picturesque style of landscape gardening; and in laying out the grounds on the former cotton terraces, I am following his lead.

Gardening in upcountry South Carolina in the antebellum era was sophisticated. It adapted old forms to new uses and blended traditional and native plant material with the latest exotics. It used its natural setting to good and picturesque advantage. Its gardens were at peace with their agrarian surroundings. Although light wooden fences kept farm animals at bay, they did not make major barriers to the eye. The gardens did not close out the world but were integral with it, in natural harmony with it, always looking to and embracing it as the acknowledged source of its life, for the fields that surrounded the gardens made the gardens possible, and the symbolism was not lost on their creators. Plantation gardeners did not need or desire to wall out the world. The world that surrounded their gardens was not a threat to the life within and did not need screening. In the fruitful and warm climate of long growing seasons, Upcountry gardeners, themselves well placed in nature, were evolving a pleasant style of charm and simple elegance, a nice balance between and blending of the homey country garden and the grand formal gardens of old-world aristocracy. Her gardens enfolded their dwellings, providing ordered seas of calm and fragrance from which to look beyond to fertile fields—and thus fully realizing Palladio's classical country ideal. They were places of family and of memory, personal landscapes humanized with associations. Her gardeners enjoyed rooting plants that took easily (like the Cape jessamine, for example). These they passed about the neighborhood and to relations. The market bulletins have continued this long tradition in our own century; and it is still interesting to note when riding through this area that particular flowers appear in many yards when they are not to be found anywhere outside the neighborhood. So the passalong tradition continues. Upcountry plantation gardens thus had certain common denominators and in some ways a communal sameness of plant material and design, but showed just as strongly an elegant variation stemming from the distinctive personalities of their creators. They were scaled and adapted well to the proportions of the particular structures that sat within them. It is truly sad that the garden history of upper Carolina has yet to be properly studied and written; when it is, the Hardy plantation will provide an important source for the story.

7

The Forest

Immediately in front of the mansion should be clustered those shrubs and flowers, which constitute true rural adornment, and their cultivation should diminish as distance leads up into the open wooded grove, which should always be retained, both for ornament and the preservation of health.
—A. G. Summer, Pomaria and Ravenscroft Plantations (1853)

From the deeds to the Hardy lands in the 1780s and '90s, one reads of the trees used for marking property lines. These give some small indication of what grew in the aboriginal forest. The deeds name post oak (14 times), red oak (10), hickory (6), white oak (3), tulip poplar (2), ash (2), holly (2), maple (2), black gum (1), and dogwood (1).

The forest today, although much abused by both monoculture pine tree farming and clear cutting, still contains, in addition to all of the above, sourwood, sycamore, sweet gum, Carolina buckthorn, winged elm, black walnut, black oak, black locust (*Robinia pseudo-acacia*), beech, red cedar (*Juniperus virginiana*), sumac, hop hornbeam, hackberry, black cherry, persimmon, redbud, and cherry laurel. Beyond this list, Robert Mills in his *Statistics* of 1826 also names as native to Newberry County the overcup oak, birch, alder, *Magnolia acuminata*, haw, pawpaw, witch hazel, service, and buckeye. The chestnut's southernmost range was said to be the Tyger River's Newberry County banks. Escaped into the woods today are also non-native privet, chinaberry, and ailanthus.

Since 1991 reintroductions have been made of native hardwoods and shrubs that probably existed in the virgin forest. These include *Mag-

nolia tripetala, *Magnolia acuminata*, Carolina silver bell (*Halesia carolina*), American snowbell (*Styrax americanus*), yellowwood (*Cladrastis lutea*), overcup oak (*Quercus lyrata*), witch hazel (*Hamamelis virginiana*), red buckeye (*Aesculus pavia*), yellow buckeye (*Aesculus octandra*), red maple (*Acer rubrum*), sugar maple (*Acer saccharum*), summer sweet (*Clethra alnifolia*), leatherwood (*Dirca palustris*), fringe tree (*Chionanthus virginicus*), and pawpaw (*Asimina triloba*), and Pinckneya (*Pinckneya pubens*).

Wildflowers and vines discovered on the plantation land are wild ginger (*Asarum*), false garlic (*Nothoscordum bivalve*), blue-eyed grass (*Sisyrinchium atlanticum*), violet wood sorrel (*Oxalis violacea*), ladies tresses (*Spiranthes*), pipsissewa (*Chimaphila*), lyre-leaved sage (*Salvia lyrata*), St. Peters-wort (*Ascyrum stans*), bluets (*Houstonia caerula*), cardinal flower (*Lobelia cardinalis*), rattlesnake plantain (*Goodyera pubescens*), field goldenrod (*Solidago altissima*), wooly mullein (*Verbascum thapsus*), daisy fleabane (*Erigeron*), field pansy (*Viola rafinesquii*), pale gentian (*Gentiana villosa*), potato vine (*Ipomoea*), coral honeysuckle (*Lonicera sempervirens*), white clover (*Trifolium repens*), common blue violet (*Viola papilionacea*), Carolina cranesbill (*Geranium carolinianum*), boneset (*Eupatorium*), heal-all (*Prunella vulgaris*), butterfly pea (*Clitoria mariana*), climbing butterfly pea (*Centrosema virginianum*), yellow jessamine (*Gelsimium sempervirens*), trumpet vine (*Campsis radicans*) and a rare white-flowering mullein (*Verbascum blattaria*) growing in three large stands. These, of course, will not be disturbed. The woods are filled with beautyberry (*Callicarpa americana*).

In 1826 Mills also listed for Newberry the gentian, snakeroot, ginseng, coltsfoot, spikenard, and sweet annies (*Artemisia annua*). In future planting, emphasis will be on native plants, particularly those given by Mills. Sweet annies returned to the land in 1991. Wildflower walks now follow along the branch that skirts the north side of the grounds. In the absence of a name, I have called this little stream *Pucpuggy*, the Cherokee word for "flower gatherer," the nickname given to the naturalist William Bartram, who passed through upcountry South Carolina in colonial times.

As of 1997, about a mile of trails has been planted in the following: trout lily (*Erythronium americanum*), shooting star (*Dodecatheon*), Virginia bluebells (*Mertensia virginica*), Heart leaf (*Hexastyles arifolium*), called locally pigs and wild ginger, lily-of-the-valley (*Convallaria montana*), rue anemone (*Anemonella*), mayapple (*Podophyllum peltatum*), Indian pink

(*Spigelia*), partridgeberry (*Mitchella repens*), bluestar (*Amsonia tabernaemontana*), *Epimedium pinnatum, Trillium catesbaei, Trillium luteum, Trillium cuneatum, Trillium discolor, Trillium grandiflorum,* bellwort (*Uvularia sessilifolia*), bloodroot (*Sanguinaria canadensis*), spiderwort (*Tradescantia virginiana*), and cranesbill (*Geranium maculatum*). Columbine seed (*Aquilegia canadensis*) was sowed in the summers of 1990 and 1991, and the resulting plants are now reseeding themselves. Cinnamon, leatherleaf, royal, shield, and other ferns have been added to the many native Christmas ferns and ebony spleenwort already in the area.

The cranesbill, *Spigelia, Trillium discolor,* and *Trillium catesbei* were originally salvaged from the Lake Russell dam site on the Savannah River in 1983, a contested Army Corps of Engineers project that destroyed their habitat. *Trillium discolor* was already deemed rare; but since the new impoundment, its number has been seriously reduced.

Several native azaleas (*R. oconee, canescens,* and *prunifolium*) have been brought to Pucpuggy's banks. Seeds of both the red- and rare yellow-flowered sweet shrub (*Calycanthus var. "Athens"*) have now germinated along the stream. *Sabal minor* palmetto seedlings are also growing there. The woods through which these wildflower paths run are called The Grove, a name borrowed from the sage of Monticello, and will serve as a bosquet between forest and plantation grounds. Here the tangle of privet has been removed and the resulting spaces are being planted with trees and shrubs native to the South. The rare *Magnolia ashei* was the first tree to go there in June 1992. It has been followed by Carolina silver bell, Washington hawthorn, yellowwood, red buckeye, yellow buckeye, rare *Elliottia racemosa,* and bald cypress. Appropriately for The Grove, the silver bell was a tree much loved by Jefferson. It, the yellowwood, and the big-leaf magnolia (*Magnolia macrophylla*) will become the signature understory trees of this wood. Forty small *Magnolia macrophylla* now grow along the trails. The tract contains 18 acres and can be enlarged as desired.

In 1860 a minimum of 300 acres of the plantation, or one-half the amount of its cultivated acreage, was left in forest to allow the wise practice of interspersing woodlands and fields. This excellent, wise practice provided diversity, a place for wildlife and native flora, a barrier against erosion, an enhancer of the water table, a mediator of temperature, a source of firewood, timber, and medicinal herbs, and last but not least, the aesthetic pleasure of forest, a place (as one Carolina planter of the day put it) "to ride, to hunt, to ramble." Although in the short term these virgin forests if converted to rich cotton lands would have yielded a small fortune, the total destruction of the plantation's forest would in the long run have been very unwise. Most upcountry Carolina planters knew this, and many said so. As they declared, a farmer "should not jeopardize both his children's future and heritage for the quick profit" or, in the words of current conservationists, "We do not inherit the land from our ancestors but instead borrow it from our children." One of the best of many such statements on this topic came from the Newberry County horticulturist William Summer of Pomaria plantation, an acquaintance of the Hardys just down the State Road. His lengthy "Essay on Reforesting the Country" won the State Agricultural Society prize in 1859. A briefer, simpler declaration came from lowcountry Carolinian William G. Simms, a friend of Summer's. In 1847 he wrote that the good planter will be "fond of trees and foliage" and so contrive his fields "as to maintain a body of woods between each." Through these forests would "meander roads on which the master could pass to the survey of one field after another without once leaving the shelter of the original forests." His fields on one side could be covered in wheat, and on the other "a broad tract of rye, green and growing; while beyond, on every hand" would "spread a wall of thickly wooded copse and forest, by which each of his fields was girdled, and through which lay pleasant walks and openings to the corn and cotton fields still further distant." For these objects, the sensitive planter "had an eye." In other words, the better plantations would not be so thickly settled or intensively cultivated as to "club nature into submission." Instead, the planter would live in nature, which must be properly revered and nourished with sensitive stewardship.

Many antebellum Carolina planters obviously had this same keen eye for nature and were thus far wiser in conservation than we are prone to give them credit. Their philosophy of stewardship was often similar to that of our own day's ecologists. The 2,000-acre Hardy plantation was always left over half uncultivated, with a sizable portion preserved as virgin forest and conscientiously protected for the above enumerated reasons. These good early stewards of the land remain an inspiration out of the Southern past that should strengthen our resolve today.

In their living so close to nature, many an upcountry planter had learned to respect land properly as the source of his life and livelihood. As they said, to abuse it was "to destroy happiness, one's own character, and the future—in effect to commit murder of self and future generations." A planter's general wisdom partly derived from knowing this specific truth. As the case of William Eppes Hardy shows us, the Southern planter did not fear nature or wish to make wholesale conquest of it as the source of evil and the devil, as his urban-born New England Puritan counterpart so often did. The New England colonist, from a merchant and business background, had no tradition on the land and thus immediately and relentlessly set about endeavoring to remove nature's mystery, while he himself held up in villages as if in so many stockades. As Hugh Johnson writes in his *International Book of Trees*, the "old New England forest . . . was relentlessly butchered." Conversely, a planter like Hardy, bred from a markedly different country heritage, sought to live peacefully in nature, to revere and celebrate its mystery, not fear it, to fit himself to its rhythms and coexist in harmony in his "fruitful green valley"—rather than in an unnatural, man-made, wholly tamed, and sterile City on a Hill. In its fruitful valley, an agrarian society would make no such mistake. What wonder that the Puritan colony, totally unaccustomed to rural life, had come ill-equipped to fish, till the soil, and hunt. If the Native American had not taught these urbanites the basics of life on the land, they would not have survived their first winter. It is very significant that in America, as soon as possible, the Puritans built towns, realizing John Winthrop's "shining City on a Hill" ideal. A life otherwise was disquieting. Not so in the South. As Jefferson wrote, large cities are to a country like sores to a healthy body.

In the final analysis, a life on the land such as William Eppes Hardy's forces the acknowledgment of the primacy of the natural realm and its Creator. Hardy reveals in several letters that he has learned this truth and learned it well. Man's role is always "to augment rather than bring into submission and destroy the world through perverse willfulness," to work with rather than against it, "using the elemental gifts of the Creator with respect, humility and appreciation" if not, in fact, "high spiritual awe and reverence." All a planter's actions are to be to that end, or he and his life are doomed to "folly, frustration and eventual destruction." These two are roots of Southern agrarian wisdom both intuitively felt and practically learned from long unbroken generations of life on the land, in the old world and the new. From all indications, including the hard statistics of his land use, William Eppes Hardy possessed this wisdom in full measure. It is a far cry from the current terrible abuse of lands of the old plantation at the hands of clear-cutting tree-farming businesses and corporations, often owned by men from cities on hills who never see or touch the soil that provides them profit and thus do not even witness the results of their abuse, much less have to live with them. One is left with the important question of whose generation was the wiser and whose philosophy of stewardship the sounder.

8

Their Fathers' Fields
The Working Plantation in 1850

There is a pleasure in aiding Nature to perfect her works, which those who till the soil can only know.
— William Summer, Pomaria Plantation (1860)

Every task had a master, and each season its round of work. Each person had some special talent or gift. Those blessed with skill or knack in one line lacked a good hand for doing something else. It was the plantation's way.
— Julia Peterkin, Lang Syne Plantation (1915)

By 1820, and probably as early as 1810, cotton had become an important crop on the plantation. As we have seen, the farm inventory of 1814 already showed 7,500 pounds of green-seed cotton produced in that year on 10 to 17 acres. In 1850 corn was still being planted on the bottom lands, as it had been from the earliest times and as it continued to be into the present century. Other grain crops also checkered the landscape, but to east and south of the Great House, more extensive cotton terraces spilled down for the planting of this white gold. In the memory of those still living, the fields of September from Maybinton to Whitmire looked "like a winter scene covered with snow." In this particular locale of South Carolina, the cotton grew tall and luxuriant in the rich soils along the Tyger, Broad, and Enoree. The fine land and climate of Goshen Hill, Fish Dam, and Maybinton, along with careful and wise seed selection over the years, produced, it is said, a longer-stapled cotton than the usual upland green-seed, a grade that rivaled the legendary Sea Island cotton of the coast in both length of staple and market value. This superior grade of cotton was the basis of the rich plantation economy of the antebellum era that made this vicinity one of the wealthiest rural communities in all America and Newberry and lower Union Counties among the very wealthiest districts in South Carolina. The state itself was only behind Mississippi and Louisiana as the richest states per capita in the nation. As we have seen, a sense of style usually accompanied that wealth; and thus the society we view here had by the 1840s become among the most elegant in America. Gus Feaster, a former slave born in 1840 within a few miles of the Hardy plantation, grew to manhood in the neighborhood during the prewar period. In 1937 he was accurate in stating that when he was a lad, the "white folks of quality in Union most all came from Goshen Hill and Fish Dam."

Although now partly overgrown by woods, trenched terraces immediately adjacent to the Hardy house can still be seen to the north, south, and east. These are likely of postbellum origin, created when the plantation acreage had begun to shrink and there was dire need to use all available acreage, and to use it more intensively. These terraces are being carefully preserved in the landscape plans for the grounds. The older members of the family recall that in the Depression era and until the 1940s, cotton grew in front of the house "right up to the boxwood walks" and extended "all the way to and then across Tyger River Road some quarter mile distant," a thoroughfare from which one could see the mansion rise above its boxwood parterres on its hill looking eastward across its cotton terraces—"a peaceful and beautiful old-fashioned Southern scene," as they remember it. Cotton was still being planted on the land at John Frost Hardy's death in 1963, a year that marks the end of the cotton era for this particular plantation.

We are fortunate to have six primary groups of documents for this period that help recreate something of the day-to-day life on Squire Hardy's spread. First, there are his three extant plantation ledger and account books for 1839 to 1844, 1842 to 1846, and 1848 to 1865, in which he kept his lists of stud facts, boarding fees for horses and travelers, hog killings and sales, purchases, repairs of buggies, carriages, wagons, and wheels, repairs made at the blacksmith shop, the sales and services from the plantation shop, foundry, and commissary, his miscellaneous farm facts, farm produce sales and purchases, and a few first drafts of letters. Second, we have family and business letters to William Eppes Hardy, and third, other business receipts of sales and purchases. Fourth, there are the agricultural statistics of the United States census for 1850 and 1860 and the 1850 and 1860 census "slave schedules." Fifth, there are the 1850 and 1860 population censuses; and sixth and finally, the detailed 1870 inventory of the plantation that reveals as much about the prewar period as it does about the postwar, since little was purchased between 1861 and 1870.

In the early days of the plantation, pioneer Thomas Hardy Sr. had kept many hogs and cattle—enough, in fact, to bequeathe five cows and calves to each of eight children in 1814 and still have a balance for his widow. His cattle holdings thus numbered around sixty. The early plantation had other livestock as well. In 1814 there were five colts and a mare, eight sheep, forty-nine hogs and nine pigs, eight head of cattle, and twenty-one geese. In 1806 his son John Wesley, who also lived by his father on the land, owned fifty-two hogs, fourteen geese, eight head of cattle, one horse, and three beehives. (His less innovative parents had retained their old-fashioned bee skeps.) William Eppes Hardy continued in the family tradition of both his father and grandfather as an avid raiser of swine. These facts place the Hardys within the Celtic tradition of herdsmen as explained by historian Grady McWhiney. Although they were Anglo-Norman rather than Scots-Irish, their manner of home-steading was analogous to the Celtic.

In 1850 the agricultural census reports a plantation of 1,800 acres, 1,000 of which were "improved"—that is, in cultivation or in use as pasturage, lots, pens, orchards, stables, fields, dwellings, and gardens. This figure proves enormous growth in prosperity in a sixty-year period beginning in 1786, when the original tract had numbered only 204 acres. For the area, this growth tended to be more typical than other-wise; but in acreage it was among the largest plantations in this wealthy county and was eventually to reach its peak of 2,035 acres by the time of the war.

The 1850 acreage now included William Eppes Hardy's recent pur-chase of much of the adjacent Lyles plantation, bought in 1844 or shortly thereafter. This acquisition rounded off irregular north boundaries on the Tyger River side. The Lyles tract also included a simple two-and-a-half-story house, built around 1750, which may have been used hence-forth as an overseer's dwelling or by the Teagle family, named as residing on the Hardy lands and with the Hardy household in the 1850 census.

The family of Nathaniel (Natty) and Mary P. Teagle (or Teacle, as William Eppes Hardy spelled it in his ledger and as it sometimes appears on official documents) had helped manage and oversee the farm of the deceased John Wesley Hardy as early as 1812 and must be counted among the family retainers. Teagle, born in 1774 in Virginia, was seventy-six years old in 1850. He died 5 June 1852. His wife was a native South Carolinian. She was born 7 August 1789 and died 18 July 1851 at the age of sixty-one. They are buried in the Sims family cemetery near Carlisle, ten miles from the Hardy plantation.

The Teagles had owned some land of their own but remained associated with the Hardys into the 1850s. In 1850 they had a personal estate listed at a value of $3,070, a rather sizeable sum. Teagle is noted as repairing a cartwheel for the Hardy blacksmith establishment in 1843 (for which he was paid) and thus must have been competent at woodworking. In the 1820s and '30s, he was a great imbiber of spiritous liquors at the tavern at Orange Hall. Former slave Gus Feaster, born in 1840 on the T. A. Carlisle plantation at Goshen Hill, recalled that in the 1850s, barrels of liquor sat outside the store "in a long row" to refresh the "rich men that carried on at the race track nearby." Teagle's fancy ran toward brandy and whiskey; but the store ledger of purchases shows that he did not fail to remember his wife and daughter, for whom he bought small keepsakes, thread, and needles. In 1850 he had a son still with him in his household: James, who was twenty-five years old in that year and, like his father, was listed in the census as a farmer.

In 1850 the census also names for the plantation a thirty-five-year-old overseer, Patrick Cox. Cox is also included within the household, but, like the Teagles, he most likely had his own dwelling. Perhaps it was he who lived in the old Lyles house. No doubt there were other house sites on the plantation's 2,000 acres that are unknown to us today. There had been various overseers before Cox. The first on record was Elisha Davis, who was hired on 16 May 1838, according to the plantation ledger of that year. He was followed by Jenkins Willson on 22 November 1838. Both the Davis and Willson (Wilson) families were locals.

At the Great House itself in 1850, according to the census of that year, lived the forty-six-year-old master, known variously as Marse Billy, Squire Hardy, the Squire, the Marster, or just plain Billy; his thirty-nine-year-old wife Catharine, known as Mistis Catharine, the Missus, Missy Kate, or Kate; and their seven children: Thomas Powell, 21; Gustavus

Adolphus, 19; Charles Wesley, 18; Elmira Frances, 15; James Haywood, 11; William Dixon, 9; and George, 3.

Thus in 1850 the Hardy plantation supported nine in the master's family, four other white adults, and forty-six slaves, a total population of fifty-nine. Exemplifying Andrea Palladio's statement in his *I Quattro Libri* of 1570 that "a country house is a little city," a bird's-eye view of the estate would have revealed a little village indeed, with the L-shaped Great House backed by its detached kitchen and flanked by two rows of five slave cabins each that ran roughly from east to west on both sides of the master's house. Several hundred feet behind the kitchen building was the cook's house. It rested on large stone piers that are still to be seen. Beyond it were several low-ceilinged "huts" made of log and clapboard—still there in the 1950s, as remembered by John Hardy III. The clapboard-covered log smokehouse was at the terminus of the path that ran to the plantation yard's north side gate. According to Hardy descendants, the smokehouse sat adjacent to a large iron trough used at butchering time for scalding hogs. The smokehouse was thus only a short space from the butchering site and conveniently placed for the storing of large quantities of sausages and hams. In the mid 1850s Hardy had as many as four hundred hams curing at a time, so there may have been more than one such structure. In the smokehouse yard was a chopping block from which the meat was rationed to the slaves each week. Descendants also testify to the delicious taste of the sausages and hams still being cured there in the 1920s and '30s. There were perhaps also a small dairy building to keep milk and, considering the 220 bushels of sweet potatoes in 1850, one or more potato houses, common to Newberry County.

There was at least one large log barn and certainly several smaller ones as well. Margaret Thomas King recalls one barn as being of giant square logs one story high. It sat on the eastern terminus of the plantation "path." The log corncrib was to the north side of the smokehouse and adjacent to the log tack or harness shed, which still stands today. These were in what was the horse and mule lot from around 1900 until 1973 and likely were so in antebellum times as well. The present mule shed of rounded pine logs was probably built in the late 1800s or early 1900s. There were two privies. The women's sat beyond the detached kitchen; and the men's to the east side of the barn. They were thus positioned at opposite ends of the service path, conveniently close to the place of work of each sex.

Anna Powell Dixon Hardy of the Hardy Plantation (1783-1861). Oil portrait by
William Harrison Scarborough in 1858. Courtesy of Mrs. Calhoun L. Kennedy,
Columbia, SC.

James Freeman Eppes Hardy (1802-1880), the landscape architect of the plantation grounds in the 1820s. Oil portrait attributed to William Kennedy Barclay, around 1840. Courtesy of Anne Hardy Tennent Cecil, Spartanburg, SC.

Cordelia ("Delia") Haywood Erwin Hardy (1812-1876). Oil portrait attributed to William Kennedy Barclay, around 1840. Delia had become the bride of James F.E. Hardy in October 1839, and this may have been her wedding portrait. Courtesy of Charles Tennent, Simpsonville, SC.

William Eppes Hardy (1804-1870), master of the Hardy Plantation, around 1850. Courtesy of the Hardy Plantation Archives.

Students at the University of North Carolina in 1859. James Thomas Douglass of The Oaks, Goshen Hill, is on the far right. His friend, H. Francis Jones, of Greenwood Plantation in Georgia is in the center. Courtesy of the Hargrett Rare Book and Manuscript Library---University of Georgia Libraries, Athens.

Dawkins Rogers, son of James and Nancy Dawkins Rogers of Orange Hall, and 2nd Lieutenant of 1st Company of South Carolina College Cadets in March 1861. Wearn & Hix, photographers, around 1860. Courtesy of Mrs. John Renwick, Whitmire, SC.

William W. Renwick of Orange Hall, Goshen Hill, around 1849. Courtesy of Mrs. John Renwick, Whitmire, SC.

Frances Booker Sims Hardy (1852-1896), around 1865. Courtesy of William Hardy Jr., Pacolet, SC.

William Dixon Hardy (1841-1932) in his uniform of the 5th South Carolina Volunteers, around 1862. The carte de visite is by Chas. H. Bee & Co., Richmond, Va. Courtesy of William Hardy Jr., Pacolet, SC.

William Henry ("Willie") Hardy (1842-1861), 2nd South Carolina Volunteers, Aide-de-camp of Gen. Joseph B. Kershaw. Quinby & Co., Artists, Charleston, SC. Courtesy of Charles Tennent, Simpsonville, SC.

Emma Hardy Tennent (1828-1924) in Paris in 1864. Carte de visite by G. LeGray & Cie, Paris. Courtesy of Anne Hardy Tennent Cecil.

William Dixon Hardy ("Captain Dick") while a member of the SC General Assembly, around 1880. Courtesy William Hardy Jr., Pacolet, SC.

Frances Booker Sims Hardy, around 1880. Courtesy of the Hardy Plantation Archives.

George Briggs, a former slave from a neighboring plantation, around 1936. Courtesy of the Union County Historical Society.

Paul H. Hardy (1888-1954), around 1918. Courtesy of the Hardy Plantation Archives.

Captain Dick and his family in June 1925 in the plantation yard. Front row (left to right): William Dixon Hardy (grandson), Frances Booker Henderson, John Frost Hardy Jr., William Dixon Henderson, Frances Scott, Mary Ella Henderson, Haywood Hardy Henderson, and Hugh Henderson Jr. Middle row (left to right): John Frost Hardy, Epps Hardy, Captain Dick, Ben Hardy, and Haywood Hardy. Back row (left to right): Frank Hardy, Mary Hardy Scott, Helen Hardy Henderson holding Addie Sims Henderson, and Paul H. Hardy. Lower photograph is of the same group on the plantation steps. Courtesy of Haywood Hardy Henderson.

Captain Dick on his 91st birthday, napping on the back veranda of the Hardy Plantation in April 1932. Courtesy of the Hardy Plantation Archives.

Hardy Plantation Great House in December 1907. Photograph by Stevenson. Courtesy of the Hardy Plantation Archives.

Rose Cottage around 1920. Ethel Setzler Renwick (Mrs. John Renwick Sr.) and her children (left to right): Pat (in front), William, John Jr., and twins Ben and Jim. Courtesy of Mrs. John Renwick, Whitmire, SC.

Hardy Plantation Great House in April 1932. Courtesy of the Hardy Plantation Archives.

Hardy Plantation Great House, 21 May 1985. Photographs by Nancy Fox.
Courtesy of the South Carolina Department of Archives and History.

Hardy Plantation Great House in December 1993. Photograph by J.E. Kibler. Courtesy of the Hardy Plantation Archives.

The rear of the Hardy Plantation Great House in 1993. Photograph by J.E. Kibler. Courtesy of the Hardy Plantation Archives.

The Oaks Plantation, Goshen Hill, in 1973. Photograph by George Douglass, Charleston, SC. Courtesy of George Douglass.

William Dixon Henderson recalled a log house used around 1930 for storing cottonseed hulls. It sat about 100 feet to the northwest of the house near the present well. The plantation blacksmith shop, that in the 1830s and '40s did such an extensive business of horseshoeing, plow making and repair, carriage, oxcart, barouche, wagon, and wheel repair, and tool making and mending, was located in the barnyard area near the main road to Gordon's Bridge over the Tyger. This activity was overseen by the eldest son, Thomas Powell Hardy, twenty-one years old in 1850 and listed as "tradesman" in the census of 1860. The commissary was either a part of the blacksmith's shop or adjacent to it, for a single plantation ledger is kept for both activities. This conglomerate of buildings thus served as an office area. Associated with the blacksmithing activity, there were a nailery for nail production and a foundry where the Hardys oversaw the melting and founding of iron and steel both for sale and for use in the plantation's own shop.

Doubtless there were also horse, mule, and cow stables. The sheep, goats, and cattle, however, would have been placed in grazing pasturage, which in the 1920s ran from the stable area northward toward Tyger River. The location of the overseer's house is as yet unknown.

A plantation bell stood near the detached kitchen for ringing the hands in from the fields. In the absence of a bell, another tradition in the Tyger area was for the women to climb the stairs "to the top of the house" and through open windows blow on a conch shell. This was done by the neighboring Thomas family of Peters Creek well into the present century.

The presence on the plantation of both a buggy and carriage presupposes a carriage house, for such expensive items would have been protected from the elements. Where the carriage house was located and what it was like are unknown; but it is probable that such a building did exist near the main house and within close proximity to the stables that housed the horses that pulled the vehicles. Because the plantation had five wagons and a cart by 1860, structures likely existed for their protection as well. These outbuildings would have been near the barns and stables. Perhaps some were sheltered in lean-to sheds attached to various cribs and barns. William Dixon Henderson remembered the plantation in 1930 as having a minimum of the structures represented in the sketch on the following page.

In 1850 the livestock on the plantation was comprised of 9 horses, 16 asses and mules, 20 cows, 6 oxen used for plowing wet lowlands, 15 "other cattle," 25 sheep, and a number of goats. Although goats are not

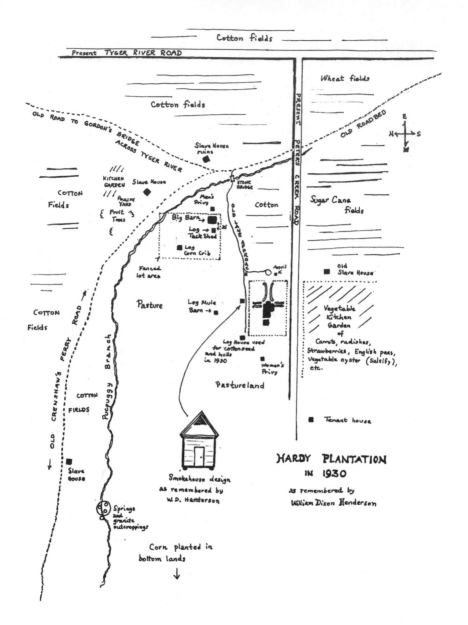

Cotton fields

Present TYGER RIVER ROAD

Wheat fields

OLD ROAD TO GORDON'S BRIDGE ACROSS TYGER RIVER

Cotton fields

OLD ROAD BED

PRESENT PETERS CREEK ROAD

Slave House ruins

KITCHEN GARDEN

Slave House

POULTRY YARD

STONE BRIDGE

COTTON Fields

Fruit Trees

Men's Privy

Cotton

Sugar Cane fields

Big Barn

Log → Tack Shed

Log Corn Crib

Anvil

Old Slave House

Fenced lot area

Pasture

Log Mule Barn →

Vegetable Kitchen Garden of Carrots, radishes, Strawberries, English peas, Vegetable oyster (Salsify), etc.

COTTON Fields

OLD CRENSHAW'S FERRY ROAD

Pucpuggy Branch

Log House used for cottonseed and hulls in 1930

Woman's Privy

Pastureland

COTTON FIELDS

Tenant house

Slave House

Smokehouse design as remembered by W.D. Henderson

HARDY PLANTATION IN 1930

as remembered by William Dixon Henderson

Springs and granite outcroppings

Corn planted in bottom lands

mentioned in the 1850 census of farm statistics, the plantation ledger throughout the 1840s notes the sale of their hides. Perhaps it is they that comprise the "other cattle" category. Goats were a common item at barbecues all over the area, as reported in numerous narratives by former slaves. The extraordinary statistic is for 220 hogs in mid-1850, even after

Hardy's ledger records the butchering of 70 or more the preceding winter. His livestock was valued at $5,250, or about $100,000 in today's currency. The large number of hogs is corroborated by many plantation ledger entries in 1848, 1849, and 1850 detailing their weights, slaughter, and sales. During this period the good squire acquired some of his new, blooded swine stock from M. S. Temple & Alexander of Tennessee and had dealings with them both for his own plantation and on his neighbors' behalf throughout the 1850s. As we have seen earlier, among the newly married master's first purchases in 1829 were three sets of sows and pigs ("spotted," "red spotted," and "banded"), showing that he was intent from the start on building up this sphere of plantation activity and self-sufficiency. In 1862, in referring to his father as a "Hog man" and himself as a "Horse man," Haywood confirms the master's continuing strong interest in this sphere of plantation activity.

The value of the plantation's farm machinery at this time tops out at $500, or approximately $10,000 in today's currency. Hardy also had a gin at which he processed his own cotton, thus maximizing his profits and furthering self-sufficiency, as did the major sideline of the plantation blacksmith shop, foundry, and commissary. The plantation ledger and account book for 1842–1846 shows just how extensive this blacksmithing enterprise had become. The shop not only performed all the services for the home plantation but also filled the needs of neighboring spreads as far away as Maybinton and Goshen Hill. Frequent customers were the families Lyles, Gordon, Maybin, Clarke, Shell, Hancock, Gilliam, Wilson, Chick, Pearson, Murphy, Tucker, Stewart, Valentine, Caldwell, and Davis. Individuals included Hardy's brother-in-law Dr. George Douglass, mother-in-law Anna Hardy, Thomas Valentine, James Henderson, J. C. Wells, Emanuel Oxner, George Ashford, P. W. and Burrell Chick, John Finger, William B. Smith, Robert Beauford, Silas Tygart, Benjamin McJunkin, Nathan Parrot, John Rogers, and scores of other one-, two-, or three-time customers in a four-year span. The services performed here were wide-ranging. The briskest business was in horseshoeing and making plow points and colters (special plow points for making verticle cuts in soil). This is what one would expect in an agricultural community. In this four-year period, the ledger records an impressive 2,025 plow points made and sold; and this figure does not include those made for the home plantation. The shop also constructed plow handles and complete plows. Over 125 plows were made and sold between 1842 and 1845. Some of these were designated "Eagle plows," "Hawk plows," and "Wing plows." The "Eagle" was, after 1843, the most popular by far, with more than 25 sold during this four-year span. The shop, as might be expected, also repaired and sharpened plows.

The records show the making and repairing of horse and mule harness, singletrees, clavises, chains, rings, ox rings, iron yokes, collar needles, halters, halter chains, hooks, backband hooks, stirrups, stretcher hooks, bridle bits, traces, and trace chains. The smithy even did intricate work (like making buckles) and was thus possessed of some skill. Agricultural tools and implements issued in great quantity from his anvil. Sales and repairs of hoes, weeding hoes, garden hoes, sprouting hoes, spades, shovels, mattocks, thrashers, "falsecotters," scythe blades and handles, and grass blades are noted with regularity from 1842 to 1845. Less often produced were "spaying needles," stilyard hooks and repairs, wheelbarrows, wagon body irons, cradle rods, and "cranks for shelling machines." There is not a single mention of the repairing or making of slave shackles or irons, an item that the modern imagination sometimes identifies most readily with plantation life. Throughout the numerous narratives of the former slaves of this vicinity given from 1936 to 1938, there is no mention of chains or chaining.

Woodworking and other tools were especially popular sellers. The plantation smithy produced an amazing volume of nails of several descriptions and sizes ("square nails"; 6-, 10-, and 12-penny nails; "spike nails"), tent spikes (in 1859), hooks, "steeples" (staples), axes, broad axes, "hand axes," log hooks (for rolling logs), iron wedges, drawing knives, chisels, sugar handles, iron stone-hammers, bolts (including the giant bolts to repair nearby Gordon's Bridge over the Tyger), drills, "twisters," "bed staples," crank handles for grindstones, and pump irons.

Creation of household and cooking utensils was common. The ledger lists several ladles, many pothooks, "flesh forks," keys, key rings, door hinges, window hinges, clock weights, bell clappers, and one "bread baker." Mending was done on coffee mill handles, trivets, teakettles, pots, spiders, pot legs, locks, guns, flax wheels, looms, currycombs, firedogs, fire tongs, fire shovels, hobbles, and several waffle irons.

The iron and steel for all this extensive activity may have been smelted on the plantation itself or boated downriver to the plantation landing from a source such as the large Cherokee Iron Works in upper South Carolina. The frequent sale of large poundages of iron and steel "by the weight" is also recorded in the ledger. Very little is known of this plantation business. A piece of smelted steel was dug from the plantation grounds in 1989 and was identified as the by-product of the ore-refining and steel-making processes. Where this activity might have occurred on the plantation is unknown.

Associated with the blacksmith shop was a rather lucrative business in horseshoeing and repairing the vehicles of the day. During the four-year period there are entries for various repairs to barouches, a sulkey, several carriages, many wagons, and half a dozen oxcarts. Braces were made for a carriage top. Many "tyres" were put on wagons, on three "carry-alls," and on sulkeys. Many gudgeons (axle pins), axles, axletrees, wagon harnesses, coupling poles, cart tongues, wagon gate latches, and band wheel-irons were made or repaired as well. Tires were "shrunk" and wheel spokes made and mended.

Then the blacksmith's various services for businesses in the area should also be recognized. The smithy provided twenty-nine bolts for Gordon's Bridge (16 September 1844), repaired forty-nine gin ribs, worked on several other gin repairs, worked on the mill irons and screws at Maybin's Sawmill (February 1845). There he also sharpened and "put steel in the mill-pick" (April 1845). He provided steel pins, boat spikes, rings, and staples for several flatboats for Bennet Hancock and James M. Henderson. (Ben Hancock, the ferryman at Henderson Ferry on the Enoree at its confluence with the Broad, was remembered by ex-slave Charles Harvey as "the best boatman in his day.")

Showing great versatility and ingenuity, the plantation also sold hides (recorded in the ledger as either "green," "raw," or "dry"), at least one saddle, and pairs of plantation-made boots and shoes. These last must have been a good product because they were requested in the 1830s by James, the dandyish brother of the master now living in Asheville. The cobblering continued into the 1860s, for son Haywood in Richmond in 1862 was requesting the shoes promised him by his father. The plantation tanned and made its own leather for these purposes and recorded sales of this article.

Perhaps most interesting of all is the evidence of a small coopering activity. In the four years between 1842 and 1845, the plantation made and sold twenty-four "large buckets," twenty-one barrels, and many small buckets. Its cooper also put the irons on several well buckets and the hoops on several tubs. This knowledge suggests that the plantation's kegs, buckets, barrels, and pails were made on the place and were no doubt plentiful there. As we have noted, the early plantation had the capacity to make casks, tubs, kegs, and barrels. The skill thus likely derived in Virginia with the early Hardys and was passed down to and kept up by their Carolina descendants.

A bill of purchase by William Eppes Hardy dated 7 November 1851 indicates that in fall 1851, the plantation coopering and woodworking activity was continuing. From Scott & Ewart Hardware in Columbia, Hardy purchased implements expressly used by the cooperer: a "Coopers Draw Knife ($1.50), a "Coopers Broad Axe" (1.50), a "Coopers Tool," a "Coopers Crow" (Crowse) (.25), a "Coopers Adze" (1.00), a drawing knife (.75), a "Spoke Shave" (.38), and a handsaw (1.00). These purchases prove the significance of this sphere of plantation enterprise. And the activity made the plantation some profit. In addition to providing kegs and barrels for its own use, the plantation could also sell nineteen "Iron Bound Kegs" and seven "Wood Bound Kegs" to Whitmire & Bros. in Newberry village on 16 July 1852. These brought a credited sum of $21.78, from which Hardy drew "100 pounds of Hoop Iron" (at $8.00), 5 pounds of "Cast Steel" (1.00), one keg (.37$^{1}/_{2}$), and the balance in 124 pounds of brown sugar (12.40). Plantation-made barrels were thus converted by barter into steel and brown sugar, in proof of yet another way in which the plantation had a diverse economic base.

The plantation also did a modest amount of hauling for the builders Absalom and Jacob Shell, for the plasterer John Finger, and for others. The hauling was largely from Boyd's Mill and Maybin's Mill and from nearby Gordon's Bridge. The plantation landing, via the navigable Tyger and Broad Rivers, gave easy access from Spartanburg District to the north and Columbia and Charleston to the south. When the master made his trips to purchase from the merchants Scott & Ewart, Birge, Gracey, or R. C. Anderson in Columbia, he also bought certain supplies for neighbors to have on hand for sale in the blacksmith shop and commissary. Manufactured shoes, "fine shoes," "negro blankets," lime, linseed oil, cloth, salt, and bluestone (to cure saddlesores) were among the items he notes selling during the 1840s.

The small 1839–1844 ledger, although mainly an account book for farm animals and stock, also has entries that prove that these various enterprises had been going on since 1836 or earlier. A loose-leaf sheet in William Eppes Hardy's hand from 1836 corroborates this assertion. It records Samuel Gordon's debt to the Hardy plantation for shoeing mules, carriage mending, repair of chains, a pot, and a bridle, and for making a bit. On this same sheet are the bills to Mrs. Stewart for putting steel in an ax and to Mr. John Lyles for whetting an ax. Thus many loose-leaf accounts were no doubt kept for the blacksmithing activity and unfortunately have not come down to us. The large 1842–1846 plantation ledger is noted on its cover as a gift from brother James Hardy in 1842. It is from this year on that the blacksmithing accounts were kept in bound form and thus better preserved.

Squire Hardy received payments for most of his goods and services either in cash or trade, but two particular entries are of amusing interest. One fee for fixing the Reverend B. S. Ogletree's carriage is unpaid and annotated "GONE TO TEXAS." Another for a Mr. Daniel Mansfield is noted "RANAWAY WEST." Such were the hazards of dealing with those men who had "western fever." To the credit of T. J. Valentine, a ledger entry notes that he paid his account of $298 "in full" and "left this country for Mississippi the 7th day of December 1848 on Thursday morning about 10 o'clock." In this notation, Hardy sounds like he is trying to record the history of stirring, changing times—as indeed he was.

Despite much and busy peripheral activity, the plantation's principal focus was, of course, on farming. On the agricultural front, the 1850 census reports a yearly produce of 2,500 bushels of corn. This was used for livestock feed, grits, and cornmeal, and for sale and barter. The plantation ledgers reveal that Hardy also sold a surplus of corn, flour, and fodder throughout the previous decade. In August 1842, for example, the master notes sending 20 barrels of 4,380 pounds of flour to Columbia—over two tons. Mills's *Statistics* lists the yield of from 10 to 40 bushels of corn per acre in Newberry County in 1826. At an average of 25 bushels per acre, Hardy thus had approximately 100 acres of land in corn cultivation in the year 1850. Cotton was king, but corn was the crown prince of the plantation. Corn was especially essential on the Hardy plantation for feeding the many hogs and other livestock. Corn fodder as well provided valuable winter food for the livestock. Corn supplied half of the essential duo of "hog and hominy" for both white and black alike. Although the white table probably had greater variety, both races had the same basic dietary underpinning in corn. The plantation cook of the colonial South had evolved imaginative new ways of using the Indian grain in dishes like corn pudding, hush puppies, the local favorite "ash-cake," and corn fritters. Three former slaves of nearby plantations, born in 1840, 1844, and 1854, recalled that each person on the place received a ration of a peck of cornmeal per week—a quantity far greater than the quart or 2 to 3 pounds of flour mentioned as given each person at the same time. All who narrate in 1937 note that this is more than they now get during the current hard times.

For the purpose of providing grits for plantation tables, Hardy had an "iron grits mill" to grind the corn. This items is just one more indication that the Hardy masters of each generation were ever mindful of the goal of plantation self-sufficiency. Incidentally, grits may not always have been standard fare on the black tables, if we can judge from former slave Gus Feaster. He recalled that at Goshen Hill, the slaves were treated to grits only on Sunday mornings—a special treat. With grits, they had "shoulder meat and gravy" (the usual "grits and gravy"). This treatment was not common at other plantations, he recollected, where slaves "never got such 'siderations as I ever heard of."

The corn crop took far less labor than cotton. It was less complicated to grow and benefited from plowing, whereas cotton had to be mostly hoe-cultivated. One plowman could usually do the work of four field hands with hoes. The crop was thus far less labor-intensive, but of course brought no such cash at market as did the "white gold." In 1850 Hardy also raised 500 bushels of wheat. Mills's *Statistics* reports an average yield of from 10 to 15 bushels of wheat per acre in Newberry County. At an average yield of 13 bushels per acre, Hardy thus had about 40 acres planted in this crop. Wheat was used to make the flour given as rations to all on the plantation. A quart of flour per adult was allotted each week on several of the neighboring plantations, and likely was the outlay here as well.

The plantation produced 500 bushels of oats. Mills listed the yield for oats as being slightly higher than that for wheat. At an average of 16 bushels per acre, Hardy thus had about 32 acres in cultivation. In 1850 he grew 200 bushels of peas and beans, a token 5 bushels of barley, 20 bushels of Irish potatoes, and a whopping 500 bushels of sweet potatoes, a popular food with black and white alike on this plantation and, as David Ramsay, an early-nineteenth-century Carolina historian, describes it, an "essential article of sustenance" for half the year or more. Sweet potatoes were, in fact, an absolutely necessary staple from January to June before the kitchen gardens could start yielding in earnest. Potatoes could be banked all fall and winter and conveniently drawn for baking, roasting, making pies, custards, puddings, and sweet potato bread. The fail-proof simplicity of taking these brown delights, with the dark sugar oozing from their jackets, from ovens or the hearth-fire coals of kitchen, Big House, and slave cabin, endeared them to cook and eater alike. At an average of 50 bushels per acre, Hardy had about 10 acres of sweet potatoes in cultivation. In the Lowcountry, a planter might get in two crops a year; but here where the growing season was shorter by a month or so, he could not easily squeeze a second in.

Another important plantation staple was sugar cane. There is no record of the acreage Hardy devoted to it or of the amount he harvested. The agricultural statistics do not survey its production; but the presence of molasses boilers and skimmers in the Hardy plantation inventory of 1870 proves its importance. Black strap molasses was a staple of the diets of both races on the antebellum plantation, as we shall see. There is no record of the purchase of molasses except in very small supplemental quantities; and so the plantation must always have supplied most of its own. In the years before the War, it was supplying all of its own.

In 1850 Hardy's milk cows produced a total of 600 pounds of butter. Because there is no mention of butter sales in the plantation ledger, most of this product must have been used on the place. This was a necessary ingredient for many of the excellent desserts and "sweet-treats" that this particular plantation was noted for, and which were shared by black and white alike the whole year round, but most copiously at berry and peach and apple cobbler time, camp meeting weeks, barbecues, and Christmas. Former slave Gus Feaster recalled of plantation life at Goshen Hill: "Every master wanted his darkies to be thought well of at de barbecues by de darkies from all de other plantations. Dey had pigs barbecued, goats; and de Missus let de wimmen folks bake pies, cakes, and custards fer de barbecue, jes 'zactly like hit was fer de white folk barbecue des-self." There were no plantation orchards listed in the 1850 census statistics; but pears, apples, peaches, and apricots grew on the place for the use of the plantation community. One very old pear tree still grows here, perhaps a descendant of one of these trees. The glory of the traditional dance or wedding party in this area was always the dessert table, which would never fail to have on it at least six kinds of pies and six of cakes. Large quantities of butter were thus essential to life on this plantation.

The great primary cash crop of cotton, as reported in 1850, yielded a very respectable 110 bales of ginned cotton, of 400 pounds each. Since about two-thirds of the weight of freshly picked cotton was in seeds, a 400-pound bale of ginned lint thus required about 1,200 pounds of raw cotton. The 110 bales therefore amounted to 132,000 pounds in the field, or 44,000 ginned. Using Mills's 1826 average yield of from 150 to

200 pounds of deseeded cotton per general acre in Newberry County, one computes that this was accomplished on from 220 to 293 acres, only about a quarter of the plantation's improved acreage of 1,000 acres and one-eighth of the 2,000. Although by 1850 the Hardy soil may have lost some of its richness from Mills's time, it had been more fertile than the average for the county in the first place, and Hardy was composting with plenty of hog manure. So I surmise this spread of figures would be close enough to give us a good approximation.

From pioneer Thomas Hardy's approximately 24 to 40 acres of cotton in 1814, the figure had thus risen dramatically for his grandson to from 220 to 293 acres in 1850. When to this cotton acreage are added 100 acres of corn, 40 acres of wheat, 32 of oats, and 10 of sweet potatoes, about 520 to 600 acres were left for the remaining crops (like sorghum cane), for pasturage, lots, barnyards, orchards, vegetable gardens, and livestock—that is, over half of his improved acreage. The plantation acreage was thus far from being dominated by cotton, as some stereotypical views of the plantation South would have it. For this particular area of South Carolina, farm statistics show that the Hardy spread was not unusual in this.

The 2 to 300 acres of cotton in full summer blow spilling down terraces from the Great House and punctuated by several hundred more acres of pasture lands and grain fields in various hues of green and gold—these set against and divided by about 300 acres of original hardwood forest in groves, copses, and virgin tracts—must have been a truly impressive sight to behold. The master's view of his fruitful landscape from the windows of his high rooms across flower parterres, fields, and forests, to the backdrop of the distant blue hills of the Tyger valley, was food for the soul on rising each morning. No matter how hard his work, the landscape he had helped create shaped the family's spirit with its beauty and was recompense in full. As a couple sensitive to this beauty, the scene was never lost on Squire Billy and Mistress Kate; and familiarity did not dull its luster. No matter where the master went, as he wrote a son in 1849, he carried this picture of his "valley home, hills, and fields with me always in the mind's eye and I see it last when falling to sleep on strange linens."

With a total of all his farming activity on the 1,000 acres listed in the 1850 census, his agricultural yield per acre was relatively high, therefore suggesting careful farm management and intelligent plantation practice. As we have noted, Hardy was assisted in 1850 by overseer Patrick Cox, a thirty-five-year-old native South Carolinian, who by 1860 had left the plantation overseeing duties to Hardy and his sons.

Hardy's 110 bales of cotton at average price in 1850 would have brought him about $100,000 in today's currency; and the Hardy cotton, owing to its length of staple, probably brought more than the average. These were flush times indeed; and the cotton plantation, supplemented by its sale of corn and slaughtered hogs, probably yielded revenue sufficient to place William Eppes Hardy near the top of Newberry and Union Counties in wealth—in fact, in the top one percent in the nation as a whole. The real estate value of his plantation in 1850 was listed at $18,000 (roughly 350,000 today). This figure did not include his personal property and slaves. The latter, even over the land, were his most valuable monetary assets. In 1853 a prime male field hand brought an average price of $900 in Charleston. In 1860 he brought $1,200. At an average value of $500 per person, his forty-six slaves were worth a minimum of $23,800 in 1850, or about half a million dollars in today's currency. Hardy and the eight men in Newberry County who were wealthier than he in real estate value compared this way:

Planter	Acreage	Real Estate Value
Charles Floyd	2,700	$57,000
John Belton O'Neall	2,000	$45,000
John Williamson	1,200	$34,000
Job Johnstone	2,500	$30,000
Richard Sondley	2,300	$30,000
Dr. Peter Moon	2,000	$30,000
John N. Herndon	[unavailable]	$20,000
John Summer	[unavailable]	$20,000
William Eppes Hardy	1,800	$18,000

Hardy's nearest wealthy neighbors in Newberry County were the Chicks, with a real estate value of $12,000, and the Maybins of Maybinton, at $10,000. The Rogers family of Orange Hall and Hardy's kinsmen the Douglasses of The Oaks, both in adjacent Goshen Hill community, Union County, were roughly on an equal plane with him. In 1850 James Rogers's real estate value was $11,400 and his acreage 950 (it increased to 1,400 acres in 1860). Dr. George Douglass's was $20,000, with 1,200 acres. Anna Hardy, William's mother-in-law, had real estate at Goshen Hill valued at $8,000 and 225 acres (that increased to 750 acres in 1860).

The good squire also raised and sold horses. One sorrel in 1845 brought $100, a considerable sum. A bill of sale for a horse to Wells & Anderson for the large sum of $200 is dated 11 November 1852. This payment was used as credit for goods that Hardy bought at this establishment. Hardy paid an additional $390 to settle this account. The plantation ledgers also record receipts of $8 for stud fees. There is evidence that Hardy also bred a significant number of mules, some of which he sold.

Another significant statistic is that the Hardy plantation produced 100 pounds of wool from 25 sheep. This figure again points to the self-sufficiency of this planting community, for it would have been used for making cloth for the plantation, fabric from which the ladies themselves made clothes, coverlets, counterpanes, and blankets. Five spinning wheels and a loom (listed in an 1870 inventory of the place) vouch for this activity, which was common in the neighborhood. Standard winter slave clothing, as recorded by most former slaves of the area, was of a cotton and wool blend made on their own plantation looms, from sheep raised on the place. There was one elderly slave woman whose duty it was to oversee this activity. There was often also a head seamstress who directed the clothes making. These ladies were most often too old for field work, so performed these duties instead. They also made many of the blankets, coverlets, quilts, sheets, and "bed-clothing." They wove cotton cloth for summer attire. For Sundays and special occasions there were brighter homemade clothes and some purchased ready-mades.

William Eppes Hardy's plantation ledger of 1842–1846 reveals that he and the mistress found it necessary to buy only the finer, special commodities from outside his domain. For example, from John I. Gracey & Co. of Columbia (in December 1831), as a newly married young gentleman, he purchased for his wife 10 yards of silk at $1 per yard, two lady's cloaks at $21, 4 yards of white flannel, 56½ yards of calico, 3 yards of "blue cirusham," 5 yards of muslin, bobinet, a black bobinet veil at $5.00, cambric, cambric handkerchiefs, 14 yards of white satin in figured design, 30¾ yards of "bleached shirting," 6 yards of black "grosenap" at $9.00, hooks and eyes, a pair of side combs, kid gloves, buckskin gloves, and belt and cap "ribleands" (ribbons). He also ordered letter paper and a bottle of snuff. The previous year (from William Birge & Co. of Columbia) he bought cotton handkerchiefs, three pairs of cotton stockings at $2.07, and a muslin cravat.

On the more practical side, the ledger of 1842–1846 shows that

Hardy purchased from other sources wagon loads of wood, sack salt, borax, some flour (only in lean years), a gross of 1½-gallon stoneware jugs, and some molasses to supplement what the plantation itself produced. By 1860 he was no longer having to buy molasses because now himself planting sufficient cane and rendering it in three new molasses boilers. (William Dixon Hardy Sr. recalls that cane continued to grow on the place into the 1930s, across Peters Creek Road adjacent to the main house.) It was usual to include "black [strap] molasses" in the slaves' rations. All the former slaves of the area recalled a ration of from a quart to a half-gallon of molasses a week for each adult.

Against this short list of debts in the plantation ledgers were noted the sales from the plantation bounty. Sales statistics are sporadic. Only those notes and scraps of accounts that survive can serve to give a very sketchy suggestion of the whole picture of his sales:

179 pounds of fodder and 8 bushels of corn	June 1836
600 bushels of oats and 30 bushels of corn	October 1836
22½ bushels of oats	20 February 1842
17 bushels of corn	June 1842
4,380 pounds of flour	16 August 1842
Pork and 180 pounds of flour	September 1842
43 pounds of beef	4 October 1842
5 bushels of wheat	22 November 1842
1½ bushels of peas	20 May 1843
88 pounds of lard and 11 pounds of bacon	July 1843
5 bushels of seed wheat and 374 pounds of flour	12 August 1843
35½ bushels of corn	August 1843
237 pounds of flour	24 July 1844
Butter, flour, and ham	August 1844
200 pounds of flour	September 1844
86 pounds of bacon	31 October 1844
10 bushels of seed oats	24 February 1845
10 bushels of wheat	10 June 1845
1,583 pounds of fodder	August 1845
966 bundles of fodder at 39,606 pounds	September 1845
18 bushels of seed oats and 10 bushels of seed wheat	8 November 1845
156½ pounds of lard	21 May 1846

In 1848 he sold William Nance 90 bushels of corn and Mark Tygart 30 pounds of lard and 30 pounds of meat. On 24 March 1849 he sold James Cotter "30 dozen of fodder and 32 bushels of corn."

On 22 December 1843 Hardy killed 40 hogs at 7,210 pounds. On 30 December of the same year he slaughtered around 10 more at 1,792 pounds. On 8 December 1844 he killed 37 hogs at 7,123 pounds. In 1844 these were noted as being "of my own raising," whereas in the previous year he purchased from Thomas Gaines and James Lockname 19 of the 50 hogs he slaughtered. On 26 December 1845 Hardy noted 39 hogs killed for sale to R. A. Barnet at 9,378 pounds. On 30 November 1849 he recorded 20 hogs killed at 2,851 pounds. Hardy's second butchering in 1849 was for 14 hogs at 2,056 pounds. His third, of 18 hogs, netted 2,631 pounds. His December 1849 slaughtering (as shown in the entry for 7 December) was for 21 hogs at 3,865 pounds. His November–December 1849 total was therefore 73 hogs at 11,403 pounds. The 1850 census reported a balance of 220 hogs on the plantation during midyear 1850. Thus there were likely close to 300 on the place before the butchering in winter 1849. No sale of pork is reported in the extant accounts. The number of hogs Hardy killed was not untypical in the neighborhood. Zack Herndon, a former slave born in 1844, recalled in 1937 that his master at Santuc always killed no fewer than 25 to 30 hogs at a time.

Of the four former slaves from the immediate Maybinton–Santuc–Goshen Hill vicinity who report the amount of weekly slave rations, three of them note 3 pounds of bacon given each adult per week, and one notes 4 pounds per person per week. The 3 pounds must have been a minimum standard; and all four of these narrators record additional ham, goat, beef, wild game, and mutton at summer barbecues, the week-long camp meetings, and holidays like Christmas, New Year's, and the Fourth of July. Thus if Squire Hardy rationed his forty-six slaves the minimum average of 3 pounds of bacon per week, he needed 7,176 pounds to feed them. There were thirteen others on the place to feed as well, including his own family and the overseers. Their minimum 3 pounds per week average would come to 2,028 pounds. Together this would total 9,204 pounds. If no pork was sold in 1849, the 2,199 pounds of pork remaining after the total rationing suggests that the Hardy domain had ample fare indeed, for our ration figures have been computed for all adults, and many were children. The recollection of Hardy slave descendants is that when it came to food, they were "treated like kings."

Beef, mutton, goat, poultry, rabbit, squirrel, deer, duck, wild turkey, opossum, and fish from the Tyger and Broad also supplemented the diets of black and white alike throughout the year.

The raising of pork on the plantation continued to increase into the 1850s. In May 1855, as recorded by a note of payment, Hardy sold 298 hams weighing 4,114 pounds to S. J. Keller & Co. of Columbia. Also in May 1855 he sold 4,056 pounds of pork—301 slabs of bacon, 120 shoulders, 118 sides, and 64 "joules" (jowles)—to his neighbors Samuel Gordon, Joshua Bishop, Mrs. Marden, Tom Gilliam, Tom Glenn, Lucy Kenner, R. S. Lyles, G. B. Tucker, and Mr. Roebuck for a total of $460 (almost $10,000 in today's currency). His hams likely brought him nearly twice this amount. These figures indicate a total of approximately 70 hogs butchered and cured for sale alone. And considering the fact that about sixty individuals on the plantation had to be fed as well from additional butcherings, the winter of 1854–1855 must have presented a bustling scene of activity. Certainly no one on the plantation went hungry for pork in the midst of this plantation bounty.

In general, during the decade of the 1850s the master's expenditures increased when he decreased his usual tilled acreage from 1,000 to 600; but it was still necessary to purchase little. We are indeed fortunate to have preserved a record of his specific purchases throughout this decade. And they are worth reporting in full for what they reveal of the social scene and the economics of life on this plantation. From George Ashford & Co., Squire Hardy bought the following during 1852: (for sewing and clothing), 35½ yards of homespun at $3.36, 12 yards of black homespun (.84), 3 yards of brown linen (1.20), 5¾ yards of muslin (1.47), 5½ yards of jean cloth (.82), 2⅛ yards of cassimere (5.31), 1 yard of merino (1.50), 2 yards of black silk (4.00), 2 yards of gingham (.50), 4 yards of poplin (1.20), 6 yards of cambric (.75), 6 spools of cotton (.55), 4 spools of thread (.30), 2 skeins of silk (.10), 4½ yards of edging (1.69), 2 yards of insertion (.70), 10 bunches of braid (.50), 1 bunch of tape (.12), trimming for coat (1.75), trimming for pants (.50), gilt buttons (.25), 1 boy's hat (1.25), and 1 pair of shoes (1.75); (for cooking) 1 pound of soda ($.25), 1 pound of ginger (.15), 2 boxes of mustard (.50), and 2 butter tubs (1.20); (for the farm) 2 kegs of nails (10.00), "30 pounds of nails for son" (1.85), 1 "stock lock" (.88), 1 hank of twine (.25), 1 horse rasp (.87), and 1 side of "W. leather" (1.38); and for the men, 5 plugs of tobacco at $1.62.

Included in this account is a listing for "Your Negroes Amt.": Pleas-

(.30). Passenger train freight on this amount was 50¢. Of the total, $19.47 was debited to son Thomas P. Hardy.

From May to December 1858, from R. C. Anderson & Co. of Columbia, a fashionable gentleman's clothier, Hardy purchased 4 linen sack coats ($14.00), a linen coat (4.00), an Alpaca coat (7.00), a "Cass Coat" (14.00), another "Cass Coat" (6.00), a linen Frock coat (4.00), three cloth coats (one designated for his nineteen-year-old son Haywood, at 20.00@ for a total of 60.00), a pair of "Black Cass Pants" (7.00), a pair of linen pants (2.00), two black hats (6.00), a drab hat (1.50), 2 Leghorn hats (2.00), a velvet cap (3.50), a "Cass Vest" (4.00), a Marseilles vest (2.00), a white vest (3.50), 4 shirts (10.00), 6 collars (1.50), and a "Boy's Alpaca Coat" (2.50). The plantation counted among its number a young son. Young George Hardy was eleven years old in 1858. No doubt some of his clothes were hand-me-downs from his five older brothers, but several of the above listed articles other than the "Boy's Alpaca Coat" were probably his as well.

Although the plantation strove successfully for self-sufficiency, Hardy's purchases in the 1850s show that life was not puritanically severe and spartan. It had its velvet caps and linen vests and frock coats, its sugar, silver, and silk, its ginger and Brazil coffee, items which could not be produced on the place; but whenever Squire Hardy found a way to do so, he did, and when he could not, he raised and sold horses and hogs, made barrels, blacksmithed, made plows, tanned leather and made and sold shoes from it, educated a son in medicine to provide service to their own, sold the surplus corn, fodder, wheat, and flour from the plantation bounty—in other words, minimized in a large way the dependence on the cash staple crop, cotton. As son Haywood wrote his father in 1862, "Hogs and Corn . . . are the foundation of a Plantation." The Squire had thus taught his son well. Hardy was thus practicing smart conservation while diversifying his base—enlightened agricultural practices that are much to the Squire's credit. He ditched, terraced, rotated crops, and fertilized his fields with composts and animal manures, particularly from the hundreds of hogs on the place. With only a quarter of his improved acreage and about an eighth of his total in cotton cultivation, he had certainly not sold his soul to cotton, as some have said unfairly of the antebellum planter. From my knowledge of this section of upcountry South Carolina, I believe such a generalization to be very wrong, for judging from the evidence presented in the agricultural statistics for Newberry and Union Counties in 1850 and 1860, the Hardy plantation's practices were more typical than not. A more comprehensive future study should, at the least, dispel some unfortunate modern myths about the planter of this particular region of this particular state.

Society in Carolina during the antebellum years was decidedly courtly and high-toned. At the Hardy plantation the master and his family conformed well to the era's pattern of dignity and noble endeavor; but despite the romance of life during the day, Hardy was preeminently a solid, practical, wise, and realistic farmer. Perhaps it was his family's upcountry pioneering heritage or simply its continued interest in pig farming that kept its members' feet solidly on the ground. There were indeed boxwood-bordered flower parterres, personal servants for the children, silver on the sideboard, engraved invitations to tell their friends when they were "At Home" on special occasions, knightly jousting tournaments, festive fancy dances, reel dances, and hoedowns, barbecues a-plenty, fine setters and hounds, and carriages with high-stepping horses; but there were also sufficiently the smell of the stable and pigsty, the ring of the anvil, and closely observed animal behavior, to temper romance with realism. Such a broad and comprehensive view was a part of the wisdom to be gained from an agricultural way of life. All in all, these plantation years of the '50s appear to have been a healthy time of balance between extremes of high and low, of fancy and folk-homely, of religious and secular, of humor and seriousness, of work and play, of dignity and commonplaceness, of controlled and yet deeply felt emotion—thus, in a phrase, of the integrated sensibility that makes for wholeness and happiness—a full possibility in an agricultural society of this kind.

The master, no doubt, like most planters of the South, probably never knew his "worth" in dollars. With our facts and figures in this chronicle, we probably know, more than he, his material "ranking" in society. Today, most often it is "assets" or gross income that determines one's status; and we can tally them in a moment or at least easily enough with the aid of broker, accountant, or the Internal Revenue Service. For Hardy and his era, however, the end result by which success would be measured from the family's endeavor on the land, would not be merely material fortune but the degree of physical and spiritual wholeness and well-being of the plantation's people and of how they themselves measured up to the codes of gentlemanliness, self-control, kindness, loyalty, fidelity, honesty, duty, decency, generosity, patience, and graciousness, all summed up so succinctly in Galatians: "The fruit of the Spirit is love, joy, peace, long-suffering, gentleness, goodness, faith, meekness, temperance." Galatians also presents a description of the opposite, "the works of the Flesh": envy, vainglory, selfishness, fornication, idolatry, witchcraft, sedition, heresy, wrath, strife, murder—unfortunately, an apt litany of the evils so prevalent in a day closer to our own.

It should be noted in conclusion that in antebellum society, these good attributes, these "fruits of the Spirit," despite the institution of slavery, cut across lines of race, class, and gender in perhaps the most democratic of ways. The measure of success for William Eppes Hardy and his wife would therefore not be in the statistics of "fleshly" possessions as we have given them in this chapter, but in the relative spiritual health and wholesomeness of family and community. Ordering this world properly and according to the high ideals of Christian chivalry was a sober duty and serious responsibility; and the family, from all appearances, met the challenge admirably.

9

Works and Days in the Quarters

Maybinton the place I love best in all the world. Most my life is right here. I'll be buried in Hardy graveyard, whar my white folks dat was so good to me lie sleeping, and dat's whar my ma and pa and others that I loves lies too.

—Pick Gladdeny, former Hardy slave (1936)

In 1850 William Eppes Hardy was master to forty-six slaves who lived in ten slave houses. Each family unit had its separate dwelling, and the family unit was honored and encouraged. The Quarters were divided into two primary "streets" (or rows) of approximately five cabins to the north of the Big House across the little creek and toward the spring, and five to the south side. There was also a cook's house next to the detached kitchen in the Big House yard. Both "streets" paralleled the sides of the Great House about three hundred yards from it. They began some four hundred yards in front of it (to the east) and then continued behind it to the west some four hundred yards. The Great House thus sat approximately at the midpoint of the flanking streets, and its high windows afforded a good view of them, as the cabins themselves did of the Big House.

On the north street, one slave cabin still exists in ruins. Its one room measures 16 feet 7 inches long and 13 feet 4 inches deep. The height of the living space is 8 feet, and there may have been a sleeping loft. Like the 1825 section of the Great House itself, it faces east. It sits on field-stone piers that raise the structure about 2 feet from the ground in order to provide air circulation. The substructure is of heavy hewn timbers and is well constructed. The roof, like that of the Great House, was of wooden shingles. During tenant occupation in this century, these had been replaced with tin, which in 1997 lies collapsed within the structure. On what was the north wall is a chimney whose base is 3 feet 10 inches across. (A chimney at the plantation house is also on the north wall.) The fireplace opening is 30 × 30 inches and is 25 inches deep. The lower 5-foot section of the chimney is made of local fieldstone neatly fitted and cemented with a yellow-sand cement similar to that used for the mortar and stucco of the chimney of the Big House. As in the main house, this sand likely came from the little creek branch nearby, for there are large deposits of sand of this color along it. The fieldstone base is topped with brick, stepped at angles for better support, and thus constructed like that of the plantation house itself. The bricks are neatly laid and covered with yellow clay on the protected interior face and with a yellow-sand cement on the three exposed exterior sides. A former slave from the nearby Jim Hunter plantation on Enoree recalled in 1937 that as a child, one of his annual tasks in preparing for winter was digging clay (in his case, a white clay) "to keep the hearth white through de winter." The hearth itself is of fieldstone. The stone in the fireplace is faced with neatly set handmade brick in the manner of the fireplaces of the Great House. A flat steel bar keeps the top brick row of the opening from sagging (again, as in the Great House). This iron bar is undoubtedly of antebellum origin and made at the plantation blacksmith shop, for "chimney rods and irons" are often noted in the plantation ledger as being forged from 1842 to 1846. I date the stone chimney base and brick work no later than 1840.

All in all, the cabin was modest and simple, but it is obvious that care was taken in its construction. Its distance off the ground allowed for air circulation and dryness and thus increased the health and comfort of its dwellers. The floor was of heart-pine and tightly fitted. Some of it has survived even after being exposed to rain for many years. The position of all these cabins on high ground also improved their healthfulness. Some of the best views of both the Great House and surrounding countryside are from these yards. They were, in effect, built on choice house-sites on a ridge paralleling the rise on which the Big House sits. Today their ruins are surrounded by roses, wisteria, jonquils, daffodils, narcissus, vinca, and breath of spring *(Lonicera fragrantissima)*.

During the era of tenant farming in the present century, another room of approximately the same size was added to this cabin. This section rests on stacked concrete blocks rather than fieldstone piers. It was not as well constructed as the antebellum part and although much newer, is more completely deteriorated. One surmises that the economic well-being of the plantation is reflected in the relative degree of craftsmanship and quality of materials exhibited in these two sections.

Former slaves of Maybinton-Goshen Hill-Santuc were very specific in their descriptions of their antebellum cabins and sometimes of the furnishings in them. Their valuable comments would likely apply to the slave houses at the Hardy plantation itself. George Briggs, raised as a field hand on the Gist Briggs plantation of Lower Cross Keys, recalled that his family's log slave house "had only one room, but some of the houses had two. Our'n had a window, a door, and a common fireplace. Now dey makes a fireplace to scare de wood away. In the old days, dey make fireplaces to take care of de chilluns in de cold weather. It warm de whole house, 'cayse it was so big and dar was plenty of wood. Wood wasn't no problem den. . . . In town it is, and I ain't guessing. I done seed so." In 1937 Briggs said that he suffered from the cold. Another field hand, Gus Feaster, born in 1840 and raised within a few miles of the Hardys, recalled that the log houses "were daubed with mud" between the cracks and were warm. He continued, "Fire last all night from dat big wood and de house didn't get cold. Us haul wood eight or ten feet long." He summed up: "Plenty to eat; plenty to wear; plenty wood to burn; good house to live in; and no worry 'bout where it was a-coming from. . . . Dem was de times when everybody had enough to eat and more dan dey wanted, and plenty clothes to wear."

Zack Herndon, born in 1844, described his Union County home in the Quarters as "a one-room log house"; but as George Briggs noted, the "larger families, dey had two rooms wid de fireplace in de middle of the room. Our'n was at de end by the winder. It had white or red oak, or pine shingles to kivver de roof . . . hand-made." Richard Jones, born in 1844 on the Jim Gist plantation, remembered, "We lived in a one-room log cabin that had to be well-kept all of de time."

In all the descriptions of the beds in these houses, the former slaves of this area remembered "cord" (that is, rope) beds, the kind also used by all classes of whites in those days. On these slave beds were homemade mattresses called straw ticks. These were often filled with wheat straw. One narrator, Charlie Meadow of Santuc, recalled straw ticks in summer and feather bed mattresses in winter. He also remembered warm quilts "made from many pretty home-made patterns" and light-wood knots to give light at night. Fires were lit from flint rock or from the kitchen hearth, where they burned the year round. Meadow continued: "We made our bedclothes on de home looms wid wool from our master's sheep. De barns was always full and so was de smokehouse. Dey give me plenty of food, clothes, a good house, and good clean bed." Zack Herndon of Santuc remembered having no chairs, but his father's hand-made benches for "us to set by de fire on. Marse Zack let de overseer git planks fer us. . . . We had a large plank table dat paw made. Never had no mirrors. Went to de spring to see oursefs on a Sunday morning. Never had no sech things as dressers in dem days. All us had was a table, benches, and bed. Had plenty of wood fer fire and pine-knots fer light when de fire git low, . . . had tallow candles. Why everybody knowed how to make taller candles in dem days; dat wudd'n nothing out de ordinary." Richard Jones, who recalled life in Union County from 1849, when he was five years old, related that his family "had comfortable home-made beds and chairs. We had nice tables and plenty to eat." George Briggs supplies more interesting details: "All de chair bottoms of straight chairs was made from white oak splits, and de straight chairs was made in de shop" on the plantation. He also recalled making split-oak sewing baskets, feed baskets, and firewood baskets.

These descriptions do indeed provide a likely picture of the Hardy Quarters. As we know from the extant furniture made on the place for the Great House, there were excellent in-house craftsmen, and the slave cabins also probably benefited in the way of good, serviceable furniture.

This sketch shows the floor plan of the westernmost extant slave cabin, drawn from the ruins of the structure in 1989:

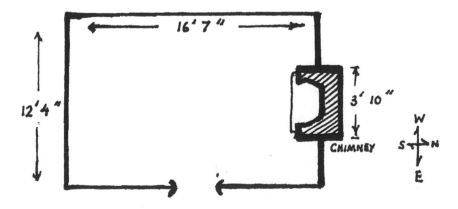

Another Hardy tenant cottage near the eastern end of the street to the north side of the house was enlarged from a slave house. It has the same stone-based, brick-topped chimney as in the sketch, only the chimney has two faces, thus suggesting that it was a two-room dwelling. As we have seen, Briggs and Herndon described such two-room houses as being for the larger families; and this was likely the practice on the Hardy plantation as well. In our century this was the home of descendants of Hardy slaves—tenants on the place until 1973. It is surrounded by a smokehouse made of round pine logs, a privy, and various chicken and animal pens. In an outbuilding are the rusting tools of cotton cultivation: a seeder, a plow, a cotton duster, a guano spreader. The farm layout is small but convenient. Several rows of daffodils, spider lilies, and jonquils mark the entrance to the cottage. To its rear, a row of garlic indicates what was probably the family kitchen and vegetable garden.

About a hundred yards east of this cabin are the much more deteriorated remains of a third cabin. Its foundation stones and stacked-stone chimney base provide the outline of a structure smaller than the other two. Its carefully fitted chimney stones, however, are similar to those in the other cabin ruins. There are hand-made bricks fallen to the chimney's side, suggesting it was topped with them as were those in the other two cabins. The structure, however, faced north-south, as did the 1804 section of the Great House, and may thus have been built at this earlier stage of plantation history.

The yard was an extension of the cabin. Plantation records, travelers' accounts, and former slave recollections testify that much household activity in the Quarter took place outdoors. Whenever possible, slaves did their cooking, washing, and socializing outside of their houses. Cabins were shelters and sources of privacy, but slave life was not confined within four walls. Aunt Ciller, a slave on the Ben Sims plantation just across the Tyger from the Hardys, was remembered as being "fond of having the Bible and *Pilgrim's Progress* read to her, which was frequently done by her young mistress, Miss Addie Sims, sitting out under the oak trees surrounded by her household goods and kitchen utensils, as she would never occupy her log cabin, except in bad weather."

Aunt Ciller said she was the daughter of a king from Madagascar, and her closeness to her roots may at least partially explain her propensities. Her story, as recorded in 1912, is an interesting one: "Her Daddy was taken prisoner in battle by another king, and instead of being beheaded, as was their custom, the victorious king sold him and his family" to a Spanish slave trade ship that took them to Virginia sometime before the Revolution. In 1783 Charles Sims brought his slaves to the new home he was creating on the Tyger at about the same time the Hardys were settling there. Aunt Ciller was among them. Her royal father had died in Virginia before the removal to Carolina. Then a girl, "she always said, 'I no African, I from Madagascar, daughter of a King.' " As the account concludes, "She was no slave either, for she never was known to do a day's work. . . . She had dark brown skin, regular features, very small hands and feet. In disposition, she was high-tempered, high-strung, and ungovernable, but very loyal and true to her own 'white folks.' She was fanatically religious . . . and died at the age of ninety." Slaves of the neighborhood sometimes got a little out of patience with what they considered her bragging. That story about being the daughter of a king "has been travelling ever since she got to dese shores, and it still a-gwine," one declared with a strong hint of sarcasm in 1937. Ciller's mistress painted her portrait sometime before 1860, but I have been unable to locate it.

The lives and material circumstances of the Hardy slaves can be recreated in general terms. The recollections of more than 25 ex-slaves from the Tyger River region, including one who lived on the plantation itself and six from neighboring farms, bring to life something of the rhythm of works and days on the place. These important life histories were recorded by Works Progress Administration field workers, particularly Caldwell Sims, during the years 1936, 1937, and 1938. Sims was a Tyger River native. His family hailed from the Maybinton area, and he had come home after earning a graduate degree in history from Columbia University. He gathered numerous interviews that provide a wealth of detailed information, perhaps the most complete picture of slavery in any one Southern neighborhood to be found in the WPA narratives. More importantly, many of Sims's respondents, as we have been seeing from the former slaves already quoted in this chapter, were young adults and not children during slavery times.

Taken together, the recollections of these narrators depict a slave culture that often differs considerably from that found on Lowcountry rice plantations and the vast cotton plantations of the Old Southwest. From these interviews, surviving plantation records, and other accounts by white Union and Newberry County residents, we can surmise that in actual practice slavery was not a monolithic institution, that it differed from region to region, community to community, and crop to crop.

As befits an agrarian chronicle, our story of the plantation's daily routine begins with sunrise over the fields; and we find from the testimony of all those interviewed that both black and white families rose with it, or, in fact, before it. For some, as recollected by Gus Feaster, the birds' singing at daybreak was the signal to get up. He reported, "We eat breakfast when de birds furs' commence singing off'n de roost. Jay birds 'ud allus call de slaves. Dey 'lowed: 'It's day; it's day,' and you had to git up" (vol. 2, pt. 2, pp. 43–44). Others like Charlie Meadow of Santuc had overseers or black drivers to "hoop" or "holler" them awake (vol. 3, pt. 3, p. 180). Feaster remembered his Goshen Hill master buying a plantation bell and the driver ringing it to wake them (vol. 2, pt. 2, p. 49). All ate breakfast; and the hours one worked depended upon the season of the year and the duties of the particular slave. During rush times of planting, laying by, and harvest, work continued until dark. No slave remembered working into the night.

There was a slower pace and shorter hours after the crops were laid by, which always occurred before the Fourth of July and the hottest time of the year. Feaster recalled, "It was unheard of fer anybody to let de Fourth come widout de crops out'n de way." "Times has changed now," he continued. "Then de fields was heavy wid corn head high and cotton around de darky's waist. Grass was all cleaned out of de furrows on de last go round. De fields and even de terraces was put in apple pie order fer de gathering of de crops in de fall" (vol. 2, pt. 2, p. 58).

All those interviewed remembered that the slaves had Sundays off. Except for some routine chores like cooking or seeing to the farm animals, the day was theirs. We see this corroborated for the Hardy plantation by the master's Sunday schedule for rotating the cooking duties. Former slave Lila Rutherford recalled: "On Sundays we just rested and went to the neighbor's house or go to church" (vol. 3, pt. 3, p. 58). Many recollected that their masters sometimes required them to attend their white Methodist, Baptist, Lutheran, or Presbyterian churches, where they would sit in the gallery or at the back. A former slave on the Hardy plantation remembered that because the blacks had no churches of their own in Maybinton, sometimes the slaves "from the Hardy plantation walked five miles" to Chapman's Stand to hear the black preacher. The blacks of this congregation boarded him and took care of the mule that pulled his one-horse wagon. "He stayed around from place to place." The church had "a brush top and log seats" and was thus what was called a brush arbor (vol. 2, pt. 2, p. 128). Most ex-slaves, however, reported enjoying going to church with "our white folks," as they called them. Charlie Meadow reported that his Santuc master and mistress gathered the slaves together "every two or three afternoons in summer" to read the Bible and pray with them on the kitchen porch. "In winter we went in de kitchen where I built a big fire, to hear de Bible read. We was Methodist" (vol. 3, pt. 3, p. 180). Mary Smith, born in 1853 on the George Young plantation of Enoree River, remembered her master "read de Bible to us, but sometimes others read it to us, too. His son, Bud, dat was killed in de first battle, used to come to de Quarters and read de Bible to us." (vol. 3, pt. 4, p. 114). As a small girl, Mary Smith attended church with her mother every Sunday and would cry when she could not. She remembered that her master gave her mother the "spot of ground and de lumber for our church. . . . De first preaching was held under a oak tree or arbor."

Most of the former slaves recalled that the men and boys often spent Sunday hunting and fishing. This area was celebrated for its wealth of game as a hunter's true paradise; and with the three great rivers in the community, the slaves were, no doubt, very successful fishermen. Several narrators recalled that often on the weekdays, slaves, "when their work was done in evening," also "went hunting and caught rabbits, squirrels, or 'possums." Young lads of the Jim Gist plantation bought fishhooks, Jew's harps, and marbles with the spending money they earned or were given, for "boys did not use tobacco den until dey got twenty-one or over" and therefore didn't have "much use for money" (vol. 3, pt. 3, p. 66). Judging from these narratives, we can conclude that hunting and fishing were the male slaves' chief recreations, and so much so, that the master sometimes tried to curb what he considered "excesses."

The Hardy slaves participated in these manly sports in the way that slaves of the neighboring plantations did. With the Tyger River flowing through their plantation and the Broad less than two miles away, fishing was a favorite activity. Several former slaves remembered using cane poles and fishhooks, but also recalled that they set fish baskets just as often. These were called "mud baskets"—that is, traps sunk into the mud and tied to the shore with grapevine in order to catch catfish, which are bottom feeders. Several others mention fish traps plaited of split white oak or hickory. Moses Davenport, of the Gilliam plantation on Little River, recalled the usual practice of setting "fish baskets of wooden splits." He noted: "If they were set anytime, day or night, a few hours afterwards would be enough time to catch some fish." He concluded, "Fishing in the rivers was much done" (vol. 2, pt. 1, p. 244). Feaster recalled buying seines and setting nets: "Pull up seine after a rain and have seventy-five or eighty fish; sometimes have none. Peter Mills made our catfish stew and cooked ash-cake bread for us to eat it with. Water come to our necks while we seining and we git de fish while we drifting down stream" (vol. 2, pt. 2, p. 46). As recalled by George Briggs of Lower Cross Keys, the fish were distributed to fellow slaves or sold to the master for his table (vol. 2, pt. 1, p. 85).

The former slave of a pious mistress on a plantation near the Hardys' remembered that children were allowed to play on Sunday "unless the mistress calls us in and stops us. . . . On Sundays we go to church . . . de white folks' church, and set in the gallery" (vol. 2, pt. 1, p. 167). At the Burton Maybin plantation of Maybinton, Milton Marshall recollected that his master "wouldn't allow fishing and hunting on Sunday . . . wouldn't let anybody work on Sunday," then reported that the slaves would "slip off" and fish anyway (vol. 3, pt. 3, p. 174). From the two accounts from Maybin's former slaves, he appears to have been a stricter master than the usual, and because his slaves knew they were getting a harder time of it than others on neighboring plantations, they thus compensated on the sly.

Even with the strictest masters, then, it was universal throughout the neighborhood for no work to be done on the Sabbath. Saturday's routine, however, varied markedly from plantation to plantation, even in this small area. Over twenty of the narrators reported that work for their masters ended at Saturday noon and that they had the rest of the day for themselves. The great majority of these narratives state that the women usually did their washing on this afternoon and cleaned up around their cabins. Often both men and women tidied themselves up at the day's end and got their clothes ready for Sunday—more or less what the white families were doing. Some men recalled: "We didn't do work on Saturday afternoons, but went hunting and fishing den, while de women folks cleaned up around de place (vol. 2, pt. 1, p. 152).

The narrators, being "awful to hunt," as one expressed it, were specific in naming their quarry. They hunted or trapped rabbits and hunted deer, wild turkey, wild geese, wild ducks, squirrels, opposums, raccoons, and various birds. Balaam Lyles recalled of Goshen Hill: "Birds of all kinds, rabbits, foxes, coons, 'possums, and squirrels was plentiful. In dem times nobody never thought of raising no tame turkey. You could go anywhere in Union County and shoot as many turkeys as you wanted to in a little while. Den in de season, dere was de wild geese and wild ducks dat went over in big droves." Lyles was a hunter who knew his game history: "Way back fo' my time, de old folks tells about de buffalo. . . . Today [in 1937], wid all de changes, hit ain't nothing dar but fish, some partridges and rabbits." Feaster also recalled "bird-thrashings," a night sport in which birds were attracted to pine-knot torches or lanterns and then killed with dogwood switches (vol. 2, pt. 2, pp. 51–52).

The slaves also killed many wild hogs that roamed the area. This was tricky business in two ways: first, it was dangerous, and then one had to be careful not to get someone's branded domestic hog that took up with the wild ones. George Patterson of Enoree River noted that "plenty of meat" could be gotten "by shooting the wild hogs that roamed the woods" (vol. 3, pt. 3, p. 230). Feaster recalled that slaves on his plantation were not allowed to kill doves, for which his master had a fondness. These birds were so trusting that they would follow in the tracks of the ploughman. "Dove," he reflected, "was first thing that bring something back to Noah when de flood done gone from over de land" (vol. 2, pt. 2, p. 44). Partridge was fair and popular game, however, with slave and master alike. As Hardy neighbor Milton Marshall observed, there "were many dogs on de farms, mostly hounds and bird dogs," and they provided excellent hunting companions (vol. 3, pt. 3, p. 174). The game taken on these hunts supplied excellent supplements year-round for the formal rations given out by the master.

Granny Cain, born on a Maybinton plantation in 1847, also recalled that slaves used their free Saturday afternoons to "stay home, go fishing, or wash up." She adds another brush stroke to our picture of slave life in the community by recalling that sometimes they would go to the banks of the Broad in the fall and winter just to sit and watch the boats stacked high with cotton going by on their way to market in Columbia, and to listen all evening to the boatmen's singing (vol. 2, pt. 1, p. 166). What leisure time there was, was thus not always pursued strenuously or for practical results. Indeed, many of the former slave narrators remembered that after a long week's work, Saturday nights were often used for "frolics—men and women" (vol. 2, pt. 1, p. 304).

Only two narrators recalled that the slaves on their plantations had all day Saturday off (vol. 2, pt. 2, p. 105; vol. 3, pt. 3, p. 118). This practice was thus decidedly unusual. But many narrators remembered having the late afternoons or evenings after work during the week to tend their own watermelon patches or vegetable gardens. For example, Lila Rutherford recalled that "our white folks sometime give us patches of ground to work. . . . We raised corn and vegetables. . . . [But] on Sunday, we just rested and went to neighbors' house or go to church" (vol. 3, pt. 4, p. 56). Emoline Glasgow of the Gilliam plantation on Indian Creek likewise remembered: "Dey give us a small patch of about half an acre to raise cotton or anything we wanted to on it. De master had a big garden and give his slaves plenty vegetables" (vol. 2, pt. 2, p. 134).

The slaves' watermelon patches were more common than vegetable plots because the master usually had an extensive kitchen garden from which he dispensed produce. The slaves worked this garden and used produce from it; but they had their own private melon patches. For this area, the vegetables most frequently mentioned in the late 1840s through the 1860s were cabbages, collards, turnips, cow peas, beans, tomatoes ("matises," as one called them), sweet potatoes, Irish potatoes, okra, peanuts, cantaloupes, and pumpkins. Corn, of course, grew extensively in the fields, interplanted with black-eyed peas. Common herbs for seasoning were coriander, sage, and basil.

The melon patch was the subject of a surprisingly large number of narratives. It was serious business for the young and adventurous, who would endure certain punishment to raid it. The melon patch was the frequent cause of lectures on theft, and in a few cases, of whippings from a slave's parents. One master had gone so far as to have all his youngsters' feet measured so that when melons were missing and tracks found, he could consult his track file and know whom to blame (vol. 2, pt. 2, pp. 46–47). No doubt one reason the melon patch was so often a subject in the WPA interviews is that the narrators, many of whom were born in the 1850s or before, were just the right age to get into such mischief. One Goshen Hill narrator recalled that he and his friends were caught at the age of twelve and as a result got graduated from the light yard and farm-lot duties of childhood to the field hand duties of grownups; for, as the master reasoned, if they were old enough to "study up such mischievousness" on the Sabbath, they are "big enough to work in de crops" (vol. 1, supplement series 2, pp. 370–80).

Another indication of routine slave treatment for the area is described in the recollection of Gus Feaster, who remembered that a female field hand who had a child took lighter duties for a year thereafter—carding cotton, weaving, sewing, cooking, and tending her young (vol. 2, pt. 2, p. 68). There thus appears to have been a close and careful division of labor on the plantations of the community. Several former slaves remarked that the elderly women, the "Mammies" or "Aunties," as they were called with a respect that amounted to awe, had the sole responsibility of feeding and caring for the children aged one to five or six while their mothers were at work elsewhere. Elias Dawkins of the Starke Sims plantation recalled in vivid detail:

> Marse Starke . . . had in de Quarter what was knowed as a chilluns' house. A nurse stayed in it all de time to care fer all de plantation chilluns. My granny "Kissy" acted as nurse dar some. Aunt Peggy and Aunt Ciller was two more. . . . All dese helped to nurse me. Dey fed us on milk, plenty of it. We had honey, molasses, and lots of good things. . . . My marster give me a biscuit sometime from his plate, and I wouldn't have tuck 25 cents for it. He allus put butter in it or ham and gravy. He would say, "Dat's de doctrine. Be kind." (vol. 2, pt. 1, p. 317).

The routine of the "Mammies" and "Aunties" is carefully recorded by Feaster. When he was a wee child, Auntie Abbie fed him his breakfasts. He recalled:

> Young chilluns and babes was kept at home by de fire and nursed and cared for by de ole wimmens dat couldn't do no field work. De chief one on our plantation during my 'membrance was ole Aunt Abbie. . . . Abbie had to see to it dat dey was kept warm by de fire and dat dey clothes was kept up wid. . . . De seamstresses also kept our work clothes patched and darned, til new ones was wove fer us. De other ole ladies helped wid de preparations of dey masses of vittles. One ole woman went her rounds wid a wet rag a-wiping dem chilluns' dresses when dey would spill dey milk and bread. Marse Tom and sometime Missus come to see de lil' babies whilst dey was a-eating. De other ole ladies tended to de small babies. Sometimes it was many as fifteen on de plantation at one time dat was too little to walk. . . . Dem babies was washed every day. If dey mammies was in de field,

dat never made no diffuns, kaise it was de old ladies' jobs to see to it dat dey was. Younguns on de plantation was bathed two or three times a week. Mullein leaves and salt was bilt in great big pots to put in de babies' washwater and also in de chilluns' water. Dis would keep 'em from gitting sick. Den dey was allus greased atter de washing to keep de skin from bustin' open. Mostly dey was greased wid tallow from de mutton. Mr. Anderson [the master's son, Anderson Carlisle] took medicine, and atter dat, he doctor all de slaves for his pa free (vol. 2, pt. 2, pp. 67–68).

An elderly slave whose special duty was to serve as seamstress for the field hands was commonly mentioned in these narratives (vol. 3, pt. 3, p. 64). Feaster also noted that "on all de plantations" of his area, the old slave women would, in addition,

study what to do fer de ailments of grown folks and lil' chilluns. Fer de lil' chilluns and babies [who had colic], dey would take and chew up pine needles and den spit it in de lil' chilluns' mouths and make dem swallow. Den when dey was a teachin' de babies to eat, dey done de food de very same way. Dem ole wimmens made pine rosin pills . . . from de pine trees and give de pills to de folks to take fer back ache. Dey allus kept de pine trees gashed fer dis purpose. Den dey also gashed de sweet gum fer to git gum to chaw. (vol. 2, pt. 2, p. 55).

At the T. A. Carlisle plantation Auntie Abbie likewise presided over the plantation rations. When the slaves ate, she was there. At table, "de mens eat on one side, and de gals on t'other" (vol. 2, pt. 2, p. 43). Abbie oversaw the plantation breakfasts of mush and milk with "shorts" (tan-colored flour seconds) and "seconds" mixed with the mush. Feaster and his fellow field hands got "no grease in de morning a-tall. Twelve o'clock brung plenty cow-peas, meat, bread, and water. At night, us drunk milk and et bread, black bread made from de shorts. Jes' had meat at twelve o'clock. 'Course 'sharpers' would eat meat when marster didn't know. Dey go out and git 'em a hog from a drove of seventy-five or a hundred. Dat one never missed" (vol. 2, pt 2, p. 44).

For the hands at work in the fields, the noonday meal was eaten on the job. Feaster recalled in careful detail how it was done at Goshen Hill in the 1850s. In doing so, he likely described the scene at nearby Hardy plantation as well:

> All de fields was enclosed wid a split rail fence in dem days. De hands took dry rations to de field early every morning and de wimmens slack work round eleven by de sun fer to build de fire and cook dinner. Missus 'low her niggers to git buttermilk and clabber, when de cows is full, to carry to de field for drinking at noon. All de things was fetched in wagons and de fire was built and a pot was put to bile wid greens when dey was in season. Over coals, meat was baked and meal in pones was wrapped in poplar leaves to bake in de ashes [ash-cake]. 'Taters was done de same way, both sweet 'taters and irish. Dat made a good field hand dinner. Plenty was allus had; and den molasses was also fetched along (vol. 2, pt. 2, pp. 66–67).

Workers "does on less dese days," he concluded. For the popular ash-cake, Feaster recollected: "De poplar leaves was wet afo' de meal pone was put in it. When it got done de ashes was blowed off and den de parched leaves folded back. De poplar leaves give de ash-cake a nice fresh sweet taste. All forks and spoons was made out'n sticks den; even dem in de Big House kitchen. Bread bowls and dough trays was all made by de skilled slaves in de marse's shop, by hands dat was skilled to sech as dat" (vol. 2, pt. 2, pp. 66–67). Again we see the division of labor, each according to his skill and craft. Feaster's comments have all the more authenticity because he was twenty-one years old when the war began and had thus experienced as a grownup all that he reported.

Feaster's narrative leads us to the subject of food. When they discussed slavery times in their 1930s interviews, many former slaves vividly recalled customs and habits respecting rations and diet. The consensus of recollections thus provides a likely picture of what was eaten on the Hardy plantation. Ration days always came at the end of the week. Here the "heavy rations," as Feaster called them—a peck of cornmeal and quart of black molasses—were distributed on Friday. On Saturday they came again to receive a quart of flour, some "shoulder meat" (front hams) "fer Sunday morning breakfast," and four pounds of bacon. On Saturday, too, meat was chopped on a block near the smokehouse. This

procedure was the cause of an altercation one Saturday morning between Feaster and his brother John:

> When de red meat choppin' was done . . . one day John
> 'lowed to me, "If you puts your ol' black hand on dat block
> 'fore I does today, I is a-gwine to chop it off." I never said
> narry a word, but I jes' roll my eyes at him. I got dar and
> broke and run fer de block. I got a big piece and when John
> come up I was eating it. I say, "Nigger, you is too late and
> lazy fer anything." 'Bout dat time he reach over fer a scrap I
> never seed. I push him back and reach for hit. John took up
> de choppin' axe and come right down on my finger . . . jes'
> left it a-hangin'. Marse's doctor come and he fix it back"
> (vol. 2, pt. 2, pp. 56–57).

John Boyd, field hand of the Polly Meador plantation on Broad River,
also recalled the "meat block," where a slave named Morg would sit and
cut the meat for her mistress to portion and hand out. Boyd recalled that
Morg "would eat her three pounds of raw meat right there. The master
asked her what she would do all the week without any meat. She said
that she would take the skin and grease her mouth every morning; then
go on to the field or house and do her work, and wait until the next
Saturday for more" (vol. 2, pt. 1, p. 72).

At the Tom Bates plantation in Santuc, Zack Herndon, born in
1844, also recalled there were two ration days, but he remembered them
as Saturday and Sunday instead of Friday and Saturday. On Saturday
each adult got one peck of cornmeal, three pounds of bacon, and a half
gallon of black molasses. On Sunday mornings each received two or
three pounds of flour. Herndon noted emphatically that in those days
they didn't eat fatback, didn't "know nothing 'bout no fat-back in dem
times." He was offended by the very suggestion, for he was proud that
he and his slave community got ham and bacon (vol. 2, pt. 2, pp. 274–
75). The measuring and distributing of rations were done by various
individuals, sometimes the master or mistress, sometimes an overseer, or
a slave him or herself. One such slave rationer, Nellie Loyd, her master's
head cook, kept the keys to the smokehouse of the George Buchanan
plantation at Goshen Hill (vol. 3, pt. 4, p. 127).

Although the specifics of ration days at the Hardy plantation cannot
be proved, we can assume that they occurred on two days at week's end,

probably Friday and Saturday, as the Hardys were rather pious church-goers. At minimum, the rations per person likely included a peck of cornmeal, two or three pounds of flour, from a quart to a half-gallon of molasses, and three to four pounds of bacon. These were universally the basic foodstuffs and portions distributed in the community. But we know also from the agricultural statistics for the Hardy plantation that a whopping five hundred bushels of sweet potatoes were raised in a single year. These must also have been distributed, as well as vegetables and melons from the gardens. We know that goats, beef, pork, and mutton were also barbecued on holidays, during the six weeks of camp meetings in July and August, and at other times throughout the year. As we have seen, slaves also supplemented their rations with game (turkeys, deer, rabbits, squirrels, 'possums, raccoons, wild hogs, geese, ducks, and birds) and fish, particularly, large quantities of catfish, from which stews were made.

Then there were the spontaneous productions of an abundant nature that both blacks and whites were adept at using. One former slave enjoyed the wild poke stalk for cooked greens. It grew everywhere and could be gathered at the slave's initiative. He recalled:

> Poke salad was et in dem days to clean a feller out. Hit come up tender every spring and when it cut deep down in sand, it looked white. . . . Cut it; wash it and par boil; pour off water and ball up in balls in your hand; put in frying pan of hot grease from ham or strip meat and fry. Season with black pepper and salt and eat with new spring onions. Tender white stems are better than the salad and of course earlier. Ash cake was good with poke salad and clabber or buttermilk and best of all with sweet milk (vol. 2, pt. 2, p. 55).

This from a man who obviously relished his poke salad.

Persimmon trees grew everywhere along the lanes of all the plantations, and ripe fruit in late fall was there for the gathering. "Simmon bread was made" at this time, recalled Caroline Farrow, who also baked corn bread every day "wid plenty of milk, eggs, and lard, and sometimes wid sweet potatoes" (vol. 2, pt. 2, p. 40). Children and their mothers picked blackberries for themselves, for their mistresses, or to sell. Blackberry pies and cobblers were the usual results. And no one picks blackberries without eating them while doing so. Feaster remembered gathering the berries to sell to a white lady at Goshen Hill to make wine. This is how he made his "first money" before the war, money with which he bought candy at Orange Hall store. In those days, Feaster reflected, "people was crazy 'bout candy; dat's de reason I ain't got no toofies now" (vol. 2, pt. 2, p. 43). The honey that nature provided in bee-trees in the forest would occasionally supplement the slave's ration of molasses. It was honey that usually sweetened the spring tea made from sassafras root.

Cakes, pies, cobblers, gingerbread, and custards were common fare on Sundays, holidays, and at barbecues and camp meetings. Zack Herndon, born in 1844 at the Herndon plantation, recounted a childhood tale of gingerbread and how cooking was done in the individual slave houses:

> Furs' remembrance was at de age o' three [1847] when as yet I couldn't walk none. My mother cooked some gingerbread. She told de chilluns to go down a hill and git her some oak bark. De furs' one back wid de bark 'ud git de furs' ginger-bread cake dat was done. My sister sot me down, a sliding down de side o' her laag, atter she had carried me wid her down de side o' de hill. Dem big chaps started to fooling time away. I grab some bark in my hand and went toddling and a-crawling up to de house. . . . When de other chilluns got back, I was a-setting up eating de furs' cake. She put gingerbread dough in a round oven dat had laags on hit. . . . It had a lid to go on top wid a groove to hold live coals. Pots biled in de back o' de chimney, a-hanging from a pot rack over de blazing fire. It had pot hooks to git it down. Bread was cooked in a baker like de ginger cake. Dey roasted both kinds o' taters in de ashes and made corn bread in de ashes and called it ash cake (vol. 2, pt. 2, pp. 271–72).

Recollections of Christmas and other holidays filled the WPA narratives. Many former slave narrators were children in the 1850s and the wonder of Christmas seems never to have left their memories. Holiday breaks from plantation routine were marked by festivities at the Great House, in the Quarters, and throughout the neighborhood. Christmas called for particular enjoyment of food, drink, and dancing—"dances wid fiddles, pattin' feet and stick rattlin' . . . everything lively at Christmas time" (vol. 3, pt. 3, p. 3). Work ceased for Christmas Day and some former slaves reported that they had two or more days respite. Whatever the duration of the holiday, "big eats" and occasional rations of spirits made the time special. Nellie Loyd of Goshen Hill recalled, "On Christmas we had a good time and good things to eat. De men would drink beer and whiskey. Beer was made from locusts and persimmons, and everybody would drink some of it" (vol. 3, pt. 3, p. 128). The Hardys had operated a still from the early days of their migration from Virginia and likely allowed a Christmas dram if the slaves so desired.

Some masters distributed Christmas gifts, candy, or coins to the children. Others were more magnanimous. Dick Johnson of the Jim Gist plantation recalled a memorable Christmas scene:

> Marse allus carried a roll of money as big as my arm. He would come to de Quarters on Christmas, July 4th, and Thanksgiving, and get on a stump and call all the chilluns out. Den he would throw money to 'em. De chilluns got dimes, nickels, quarters, half-dollars, and dollars. At Christmas, he would throw ten dollar bills. De parents would take de five and ten dollar bills in charge, but Marse made dem let de chillun keep de small change (vol. 3, pt. 3, p. 66).

Gist may have been the most magnanimous, but even the strictest master gave Christmas day as a big day of feasting and celebration. Again, it was the custom of the country, and the Hardy plantation would likely have been no exception to it.

Other holidays varied from plantation to plantation. Some slaves recounted holidays on the Fourth of July, Thanksgiving, and New Year's (vol. 2, pt. 1, p. 303; vol. 3, pt. 3, p. 66). A few remember only Christmas and New Year's; others, only Christmas and the Fourth of July or Easter. The rhythms of agricultural labor, however, also provided other occasions for celebration. Communal work like corn shucking, log rolling, cotton picking, spinning and quilting bees, and peanut-pulling had a festive air because folks from neighboring plantations would be there, as would special foods like pies and cakes. Seasonal "eats" like pumpkin pies and custards and strong spirits for the men were part of fall harvest gatherings (vol. 2, pt. 3, p. 213.).

The plantations of the community set particularly great store by the Fourth of July. Several factors converged to make this midsummer holiday particularly joyous. Most of the plantations had laid by their corn and cotton crops before July 4th, and that in itself was a cause for celebration, a signal to slow down the pace of heavy labor for the hot summer. Immediately after the Fourth, the white folks' six weeks' camp meeting, or "Big Meeting," as former slaves called it, got underway. Thus, bridging lay-by and the camp meeting was July 4th, a day that was celebrated by what seems to have been a community-wide barbecue. Former slaves from Goshen Hill, Santuc, Maybinton, and Fish Dam recounted in loving detail feasting and frolicking on that day. Feaster of Goshen Hill, one of the most talented and loquacious chroniclers of the region, was twenty years old in 1860 and vividly remembered Fourth of July barbecues:

> Marse and Missus had good rations fer us early on de Fourth. Den us went to barbecues after de mornin' chores was done. In dem days, de barbecues was usually held on de [Hillside] plantation o' Mars Jim Hill in Fish Dam. . . . . Old Marse, he give us de rations for de barbecues. Every master wanted his darkies to be thought well of at de barbecues by de darkies from all de other plantations. Dey had pigs barbecued; goats; and de Missus let de wimmen folks bake pies, cakes, and custards fer de barbecue, 'jes 'zactly like hit was fer de white folk barbecue desself. Young ones carried on like young colts in de pasture til dey had got so full o' vittles dat dey could not eat another bite (vol. 2, pt. 2, pp. 58–59).

Feaster saw and socialized with slaves from surrounding plantations at the Fish Dam Fourth of July, and perhaps the Hardy slaves were among them.

Wesley Jones of John Hill's plantation in the Sardis section also recalled the local barbecues with relish. Like Feaster, Jones was born in 1840 and was a young adult before the war. He was an all-night cook at these barbecues and recalled not only the way the meat was prepared but also his barbecue sauce recipe: "vinegar, black and red pepper, salt, butter, a little sage, coriander, basil, onion, and garlic. Some folks drop a little sugar in it." He was obviously a man who knew his barbecue, and it is no wonder that he took pride in his culinary skill.

He recollected further that speeches were held during the day and that "all de fiddlers from everywhars" came to "fiddle fer de dances." Jones continued: "Dey had a platform, built not fer from de barbecue tables, to dance on. Any darky dat could cut de buck and pigeon wing was called up to de platform to perform fer everybody" (vol. 3, pt. 3, p. 73). Often there was whiskey. Former slave Al Oxner recalled that at barbecues almost every man would drink his dram, and some to excess (vol. 3, pt. 4, p. 222). Mad Griffin of Goshen Hill summed up the situation admirably when he said that he and his friends had "de mos'es fun at a barbecue dare is to be had" (vol. 2, pt. 1, p. 2). Jones agreed: "barbecues was de most source of amusement fer everybody, all de white folks and de darkies de whole day long."

For the slave, music and dancing were thus apparently important parts of the barbecue, as they were on other holidays and "Saturday night frolics"—so much so, in fact, that the master would try to impose a midnight limit on them. In this he was often foiled by slave ingenuity. When the master wouldn't let them dance, Mad Griffin remembered, they "shut up the doors" and had "secret dances" anyway, out of his hearing (vol. 2, pt. 2, p. 213).

Sketchy but important details of the slaves' dance customs can be pieced together from these narratives. Wesley Jones has already given us the description of the buck-and-pigeon-wing performed on platforms near the barbecue tables; but this was a more formal affair—most literally, a staged presentation. C. B. Burton of the Henry Burton plantation remembered the private ones: "We danced and had jigs. Some played de fiddle and some made whistles from canes, having different lengths for different notes, and blowed 'em like mouth organs" (vol. 2, pt. 1, p. 152). Remembered Adeline Jackson: "Dances wid fiddles, pattin' feet, and stick rattlin' " were lively affairs much enjoyed (vol. 3, pt. 3, p. 3). In the absence of fiddles and banjos, "Pats our feet and knocks tin pans was the music . . . danced to all night long," recalled a former slave of the Hardy plantation itself. He reflected on his love for the dance when he was young: "Used to rather dance than eat. Started out at sundown and git back to Maybinton at daybreak, den from dar run all de way to Squire Hardy's to git dar by sunup" (vol. 2, pt. 2, p. 127). John Davenport recalled one particular slave dance. A fellow "would jump up and down while tripping and dancing in de same spot. Sometimes he say, 'Every time I jump, I jump Jim Crow.' We had what was called a 'Juber' game. We would dance a jig and sing, 'Juber this, Juber that, Juber killed a yellow cat' " (vol. 2, pt. 1, p. 242). William Pratt also remembered:

We used to dance jigs by ourself, and we danced the "hack-back," skipping backwards and forwards facing each other.

> When one danced a jig, he would sing, "Juber this, Juber that, Juber kills a yellow cat." My brother used to sing a cotton-picking song: "My mammy got meat skin laid away; grease my belly three times a day" (vol. 3, pt. 4, p. 278).

This last rhyme was not total nonsense, for, as we recollect from an earlier section, the mammies greased the babies after washing them with mullein water. Nellie Loyd of Goshen Hill recalled that slaves "had lots of dancing and frolics. Dey danced de 'flat-foot.' " One "would slam his foot flat down on de floor. De wooden bottom shoes sho would make a loud noise. Leather was tacked to de wood soles to make our shoes. At weddings, everybody would eat and frolic" (vol. 3, pt. 3, p. 128). Several former slaves stated that they quit their heavy frolicking and dancing when they matured, married, and joined the church (vol. 3, pt. 3, p. 3; vol. 2, pt. 2, p. 41). The activity was thus largely for the young, the unmarried, and the lighter of heart and feet.

An occasion at the Hardy plantation that was as memorable as dance frolics, Christmas, and the Fourth of July was the six weeks of the white folks' Methodist camp meeting. For an account of this important community event, which ran through July into August, we must rely on one chief source—a wonderful narrative by Gus Feaster. Feaster's Methodist master attended church at Goshen Hill, a church that rivaled the Hardys' nearby Ebenezer "in de way o' finery and style." The Jeters, Carlisles, Simses, Selbys, and Glenns attended Rogers Chapel with their slaves, while the Hardys, Douglasses, Cofields, Chicks, and Oxners were the most prominent members of Ebenezer. Feaster's account of the Rogers Camp Meeting contains so much detail about white and slave social activities that it bears extensive quotation. In addition, it is worth comment that the family of WPA field worker, Caldwell Sims, who recorded Feaster's story, were antebellum communicants at Rogers Chapel. Feaster narrates:

> Every summer, dey carried on Camp Meetin' at Rogers. All de big Methodist preachers would come from way off den. Dey was entertained at de Carlisle Big House. Missus put on de dog den. Everything was cleaned up jes' 'fore de meetin' like us did fer de early spring cleanin'. Camp Meetin' come jes' after de craps was done laid by befo' July de Fourth. . . . De chilluns was put in one room to sleep and dat make more

room for de preachers and guests dat gwine to visit in de Big House fer de nex' six weeks. Den de plans fer cooking had to be brung 'bout. Dey never had no ice in dem days as you well knows; but us had a dry well under our big house. . . . Steps led down into it, and it allus be real dark down dar . . . de younguns skeert to go down fer anything. So us carry a lightwood knot fer light . . . it was de talk o' de country 'bout what nice fresh milk and butter de missus allus had. A hollow oak log was used fer de milk trough. Three times a day, Cilla [the head cook] had her little boy run fresh cool well water all through de trough. Dat keep de milk from gwine to whey and de butter fresh and cool. In a dry well, we also kept de canned things and dough to set til it had done ris. When company come like day allus did fer de camp meetings, shoats and goats, and maybe a sheep or lamb or two, was kilt fer barbecue out by Cilla's cabin. Dese carcasses was kept down in de dry well over night and put over de pit early de next morning after it had done took salt. Den dar was a big box kivvered wid screen wire dat victuals was kept in in de dry well. Dese boxes was made rat proof.

Whilst de meats fer de company table was kept barbe-cued out in de yard, de cakes, pies, breads, and t'other fixings was done in de kitchen out in de Big House yard. Baskets had ter be packed to go to camp meetin'. Tables was built up at Rogers under de big oak trees dat has all been cut down now. De tables jes' groaned and creeked and sighed wid vict-uals at dinner hour every day durin' de camp meetin'.

Missus fetch her finest linens and silver and glasses to outshine dem brung by de t'other white folks o' quality. . . . After de white folks done et all dey could hold, den de slaves what had done come to church and to help wid de tables and de carriages would have dey dinner on a smaller table over clost to de spring. Us had table cloths on our table also, and us et from de kitchen china and de kitchen silver.

Young gals couldn't eat much in public, kaise it ain't stylish fer young courting gals to let on like dey has any appe-tite to speak of. I sees dat still goes amongst de wimmen folks, not to eat so heavy. Cullud gals tried to do jes' like de young white missus would do.

After everything was done eat, it would be enough to pack up and fetch back home to feed all de hungry niggers what roams roun' here in Union now. Dem was de times when everybody had 'nough to eat and more dan dey wanted and plenty clothes to wear.

During de preaching, us darkies sot in de back o' de church. Our white folks had some benches dar dat didn't nobody set on 'cept de slaves. Us wore de best clothes dat us had. De Marse give us a coat and a hat; and his sons give all dey old hats and coats 'round. Us wore shirts and pants made from de looms. Us kept dem cleaned and ironed jes' like de Marster and de young marsters done their'n. Den us wore a string tie, dat de white folks done let us have, to church. Dat 'bout de onliest time dat a darky was seed wid a tie. Some de oldest men even wore a cravat, dat dey had done got from de old marster. Us combed our hair on Sunday fer church. But us never bothered much wid it no other time. During slavery, some o' de old men had short plaits o' hair.

De gals come out in de starch dresses fer de camp meeting. Dey took dey hair down out'n de strings fer de meeting. In dem days all de darky wimmens wore dey hair in string 'cep when dey 'tended church or a wedding. At de camp meetings de wimmens pulled off de head rags, 'cept de mammies. On dis occasion, de mammies wore linen head rags fresh-laundered. Dey wore de best aprons wid long streamers ironed and starched out a-hanging down dey backs. All de other darky wimmens wore de black dresses and dey got hats from some dey white lady folks, jes' as us mens got hats from our'n. Dem wimmens dat couldn't git no hats, mostly wore black bonnets. De nigger gals and wenches did all de dressing up dat dey could fer de meeting and also fer de barbecue.

At night when de meeting done busted til nex' day, was when de darkies really did have dey freedom o' spirit. As de waggin be creeping along in de late hours o' moonlight, de darkies would raise a tune. Den de air soon be filled wid the sweetest tune as us rid on home and sung all de old hymns dat us loved. It was allus some big black nigger wid a deep bass voice like a frog dat 'ud start up de tune. Den de other mens jine in, followed by de fine lil' voices o' de gals and de cracked voices o' de old wimmens and de grannies. When us reach near de Big House us soften down to a deep hum dat de missus like! Sometime she his't up de window and tell us sing "Swing Low Sweet Cha'ot" for her and de visiting guests. Dat all us want to hear. Us open up and de niggers near de Big House dat hain't been to church would wake up and come out to de cabin door and jine in the refrain. From dat, we'd swing on into all de old spirituals dat us love so well and dat us knowed how to sing. Missus often 'low dat her darkies could sing wid heaven's 'spiration. Now and den, some old mammie would fall out'n de waggin a-shoutin' "Glory and Hallelujah and Amen!" After dat, us went off to lay down fer de night (vol. 2, pt. 2, pp. 58–63).

There can be little doubt that the Hardys and their slaves attended either this Big Meeting or one very similar, and entertained visitors in like manner. As we have seen in an earlier chapter, Bishop Francis Asbury often stayed at the Hardy plantation at the turn of the nineteenth century, and to house and care for visiting clergy was traditional with them.

Feaster's description of black church attire at Big Meeting was likely very accurate and not extraordinary, for there is substantiation for it elsewhere in these narratives. Former slave Henry Coleman from a plantation near Carlisle recalled that the "Missus 'ud gib some of de gals some short [peacock] feathers to put in dere Sunday hats. When dem gals got dem hats on, I used to git so disgusted wid 'em I'd leave 'em at church and walk home by my self" (vol. 2, pt. 1, p. 211). Feaster recalled that his mother, a field hand, exchanged $10 worth of cotton for a Sunday bonnet at the Orange Hall store (vol. 2, pt. 2, p. 69). Sunday clothes were so highly prized that on one occasion a female slave was jailed for stealing them from a fellow slave on a neighboring plantation (vol. 3, pt. 4, p. 113).

The great majority of references to clothes by these narrators was to homespun of wool, cotton, or wool-and-cotton blends. These were made on the spinning wheels and looms on the place by the slaves and the womenfolks of the Big House. Feaster recalled that everyday-wear was "cotton clothes in hot weather, dyed wid red dirt or mulberries, or stained wid green walnuts [to make brown] . . . heavy shoes wid wood soles; heavy cotton socks which was wore de whole year through de cold weather; but we allus go barefooted in hot weather. . . . Sunday clothes was dyed red fer de gals; boys wore de same. We made de gals hoops out'n grape vines. Dey give us a dime, if dey had one, fer a set of hoops" (vol. 2, pt. 2, pp. 46–47). Feaster also remembered that the slave girls of Goshen Hill "charmed us wid honeysuckle and rose petals hid in dere bosoms [a practice of the white ladies as well]. Now, de gals goes to de ten-cent sto' and buys cheap perfume. In dem days, dey dried cheneyberries and painted dem and wo' dem on a string around dere necks to charm us" (vol. 2, pt. 2, p. 52). Moses Lyles recollected that his girl friend wore a beautiful dress dyed purple with pokeberry juice (vol. 3, pt. 3, p. 141). Other colors were achieved with yellow clay, a gray from maple tree bark (vol. 3, pt. 3, p. 90), and a green made from dye bought at a store in Union. Maple bark and copperas (a green hydrated ferrous sulfate) made a "pretty yellow" (vol. 3, pt. 3, p. 180). Charlie Meadow of Santuc recalled:

> For our summer clothes, we plaited de hanks [of yarn] to make a mixtry of colors. De winter clothes was heavy, drab, and plain. . . . Us wore thin home-made clothes [in summer] and dey sho' was better dan what I has now, kaise us made dem on de home looms and spinning wheel, and dey was good. Cloth ain't no count, kaise it ain't made good in no mills like dat what us made at home. . . . Ain't never seed no garments as strong as dem we wore back dar. Everything was made out of plaited cotton and it lasted fer years and years. Winter time, we wore all wool clothes. . . . Marster had enough sheep to give his folks wool. . . . I'se 'bout ten years old when I could card and spin good (vol. 3, pt. 3, pp. 177, 180).

In Maybinton, Milton Marshall recalled: "Our clothes was made at home, spun and wove by de woman folks and made by dem. . . . Our shoes was made by a shoemaker in de neighborhood named Lyles. Dey was made wid wooden soles" (vol. 2, pt. 2, p. 172).

Pick Gladdeny, one of Squire Hardy's own slaves, described the clothes he wore on the Hardy plantation. For his Saturday night frolics, Gladdeny wore clothes that were "made right on the plantation. . . . My britches were copperas colored, and I had on a home-wove shirt with a pleated bosom. It was dyed red and had wristbands. I wore that shirt for five year. Gals wore their homespun stockings. Wore the dresses so long dat they kivered their shoes" (vol. 2, pt. 2, pp. 127–28). Obviously both sexes cared about their appearance and took pride in their clothes. They made do the best they could with grapevine hoops, purple pokeberry dye, chinaberry-seed beads, pleated shirt bosoms, second-hand string ties and cravats, store-bought bonnets, and peacock-feathered hats in order to be as much in fashion as their circumstances allowed. Considering their situation, they succeeded most admirably. The slave's sense of pride and decorum, and often a nice delicacy of manners approaching re-finement, are often demonstrated in these narratives.

In addition to holidays and Big Meeting, there were other rituals that affected black and white alike. Weddings and funerals are defining moments in individuals' lives and in the life of all communities. Slave marriages were marked by a frolic and a good supper or dinner, provided by the master. (See Emoline Wilson, vol. 3, pt. 4, p. 214; Caroline Farrow, vol. 2, pt. 2, p. 40; and Granny Cain, vol. 2, pt. 1, p. 167.) Or, if the ceremony occurred during watermelon season, they often had a big watermelon feast after the service, which itself was a simple affair. (See Feaster, vol. 2, pt. 1, p. 46.) The melon symbolized fecundity and so was appropriate to the occasion. Slaves attended the funerals of their white masters' families. They shared bereavements, but also took comfort with their white families in their Methodist faith. Again Feaster, the oral chronicler of the community, presented an excellent vignette of slave funerals:

> Going to funerals we used all Marse's wagons. Quick as de funeral start, de preacher give out a funeral hymn. All in de procession tuck up de tune, and as de wagons move along wid de mules at a slow walk, everybody sing dat hymn. When it done, another was lined out, and dat kept up til we reach de graveyard. Den de preacher pray and we sing some mo. In dem days, funerals was slow for both de white and de black folks. Now, dey is so fast, you is home again befo' you gits dar good. On de way home from de funeral, de mules would perk up a little in dey walk, and a faster hymn was sung on de way home. When we got home, we was in a good mood from singing de faster hymns, and de funeral soon be forgot (vol. 2, pt. 2, p. 51).

The contours of country life were defined to the greatest extent by the tasks necessary to raise and harvest crops from the earth. The routines

of soil preparation, planting, cultivating, and harvesting have been identified in earlier chapters. The slaves of the Hardys, Gists, Simses, Maybins, Jeters, Colemans, and other local plantations lived by these
routines. Their calendar of works and days began in childhood and continued to old age.

A stage of life on the plantation that is documented particularly well
by the former slaves of the area is childhood. From these accounts, it is
clear that all the young had chores. The most common of these were to
lead the cows to and from the pasture and to tend the farm animals. This
included grooming the horses and feeding them—in general, "working
round the barn and taking care of de stock," as Simon Gallman put it
(vol. 2, pt. 2, p. 105). On some plantations cows and cattle were branded
and freed to roam in unfenced pastures, but those that did not roam
must be led from one fenced pasture or lot to another. Milk cows had
to be brought up, milked, and put up for the night; but the other cattle
and calves used to stay in the woods all night long. Sometimes they
would be a mile away from the house, and the boys "wouldn't mind
bringing them in, because they played so much together" as they drove
the cows in (vol. 3, pt. 4, p. 270). In winter, particularly, the stock
needed shelter and feeding, and young slaves accomplished these important chores. Some narratives reveal that many slave children often shared
barnyard duties with their master's children. Chores acquainted black
and white children with the world of nature, wild and domesticated.
They learned together to ride horses and mules, to care for livestock,
and to operate farm equipment.

At the Hardy plantation in 1860, Pick Gladdeny, at age five, carried
water into the Big House and fetched kindling to light Squire Hardy's
hearthfires. When old enough he graduated to hauling and drawing
water from the well. He remembered:

> Squire William was de man dat I worked for when I had
> done turned five. Dey teach me to bring in chips, kindling
> wood, firewood, and water. I learnt to make Marse's fire ever
> morning. Dat wont no trouble, 'cause all I had to do was
> rake back de ashes from de coals and throw some chips and
> lightwood and de fire come right up. Wont long 'fore I was
> big enough to draw water and bring in big wood. You knows
> what big fireplaces they got down dar at Squire Hardy's (vol.
> 2, pt. 2, pp. 127–28).

Jonathan Coleman, born in 1855 at the Johnson Coleman plantation across Broad River from the Hardys, recalled that his childhood chore at the Coleman Big House was to fan the table to keep flies away. There was a swing over the Colemans' dining room table and young Jonathan sat in it with a peacock feather fan. "At fus, dey had to show me jus how to hole de brush, kaise dem peacock feathers was so long, iffen you didn't mind your business, de ends of dem fethers would splash in de gravy or sumpin-nother, and den de Missus' table be all spattered up. When I got bigger, I got to be house boy" (vol. 2, pt. 1, pp. 210–12).

Other narrators also recalled fanning flies with peacock feather fans as children. At some houses, there were even small steps used for mounting the swing. Coleman's account may indeed describe a neighborhood fashion and perhaps a practice at the Hardys'. That the Hardys had many peacocks and guineas during the antebellum era is a known fact. To have peacocks wandering near the Big House eating insects and displaying their fans was yet another custom of the country.

Slave children became youths—that is, went from light childhood chores to light and simple field work—at the age of twelve or thirteen. Seventeen was generally the age when childhood was considered to end, when, as one former field hand recalled, "the marster felt my bones were hardened enough to do some field work." Richard Jones recollected that the slave children, when "dey was strong and well-developed younguns, was give tasks and learnt to do what de master and mistress thought dey would do well at. . . . All de chilluns in de Gist quarter had very small tasks until dey was seventeen or eighteen years old" (vol. 3, pt. 3, p. 63). Feaster remembered graduating to field hand work by dropping peas—that is, sowing the seed after his older brother Albert ran the furrough. (Albert's main chore was to plough.) His older sister Harriet also planted peas and corn. He recalled: "I had to drap peas in every other hill and John had to drap de corn in de rest" (vol. 2, pt. 2, p. 43). Feaster then related how he got punished by a cruel overseer:

De overseer, ol' man Wash Evans, come down dar to see how us was doing. Den us got dat skeert dat us got de corn and peas mixed up. He started to hit us wid de whip dat he hung 'round his waist. 'Bout dat time Marse Tom [Carlisle] rid up. He made de overseer git out'n dem corn rows and let us 'lone. After dat, us got 'long fine wid our drapping. When it come up, everybody could see dem rows dat us had done got mixed up on when de overseer was dar. . . . But one day when ol' man Evans come through de field and see dem rows, he did call me and John off and whip us. . . . Marse got shed o' de overseer soon atter dat (vol. 2, pt. 2, pp. 64–65).

Evans was a real source of grief for the slaves on this plantation. Feaster contributed another priceless account of an event he witnessed as a child—the scene, in fact, that led to Evans's dismissal:

Ol' man Evans was a wicked man. He take 'vantage of all de slaves when he git half chance. He was great source of worri- ment to my mammy, ol' lady Lucy Price and 'nother 'oman, ol' lady Lucy Charles. Course he 'vantage over all de darkies and fer dat reason he could sway everything his way, most all de time. But my mammy and ol' lady Lucy was 'ligious wimmens. Dat didn't make no diffuns wid wicked ol' man Evans. One day Missus sont my mammy and de other ol' lady to fetch her some blackberries by dinner. Me and John was wid dem a-pickin' and fillin' o' de big buckets from de lil' buckets when ol' man Evans come riding up. He argued wid both mammy and ol' lady Lucy; and dey kept telling him dat de missus want her berries and dat dey was 'ligious wimmens anyhow and didn't practice no life o' sin and vile wickedness. Finally he got down off'n his hoss and pull out his whip and 'low if dey didn't submit to him he gwine to beat dem half to death. At that, me and John took to de woods. But we peep. My mammy and ol' lady Lucy start to crying and axing him not to whip dem. Finally dey act like dey gwine to indulge in de wickedness wid dat ol' man. But when he tuck off his whip and some other garments, my mammy and ol' lady Lucy grab him by his goatee and further down, and hist him over in de middle of dem blackberry bushes. Wid dat dey call me and John. Us grab all de buckets, and us all put out fer de Big House fas' as our legs could carry us. Ol' man Evans jest er hollering and er cussing down in dem briars. Quick as us git to de Big House us run in de kitchen. Cilla [the head cook] call Missus. She come and ax what ailing us and why we is so ashy looking. Well, my

mammy and 'ol lady Lucy tell de whole story of dey humilia-
tions down on de creek.

Missus 'lowed dat it didn't make no diffuns if Marse was
in Union, she gwinter act prompt. So she sent fer Mr. Evans,
and he took real long to git der; but when he do come,
Missus, she 'low—"I does not want to argue de point wid
ye, Mr. Evans, fer yo' services has come to an end on dis
plantation!" Wid dat, ol' man Evans go off wid his head a-
hanging in shame. Us niggers went out and tole de news wid
gladness shining out from our eyes, kaise us was dat glad dat
we did not know what to do (vol. 2, pt. 2, pp. 65–66).

Thus his mother's ingenuity, strength of character, and resourcefulness
saved the day in what otherwise might have been a tragic scene. Feaster
went on to relate that since the war, the Evanses had risen high in the
world, whereas his master's family had not. He obviously saw the irony
in all this. Virtue had neither triumphed nor been rewarded; the war
had raised the bad element and weakened the good and kindly. It was
such scenes as the above that ushered young Feaster into the realities of
manhood. Here, his narrative becomes a sophisticated parable of the loss
of childhood innocence.

Despite the shortage of direct testimony by Hardy slaves, documents
and letters from the white family can fortunately provide us with some
significant hard information about the Hardy slave community and the
specific individuals who comprised it. The core and progenitors of the
Hardy blacks were eleven slaves who came from Virginia with the old
pioneer in 1785. We know something about them from extant wills and
estate appraisements.

In 1806 Thomas Hardy Sr. made a gift of two slaves, likely born in
Virginia, or of parents who were, to his son John Wesley, who lived
adjacent to him. They were Mak and Moriah. Their names are the earliest that have come down to us. Moriah (who apparently pronounced
her name "Mora," judging from the way the master usually spelled it)
was still alive and on the plantation in 1844.

Later in 1806, several other family slave names were recorded. They
were Amey and her two children Anderson and Henry (the three valued
at $600); again Moriah, this time noted as having a son named Tom
(both valued together at $450); a woman named Rachael (valued at
$325, and who by 1809 had borne a son named Jack); a boy named Matt

(valued at $300); and a girl named Holley (valued at $270). Both Rachael and Holley were alive in 1844. Amey, Henry, Rachael, Matt, and Jack were all visited by Dr. J. L. Reid in 1854. Amey was visited thirty-seven times that year, Henry eighteen, Rachael thirteen, Matt seventeen, and Jack four. Henry also appears in plantation documents as being on the plantation in January 1861. In 1852 Matt was allowed to purchase items on his own credit at George Ashford & Co., a fact that indicates he was among the most trusted slaves. Jack was entrusted with the young Hardy sons in war and was thus alive in the 1860s. Rachael shared in the cooking duties for Sundays in 1846, and her age at this time must have exceeded fifty. These then are the surviving names of the original pioneering black settlers from Virginia, or their immediate descendants.

From 1814 we have record of the names of two more women in the household of Thomas Hardy Sr.—Dillar and Rose. Dillar's valuation at $37 suggests advanced age and thus also that she was one of the original pioneers, and very possibly the matriarch of the family. Rose, Isham, and Ben were grouped together at the value of $900, and in 1815 went to live with Thomas's daughter, by this time the wife of the Reverend George Clarke, who resided nearby on Enoree River. Dillar also went with them, suggesting that she may have been related to Rose, Isham, and Ben. Their new master was a very well-respected man of substance, known in the community for his unassuming nature, simplicity, piety, and humility.

Seven men are named in the household of the old pioneer in 1814: Manuel (valued at $601); Isham, Ben, and James (valued at $301); Sirus Sr. (valued at $628); Sirus Jr. (valued at $360); and Ephraim. None of these men appear in the extant partial slave lists for 1844–1846, 1851–1854, or 1861. They were likely dispersed to family members at the sale of Thomas Hardy Sr.'s estate in December 1814. Only Thomas Jr.'s purchase of Manuel retained him on the plantation. The others were moved into the households of the old pioneer's other five children. The name of the slave Isham is significant. It no doubt originated with the Isham family of Virginia that married into the Hardy clan about 1747. Slave Isham, therefore, undoubtedly had roots in that distant Virginia past.

In 1818 William Eppes Hardy inherited his mother's slave Ben; and his two older brothers received Delphy (sometimes called Delph), Jim, and George. Fanny went with William Eppes Hardy's half-brother Charles Wesley Shell. His mother's maidservant Guinea was given the choice of her freedom or of going with her pick of the Hardy sons. As we saw earlier, she chose to live with Charles Wesley, then under the care of Thomas and Precious Shell in Newberry village. All these men and women were likely descended from Hardy slaves.

I find no indication that the Hardys ever sold slaves out of the family; and from all evidence it appears that they sold no slaves at all. Even when the young orphans William Eppes, James, and Hamlin had no plantations to farm, the family slaves they inherited were kept in the family by the children's guardians and hired out rather than sold. (The hiring out in this particular case lasted for eleven years.) When the three children came of age, each continued to retain his servants. This was also the case with the slaves of Nancy Hardy Shell from the time of her death in 1818 until her children came of age and took charge of them officially in 1825. During this period their slaves were hired out at various times to different relations, neighbors, and friends: William Beard; James, Asbury, and Isham Shell; Dr. Tom Shell; Dr. James Shell; Dr. Curtis Atwood; and John Hatton. William Eppes Hardy's Ben was valued at $1,000 in 1818 (around $20,000 in today's currency). He thus must have been an especially skilled man, perhaps a driver, overseer, or artisan (maybe a builder or blacksmith). Like Matt, Ben appears on a list of seven Hardy slaves in 1852 who could buy on credit in their own names from George Ashford & Co. Ben was thus among the most trusted men on the plantation. Guinea's value was listed at $620, a sum that proves she was an excellent houseservant and waiting maid and not elderly. Nancy Shell's freeing her indicates that she felt Guinea to be capable of making her own way. It was a costly decision for her estate and reflects the bond of friendship, mistress to slave. In summary, from all indications, we can therefore conclude that the Hardys tried every means possible to avoid selling their black retainers out of the family's sphere. Even when Hardy children were orphaned, they, with the aid of guardians appointed from within the family, kept ownership and responsibility. ✓

The Hardys did buy slaves, however. One such sale document dated 28 December 1832 records Dr. Curtis Atwood's conveyance to William Eppes Hardy of a "family" consisting of a woman named Chaney ("about 28 years old") and her two children, Anna ("about 7 or 8") and Judge ("about 2")—the three for the sum of $628. The mother was thus not separated from her two children. In fact, she may have been related to, or at least acquainted with, some of the Hardy slaves whose community she joined in 1832, for Dr. Atwood was Nancy Hardy Shell's close neighbor and friend. She had made him executor of her will and of her children's trust, a duty that he performed from 1818 to 1826. Thus, from all appearances, Hardy was not buying slaves at slave auctions, as in the popular conception of the institution, but instead was choosing them locally, and very possibly those who already had ties and friendships with his own people and wished to move. In fact, it is possible that Chaney may have been joining her husband as a result of the sale.

All three of the Atwood slaves, Chaney, Anna, and Judge, were still on the Hardy plantation in 1844, when they were mentioned by their Marse Billy. Chaney and Judge were still present in 1854, when Dr. J. L. Reid provided them medical care. (As we shall see, in this year alone, he treated Chaney twenty-nine times and Judge fifteen.) At the time, Chaney was fifty years old and Judge twenty-four. The 1832 purchase occurs in the period in which Squire William, now married four years, was establishing the plantation on a grander scale. It was also at this time that its acreage had begun to increase dramatically.

Luckily, Hardy jotted several groupings of slave names in his plantation ledgers of 1839–1844 and 1842–1846 and on the verso of a letter that he received in 1844. From these documents we can assemble the following list of forty-two slaves for the period circa 1846. This number is only four short of the forty-six slaves of the 1850 census total:

Women

1. Addy (or Adeline)
2. Ann (also written "Anna")
3. Caroline (later Caroline Lyles)
4. Chany (also written "Chaney")
5. Eglace (also written "Egles" and "Eglan")
6. Ellen
7. Emmaline (later Emmeline Hodge or Hodges)
8. Emalee (enumerated as different from Emmaline in the lists)

Men

1. Calvin
2. Dan
3. Daniel (enumerated separately from Dan in the lists)
4. Frank
5. Goodman
6. Hilliard
7. Hores
8. Jack
9. Little Jack
10. Jerry
11. Judge
12. Monford (also written "Manford" and "Manfred")

9. Harriet (later Harriet Lyles)
10. Hannah
11. Holly (sometimes written "Holley")
12. Irene
13. Lulum
14. Mary
15. Milly
16. Mora (also written "Moriah")
17. Martha
18. Nancy (also written "Nance")
19. Rachel (also written "Rachael")
20. Sary
21. Sook (also written "Sooky")
22. Susy
23. Tempy (also written "Tem")
24. Vilet

13. Neely
14. Pleasant
15. Simon
16. Tom
17. Warren
18. Warner

Around 1844 the master listed the following to "cook Sundays": Caroline, Rachael, Susy, Hannah, Milly, Vilet, Anna, Sary, Martha, Emmeline, and Harriet. Besides supplying names, this ledger entry is significant because it suggests that Hardy let the slave community have Sundays for themselves. These slave women took turns cooking in the Big House on the Sabbath. The family was thus not so pious as to disallow all work on Sundays. People were fed and likely fed well. Into the present century, descendants of these slaves recall that the Hardy servants ate their cured ham, barbecue, and bacon just like the white family. It is doubtful that there were any empty stomachs on the place.

There are five other significant documents that help shed light on these men and women and the manner in which William Eppes Hardy treated them. The first is an 1842 entry in the 1842–1846 plantation ledger. Here Hardy notes small payments to five of his slaves: Pleasant ($1.50), Warren and Frank (1.00), Monford and Frank (.62½), Simon (.62½), and Jack (.25). In his 1839–1844 ledger, Hardy similarly pays sums on 3 October 1844 to Jack ($2.50), Pleasant (2.50), Warner (1.25), Holley (1.25), Frank (1.25), Little Jack (1.25), Goodman (1.25), and Hannah (1.25). The documents provide us the three new names Warner,

169

Little Jack, and Goodman and show that these slaves were thus allowed to make spending money of their own on their own time.

The third document, perhaps even more signficant than the first two, is an entry among the items of an 1852 account bill with George Ashford & Co. in which Ashford notes "Your Negroes' Amount" of debts incurred at his store. The men listed are: Pleasant ($2.50 and 1.25), George (2.50), Warren (1.25), Matt (1.25), Ben (4.65), Simon (1.25), and Mose (1.25). Ashford's entry contributes three additional slaves' names—Matt, Ben, and Mose—and also reveals that the seven men on the list were allowed to go to his store and purchase items on their own credit and in their own names.

The fourth document is a jotting of names on the verso of a letter to William Eppes Hardy dated 15 January 1861. It is thus our last list in time. The decipherable names are Caroline, Mary, Amy, Felix, Adam, Silas, Henry, Ann, Jim, Warner, Manfred, Charles, Jake, "7 children," Chatty, Mimy, Stevens, Jerry, Eliza, "2 children," Molly, Mary, and "a child." This list provides twelve new Hardy slave names: Adam, Amy, Charles, Eliza, Henry, Jake, Jim, Felix, Molly, Mimy, Silas, and Stevens. Another slave, "Pomp," is mentioned in a letter of 1862. From the war front, Haywood writes his father about hounds and hunting. "Let me know how Pomp comes on in the Patridge line," he says.

In 1862 Hardy slaves Jack and Silas accompanied the young Hardy's in gray to Richmond, Virginia, and attended them in battle as valets and body servants. As we have seen, a child named Jack had been born to Rachael by 1809; it may have been he or his son "Little Jack" who went to war with his master's children. A body servant by the name of Tom Hardy also attended Squire Hardy's son William Dixon Hardy and lived to care for him until his death in 1932.

The fifth and by far the most important document dates from 1854 and is a careful list of Dr. J. L. Reid's visits during that year to the Hardy family. This list shows that Reid treated a total of twenty-two slaves (almost half the total of forty-six that Hardy owned) at least once during the year. Of these twenty-two individuals, Amey required thirty-seven visits, Chaney twenty-nine, Caroline twenty-two, Henry eighteen, Matt seventeen, Simon sixteen, Judge fifteen, Rachael thirteen, and Mose and Monford twelve each. Dr. Reid attended Silvy at her "accouchement," as he called the event. The Hardys thus did not rely on midwife delivery. Perhaps the most significant detail of all is that both Hardy's daughter Elmira and his son Haywood were also treated by Reid at the same time and listed alongside the entries for the Hardy slaves. It is obvious that in 1854 the Hardy slaves received good medical care, for the same physician that attended his children attended his slaves. Those costing the most were the elderly slaves like Amey and Chaney; and it is thus clear that Hardy, even though their "value" had decreased, did not consider this in providing them with care as good as he gave the prime field hands. The list of these twenty-two slaves includes five names not found on any other lists: America, Bet, Joe, Minerva, and Silvy. The sixteen other slaves treated were Amey, Caroline, Chaney, Henry, Jack, Judge, Matt, Milly, Mimy, Monford, Mose, Rachael, Sarah, Simon, Sooky, and Vilet.

Also caring for the Hardy slaves in the 1840s and 1850s was Dr. George Douglass of The Oaks. In the most enduring folk tale from the area (a ghost story called "Happy Dog"), it was to The Oaks that the Hardy slave Ben was sent to get Dr. Douglass for treating a sick slave back in the Hardy Quarters. The events which comprise the folk tale were reputed to have occurred in spring 1855. After son Charles Wesley received his medical degree in 1855, he took over the medical duties on the place. He was listed as being still in residence on the plantation in the 1860 census. It was common enough in the area for a planter's younger son to become a doctor, and was certainly a practical move, considering the number of people on the plantation requiring health care. The medical bill Dr. Reid presented to Squire Hardy in 1854 totaled $329, or over $6,000 in today's currency. As we have seen, Charles Wesley's learning medicine was thus one more way in which the Hardys were striving for plantation self-sufficiency in changing times. It is yet another example of the family's resilience in adapting to modern realities.

Compiling now the names of Hardy plantation slaves from all sources yields a list of eighty-eight men and women who lived on the place at some time during the plantation's history:

Women: (1) Addy (also written as "Adeline," born 1835)

        (2) Amey (on the plantation in 1806)

        (3) Ann (also written "Anna," daughter of Chaney, born c. 1815)

        (4) Bet

        (5) Caroline (later Caroline Lyles, born c. 1828)

        (6) Chaney (also writeen "Chany," born c. 1804)

(7) Chatty

(8) Cornelia (daughter of Eglan)

(9) Dillar (born prior to 1800, on the place in 1814)

(10) Eglan (also written as "Egles" and "Eglace")

(11) Eliza (born 1837)

(12) Ellen

(13) Elvira (daughter of Eliza, born 1858)

(14) Emma (daughter of Eglan)

(15) Emmaline (later Emmaline Hodge)

(16) Emalee

(17) Harriet (later Harriet Lyles)

(18) Hannah

(19) Holly (also written "Holley," daughter of Rachael, born prior to 1809)

(20) Irene

(21) Jinny (born c. 1800)

(22) Lulum

(23) Mary (daughter of Caroline, wife of Anderson)

(24) Milly (born c. 1806)

(25) Mimy (also written "Mimey")

(26) Minerva

(27) Molly

(28) Mora (also written "Moriah," wife of Mak, born c. 1780)

(29) Martha

(30) Nancy (also written "Nance," daughter of Caroline, born c. 1845)

(31) Rachael (born c. 1795)

(32) Rose (on the place in 1814)

(33) Sally (later Sally Murphy, came to the plantation c. 1860)

(34) Sary

(35) Silvy (bore a child in 1854)

(36) Sook (also called Sooky)

(37) Susy

(38) Tempy (also written "Tem," born c. 1826)

(39) Vilet (wife of Pleasant, born c. 1820)

Men:

(1) Abram (son of Eliza, born 1856)

(2) Adam

(3) America

(4) Anderson (son of Amey, born prior to 1806)

(5) Anderson (husband of Mary)

(6) Ben

(7) Calvin

(8) Charles

(9) Chuky (son of Mary)

(10) Dan

(11) Daniel

(12) Dock (born c. 1850)

(13) Ephraim (on the place in 1814)

(14) Felix (mulatto, son of Caroline, born 1853)

(15) Frank

(16) Goodman

(17) George

(18) Henry (son of Amey, born prior to 1806)

(19) Henry (born 1852)

(20) Hilliard (mulatto, born 1849)

(21) Hores

(22) Isham (on the place in 1814)

(23) Jack (son of Rachael, born prior to 1809)

(24) Little Jack

(25) Jake

(26) Jerry

(27) James (on the place in 1814)

(28) Jim (on the place in 1860)

(29) Joe

(30) Judge (son of Chaney, born c. 1830)

(31) Mak (husband of Mora, born c. 1780)

(32) Manuel (on the place in 1814)

(33) Matt (son of Rachael, born prior to 1809)

(34) Monford (also written Manford, born in 1825)

(35) Mose (also written "Moses," born in 1805)

(36) Neely

(37) Pleasant (husband of Vilet)

(38) Pick (later Pick Gladdeny, son of Sally, born c. 1855)

(39) Pomp

(40) Silas (body servant during the war)

(41) Simon

(42) Sirus Sr. (born prior to 1800, on the place in 1814)
(43) Sirus Jr. (on the place in 1814)
(44) Stephens (also written "Stevens," born in 1818)
(45) Tom (son of Mora, born prior to 1806)
(46) Tom Hardy (body servant of William Dixon Hardy during the war)
(47) Uriah (born in 1855)
(48) Warren
(49) Warner (born in 1840)

From the 1860 slave statistics of the South Carolina census, we learn yet more about the blacks of the Hardy domain. In 1860 there were now forty-five slaves who still lived in ten slave houses. The names of the twenty-five males were not given, but their ages were listed as 70, 60, 42, 41, 40 (3), 30 (2), 25 (2), 23, 22, 18 (2), 12, 10 (mulatto), 10 (2), 7 (mulatto), 6, 5 (2), 2, 1. The twenty unnamed females were ages 45, 40, 32, 30 (2), 28 (2), 25 (mulatto), 20 (2), 15 (4), 14, 11, 10, 8 (2), and 1 (mulatto). These ages indicate that Chaney, Amey, and Rachael had died by 1860. Of men and women 15 to 45, there were twenty-eight. This is the number of prime hands who could be put in the field at maximum work times of planting and harvest. The master had to hire hands to help with various seasonal duties in times of peak activity, especially during the cotton harvest, when time was of the essence. His land thus always exceeded his work force—at least during the period from 1835 to 1842, when fairly complete records are available through the plantation ledgers. During these years the squire notes hiring James Pearson's man to "pick out 1,000 pounds of cotton at 50 cts per count" in 1839, and Pearson's same man to "cut wheat 3 days and oats 3½ days" in 1841. In May 1842 the "hands" of Evans and Abrams "picked out for me in all cotton to the amount of 1800 pounds."

One of the five-year-olds enumerated in the 1860 census can be identified as Pick Gladdeny, who had recently come to the Hardy plantation. In 1936 Gladdeny recalled that his mother was the slave of David Murphy of Maybinton. Murphy was overseer for Captain Tom Lyles two miles from Lyles' Ford on the Broad. Gladdeny's mother's name was Sally Murphy, and she and her child had come to live on the Hardy place by 1860. In 1936 Pick stated that he would "be buried in Hardy graveyard, whar my white folks dat was so good to me lie sleeping, and dat's whar my ma and pa and others that I loves lies too." Gladdeny was about fifteen years old when Squire William died and knew the master well enough to say, "Squire Hardy was a good man: so was Mr. Dick [his son]." Gladdeny recalled that Hardy was a strict master who acted decisively. Gladdeny was duly impressed by one event he witnessed as a child, an event that likely occurred during the war:

> Droves of niggers used to come down the road by Squire Hardy's front gate. Yes, sir, a overseer used to come through here driving niggers; just like us drives cows and hogs up around this big road. . . . One day Squire Hardy went out and stopped a drove coming down de road in the dust. He pick him out a good-natured looking darky and give the overseer one our contrary niggers, what nobody didn't like, for the good-natured one.

The three mulatto children, ages 1, 7, and 10, as given in the 1860 census, may have been the offspring of the 25-year-old mulatto woman listed therein, who would thus have been born in 1834 or 1835. Two of their names have come down to us in the census of 1870 as Hilliard (age 21 in 1870), and Henry (age 18). A fourth mulatto, Felix (17 in 1870) is listed as the son of Caroline and hence could not have been borne by the mulatto female. Caroline was born around 1828. The name Hilliard was a Hardy family name. The old pioneer's brother, John Hardy, who settled in Edgefield District in 1785, had a son with this name; but this is no conclusive proof that these slaves had blood connections to the family, for many of the Hardy slaves, as far back as Virginia, took names from the white family.

In 1860, 75-year-old Anna Powell Dixon Hardy of Goshen Hill, living next to her younger daughter Frances Hardy Douglass of The Oaks, was running her own plantation. Here she owned an additional thirty-one slaves, some doubtless part of the Hardy patrimony and perhaps even more closely connected to the original blacks who came to Carolina from Virginia with the old pioneer. Little is known of them but their names and ages. The latter derive from the 1860 census: Males—44, 30, 28, 26, 25, 24, 22, 16, 15, 13, 10, 6 (2), 3, 1; Females—55, 45, 32, 26, 25, 20, 19, 18, 14, 12, 9 (2), 7, 5, 2 (2). All their names come from Anna Hardy's will of 1859.

Here they are listed in four groups. First are the elderly: Stephens, Jinny (age 59), and Molly. These three slaves were given the choice of going (at Anna Hardy's death in 1861) to either of her daughters, Catharine Hardy or Frances Hardy Douglass. The second category is of slaves who were already with Catharine and working for William Eppes Hardy: Manford, or Monford (age 34); Silas; Henry (7); Anderson; Mary and her child, Chuky; and Caroline and her children, Mary, Nance (13), and Felix (6). The third group is slaves who were with Frances Douglass at the time and in "the employ" of Dr. Douglass: Jacob and Mimey, Winny and Caesar, Pelina and Thom, Milly and John, Chatty and her child, and Charles. These appear to be grouped in five family units. In the 1854 list made by Dr. Reid, Mimey and Milly are at the Hardy plantation. In the fourth group are slaves in Anna Hardy's employ in 1859: Warner (19) and Jim, who at Anna Hardy's death would go to the Hardy plantation as the property of Catharine Hardy; and Amanda, Caroline, and Eliza (22) and her children Abram (3) and Elvira (1), who at Anna's death were to go to The Oaks as the property of Frances Douglass. For some reason, all but Amanda went instead to the Hardy plantation. From the records it appears that some of the Hardy slaves must have moved rather freely back and forth between the Hardy plantation and Goshen Hill, working for the extended family. Perhaps the specifics of the work at hand required it, or perhaps it was the relationships between the slaves themselves.

In 1860 Hardy's immediate neighbors in Newberry County had fewer slaves than he. John Gilliam came closest with thirty-eight. Abraham Gordon had nine; Colonel John Lyles thirty; and Berry Richards sixteen. From a letter to Orange Hall written by a Renwick cousin in March 1862, we learn that the blacks also had their friends and relations among these slave families owned by their masters' friends and relatives. Cousin Sallie writes her cousin Rogers Renwick: "The Black folks all send howdies to yours. Tell them howdy for me too." There was a complicated and close network of slave relationships and friendships in the extended community, just as there was in the white sphere.

Today there are black families in the area who still bear the Hardy name and descend from Hardy slaves. In southern Spartanburg County, a white Hardy descendant attends school with several black Hardys. These probably descend from the plantation. They moved to the towns just as the white Hardys were forced to. The Hodges family of Maybinton are perhaps descended from the Emmeline Hodges listed in the cook's list for Sundays in 1844. In the 1860s this family also included Wade and Viney Hodges, or "Aunt Viney," as she was called. Their patronym likely originated from Dr. Charles Hodges of Maybinton, who was practicing medicine there by the year 1850. After emancipation, they, like many of the other families, stayed on the land as tenant farmers. So did ex-slave Eglan and her two daughters Cornelia and Emma, and ex-slaves Pleasant and his wife Vilet, with all of whom Hardy signed freedman's agreements in 1866. In 1866 also, it may have been the Tom of the slave lists of 1845–1846 who entered into a sharecropping agreement with his ex-master. He made his mark, and William wrote for him: "Tom Suber, Freedman." The white Suber family, whose name Tom bore, was of German heritage and originated in the Dutch Fork section to the south.

The 1870 census of William Eppes Hardy's family throws more light on the black population. Living in the Hardy household in 1870 were fifteen blacks and three mulattoes, all of whom had taken the surname Hardy. The males were named Moses (age 65), Stephens (52), Manford (45), Warner (30), Hilliard (21, mulatto), Dock (20), Henry (18, mulatto), Felix (17, mulatto, the son of Caroline), Uriah (15), and Abram (14 and the son of Eliza). The female Hardys were Jinny (70), Milly (64), Violet (50), Tempy (44), Adeline (35), Eliza (33), Nancy (24, the daughter of Caroline), and Elvira (12, the daughter of Eliza). Of these, Stephens, Manford, Warner, Henry, Felix, Abram, Jinny, Eliza, Nancy, and Elvira had come from the bequest of Anna Hardy in 1861, though all but Jinny had already been on the plantation before that time in the master's employ. Jinny came there by virtue of the choice allowed her in Anna Hardy's will. These were likely the truest family retainers, the descendents of the original slaves who had been part of the pioneering adventure with the first white Hardys.

Tom Hardy, William Dixon Hardy's manservant, who had gone to war with him as his "bodyguard," attended his friend until William's death in October 1932. He was said always to be at his deaf and blind comrade's side to hand him his cheroots. Tom, also now of advanced age, had many grown grandchildren in the area. If it could be known, the story of their complex friendship and intertwined lives would probably make an interesting chronicle in its own right.

In the 1920s and '30s, the Great House was still surrounded by no fewer than five black families, at least the majority of them living in remodeled and expanded slave houses. The Henry Renwick family lived on Peters Creek in the 1930s. Henry's wife Eva cooked for the Hardys. Two of these households were headed by John Rooks and Clarence

Hodges. It was the Hodges, Ruff, and Sanders families who, as tenants, helped John Frost Hardy Sr. raise and market the last eight bales of cotton on the land in 1963. Clarence's wife, Thad, helped Mrs. Hardy around the house in the 1950s and '60s and made it possible for her to stay there after her husband's death in 1963. As her grandson recalls, Mrs. Hardy and Thad made soap at the spring and in many ways carried on the old rural rituals. It was said that Clarence still made his moonshine as his father had in the generation before and John would often have to go post his bail in Newberry when he got caught. Life on the land went on in the well-worn patterns. Clarence's sister Ellen Hodges was cook for Frank and Paul Hardy in the 1930s and '40s. Ellen's and Clarence's mother, Wren Hodges, also lived on the place and was much in demand as a midwife. She was "a tiny ancient lady" in the 1960s. When John Hardy III would go to town with his grandfather and Clarence every Saturday, John Sr. would always buy her a can of snuff, her one "vice." On occasion, as grandson John recalls, she would also use this snuff to "snuff" a pregnant woman. The method was to put the snuff in her apron and shake it in the woman's face to cause her to sneeze and thus induce childbirth.

The Hardy slave cemetery is on the family land just off present Tyger River Road less than a quarter of a mile from the Great House. This burying ground was still being used by descendants as late as the 1930s, when John Tucker remembers attending a funeral there as a young man. The white Hardys are buried at Ebenezer Cemetery and at a plot near the Comer plantation in Tuckertown, north of the Tyger. As we have seen in this chapter, former slave Pick Gladdeny, in 1936, described a "Hardy graveyard, whar my white folks dat was so good to me lie sleeping, and whar my ma and pa and others that I loves lies too." If he was referring to Ebenezer, the blacks' graves are unidentified. There are fieldstone markers at Ebenezer and empty spaces around the Hardy plots, so Gladdeny may indeed be referring to this cemetery. Possibly, however, he was thinking of the Hardy slave cemetery off Tyger River Road.

Perhaps our chapter should end with a consideration of a fact of plantation life made patently obvious in the narratives of former slaves: the closeness of the two races in their works and days. For the slaves, it was truly, as they phrased it, "life with our white folks." A few more specifics from these narratives should suffice to illustrate this point. Granny Cain of Maybinton recalled: "I stayed with my mama at Squire

Kenner's and waited on my mistress, Mrs. Lucy Kenner, who was the best white woman I know of—just like a mother to me. I stayed there til my mistress died; was right by her bed. . . . I wish I was living with her now" (vol. 2, pt. 1, pp. 166, 168). Jimmie Johnson recalled that his "Missus told me I was free, but I told her I was going to stay on where I was and protect her until I died. And when Masser died, I grieved and grieved about him. I loved him dearly and I know he loved me. . . . I grieve about my masser to this day" (vol. 2, pt. 2, p. 54). Or Maggie Perkins, who remembered that as a young girl at Colonel Robert Beaty's plantation, she would sit at her mistress's feet and sometimes "fall asleep against her knees." Or George Briggs of Cross Keys: "Union County is whar I was born and raised, and it's whar I is gwine to be buried. Ain't never left de county but once in my life, and if de Lawd see fitten, ain't gwine to leave it no mo', 'cept to reach de Promise Land. . . . I loves it and I is fit throughout and enduring de time dem Yankees tried to git de county, to save it. . . . All de white folks is good to me since my marse done gone and left his earthly home. And he is waiting up dar wid Missie to see me agin. Dat I is sho of" (vol. 2, pt. 1, p. 81). Or again, Gus Feaster, who recalled how his playmates, the young masters Newt and Anderson Carlisle,

> would tell me and John to come and git under de steps while
> ol' Marse was eating his supper. . . . When he go into de
> missus' room to set by de fire, warm his feets, and have his
> Julep, quick as lightning me and John scamper from under de
> steps and break fer de big cape jessamine bushes long de front
> walk. Dar we hide, til Anderson and Newt come out a fetch-
> ing ham biscuit in dey hands fer us. It would be so full of
> gravy, dat sometime de gravy would take and run plumb
> down to de end o' my elbow and drap off. . . . When dey
> had honey on de white folks' table, de boys never did fail to
> fetch a honey biscuit wid dem. Dat was so good dat I jest
> take one measly lil' bite of honey and melted butter on my
> way to de Quarters. . . . When I git to Mammy, den me and
> Mammy set off to ourselfs and taste it til it done all gone.
> (vol. 2, pt. 2, p. 64).

Feaster was about ten years old at this time (in the year 1850); and, when a little older, as he recalled, he groomed and cared for the young masters' horses when they rode home from Renwick Academy (vol. 2, pt. 2, p. 63).

A final small masterpiece of narration, again by Feaster, shows a society in which black and white worlds intersected and mingled daily across barriers of class; and with Feaster's words, our long chapter ends:

> Marse Tom let my mammy go up to de [Orange Hall] post to fetch her back a bonnet. . . . So Mammy took a lot of cotton. I'se gwine long wid her and so I had to wear some pants. . . . as dat was big doings fer a lil' darky boy. So Aunt Abbie fotched me a pair of new pants dat was dat stiff, dat dey made me feel like I was all closed up in a jacket, atter being used to only a shirt-tail! Well, it wasn't fur and us arriv' dar early in de day. Mammy said "howdy" to all de darkies what dar, and I look at dem from behind her skirts. I felt real curious-like all inside. But she never act like she knowed dat I was pulling her dress at all. I seed so many things dat I never had seed befo', not in all my born days. Red sticks o' candy was a-laying right dar fo' my eyes, jes' like de folks from de Big House brung us at Christmas. It was not near Christmas den, kaise it was jest cotton picking time and I wondered how-come dey was having candy in de store. . . .
>
> Mammy look down at me and she say to de white man wid a beard, "Marse, please sir, give me five cent worth peppermint candy." Den when he hand her de bag she break off lil' piece and hand it to me, and wall her eyes at me and say in a low voice, "Don' you dare git none dat red on yo' clean shirt, if you wants to git home widout gitting wo' plumb smack out."
>
> Den she talk about de bonnets. Finally she git one fer ten dollars worth o' cotton. Money wasn't nothing in dem times. By dis time us had done started on our return home and I was starting to feel more like I allus felt. . . . "Look dar a-streaming down off'n your chin at dat red. . . . When we gits to dat branch, now I's got to stop and wash dat dirty black mouth and den I can't git dat red candy off'n dat shirt. What ol' lady Abbie gwine to say to ye when she see you done gone and act like you ain't never seed no quality befo'. . . . Ain't never gwine to carry you nowhars 'gin long

as I lives. . . . Gimme dat candy right now; I gwine to see to it dat you gits back home looking like someting after all my worriments wid ye."

Mammy seed dust a-flying and de hoss come a-bringing Marse Tom down de road. Mammy drap everything in the dust and grab her apron to drap a curtsy. She 'low: "Git dat hat off dat head and bow your head fo' he git here!"

"Howdy, Lucy, whar is you and dat youngun been, anyhow?"

"Us been to git me a bonnet, Marse Tom, and it took all de ten dollars worth of cotton to fetch it back wid."

"Yes, Lucy, money does not go far these days, since the Yankees got everything."

"No Sir, No Sir, Marse."

And he rid on, leaving us behind in de dust (vol. 2, pt. 2, pp. 69–71).

10

In the Way o' Finery and Style
The Decade before the War

The gentry of South Carolina, descended from an old chevalier stock; and accustomed through many generations to the seclusion of country life, and that life under Southern skies, surrounded with all the appliances of wealth and homage, have acquired an ease, a grace, a generosity, and largeness of character, incompatible with the daily routine of the petty occupations, strategems and struggles of modern commercial and metropolitan life, be it in the South or the North.
—T. A. Richards, *Southern Scenery* (1857)

There is less vulgar display, and more intrinsic elegance, and habitual mental refinement in the best society of South Carolina, than in any distinct class anywhere among us.
—Frederick Law Olmsted, *Seaboard Slave States* (1856)

By the time of the 1860 agricultural census, Squire Hardy, now fifty-six, had become "old marster" to his people, but he still managed the plantation with the vigor of youth despite his duties as the county magistrate of Gilliam's Beat. He had buried six sons and daughters; but all six of his living children (five sons and one daughter), to whom he was said to be deeply devoted, were still unmarried and usually at home. By this time, eldest son Thomas (now thirty) was listed in the census as ı tradesman and thus helping to manage the plantation's commissary and ts bustling business of iron foundring and sales, plow and harness mak-

182

ing and repair, buggy, carriage, barouche, oxcart, sulkey, and wagon repair, tool making and mending, nail making and other blacksmithing of all sorts, and coopering, tanning, cobblering, and goods hauling. As we have seen, from the 1830s on, the plantation had made and sold shoes and boots and performed all the various tasks of blacksmithing for both itself and the surrounding neighborhood—even to the point of creating door and window hinges, keys, gate locks, andirons, "chimney rods and plates," hoes, shovels, axes, mattocks—and even staples, pins, and spikes for flatboats. As we have also seen, the plantation ledgers record that this activity was extensive and lucrative. Son Gustavus Adolphus (twenty-nine in 1860), and called Dolphus and Dolph by the family, helped in this varied endeavor as well as assisted his father with the planting duties. He focused on the latter.

With the eldest sons due to take over the plantation, two of the younger sons were being educated in the professions. Such was the old pattern of primogeniture established in Britain and brought with the Hardys to Virginia. Charles Wesley (twenty-eight) had become a medical doctor after attending W. W. Renwick's Academy at Orange Hall until 1849 and then Stephen Lee's Academy in Asheville from 1850 to 1852. He went on to study medicine with his uncle James Hardy in Asheville and graduated from the Medical College of South Carolina in Charleston in 1855. In 1860 he was practicing from the plantation. A letter to his father from Lee's Academy when he was eighteen speaks of his own concerns as a student but as much of what is going on back home on the plantation:

Asheville, March 20, 1850

My Dear Father,

I received your letter by Mr Neilson this morning and was very much gratified to learn that you were all well. I am very much pleased with Mr Lee. He is a very kind man. He keeps me very close indeed, not allowing me to go anywhere without his permission. We have had a great deal of rain since I left you. The streets of Asheville are very muddy indeed. I am getting along very well with my studies. I am studying Latin and Greek, Arithmetic, and Ancient Geography. We study till nine Oclock every night and from five till service every morning. You stated that you had bought the right sort of a horse, a good buggy horse, and a good riding horse. I

hope he may please you in every way. I did not see Mr Neilson. He staid at his brother's in the village last night. I was
sorry that I could not see him. Tell Mother I wish she would
have those clothes ready and send them to me. I was very
glad to hear that you had sold the balance of your cotton at a
good price.

I must close this short letter, as it is time for school to
commence. Give my love to all. I remain truly your son

C. W. Hardy

That Charles Wesley writes of his mother's readying clothes for him
shows that the women of the house are busy sewing. The mention of
"the right sort of a horse" is in keeping with the male Hardys' passion
for horseflesh. Finally, it is apparent that all the family, even students far
away at school in the midst of Ancient Geography, are ever aware of the
cotton harvest and the price it is bringing. What a volume of history this
letter provides, revealing in its well-written lines the sincerity of respect
and feeling this eighteen-year-old had for his family.

A letter from twenty-year-old Charles Wesley has also come down
to us:

Asheville, N.C. March 15, [1852]

My Dear Father,

I write you this to inform you that we arrived here safely
on Friday after we left home. We got the first night to Mrs.
McBride's a little after dark. We could have gotten there
sooner but I was mistaken in the distance. The next night we
stopped at the Widow Hunt's about nine miles from the
North Carolina line. We would have stopped at Dr. [Colum-
bus] Millses [near Tryon, N.C.], but it was too early. . . . We
made Allen's nineteen miles below Asheville. Jimmy [Doug-
lass] is here. He is in fine spirits. He is much better satisfied
than I anticipated. We will go over to Mr. Lee's on Monday
and commence School. Uncle [Dr. James] Hardy will not let
us off till then. We came very near losing our places on account of our delay in not coming sooner. Mr. Lee has rejected several applications in consequence of us. Tell Mr.
Glenn Mr. Summey [of Summey & McDowell Store in
Asheville] says the clover seed is not to be had anywhere in

Buncombe County. It is worth nine dollars per bushel. I will enclose a bill of our expenses in this, so that you and the Doctor can settle it between you. You can give Uncle Dr. [George Douglass] credit for three dollars which he gave me at Union Court House in part of our expenses. Tell him I have given that to Dick to bring him back home. Tell the Dr. I will write him soon how Jimmy [his son] is satisfied. Tell Mother, Aunt Delia [Mrs. James Hardy] is very thankful for the gourds which she sent. I will write again soon.

> I remain your dutiful son,
> Chas. W. Hardy

That Uncle James Hardy "will not let us off" before a long visit attests to the Asheville Hardys' continuing strong bonds with the Hardys of Tyger. Catharine's sending gourds from the Hardy plantation tells us both that they were grown there and that the family practiced the common gardening habit of sending passalong plants, seeds, and produce long miles from relative to relative.

Eldest daughter Elmira, who was twenty-four in 1860, had attended Renwick Academy and then graduated from Salem Academy in Salem, North Carolina. She returned home an accomplished lady. Her two letters from school during the same span Charles Wesley wrote his give glimpses of family priorities and a suggestion of the social milieu. Fourteen-year-old Elmira wrote on 6 February 1850:

My dear Pa,

I received your kind and affectionate letter on the 2nd, and I was very sorry to hear that you had been sick; but I hope that you will soon get well. I received a letter from brother Wesley last Sunday. It was very short indeed. Please tell him to write longer letters. They have no news in them at all. I am very sorry to inform you that Mr. Boner will soon leave the hotel, but we do not know who will take his place and fill it as well as he did. Eliza and Jane Moore's brother is here. I expect you are acquainted with him. He is from Tennessee. He stayed all night at Uncle George's [George Douglass]. I hope that Cousin Laura Randolph will remain with Aunt [Fannie Douglass] the whole summer, but I do not expect she will leave home so long as that. Our school is not very full at present, but new girls are coming every day. We have had very bad weather for about one week. I hope we will have fine weather now. It has been wet so long. Tell brother Thomas and Adolphus to be sure and write to me. Pussy Garland, Nannie Hair, Emma Scales [Seales?] and myself are writing letters to our relations. Mary Frost sends her love to you and says she will write to you soon. Give my love to Grandma, and tell her that I will write to her. Also ask Mother to write to me too. I believe I have given you all the news at present. Write soon.

Your affectionate daughter,
Elmira Hardy

Two weeks later, on 19 February 1850, Elmira again wrote home:

My dear Parents

Not having received a letter from you in four weeks, I thought it was my duty to write. Cousin Laura [Douglass] received a letter from Aunt Fannie [Douglass] today and we were glad to hear that you were all well. Mr DeSchweinetz received a letter from Pa about two weeks ago. I received the money you sent me and am very much obliged to you for it. He said he would answer it very soon. I am looking very patiently for a letter from either of you or any of the family. The girls are very busy preparing for an entertainment which will be on the 1st day of March, and a great many of the girls have pieces to play on the piano and guitar, and some have recitations and dialogues to recite. I am sorry to inform you that Mary Frost is sick with a sore throat, but she is getting better. I was very sorry indeed to hear that Pa and brother Wesley had been sick, but I hope they will soon be well again. It pleased me very much to hear that Pa would come to see me in May. I will be very glad if both of you will come and bring the family. I would like very much to see *you all* in Salem together. Be sure and come. Give my best love to Cousin Laura Randolph and tell her that I would like very much to receive a letter from her, and also Aunt Fannie. Please send me a lock of hair from each of the family, in the next letter. I have given you all the news. Give my best to

Aunt, Grandma, Uncle, and all my relations. Write soon to
your affectionate daughter
                          Elmira

Elmira's penmanship is expert, even artistic. She had been enrolled at
Salem at the age of twelve or younger (her father's ledger of 9 January
1849 notes a trip to take $184 to Salem to pay her tuition and to visit
her); and now, for a fourteen-year-old, she exhibits maturity and competent writing skills. Although battling homesickness, she shows herself
to be quite the brave young lady. Like her brother Charles Wesley's, her
love of *"all"* the family is obvious and again reveals the closeness of the
Hardy (and Douglass) family circle.

Elmira was still one of the 169 boarders at Salem Female Academy
the following year, when Headmaster DeSchweinetz billed her father
the sum of $262 for "Board, Tuition, etc." to 18 January 1851. Hardy
paid his account on 14 March 1851. Mr. DeSchweinetz's explanation of
Elmira's bill reveals "Elmira's having taken French & Guitar lessons."
She also received a "great quantity of [sheet] music . . . likewise caused
by her taking lessons, both on the piano and guitar." In his letter of 14
March 1851 the headmaster continues: "Elmira is well & doing well.
Her examination will be held on the 29th & 30th of May next [1852]."
The professor is aware of Squire Hardy's source of income. He con-
cludes his letter by saying: "I have perceived that cotton has been declin-
ing. I fear that many in the cotton states will be sufferers on this account.
The last accounts from England seem to be somewhat more favorable."
Such was the extent to which all kept their eyes on this agricultural
commodity.

Upon returning home to the plantation in the summer of 1852 at
age sixteen, Elmira continued her interest in music. It was she who
played the pianoforte at plantation "entertainments" and for the quiet
evenings with the family in the drawing room. The Hardy men were all
said to have some musical talent in singing and were not embarrassed to
perform before others. Their Methodist hymn tradition, as well as the
Southern Harmony influence of neighbor Singin' Billy Walker, stood
them in good stead. One or more of them stood tall at her side, singing
with her as she played. This fondness for music continued well into the
twentieth century, when the last of these children, William Dixon
Hardy, always importuned his children to sing well into the summer
nights from the downstairs porches while he slept upstairs. In 1860

Elmira was traveling much in the company of her "Pa" and her Douglass cousins and was often on visits to Columbia to be with Mary Frost there and on the Frost plantation in Richland County. Mary Frost was the Salem classmate with the sore throat mentioned in Elmira's letter. Elmira was now in love with Mary's brother John and would be married to him early in the following year. Already her father was having the little cards engraved that invited friends, neighbors, and relations to the plantation, where they would be "At Home, Tuesday Evening, Feb. 26th 1861, Half past 7 o'clock."

From November 1860 to December 1861, around the time of Elmira's marriage, the Hardys made an impressive list of purchases from J. & H. Richards Co. Among these items, Catharine had bills for a number of rather modest piece and millinery goods: 30 yards kersey ($6.60), 49½ yards osnaburg (5.73), 16¾ yards gray casinett (13.55), 1 yard crape (.50), 1 yard brown holland (.30), 6 yards calico (.75), 1 yard black gingham (.47), 5 yards brown homespun (.75), 2½ yards jeans cloth "for George Eppes Hardy" their fourteen-year-old son (1.25), 2 yards brown jeans cloth (.25), 4½ yards Salem jeans cloth (4.95), 7 yards bleached jeans (1.05), 1 yard of black jeans cloth (.15), 1½ yards of white jeans cloth (.22), 2 yards of Irish linen (1.50), 6 yards of flannel (6.00), 2 yards of cambric (.25), 1 yard of gingham (.38), 2 spools of silk (.50), 14 skeins of silk (.70), 37 spools of cotton (1.55), 5 papers of needles (.25), a paper of pins (.10), 2 bunches of tape (.10), 1 steel thimble (.05), 2 dozen pearl buttons (.25), 2 dozen coat buttons (.20), 8 vest buttons (.10), 1 bunch of whale bone (.10), 1 pound of indigo dye (1.50), 8 papers of tacks (.40), and 5 boxes of blacking (.50). Another item, three bunches of flax (.30), suggests that the women were weaving linsey-woolsey, a blend of linen and wool. A purchase on 8 August 1861 of 2 pairs of wool cards points to wool cloth production for the young men of the family, a necessity created by the war. In addition, six "goods boxes" ($3.00) on 3 July 1861 were probably used for sending things to the sons in camp. To have a "box on the road" was a much anticipated event for the Hardy soldiers, and often mentioned in their letters from the front. Ready-made clothing included 2 pairs of shoes ($3.40), 5 cotton handkerchiefs (1.53), 2 pairs of merino drawers (4.00), 3 merino shirts (5.25), a "Fine dress & Trimmings" (11.00), a black silk cravat (1.50), an overcoat (12.00), and a coat (8.00).

House furnishings purchased in the four months prior to Elmira's wedding in February 1861 included 10 blankets ($12.75), a set of knives and forks (1.00), 2 iron spoons (.25), 2 green buckets (.50), a meat cutter (2.50), and 2 looking-glass mirrors (.50). House furnishings after the marriage included a coffeepot (.60), 4 pounds of candles ($1.00, likely to replace those burned during the festivities), 2½ yards of table cloth (1.25), 4 cakes of honey soap (.50), a bar of toilet soap (.10), a tin bucket (.50), and 2 steak dishes (2.00). Likely for Milady Catharine's hair, we find a pair of side combs (.30). Incidental items included a barrel of Irish potatoes ($5.50) and 18 nutmegs (.60).

James Haywood (twenty years old in 1860), who had studied at Renwick Academy with his Douglass cousins and his own brothers and sisters, had completed his education at Lee's Academy in Asheville. He now helped his father and brothers on the land, and had chosen to make a life of farming. He was also raising some cotton on his own to pay some of his small debts incurred from purchases of clothes, tobacco, pocketknives and such. Like his father, he loved a good hunt and a horse race. He particularly prized his horses and even more, perhaps, his hunting hounds and setters. He was an excellent horseman and from all accounts "a handsome, smart, and lively young blade of a lad." A daguerreotype portrait of him while at Lee's Academy in the mid 1850s reveals a tall, broad-chested, dark-haired fellow who looked the photographer straight in the eye. As we will see later, he was becoming a wise young farmer, who would write his father from the war front to applaud his tilling some new bottom land for the growing of corn, saying "I am a great man for an abundance of Corn, and if the War was ended I could raise Hogs and Corn in plentiful style, as they are the foundation of a Plantation, but you are Hog man and myself the Horse man." The son is thus showing solidarity with his father across the miles and says clearly that he will strive to return home to take up the family's agrarian tradition and complement with corn and horses what his father does with corn and hogs. There is, interestingly, no mention of cotton in Haywood's letter. He obviously had no obsession with the chief cash crop of his Region.

Haywood also took an active interest in politics. His four letters preserved for us, written during the war, show excellent penmanship and a vigorous prose style. The style is the man indeed with Haywood. He was a spirited and bold man of action. A list of his purchases from the local store of D. Gross in 1858, when Haywood was eighteen years old, reveals the degree to which he was both a horseman and a sportsman. In this year alone, and from this one establishment, he bought 6 pairs of riding gloves, "Foxing" (fox-hunting) boots, riding boots, a riding whip, a saddle blanket, a currycomb, a pair of bridle reins, powder, shot, and caps. He also loved his tobacco while hunting and riding; from D. Gross in this year he bought 31 plugs of tobacco. Since he was a young country squire, it is fitting that he also purchased a "fine Hat," a "fine Shirt," a coat, a silk handkerchief, a vest, 2 cravats, 10 shirt collars, 4 linen hankerchiefs, a pair of pants, a pair of suspenders, 2 hairbrushes, a coarse brush, a blacking brush, 4 pairs of socks, a pair of "half Hose," soap, and drawers. To round out the picture, his incidentals included a pocketknife, a small blank book, a memorandum book, a lead pencil, a padlock, and nails. Haywood's father also bought him a costly "Cloth Coat" from the Columbia firm of R. C. Anderson on 13 November of this year. There were no doubt other purchases from other sources; but only these two receipts have come down to us.

From Lee's Academy in 1857, when Haywood and Dickie were still in school there, Headmaster Lee had sent a letter that reveals Squire Hardy's complaints about his sons' tendency to spend their father's money too "extravagantly." More seriously, Lee himself felt that the young men, seventeen and sixteen years old, were "practicing deception" in the way they were doing so:

Buncombe N.C. July 22 [18]57

W. E. Hardy Esqr.

Dear Sir,

I have just received your letter and tho' I regret very much that your boys have been so extravagant, yet I do not feel that I am to blame except in believing their promise, formally made to me, not to buy anything that you would not approve. It is certain that only a few weeks after Dixon came to me, he was out at elbows & told me that he had only a Sunday coat & the one so worn, I allowed him then to get an every-day coat.

When the time came to get summer clothes, they said that they had none & I gave them the order accordingly, after they had made me the promise above alluded to. I found that both Haywood & Dixon have since both got things in Asheville *not at Summey & McDowell's store* where I deal, without my order & which I would not sanction & which you are not bound to pay for.

I asked you in my last to limit Haywood & Dixon in the number of pieces that they send to the wash. They do not send more than some others, but more than I expect you would approve—something like an average of 16 pieces per week lately.

They never wore out here the 4 pairs of shoes you gave them; but what could I do, when they told me that they had none.

I shall let them buy nothing hereafter whether they be offended or not, tho' it is impossible to watch young men all the time, like children. If they had not practised deception towards me, they would not have bought as they did. I shall know how to trust them hereafter.

Very truly yours
Stephen Lee

These younger Hardy lads were more like their Uncle James Hardy than their father and their more sober farmer brothers back home. They were, like James Hardy at the same age, intent on making a dashing appearance. Haywood's bill of purchases for 1858, given in his own name, might suggest that Haywood, his father, or both felt that Haywood should learn the value of money by having to pay for the things he purchased. It is interesting that the $20 credit from Haywood's exchange of cotton on 31 January 1859 paid for less than one–third of his bill.

Haywood's younger brother, William Dixon (or "Dickie" as he was called by the family), now nineteen years old in 1860, had since late 1857 or early 1858 become an employee of Hardy & Agnew, a mercantile establishment in Spartanburg run by his first cousin John Wesley Hardy, Uncle Hamlin Hardy's son. Dickie was now enrolled at Wofford College in Spartanburg, a natural move for this staunchly Methodist family, since Methodists created the college. Like Wesley and Haywood, Dickie had been educated at Renwick Academy and finished his schooling at Lee's, under both brother Wesley's and his Uncle James Hardy's tutelage. Dickie studied with Lee from 1854 to 1857, from the age of thirteen to sixteen.

Perhaps something should be said here of Stephen Lee, who played such an important role in the education of the young men of both William and James Hardy's families. He was born of an old Barbadian family in Charleston in 1801 and was thus roughly the same age as William and James. He was educated at West Point and the College of Charleston, from which he graduated in 1828, the year James Hardy had himself moved to the city. They may have known each other there. Lee had been running his excellent boys' boarding school at the Thornton place (Mountain Home) on the banks of the Swannanoa since 1846. His younger brother Thomas Lee had been in medical school with James Hardy, and it may very well have been through "Dr. Jim" that the schoolmaster found his way to Asheville. Young Wesley got good training from Lee, schooling that prepared him for his medical studies. In 1851 Headmaster Lee, very much as Professor DeSchweinetz had done from Salem in the same year, wrote Squire William a letter that reveals how interested even headmasters were in agricultural concerns—"the life blood of us all," as well they knew and as William himself expressed it.

> Mountain Home, near Asheville
> June 30th 1851
>
> W. E. Hardy Esq
> My dear Sir
>
> I received yesterday your letter covering $70 and will apply it as you direct, the whole being entered to your credit, in account.
>
> Wesley is not at home now: it being vacation, he is spending a few days with his Uncle James and family. He however is well and shall read your letter.
>
> I regret that the drought has so nearly destroyed your crop of oats. This dry spell seems to have been very extensive and I fear in many parts of our country, will shorten the corn crop very considerably. 'Tho' the wheat is good in this vicinity, we are still paying $7 for flour and that not the best.
>
> We shall be very glad to see you & trust that your youngest child [William Dixon] is now perfectly well. Our school commences again tomorrow.
>
> My best respects to Mrs. Hardy.
>
> > With gt. respect
> > Your friend
> > Stephen Lee

Through Lee's Academy the three Hardy sons shared a common tie to the famous Stephen D. Lee, a lieutenant-general of the Confederacy, nephew of the headmaster, and a pupil there during Wesley's and Haywood's student days. The boys were no doubt well acquainted. Haywood would meet Lee again as a comrade on the battlefield. Young William Dixon, whom Headmaster Lee mentions in his letter, as we have seen, also was to receive excellent training from Lee that prepared him well for more than fifty years of political service to the state.

Something should also be said of William W. Renwick, founder and headmaster of Renwick Academy and all these children's first schoolmaster. Renwick was a successful cotton planter and after 1848, the master of Orange Hall plantation at Goshen Hill. He was descended from Scots-Irish dissenting ("Covenanter") Presbyterians from County Antrim, Ireland. In 1839 he graduated from South Carolina College, where he had been a brilliant and much-admired student. A letter to him from his old college classmate William J. Rivers, now president of South Carolina College, hints at his intellectual abilities:

24 October 1859

Dear Sir

   I thank you for your kind enquiries. I have not seen you since your graduation, but have you most distinctly before my mind. Are you as fond of Mathematics as you were then? Do you remember the discussion with Bishop Elliott on the principles regulating the motions of worms and reptiles? He maintaining one principle and you another? I believe both were right, were you not? I was several classes below you—but the firmness and decision of your character, and the manliness with which you devoted yourself to study—as if you appreciated the great realities of life and all its high principles—made a deep impression upon me. . . . Very many pleasing reminiscences occur to me, as no doubt they do to yourself.

Very respectfully yours,
Wm. J. Rivers

In Renwick's papers from the 1850s are receipts for subscriptions to many magazines and periodicals, among them the *Southern Literary Gazette*, *Southern Quarterly Review*, *Charleston Mercury*, *Newberry Mirror*,

Southern Guardian, Orion (a literary magazine), *Farmer and Planter,* and *Southern Presbyterian Review.* These speak well of the continued varied intellectual interests of this planter–educator. As also revealed by his papers, he was a friend of the Hardys, Douglasses, Moormans, and Gists. Governor and Mrs. Gist of Rose Hill plantation were on familiar terms with him. Gist owned land adjacent to both him and the Douglasses and was, in a manner of speaking, their neighbor at Goshen Hill. This, then, is the man who first guided the Hardy and Douglass children in their paths of learning. They apparently had excellent training that equipped them to go on to institutions like Salem Academy, Lee's Academy, Mt. Zion, and South Carolina College and the University of North Carolina. Renwick, like Lee, prepared the children for the difficult lives they were soon to lead.

It was young Dickie's lot to succeed Old Master at his death in 1870. By this time, however, both the titles Young Master and Old Master would be practically obsolete, and the new *paterfamilias* would rule over a diminished estate of ruined fortunes in which the struggle for survival for both black and white had become desperate. But in 1859 this was still what amounted to light years away. In 1860 the plantation's real estate value alone tallied $40,700 (or about $800,000 in today's currency). The addition of William Eppes Hardy's personal property worth $45,000 (about $900,000 today) made him twice a millionaire and, as we have seen, in the top 1 percent of personal wealth in America, although not nearly so high in rank in the wealthy South as a whole.

There were eleven plantations in Newberry County in 1860 that exceeded 1,000 acres, and Hardy's exceeded 2,000. His land per acre was valued at more than twice the South Carolina average. In fact, Newberry County had the second-highest land value in the state at $14.85 per acre; and the Hardy land was valued at $20, well over even the high Newberry County figure. The seven highest land values in South Carolina counties in 1860 were as follows: Georgetown, $15.75; Newberry, 14.83; Fairfield, 12.20; Union, 12.00; Beaufort, 11.11; Edgefield, 8.78; and Charleston, 7.31. With the valuable rich new lands of the Deep South, the Hardy plantation also ranked high. At $20 per acre, the plantation fell just below the highest land average for a state, and nearly double the second. The land values per acre in the five wealthiest Southern states ranked this way in 1860: Louisiana, $22.02; Mississippi, 12.02; Alabama, 9.20; South Carolina, 8.62; and Georgia, 5.89.

From 1850 to 1860 William Eppes Hardy had also made steady gains on the per capita income of the wealthiest citizens of his wealthy county, in a state that (with Mississippi and Louisiana) had the highest per capita income of all the states in the Republic. In 1860 the thirty-five states of the nation ranked this way in the order of the per capita income of their free citizens: (1) *Mississippi*, $2,128; (2) *South Carolina*, 2,017; (3) *Louisiana*, 1,677; (4) *Alabama*, 1,497; (5) *Virginia*, present borders, 1,204; 1860 borders, 980; (6) *Georgia*, 1,153; (7) *Texas*, 1,075; (8) *Florida*, 1,050; (9) *Tennessee*, 1,005; (10) *North Carolina*, 832; (11) *Kentucky*, 814; (12) *Arkansas*, 811; (13) Connecticut, 771; (14) New Jersey, 734; (15) Oregon, 726; (16) *Maryland*, 696; (17) Delaware, 656; (18) Massachusetts, 625; (19) *Missouri*, 612; (20) New York, 597; (21) Rhode Island, 593; (22) California, 571; tied with Pennsylvania; (24) Vermont, 570; (25) Ohio, 543; (26) New Hampshire, 530; (27) Illinois, 528; (28) West Virginia, present borders, 467; (29) Indiana, 463; (30) Michigan, 461; (31) Iowa, 402; (32) Wisconsin, 380; (33) Maine, 354; (34) Minnesota, 350; and (35) Kansas, 288.

The even more astonishing ranking is the per capita income of the total population, including the slaves as potential wealth-holders. In 1860 the states in order of average total black and white per capita wealth were (1) *Mississippi*, $954; (2) *Louisiana*, 891; (3) *South Carolina*, 864; (4) *Alabama*, 822; (5) Connecticut, 771; (6) *Tennessee*, 756; (7) *Texas*, 750; (8) *Virginia*, present borders, 746; 1860 borders, 679; (9) New Jersey, 734; (10) Oregon, 726; (11) Delaware, 656; (12) *Kentucky*, 655; (13) *Georgia*, 649; (14) Massachusetts, 625; (15) *Maryland*, 607; (16) *Arkansas*, 604; (17) New York, 597; (18) Rhode Island, 593; (19) *Florida*, 588; (20) California, 571; tied with Pennsylvania; (22) Vermont, 570; (23) *North Carolina*, 554; (24) *Missouri*, 552; (25) Ohio, 543; (26) New Hampshire, 530; (27) Illinois, 528; (28) Indiana, 463; (29) Michigan, 461; (30) West Virginia, present borders, 444; (31) Iowa, 402; (32) Wisconsin, 380; (33) Maine, 354; (34) Minnesota, 350; and (35) Kansas, 288.

Parenthetically, it is interesting to note some 1990 per capita rankings of these same states: (1) Connecticut, $25,358; (2) New Jersey, 24,968; (3) Massachusetts, 22,642; (4) New York, 21,975; (5) *Maryland*, 21,864; (8) New Hampshire, 20,789; (9) Illinois, 20,303; (12) *Virginia*, 19,746; (15) Rhode Island, 18,841; (18) Pennsylvania, 18,672; (20) Michigan, 18,346; (24) Ohio, 17,473; (30) *Georgia*, 16,944; (32) *Texas*, 16,759; (35) *North Carolina*, 16,203; (37) *Tennessee*, 15,798; (38) *Oklahoma*, 15,444; (42) *South Carolina*, 15,099; (43) *Kentucky*, 14,929; (44)

Alabama, 14,826; (45) *Louisiana,* 14,391; (47) *Arkansas,* 14,218; (49) West Virginia, 13,747; and (50) *Mississippi,* 12,735. The first has been made last and the last first. The top ten rankings were Southern states in 1860. In 1990 only Maryland ranks there, while seven Southern states fall in the last ten. Mississippi's plight is the most dramatic—indeed, from first to dead-last; and South Carolina's plummet from third to forty-second is no less telling.

But to return to the antebellum plantation—what the 1860 statistics show is that Hardy was, from the standpoint of possessions, one of the South's "great planters," if only marginally so. He thus fit into the lower realms of the top class of white Southern society, which today's historians divide into three primary classes: (1) the great planters, (2) the small planters, and (3) the yeoman farmers. To be in the great planter class required a minimum total of forty to fifty slaves and 800 to 1,000 acres of land. Also pertinent in their day were such matters as education, an elegant and finely appointed house, personal style, personal values and morality, subscription to the planter's code of honor, family connections, and civil responsibility. On all these counts, William Eppes Hardy qualified, although in wealth he was at the class's marginal lower reaches.

The 1860 statistics further reveal that as one of the smallest of the great planters, Hardy was doing very well indeed, and that the decade of the 1850s was a very good one for the plantation. The master could now afford to reduce his cultivated land from 1,000 to 600 acres. Accordingly, the number of his cotton bales diminished from 110 to 81 (from 132,000 pounds of raw cotton to 97,200 pounds, or from 44,000 to 32,400 pounds ginned). At 150 to 200 pounds of ginned cotton per acre, his cotton acreage must thus have been about 162 to 216 acres of the 600 improved acres, or about 27 to 36 percent of the total, thus up from the 18 percent of the total in 1850. He therefore reduced his cotton acreage from about 220–293 acres to about 162–216 acres, or by about 26 percent. His corn crop diminished even more dramatically from 2,500 bushels to 200—to less than a tenth of its previous volume, or from 100 acres in 1850 to less than 10 in 1860. His wheat production was cut from 500 to 350 bushels, his rye from 50 to 23, his sweet potatoes from 500 to 200, and his butter from 600 to 500. The number of his hogs declined from 220 to 150; he kept 5 fewer cows, got rid of his sheep and oxen, but increased his blooded horses from 9 to 16 and his mules from 16 to 19. His yield of peas and beans increased from 200 to 300 bushels, his barley from 5 to 20 bushels, his Irish potatoes from 20 to

100 bushels. His oats production remained the same at 500 bushels. He was now planting cane and extracting molasses in larger quantity.

The 1860 census lists no overseer and no Teagle family on the place, as the 1850 had done. The slave population declined by 1 to 45. The total land acreage increased, however, from 1,800 to 2,035, even though the improved acreage fell by 40 percent from 1,000 to 600. All of this is somewhat puzzling at first glance. Why was Hardy taking from 58 to 77 acres, or from 27 to 36 percent of his cotton lands, out of production at a time when cotton was paying a premium, and similarly scaling back other areas of farm activity? Perhaps because he was a wealthy man already and had educated most of his children, he did not need to push the land and its laborers to the limit. Several sons had chosen professions, and the family was certainly wealthy enough to supply its needs. Too, William was a master who foreswore ambition and greed. He was living a good and useful life, did not need to display figures in a bank account or tally sheet to tell him so, and thus needed no more of worldly possessions. His planter's code placed a premium on moderation, simple elegance, and restraint, and discouraged a vulgar display, too often bought at the expense of exploitation—whether in Southern field or Northern factory. As we have seen, from the start one of his mottoes had been the Delphic μηδέν λίαν—"Nothing to Excess." Solid instincts from his family's pioneering past no doubt reinforced his Christian teachings that simplicity, moderation, and humility were traits that ennobled and spoke both of true culture and gentlemanliness.

These surmises about his character and motives are substantiated by his letter to his son Charles Wesley, written 1 September 1854, while Wesley was at the Medical College of Charleston. Let us hear the good planter speak in his own words:

> My dear Son
>
> I sit down from the harvest to enquire after your health and to let you know that if you have any wants from the plantation, to send us word before we begin our trip to Charleston.
>
> The rich bounty of the fields would warm your heart, as they again bear nobly. I trust you are gleaning your own crop of learning and that your toil has equalled that of those hereabouts, in this busy season.
>
> Today finds me thoughtful because it is the 50th anniver-

sary of my birth. I reflect back on half a century of such joys and pains, remember when your mother and I first held you to us, the losses of your dear little brothers and sisters, of my own father who never lived long enough for me to know him, and of my mother, dead before I knew to appreciate her properly well. For all this last, my life has been so blessed with joy in your own dear mother whose smile is to me like the spring rain on the newplanted furrough. I only conclude that I am now at a place and time in life—of accomplishment, satisfaction, and some wisdom, that allows me forebearance. The deeper spirit of things tells me that overmuch and excess of wealth can bear no proper fruit. There are bounds to all things, and especially of man's earthly desiring. I forebear to exert my loyal people any further than is reasonable, for they must have their own freedoms within their bondage. Their liberties are to grow with me as long as they grow in capacity to manage and make use of them. The Soil of your ancestral lands has once again sustained us. We must also cherish and protect it, for from its furroughs we all grow and bear our modest fruit. We owe it our all. Neither must it be pushed to its limits, and must itself have its own freedoms—to lie fallow and rest. For as I grow wiser on the Land, so do I know how close all our fortunes lie with the generous fields with which our good Creator has blessed us. Fifty years has taught me this, if nothing else. God grant us all wisdom in our progress toward a reward that is not in or of this world.

Dear Wesley, though you are preparing to embarque on a useful life of service to your fellow man, never forget what you owe the Soil of Tyger, and I pray you never foreswear Family and all those many who have toiled to give you the privilege that places you there in your schooling. Some of these will require recompense from your maturity, and from your accomplishments, which they themselves are not privileged to attain.

I must see to Jack, for he calls from off the mule at the door—and then back to the fields. All the family send their love. Until we see you,

Your affectionate Pa

The letter speaks for itself. It provides the final measure of the man and of a planting society in its mature leaf.

Squire Hardy was not alone in Carolina in holding this philosophy or putting it into practice. In 1842, some twelve years before Hardy penned his letter to his son, William Gilmore Simms of Woodlands plantation in Barnwell County, South Carolina, addressed a young group of collegians with these wise words:

> We must moderate our desires—restrain our impatience,— learn to respect labor—abridge our propensity to wander [westward], and narrow our ambition as much as possible to the sphere in which our affections should move. We must give up our vague and morbid cravings after a condition which few persons can, at any time, attain. We must put on a more subdued demeanor. We must acquire a temper of more content and cheerfulness. We must concentrate our energies upon the little spot in which we take up our abodes, and, in making that lovely to the mind, we shall discover in it abundant resources to satisfy all the mind's desires.

The ideas here are the same, point by point, as those in Hardy's letter and, moreover, reflect the philosophy that guided the Squire's life— from his refusal to emigrate to western lands for quick wealth, to the moderation of his desires; from his temper of content and cheerfulness to, above all, his concentration of his love and energies on the lands of his fathers—fields that, in effect, as he phrased it, he and his family through the years had "loved into being."

It is unknown why the plantation's black population declined by one from 1850 to 1860. For whatever reason, in 1860 Squire Hardy appears to have been intent on reining in rather than expanding, on scaling down most aspects of his farming endeavor. Still his cotton sales of 81 bales netted him close to $90,000 in today's currency, so he was doing very well indeed. As his letter to his son reveals, not being a greedy man or a man of excess and extremes, he found this sufficient to his purposes.

His plantation ledgers verify the decreased yield in corn and other crops. Here he notes that he is occasionally buying certain items on credit during these years. In 1859 there are purchases of wood (by cart and wagon load), flour, potatoes, corn, oats, wheat, and pickled beef.

These debts were paid off with proceeds from the sale of cotton and other produce.

The 1870 inventory of the plantation reveals the extent of its self-sufficiency. Hardy now had a cane mill, molasses boilers and skimmers, a hominy mill, a gin, a grain thrasher, more blacksmithing tools, 2 "feed cutters," 7 grain cradles, 5 spinning wheels, and a loom. In 1870 there were 10 mules on the place; they were named Dove, Mary, Dick, Pigeon, Gin, Kate, Dennis, George, Colt, and Bill. These were the mainstays of plantation transport and ploughing. For planting, there were the usual hoes (10 in number), shovels, plows, 2 oxyokes, a rake, and a wheelbarrow. For building and furniture making, there were a crosscut saw, foot adze, augers, axes, crowbar, planer, and grindstone. For milk, cream, and butter there were 11 cows, 4 of which were named Boss, Scilla, Liza, and Sallie.

The inventory of the tools of the women's trade was no less full. The plantation kitchen and pantry (which fed at one time a minimum population of fifty-nine) housed a cookstove and "kitchen furniture," a cupboard, pine tables, and a "kitchen table," 5 trays, 4 tubs, 5 cookpots, 6 iron Dutch ovens, 2 spiders for hearth cooking, a fire shovel and tongs, 3 pairs of pothooks, 2 pot lifters, a soap trough, candle molds, boxes, barrels, one-gallon and one-half-gallon pots, a funnel, a ten-gallon keg, 2 casks, 3 troughs, cake pans, cake boxes, 2 stone jugs, a saucepan, a tin water can; a bucket and tub, three smoothing irons, a crumb brush, a grater, a mortar and pestle, teakettles, coffeepots, a coffee urn, a coffee mill, three demijohns, glassware, silver plate, a fireplace trivet, an umbrella, a bow basket, a knifebox, 2 pitchers, tin pans, milk piggins and churns, 4 tin milk buckets, milk strainers and dipper, 2 milk crocks, a milk bowl and 7 milk jars, a sausage cutter and stuffer, 3 lard jars, a scoop, a fish knife, and a "tailor's goose."

On the eve of the war, then, William Eppes Hardy was a most prosperous plantation master. When his blooded bays pulled his buggy from off his ancestral lands into the great world beyond, the men of his day regarded him with respect. His opinions were valued and his vote courted. Ex-senator Robert Moorman (1814–1873), for example, would write William Renwick at Orange Hall instructing him "to spend the day with W. E. Hardy, Esq. and his sons with the view of changing their purpose of voting against [A. C.] Garlington" in an October 1860 election. "I think Dr. [James M.] Eppes, who has lately turned away from [John P.] Kinard, has pretty well turned Esq. Hardy, and know of no man who could more effectually complete the work than yourself." The Hardys, he continues, "are just now considering as to whether they shall vote Kinard or not at all, I hear, except Haywood, who is openly for Garlington." Their votes and support obviously counted in ways that transcended the mere numerical tally.

The good squire owned some of the most valuable land in the state—in fact, in the Seaboard South—had educated his children as befits the young of a family of standing and wealth, had held public office as magistrate during the preceding decade, had been a supporter of the church, and had created and preserved an orderly world in which there was no poverty or material want for those over whom he had control and for whose well-being he was responsible. From all accounts, 1860 found him a happy and contented man, "as much a tease as ever," in the words of his niece at The Oaks, and displaying no great drive for more wealth and power, ambition now being unnecessary for the enjoyment of a healthy agrarian existence. With his family and well-ordered fruitful lands and forests around him, in a "garden" world in which nature came to the very door and in which he witnessed no distressful want, with refined neighbors tried and true for fellowship, and a large extended network of family, it must have been a halcyon age indeed—"blissful but how brief," as another Carolinian of the day expressed it in retrospect. In fine, Hardy was privileged to live in the top ranks of a civilization in which courtly behavior, gentlemanly values, and Christian chivalry more often than not were the ideals for which to strive and were powerful influences that sustained the individuals who shared them.

In 1860, on the eve of war, the young cousins of the Hardy and Douglass families painted, through their letters, a very good picture of how it was to be young in their planter society. The lads were interested in setters and hounds and horses, talked incessantly of breeding dogs with the right stock, and of the skills of this setter "huntress" or of that hound "hero." When away, the sons were always inquiring home about their dogs or how "Pomp comes along in the Partridge line," or directing their father to "have my Mare kept in good fix and attend to my Dogs." As recalled by former slave Milton Marshall of the Burton Maybin place at Maybinton, bird dogs and hounds abounded on all the plantations of the area. And as we have seen, the young fellows learned to be good horsemen at a very early age. The young Hardys, girls and boys, rode their own steeds the three miles to Renwick Academy. As we noted in the previous chapter, Gus Feaster, born in Goshen Hill in 1840, recalled that the little Carlisle lads, Newt and Anderson, did the same: "Young Newt and Anderson . . . went to school every day it was in session. Dey had dey own hosses and dey rid 'em to school. When dey come home, dey would throw de reins to me and John, and us took dem hosses and rub dem down and feed 'em." According to a list of pupils made by schoolmaster Renwick, Newt and Anderson were indeed at the Academy in April 1849, thus making Feaster nine years old if this was the particular school year of his recollection.

Before they had real horses, the lads would ride each other. Former slave George Briggs recalled this play-practice on a Cross Keys plantation: "When us was real little, we played hoss. . . . Cheney Briggs [the master's son] was our play hoss. His brother Henry was the wagoner, and I was de mule. Henry was little, and he rid our backs sometimes. Henry rid old man Sam [Briggs, the master] sometimes; and old man Sam jes' holler and haw-haw at us chilluns. Dis was in such early childhood dat it is not so I can exactly map out de exact age us was den; anyway, from dis we rid de gentle hosses and mules." It is no wonder that the boys of the neighborhood grew up to be very fine horsemen. One of two antebellum toys dug from the yard of the Hardy plantation in 1990 was a porcelain horse.

There were popular racetracks at Goshen Hill, Maybinton, and Santuc to allow indulgence of their interest in the sport. Famous races were held at all three in this twelve-mile radius. Often barbecues accompanied them. At Goshen Hill, alcohol from the rows of barrels that sat in front of the store at Orange Hall flowed in abundance to refresh the racegoers.

For the young ladies of the family, it was a world of carriage rides in silk chemises they had made over the winter in their sewing closets, of "strawberry season, when we feasted our fill" on the ripe red fruit from the cool morning fields, of having the famous artist Scarborough stay with them while painting portraits of Grandmother Hardy, and of big Fourth of July barbecues where the men could get up a horse race or a fox hunt, listen to political speeches, drink moderately (usually), watch the slaves dance the buck-and-pigeon-wing to fiddle and banjo on an improvised platform near the barbecue tables, and swap yarns and knowledge of the crops, while the women would show the handiwork of their needles in summer frocks and chemises, exchange stories of the household, and stroll the grounds and gardens. It seemed there were no great cares for the young women like Cousin Garrie Douglass beyond being frightened when a baggage car caught fire on one of her railroad junkets, or having trouble learning to operate a new sewing machine, or worrying whether or not the peach and plum trees brought into full bloom by the welcome but premature spring would be killed by another frost and thus, as she put it, "deprive me of a good many luxuries." It was a time of reading *Beulah,* "the new novel of Augusta Evans of Mobile," and of recommending, "If you have not read it, I advise you to get it, for I know it will please you." For upcountry planter gentry, these were quiet years of content, a placid and gentle era, agitated only by political ferment.

It was also a world of large family gatherings and of Saturday and Sunday afternoon picnics by the Tyger. In 1860 one young lady of the family asked another if their valley were not truly becoming a "Pick Nick country." Then in September it was time for trips to Chick Springs in Spartanburg, Warm Springs near Asheville, or to the mountains of Flat Rock. Throughout the seasonal activity, there were always the courtships and much talk and rumor of marriages to be, of who came to church in his new buggy, and of how he acted and of what figure he cut. There were also the constants of flirtations with the young men and the maidenly confidences one to another. One friend the young cousins liked especially well because she was "a good-hearted girl" and had style and spirit besides. She had gotten a new carriage for herself, and they admired her independence. "Meg [Worthy] has bought a new carriage," one wrote. "If she comes up [to Spartanburg] for Commencement, I have no doubt but what Jim Williams will be very willing to ride with her. You remember how very much disappointed he was last year." One male friend disappointed them by his "lack of temperance." He had gotten a little loud from drinking and became somewhat too "exuberant" at a church outing.

Running through all these letters was proof of an abiding, solid family loyalty. Cousins were as close as brothers and sisters and there were many of them. In early March 1860 Miss Garraphelia Douglass, nineteen, wrote her nineteen-year-old cousin Dickie Hardy, then at work as a clerk in Spartanburg, a flirtatious note of innocent cousinly closeness, filling him in on what was happening at home, and making not-so-veiled attempts at matchmaking. She had just described him as "lively," "playful," and "teasing," like her Uncle Billy, his father. She continued:

We have beautiful weather at present. Everything has the appearance of Spring's approach. Your father's family were all quite well. . . . You said in your last letter to Sall [her sister] that the height of your ambitiousness is to say "Hurrah for Christmas" [when vacation will bring him home]. I take it you must be very low down. Has Miss Hattie rejected you? You must remember, that you will have to get the key of your heart back from me, before you offer it to another. You gave it to me when you were down. I think your heart must be very small if that key can unlock it. Have you got any lemon candy? When you get some, remember me. Miss Meg Worthy has not gone to Charleston yet. You had better come down and interfere with that trip. . . . Jim Oxner was at Church last Sunday in his fine new buggy. I wish you could have seen. I understand that Mr. Sondley is to be married soon to Miss Carrie Smith of Spartanburg. He and Onie Gilliam have returned from the West. . . . Our Sunday school will commence as soon as the weather is pleasant. Mr. Morgan Dawkins is teaching this year at the Renwick Academy. Have you had the pleasure of an acquaintance with Miss Pembleton? I would not be surprised if she did not fall in love with you yet. Sister received your letter last Saturday. I am much obliged for that beautiful Valentine you sent me.

Hardys and Douglasses spent much ink in arranging trips to family or from family, trips of a day, a week, or weeks. Then there were the arrangements for family travel together "on the cars"—to the springs or "Pine Woods" for health, to Spartanburg, Columbia, and Charleston, and to Asheville, Flat Rock, and Salem, North Carolina. At Salem Academy, Garrie's sisters (like their Cousin Mira) were in school. The young cousins at The Oaks and the Hardy plantation went religiously to commencements there, as at the woman's college in Spartanburg where friends and family were studying. "How was your May party" at the Spartanburg Female College, one asked. "Who was your queen?" Then a note about the fire there and the humorous comment that "I expect the students at Wofford had a good deal of fun in assisting the girls in removing their things." Choosing proper colleges and academies was of much import to parents who squired their charges hither and yon.

For the young gentlemen, their object in writing the ladies was to be entertaining and sincere. They wrote often and well, and the students expressed the usual gladness at the prospect of holiday or graduation. From Chapel Hill, Cousin Jimmie Douglass wrote his sister at The Oaks that classes at the university would soon be over, "Hurrah!" He missed hearth, home, sisters, cousins, the plantation fields, and Uncle Peter, the black servant closest to him. Jimmie has had good friends at college, like Henry Jones of Greenwood plantation in Georgia and the son of one of the wealthiest men in that state; or Pierce Mason Butler of Edgefield and Louisiana, and R. B. Adams, son of a planter in York, South Carolina. Jones particularly was a lively friend with a flair for the gallant, especially where the ladies were concerned; and with him and Adams, Jimmie joined Chi Psi fraternity, to which he was devoted.

In 1860, among the young people, very little was said of politics; and no mention was made of the great storm clouds of war on the horizon that were to buffet all their lives, and bring a swift end to this era of strawberry feasts, picnics, summer barbecues, horse races, carriage rides, and May parties. "Rides on the cars" would soon have a new meaning and with new destinations, no longer to schools, academies, the springs, and the Pine Woods, but to the battle lines of Virginia. The very letters themselves, in less than a year, would often be feared for the messages of death they too often contained.

11

The Plantation Neighborhood

An agricultural country leaves few monuments but moral ones.
—William Gilmore Simms, "The Good Farmer" (1841)

LISLES (LYLES) HOUSE AND PLANTATION

Less than a quarter-mile from the Hardy dwelling, and thus in physical terms its closest neighbor, was the Lisles house, a true pioneer home that predated the coming of the Hardys by several decades. The Historic American Building Survey fixes its construction date as around 1760. The Lisles lands stretched to the Tyger on the north and were bounded on the south by the Hardy plantation. After 1844 the house and its 486 acres were acquired by William Eppes Hardy and made a part of his holdings.

The Lisleses had much in common with their Hardy neighbors. Both families hailed from the Old Dominion, fought in the Revolution as Patriots, and became members of Ebenezer Methodist Church. Pioneer John Lisles Sr. served in the Snow Campaign of 1775–1776. He became colonel of a regiment of militia and saw action in most of the battles of the state before the siege of Charleston. Before the war's end, the colonel resigned because of his age, but his nephew James Lisles succeeded him in command. James's five brothers, Arromanus, William (known as Big Bill), Ephraim Jr. (known as Big Eph), Henry, and John, all served in the American army. During the course of the war, Colonel Patrick Ferguson and the 71st British Regiment encamped at James's plantation. The British, in marching from Camden, crossed the Broad at Shirer's Ferry, made their way to the plantation of David Hentz at Heller's Creek, where they camped—then moved north by crossing the Enoree at Kelly's Ford, before sojourning at the Lisleses' by the Tyger. Williamson Lisles, the youngest of Colonel John Lisles's brothers, also served as captain of a company of state militia, resigning in 1780, like his brother John, owing to age.

The story is told that when the army of Lord Rawdon pursued Nathaniel Greene on his retreat from Ninety Six, they encamped about a week at Colonel Glenn's, later known as Brazzelman's Mills, on the Enoree. Marching through the Tyger valley to Lisles Ford, the British plundered everything along the way. The widow Maybin at present-day Maybinton was robbed of all food and her one horse. One soldier who visited her cabin found a piece of homespun in her loom, cut it out, and ran off with it. Later on, when Little Eph Lisles met up with him, he drubbed the soldier severely and restored the cloth to his neighbor. Mrs. Maybin's husband William had died for the Patriot cause in the war. The Maybins had immigrated from County Antrim, Ireland, via Charleston before 1771 and had just built their cabin and set up a store and tavern on this main backcountry wagon road when the war broke out.

In January 1781 Matthew Maybin, Little Eph Lisles, and others of the Tyger valley "left their homes to unite with Daniel Morgan" in the famous Battle of Cowpens. This important Patriot victory sealed the doom of the British in upcountry Carolina and made American independence possible.

But all this occurred before the Hardys had begun their trek southward. The Hardys were fighting the same revolutionary fight, however, in Virginia and would thus have experiences to share when they did finally meet on Carolina soil. John Lisles, who had himself come from the Old Dominion about thirty years earlier, was a truer pioneer. He took up the land in the teeth of Cherokee scalpings and a roaring, howling wilderness. In a sense, he paved the way for the Hardys, making life easier and safer for them. Having done so, many of his clan then pushed further west into the wilds of the uncharted frontier just as the Hardys were arriving. John Lisles Sr., however, remained behind.

Like the Hardys, the Lisles family brought slaves with them from the Old Dominion. Eison Lyles, born a slave around 1845, remembered that his parents, Aaron and Betsey Lyles, had come from Virginia, brought by their white folks "from Virginny to Maybinton." He continued, "My name was down in the Old Lyles Bible, but it done burnt up now, and Miss Ellen Lyles done dead and ain't none of my set of Lyles livin' dat I know the whar'abouts of."

During the second generation (and about 1820–1830) the Lisles name changed to Lyles. John Lyles Jr. (born 1776) married a Tyger River neighbor, Mary Sims; and when he died in December 1843, he willed the Lyles house and plantation to his son Thomas J. Lyles (26 May 1808–8 September 1879), a physician living in Maybinton village. Some time shortly thereafter William Eppes Hardy bought the house and 486 acres that adjoined him to the north and ran down to the river. It was this Lyles land that figured into the 1850 census increase of Hardy lands to 1,800 acres. The Lyles domicile itself may have functioned as a tenant or overseer's dwelling. When William Eppes died in 1870, he willed the property to his wife Catharine and his son William Dixon Hardy. In 1897, 267 acres of this land and the dwelling were resold again to the Lyles family, who thus returned to the old homeplace. The land still remains with the family; but the house was disassembled and removed to Glenn Springs in 1982. In 1996, its double-pen broad-ax hewn log barn was sold for its wood. Only the house's granite gateposts and a pile of brick from the chimney remain to mark the site.

ORANGE HALL

In the nineteenth century, the lower Tyger valley was a land of many fine plantations. The Hardy estate was an early one and one of the largest on the river, but did not go unchallenged as the place of "highest society." As the Lisles home was one of the most venerable simple dwellings, the oldest and most famous Great House and indeed the major landmark of the land between Tyger and Enoree was Orange Hall, located three miles to the northeast of the Hardys along the Old State Road. This was a massive brick mansion built in the Georgian style of English and Irish country estates.

Orange Hall's builder, John A. Rogers Sr., like the neighboring Maybins and Renwicks, was a Kings Creek Scots-Irish Covenanter Presbyterian who came directly to Carolina from County Antrim in the north of Ireland around 1773. He brought with him a wife and several children, including a son John, who was born in Ireland on 4 September 1764. The Rogerses hailed from the village of Monaghan and came to Carolina seeking religious freedom. John Sr. soon amassed a goodly fortune in colonial America by buying and reselling huge tracts of land. When the country pushed west, he speculated in those territories and made large profits. At Orange Hall he was also a planter on a large scale. The plantation was so named because the family was descended from the royal house of Orange. The family coat of arms bore a crest from this royal house.

The date Rogers built his home is subject to debate. Some say 1774, others 1796 or shortly after. A house was indeed there by 1818, when it appears on a plat map. This structure is designated Orange Hall on the Robert Mills survey of 1820 for his atlas of 1825. It faced west from its rise along the east side of the road that led from Charleston to Buncombe County, North Carolina; its back lands ran to the Tyger. No doubt it was an eighteenth-century house, judging from the detailed descriptions that have come down to us. Tradition places it there during the Revolution, when its cupola was said to have been used to view the skirmishes between Tories and Patriots; and this certainly may have been true.

From all the descriptions that we have of it, this dwelling was truly a "great mansion house." It had two full stories and a garret. It was made of brick and trimmed with carved granite. On one end there were two chimneys, one at each corner of the house, thus uniquely and "quaintly" placed, as one account puts it. The other end had either one or two exterior chimneys. Some say that the house resembled the old Riser Brick-House that still stands west of Whitmire on the Joanna Road.

There were three rooms and a "hall room" on each floor. To one side of the hall was a single room 18 feet square; to the other side there were smaller rectangular rooms, each having a fireplace on an outside corner. The downstairs great room was a formal drawing room; the upstairs one, probably a music room or another formal parlor, as in the townhouses of Charleston. In that city, formal entertainments were usually held on the second floor. At Orange Hall this large room was also used as a meeting place for the Masonic Lodge, said to be the first outside Charleston. In 1824 a letter mentions a detached kitchen. From this outbuilding, food was brought in platters to the dining room of the Great House. The top of the house was crowned by the previously mentioned wooden cupola, which was partially inset and protected by the roof. Because of the house's high positioning, it provided a particularly fine view of the plantation fields, the Tyger, and its valley.

The lumber of the house was cut on the place, sent to Columbia by flatboat down the Broad to be dressed, then returned and seasoned in the yard for a time before building. The usual practice in the area was to keep the green lumber for the period of a year before it was used for construction. The brick was said to be made in the great kiln on the Burrell Chick Quarter Place plantation a quarter of a mile south along the State Road, where Chick's and Rogers's slaves worked together to form them from the red clay dug from the site. One of the last residents of the Chick plantation recalls that "old people said that there was an old brick mill about a mile back behind the Chick house." This corroborates the earlier information that the bricks of Orange Hall were made there. "Brick tiling," however, was said to have been imported from Ireland. John Renwick, who lived in the Chick house as a child, recalls that such brick tiling also faced the Chick plantation fireplace. He surmises that this may have been the way such tiling was used at Orange Hall. That Rogers imported at least some building materials for the dwelling is likely accurate because he continued to be a frequent traveler to Ireland and an importer of mercantile goods from England and Scotland through the port of Charleston, as recorded in his plantation ledger and daybook of 1821. The tiling is said to have been brought from Charleston up the Broad River to Lyles Ford, from where it then came to the house by wagon. This was indeed likely the typical means by which heavy cargo from Europe and Charleston came to this section of the Tyger valley. Before the railroads came in the 1850s, the alternative would have been an arduous trek by wagon up the State Road, a trip of more than a week.

All doors and windows were faced with carved granite taken from the James Hill quarry at present-day Hillside plantation in Fish Dam Township (now Carlisle), thirteen miles across the Tyger. All the mantles were 6 feet high with narrow mantle shelves. The openings of the fireplaces measured 5 feet all around. The descriptions of these features do indeed sound Georgian, not Federal, again pointing to an eighteenth-century construction date, although such mantles were still being used into the 1800s where the architectural styles were lagging behind the current fashions.

An old marble milepost reading "46 m. C.S.C." stood at Orange Hall by the old coach road and told the traveler he was forty-six miles from Columbia. By the nineteenth century, Orange Hall had become a well-known landmark among the travelers from the mountains to the sea. It and the Chick Quarter Place were said to have been regular watering and stagecoach stops.

John A. Rogers Jr. became master of Orange Hall on the death of his father in late 1822. In that year, the new master, who had been born in Monaghan, Ireland, was sixty years old. Many years before, he had married Rosannah Glenn (14 January 1778–6 May 1841), daughter of the David Glenn who had fought at King's Mountain. She was called Rosey. The couple had several beautiful daughters who were soon to marry neighboring Kings Creek Scots-Irish Covenanter Presbyterians of the Renwick and Beard families. John Jr.'s sister Jane (1773–1847), also born in Monaghan before the family emigrated, had already married into the Renwick clan.

Although both John Rogers Sr. and Jr. were said to have "loved the virgin beauty and freedom of the hills of Carolina, yet their hearts yearned for ole Ireland." As a result, one or the other sailed there every two years, while also delivering Orange Hall cotton to Liverpool in person. They stayed at least six months at a time. One visit extended to nearly two years. Rogers Jr. was in Ireland, in fact, when he received news of the birth of his daughter Rosannah Pattan Rogers on 1 January 1812. She was named for her godmother, Rosannah Pattan, John Rogers's hostess on his stays in Ireland. Mrs. Pattan was so pleased with the honor of a little namesake in Carolina that she and her family shopped for gifts for the child, one of which was an oval gold watch to be worn on a chain. They also had a pianoforte shipped with Rogers for her. Rosannah Rogers grew up to marry William Renwick, headmaster of Renwick Academy, and the piano remained at Orange Hall when Renwick became its plantation master. By 1936 the piano was in the home of Mrs. J. B. Trail of Roebuck, South Carolina, and the watch was slated to be given to Rosannah Pattan Rogers Renwick at her graduation.

By the 1820s the Rogers estate had grown into a very prosperous cotton plantation, complete with its own cotton gin on the place. This was located off the Crenshaw Ford Road (later called Peters Creek Road) and appears on an 1818 plat. The tract immediately surrounding the Great House numbered a thousand acres. To the north, the adjoining plat contained 992 acres and shows another house located near the banks of the Tyger. This second tract was designated the "upper place" of Orange Hall or "Orange Hall upper place."

An 1837 entry in the Orange Hall plantation ledger corroborates this division when the plantation master records that he had turned 5 sows, 12 shoats, and 20 pigs out "at the plantation upper place" and kept 1 sow and 7 pigs "at home." Sketchy entries in the plantation ledger provide fleeting glimpses of the family activity at Orange Hall from 1821 to 1838. In 1824 Rogers made an entry for 61 bushels of wheat raised at the plantation, 2 of which would be "put up" for seed. By 17 November 1824 he could tally a total of 314 barrels of sound corn and 212 barrels of damaged corn raised on the place in that year. Rogers noted that he is cutting "cotton bags" for the plantation and sending four of them "to the plantation to sun the wheat." This bagging he had just imported from Liverpool via the port of Charleston. In the same year he reports payment of $252.30 to Charles Lucker and Archibald Armstrong for "overseeing" the plantation. In 1828 Rogers paid $225 to Lucker alone. He also promised another $3.00 per cotton bale over a minimum of 60 bales raised under his care. This likely tells us that Rogers expected at least 60 bales as a fair yield for his acreage, and anything over that yield would come from Lucker's expert management. This method of giving incentives to his overseer was probably an effective one for realizing profits. In 1829 Lucker still held his position, but there is no record of his wages.

The Orange Hall plantation ledger lists the cultivated acreage for 1827 as follows:

In Corn:

Low grounds	30 acres
Long field	10 acres
Orchard field	10 acres
New ground last year	14 acres
At home	10 acres
	74 acres

In Cotton:

Low ground	30 acres
Banister field	14 acres
Large field next the mill	20 acres
Buck field	18 acres
House field	10 acres
Other fields	14 acres
	106 acres

The final notation is for "fourteen grown hands at 18 acres to the hand." At this rate, 252 acres could be worked. The corn-cotton total of 180 acres thus leaves 72 acres of the 252 possible to other crops like the wheat mentioned earlier. (The fourteen field hands are designated as "grown." Likely there were also younger hands involved who were not expected to do this full measure of work.)

This document provides a good look at certain aspects of the workings of the plantation. It is very significant for a number of reasons. Mills's *Statistics* of 1826 judges that 250 pounds of ginned cotton was a maximum yield for the county. Rogers was therefore growing near Mills's maximum figure on his acreage, for 60 bales (at 400 pounds per bale) represents 24,000 pounds of ginned cotton, and the yield of 106 acres was therefore 226.4 pounds per acre. This figure presumes that only the minimum 60 bales were grown. If the overseer exceeded the amount and produced more than his minimum, he then realized or bettered the mark deemed possible by Mills, a real likelihood considering the richness of the Tyger valley and the wise farm practices of its families.

That Orange Hall planted about three-quarters as much corn acreage as cotton in 1827 corresponds to what we find at the Hardy plantation as late as 1850 and 1860. There was much diversity and no monopoly of cotton on the land at either farm. The other interesting fact that emerges from these figures is that this amount of work was performed by an overseer and fourteen field hands, each hand set the task of cultivating 18 acres of corn, cotton, wheat, and other crops. This points to Rogers's possible use of a sort of "task" system of slave responsibility, and possibly the method used by other planters in the area, including the Hardys. This, of course, cannot be said with assurance; but that a variation of the "task" system of the Lowcountry might be followed in upcountry South Carolina is a strong possibility, given the close ties between the locales and the proof of the Orange Hall notation of acreage allotted per "grown" hand. Ex-slaves of this area also spoke of being given "extra long tasks" as punishment for theft, and of "light tasks" while they were young.

That Orange Hall had 106 acres in cotton and 74 in corn in 1827 shows the plantation to be a relatively flush concern for its decade and among the larger cotton enterprises in the Upcountry. From its bounty, the master could afford to send his daughters Eliza and Rosannah to the women's academy at Salem, North Carolina. The family obviously put a high premium on education for both its men and women. On 12 December 1823 Rogers and his wife sent from Orange Hall to their eleven- and fourteen-year-old daughters a "bundle" containing "fine stockings," calico, "frock patterns," and a letter. These were delivered "by the politeness of" neighbor and friend Colonel Benjamin H. Maybin, who was taking his own young daughter to school at Salem. (As we have seen, in the 1850s the Hardy and Douglass neighbors were also to send their daughters there.) Rogers's epistle exhorted his daughter to pray, "keep holy the Lord's day, and also to avoid all vain and loose or proud company. . . . It will be highly pleasing to your parents and all other friends that you return Improved & Polished in your minds and actions. . . . Make high leaps and learn fast and try in all things to excell." Rosannah was later to marry William Renwick, himself a well-educated man from South Carolina College. As we have seen, Renwick's family, like the Rogerses, had also come to Carolina from County Antrim and perhaps in their company, the Renwicks having been banished from Ireland for their dissenting Covenanter Presbyterian faith. It was Rosannah's husband who would establish the academy adjacent to the Orange Hall store during the 1840s—the school where the Hardy children would begin their educations.

John Rogers Jr.'s complete letter to his daughters reveals much about the social milieu of Orange Hall in 1823, and shows its new master to be a religious, practical, common-sensical, and caring father. He had just lost his own father the year before.

> To Miss Eliza and Rosanah Rogers, Salem, N. Carolina
> Favoured by the Politeness of Col. Benjamin Mebon [Maybin]
>   One small bundle & letter
>
>   Orange Hall December 12th 1823
> My dear little Daughters, Eliza & Rosana
>   This will be handed you by Colonel Mebon [Maybin] and his daughter for Salem, and I hope it will find you both well as it leaves all here at present [except] only your grandmother who still continues in a low state and cannot be long in this Valley of tears. We have looked long for a letter from you, but as yet, none has come to hand but one from Mr. Reciel your Principle Man dated the 1st of November, giving us an account of your welfare and progress in your learning which give much comfort and satisfaction to all friends but more particularly to your aged parents. We hope to have a letter from you both by Col. Mebon to know how you are

situated & satisfied; and should you have any Little wants let us know them before we go out in the Spring.

There has died several People since you left home. Some I mention [:] John Moreton, David Priest, John Stewart, Edward Crowfield, and Mrs. Herndon with many more I cannot mind. I hope my dear Children we will have a letter from you every month in future, and I request and beseech you both to mind my last request at parting: Viz. to mind secret prayer and keep holy the Lord's day, and also to avoid all vain and loose or proud company—giving the morning and evening to God who Justly claims the same, and all the rest of your precious time which will be short, to your own Improvements, seeing it is yourselves alone can be benefitted thereby, yet it will be highly pleasing to your parents and all other friends that you return Improved & Polished in your Minds and Actions so as to pass through the world as Strangers and Pilgrims to a heavenly country which is far better.—Should you not yet have got Filonalls for undercoats, get what will be necessary and wear them till the cold weather is gone—we send you a couple of Frock patterns—and be sure to let us know of any other little matters you stand in need of or would wish to have.—All friends desire to be remembred to you, particularly your Grandmother and Uncle David Glen's family, Mr. Lyons & your Sister also.

Your Brother James has been here and is at present in Columbia; and David is here now but starts back to York in 2 or 3 days—You will find folded up in the callicoe 2 pair fine stockings and seeing you have so favourable an opportunity, we shall look for a letter from you both as Col Mebon will stay 2 or 3 days.—May saving and divine Grace and the blessings of a Father and Mother be with you both my dear Children; and that you be fitted and prepared for the full Enjoyment of the heavenly & Eternal State is the wish and desire of your Loving parents—

John & Rosey M. Rogers

P.S. Take care to keep yourselves warm with good shoes and stockings during the winter.

N.B. Make high Leaps and Learn fast and try in all things to excell.

The penmanship in the letter is superb—in fact, among the most beautiful I have witnessed in American documents of the era, thus reflecting a superior education. Unfortunately, this is the only letter to survive from Rogers's hand—passed down to us by Rosannah Renwick's descendants.

Another letter to young Rosannah and Eliza while they were at Salem the following year (1824) stated that their father was traveling in England and Ireland. He was to be written in care of Boyce & Johnson, likely merchants from whom Rogers stocked the store at Orange Hall with imported china and other goods. This letter, written by Rosannah's brother-in-law, James R. Lyons, the husband of her sister Sarah Rogers Lyons, has a vignette of a dramatic event that has just occurred at Orange Hall. On 3 August 1824 Lyons wrote from there, where he and his wife were living with his Rogers in-laws:

> Dear Rosannah & Eliza
>
> I recd. your very kind and friendly address of June 17th in due time—which reached us in health. And have withheld my answer awaiting an event in the family, which we anticipated a few weeks to bring about—
>
> Not until Saturday morning 24 July did Sarah enable me with much pleasure to present you that angelic gift I promised you.
>
> He is a fine large fellow indeed. I am flattered he is equaled by few, and excelled by none. Since his birth Sarah and him have enjoyed perfect health. I have not named him yet.
>
> With a high sense of gratification we can inform you of the reception of a letter from your Father (from last mail dated Liverpool May 23d, 1824). He stated he arrived there on 18th after a rough passage of 30 days—He made sail to the East of Ireland in 18 days. But was blown again to sea by a violent N. East wind lasting 12 days. "And though it was Summer, I have never had so cold and rough a passage not even in winter at any time before."
>
> He expected in two days from the date of his letter to take the steamboat for Dublin. Also stated if we will write and direct to the care of Boyce and Johnson, he will get it on the return of Capt. Paw, the bearer of this. And anticipates a

return to America with Capt. P. of the *Mary Catherine,* the gentleman he went with. Your Mother speaks of writing.

The Lord in the plenitude of his wisdom has many means of visitation to the frail mortals of the earth. On Friday, 30th July, about 1 o'clock P.M., the nearest lumbardy Poplar to the house of the three standing between the kitchen and dwelling, was shivered by a tremendous peal of lightning. Fan and Gabe at the time was passing from the house to the kitchen, each with a plate in their hands to bring in dinner. Fan, who was within 3 or 4 feet of the tree when it was struck, was killed for a space of half an hour to 3/4. When by a copious application of cold water life was restored. She has not since been able to do anything for the searing wound the lightning gave her. It commenced under the right cheek and continued down her side, in places burnt or crisped to the size of my hand. Gabe experienced nothing more than an electrickal shock which brought him down. He was up immediately and ran off.

Sarah and the child was lying in the room near to the tree on the bed but received no injury. Your Mother, in the hall room, felt sensibly the electricity. Camp-Meeting began on Thursday last and ended on Monday. About 24 confessed conviction and joined the Church—Nancy Anderson died of the nervous fever about 6 weeks since.

Write as soon as you rec. this. Numerous reports are in circulation that one or other are dead. We hope the contrary, but are anxious till we know the certainty.

Mother, Sarah, and son join me in love to you both, etc.

Jas. R. Lyons

This letter reveals that in 1824 the house had the usual detached kitchen and that the family ate dinner about one o'clock, after the servants brought plates kept in the dining room to receive the food that then was served back to the Great House.

Orange Hall, like the Hardy plantation, also shows self-sufficiency. On its 2,000 acres, cotton was both planted and ginned. Hogs were raised, as were cattle, horses, sheep, wheat, and corn. There was a mill for grinding flour and meal. It is significant to note that Rogers even managed to grow a token 2 pounds of rice in 1860, not too common an event this far inland. In 1831 Rogers mentions hiring a laborer to do smith work "at my shop," thus showing a forge and blacksmithing activity on the place. By 1838 he had acquired a slave named Vol to work as smithy. There was also a "coal kiln" in operation in 1831. Further, as early as the year 1820, John Jr. had been operating a lucrative plantation store and tavern (presumably, both in the same structure) to serve both travelers along the coach road and the farmers and smaller planters of the area from Goshen Hill to the Enoree River.

The tavern and store were of eighteenth-century origin, perhaps even dating from the Revolutionary era. It was constructed of local fieldstone in the manner of mid-eighteenth-century upcountry Carolina and appears on the old maps and plats as the Stone House or Stone Tavern. It may have served as the Rogerses' or another pioneer family's original house in the earliest days of settlement. The structure was located across the coach road from Orange Hall near the 46th milepost, and at the T intersection of the coach road and the Crenshaw Ford Road (now called Peters Creek Road) leading to the Hardy plantation.

This stone tavern sold its grog (a mixture of rum and water) but, like most upcountry taverns, specialized in corn whiskey, made at its own distillery on the place. An 1818 plat of Orange Hall, in fact, shows a distillery at the head of the creek that flows into Dick Creek, a tributary of the Tyger. Grog and whiskey were popular commodities in 1820. From 1821 to 1836, brandy, whiskey, gin, Jamaica rum, cordials, bottled wine, "cherry bounce," and homemade whiskey continued to be dispensed with regularity by the pint, quart, and gallon. But by 1821 the tavern had become more pronouncedly a general store selling an amazing variety of goods. This shift likely indicates the passing of a "rougher" frontier society. Rogers sold sugar by the pound, cheese, vinegar, spices, raisins by the keg, Irish potatoes, coffee, salt, tobacco, pipes, and cakes of scented soap. His cloth and sewing goods inventory included cambric, silk, bombazine, bombardelle, muslin, "superfine casimere," corduroy, white flannel, yellow flannel, Scotch plaids, shirting, brown linen, brown Holland cloth, corduroy velvet, silk velvet, and velvet ribbon. There were also calico in an array of prints and colors, plaid homespun, fustian, coat lining, "Tabinott" cloth, lace, silk cord, silk in skeins, buttons, silk buttons, pantaloon buttons, needles, pins, scissors, thread, and patterns for jackets, coats, riding habits, robes, and frocks. These were all imported from the British Isles. The imported ready-mades included cashmere shawls, silk shawls, silk handkerchiefs, "lamb's wool socks," buckskin suspenders, and slippers. Then there were various items like spectacles, lampblack, paint, and indigo dye by the pound. There were saddles, bridles, and cart wheels. Household furnishings included glass lamps, bedstraw cots, washstands, rugs, looking glasses, and printed table covers. Rogers carried guns, toys, watches, inkstands, paper by the quire, *Crooke's Almanac,* schoolbooks, hymnbooks, blank books, and other books, razors, razor "stones," shaving boxes, shaving brushes, shaving soap, and blankets (a very popular item imported from Liverpool). For the farmer, there were hoes and cotton bagging (imported from Paisley in Scotland). Hardware included nails, door locks, chains, padlocks, and keys. He carried a variety of spoons, tablespoons, dessert spoons, forks, and table knives.

Perhaps Orange Hall's most popular items were dishes and glassware of various sorts. From 1821 to 1836 Rogers sold a great quantity and tremendous variety of them—all imported from England. They included fine china: plates, cups, saucers, bowls, and pitchers. Blue Willow dishes and plates, designated as both "large" and "small," were among his best-selling items. The "large" may have been what the people of those days called chargers. "Embossed purple plates," "figured" plates, and "printed and flowered" plates were popular fancy wares. These were likely transfer ware. Both blue and red feather-edged pearlware plates (large and small), "figured" red feather-edged plates, and blue feather-edged dishes and "deep dishes" were favorites. The store also sold "copper [luster?] plates," cake plates, coffeepots, teapots, "blue basins," cutglass salt cellars, mugs, goblets, decanters, gilt tumblers, "lustre" (lusterware) pitchers, china pitchers, common pitchers, flowerpots (big and small), sugar dishes, cream pots, mustard pots, butter pots, butter plates, milk pots, bowls, chamber pots, pickling casks, and jugs, among numerous other items. Other frequent sellers were knives of various sorts, including pocketknives and "Sportsman's Knives." For malaria Rogers kept Lee's Fever and Ague Drops. His own overseer, Lucker, was a one-time purchaser of this cure in 1828. We are immensely fortunate to have Rogers's Orange Hall ledger, 1821–1836, which records all items sold at the store, and from which the preceding list has been assembled.

It is here in the ledger that we learn that both Rogers Senior and Junior imported their goods from Liverpool and Paisley. The goods they ordered came as ballast into the port of Charleston, and the ships then returned to Liverpool with their holds full of cotton for the factories of northern England. Brick, building stone, mantles, china, ironstone dishes, glassware, blankets, brass and iron locks, and other heavy items were preferred ballast to the South.

An entry for late 1824 tells us that Rogers paid $4.50 for "Freight from England on 1 crate of ware and blankets," 50 cents for "Landing and Draying the Crate in Charleston," $2.00 for "Freight to Columbia," and $2.00 freight "Up to the Country." He also noted that a 25 percent duty was paid on the crate of "crockery & blankets" at the Charleston Custom House. Interestingly, it cost exactly the same amount for sea passage of the crate to Charleston as it did to bring it from the docks to Union County. In 1823 Rogers paid William W. Glenn of Newberry $375.00 to bring a large shipment of goods from the Charleston wharves. This was a very large sum and must have been for a big shipment. At $4.50 per crate, this figures to be around 80 crates. During the 1820s the volume of dishes sold was very high.

As his ledger tells us, Rogers sold most of his merchandise during the months of December, January, and February. This was true for two reasons. First, the cotton ships that sailed into Charleston brought this merchandise as ballast; and as they were docking in time for the cotton harvest shipment, they began arriving in December, thus making the goods available for transport upcountry. Second, planters were selling their crop in December and would know how much extra money they would have to spend on such "niceties." That all of this happened at Christmas in time for Christmas giving made it doubly convenient for the planter to bring home his Orange Hall purchases. For the smaller planters and farmers who could not often go to Columbia or Charleston to visit the shops, Orange Hall was indeed a "Christmas convenience." As we have seen at the Hardy plantation, in a good year, Christmas and New Year's were very joyful times of completion and great cause for celebration. The store at Orange Hall would have been especially busy and cheerful during this season, and many of the men's cheeks no doubt glowed a little redder than usual with its grog.

Before 1821 some of the house and hardwares at the Hardy plantation may have come from the store at Orange Hall. Certainly the number of shards of Blue Willow, transfer ware, flower-decorated dishes, and red, green, and blue feather-edged dishes found on the plantation grounds today must suggest so; but the only purchase recorded as made by the plantation master during 1821–1836 is for Thomas Hardy Jr. on 17 April 1832, and this was for 4¹/₂ yards of cotton bagging. Squire William's brother James F. E. Hardy, however, purchased materials for a corduroy frock coat, buckskin suspenders, a pipe, and a pint of cordial on 19 December 1821; then on 20 December a knife, another pint of cordial, a jacket "shape" (or pattern), a yard of lining, a quire of paper, a schoolbook, and two sets of china (some of these items no doubt gifts); then another pint of cordial on 24 December, and on Christmas day itself two half-pints of whiskey, a half-pint of cordial, and a "fine shawl" (at $1.50) and two pounds of sugar "for Negroe named Grief." On 29 December he bought a knife, cordial, and three yards of "Teap," a loosely woven fabric, usually of cotton. On 30 December he ended the year with an intriguing purchase of two birds, no doubt for a young belle of the area. William's other brother, Hamlin Hardy, just establishing his new household, purchased on 28 December 1828 a set of cups and saucers, three bowls, a sugar dish, milk pots, six large Blue Willow plates, a teapot, gilt tumblers, and a quart and three pints of whiskey. Twelve days later he bought five pounds of sugar. The Hardy overseer, "Natty" Teagle, was buying an unusually high volume of spirits (from brandy to whiskey). He was, in fact, one of Rogers's best "grog" customers; but he also purchased thread and needles for his daughter.

William Eppes Hardy, the new master of the plantation beginning in November 1828, does not appear as a purchaser. Receipts in the Hardy family papers show him buying a long list of items from John I. Gracey (later Gracey & Hart, No. 8 Brick Range) and R. C. Anderson, both in Columbia. Perhaps the items from both Gracey and Anderson were to be had at better prices; perhaps they were of better quality. From the list of purchasers, it appears that Rogers did most of his business with the smaller planters, farmers, overseers, youngsters, and slaves. The Douglasses of The Oaks, like their Hardy kinsmen, also bought from Gracey in Columbia although Orange Hall was only a few miles away.

As was usually the case with country stores in the Upcountry, Orange Hall was a busy gathering place for the men of the area, who would shoot for beef (that is, hit a bulls-eye and win beef), play whist (a card game still played in the area under the name "setback"), "throw long-bullets" or ninepins, pitch dollars, spin yarns, and talk crops, weather, politics, and the world scene—or in general just pass the time of day. Here they could get a stiff drink of whiskey or good grog and be sociable. It was in a sense their neighborhood pub, not unlike those in the Ireland many of the families had just left. In the 1850s former slave Gus Feaster remembered that some folks called the store "the trading post" and that its operator had "barrels o' liquor settin' out from de store in a long row." Near the store was Renwick's Academy to one side (where the plantation children of the community rode to school on horseback), and a popular racetrack to the other. The barrels of whiskey were sold "to de rich mens dat carried on at de race track." It was a lively scene at all times. The store, racetrack, and Rogers Church were the acknowledged centers of society in the community. Robert Mills, in his *Statistics* of 1826, gives a good account of local "amusements":

> It is a prevalent custom . . . to meet at some store or place where liquor is sold, and spend their time at whist, or pitch dollars. Some will put up a beef to be shot for, or any other piece of property. Fox hunting, driving for deer, throwing long-bullets, and ninepins, make up also some of their amusements. . . . [For] the first settlers of this country, their chief amusements [were] wrestling, jumping, running foot races, fiddling, dancing, shooting, playing blind man's buff, snuffle the brogue, running the thimble, selling of pawns, crib and tailor, grinding the bottle, brother I am bobbed, black bear, dropping the glove, swimming and diving, etc.

The stone tavern and store at Orange Hall closed around 1865. It had for nearly a century been an important coach stop and stage post office that bore the name Poplar Grove—as we have seen, the name also sometimes affixed to Orange Hall itself in the earliest records. The trees alluded to were no doubt the poplars mentioned by Lyons in his letter of 1824. The continued existence on this site of huge tulip poplar trees attests to what must have been the abundance of this beautiful hardwood, for it still hangs on toughly despite the modern obsession with pines exhibited by the U.S. Forestry Service in making the forest of this area a perversion of what it was—certainly in the past a finer and ecologically richer thing. One may take some solace from the fact that if man or his government were ever to disappear from the environs, the tulip poplar would starve out the pines and again reign supreme, for the pine forests of this area would all give way to hardwoods (and the wide variety of wildlife they alone support) if left to their natural ways and devices.

When John Rogers Jr. died on 27 January 1847, he was a very wealthy man. He left slaves Elijah (25 years old) valued at $900, Billy (45) at $700, blacksmith Vol (29) at $1,200, "yellow girl" Jenny at $600, a woman and three children valued at $1,300, and Abby (elderly) at $25. John Rogers bequeathed the estate to his son James; but in 1848 William W. Renwick, his son-in-law (the husband of Rosannah Rogers Renwick) purchased 948 acres of the land and was living at Orange Hall. James and his wife, Nancy Dawkins Rogers, were living as neighbors on Orange Hall land. Renwick's wife died in 1850, but he continued as master of the place through the war years and after, until his death in 1872.

In 1859 or 1860, it was Renwick who had a pair of 10-foot-tall gateposts carved from granite from the Hill Quarry across Tyger and decorated on one side with the outlines of orange trees, a play on Orange Hall and the House of Orange from which the family descended. On the other faces were carved grapevines and clusters (like the gate posts at "Hillside" in Carlisle, in a tree-of-life pattern), and grapevines entwining a pear tree in full fruit. From ancient myth, pears and grapes are symbols of fertility and are thus appropriate for both plantation land and the family line itself. The decorations were obviously intended to have the symbolic meaning of both family continuity and successful compliance with the Biblical command to be fruitful and multiply. They stand as fitting symbols of an agrarian civilization.

This carving was done by a talented stonecutter, J. E. Sherman. The gates were removed in 1929 and taken to Pine Street in Spartanburg. In the 1970s Frank Coleman of Mountain Shoals plantation located them in the Golightly community of Spartanburg and had them positioned at the present entrance to Walnut Grove plantation in Spartanburg County. They still have with them their very fine iron gates, the twins to gates at 22 Legare Street in Charleston.

In 1860 the master of Orange Hall also employed Sherman to carve more elaborate mantels to bring the house into the latest fashion. The renovations were still going on in 1862. Also in 1860 Sherman carved the granite base of the spring at Orange Hall 325 yards north of the house. This spring, now called Jew's Harp Spring, has become legendary in the area. The base stone has a carved Jew's harp design where the water flows from the earth, and the stone surrounding the spring is laid in that configuration as well. The spring was both the chief source of water for the residents of the Big House and a place to cool perishable food.

In 1938 a former slave, Alice Dawkins Sims, recounted vignettes of life at Orange Hall. Her mistress, Nancy Dawkins Rogers (Mrs. James

Rogers), who lived on Orange Hall land next to the Great House, was of advanced age during the 1860s when Alice was her waiting maid. Her story gives a good picture of life at Orange Hall around 1865. But hear Aunt Alice:

> Miss Nancy got down wid de terribles' aliment and misery. It ailed her legs and kept on gittin' worse and worse. Ev'ybody knowed dat it wus de rheumatiz. . . . Miss Nancy finally got to usen' crutches all of the time. She made me put a pallet at the foot of her bed and I slept on it for years. Miss Nancy had five servants to wait on her all of the time, and she was able too. She was so kind and gentle to us, and we all loved her. I was the one who cared for her through the night. I would do all her rubbin', git up whenever she was having a misery dat waked her, and rub her all over. We made turpentine liniament and dat did her the most good. Sam, her carriage driver, go out in the pines wid his ax and tap a tree, ketch fresh turpentine rosin and mix it wid egg and kerosene. . . . I kept fire all night when we needed it and her room was always dry and warm. In the summer we took wet sheets and hang up at her windows to cool the air as it came through. Miss Nancy had two of the prettiest fans made out of peacock feathers that we fanned her with. She kept me dressed wid white cloths over my head and a big white clean apron all of the time. One day we was walkin' through the hog pasture where it was cool, and an ole boar got atter us. We had been to the tater house and I had a big bucket of taters. Miss Nancy took and let her crutch slip and fell. She couldn' git up and she cried and moaned. I hollered for Sam and Ree, and we picked her up and carried her into the house. Old Dr. George Douglass [of The Oaks] come and 'lowed dat she done got her hip knocked out of place. Miss Nancy lived several years, but never did walk no more. Atter dat though, she kept on gwine to Pacolet . . . to visit her brothers. Sam was the only man that she would let drive her carriage. I fixed her seat with pillows and quilts if it was cold, and sat in front of her. She trusted nobody but Sam to drive. . . . Sam driv her to the mountains every summer. I went too, but I do not like the mountains. They scare me. The folks there are so strange.

Then them North Carolina folks were not quality. But we met quality up there from Columbia and Charleston and other places in our state. The third year of the 'Federate War broke up our trips to [Pacolet]. We did go to the mountains that summer though, but that was the last time we went, for Sam died. When we got home, Sam was pullin' fodder on the Tyger bottoms one day, when he fell in the field with his heart. They brought him to the house, but he did not live long. Sam was young too and everybody cried. Miss Nancy went to goin' down fast, and she never got in her carriage no mo'. She said that she could not trust anybody wid them spirited horses and her in dat carriage, but Sam.

During the war, a descendant of Orange Hall (yet another John Rogers) was a blockade runner out of Charleston and was able to get some of his goods to Union. He thus carried on the family tradition of sea commerce established by his Irish ancestors in colonial Carolina. The statistics for Renwick's Orange Hall in 1863 and 1864 reveal what was happening to its agricultural economy. In 1863 Renwick produced 180 bushels of wheat, 1,818 bushels of corn, 5 of oats, 450 bushels of good sweet potatoes, 10,500 stacks of good fodder, 100 pounds of tobacco, 95 bushels of peas, and 20 bushels of ground peas (peanuts). In 1864 he had 533 acres of land in cultivation and 867 not in cultivation, for a total of 1,400 acres. He had thus increased his holdings from 948 to 1,400 since 1848. Thirty-five slaves over twelve years old "went to the field" in October 1864. There were thirteen work animals on the farm at that time.

After the great cataclysm of war, the Renwick, Rogers, and Lyons family fortunes rapidly decined with the rest of Goshen Hill. In 1865 the Orange Hall acreage was 1,400. Five years later it was 1,215. During the last hard years of Federal Reconstruction, the family lands dwindled at an accelerated rate. The soil, however, remained fruitful and fertile, only lacking the labor force to work it. The sons of William Renwick sold off their father's library at his death in 1872 in order to get by. The plantation remnant was inherited around 1890 by the widow Mary McCarley Renwick, who was raised at Walnut Grove plantation in Spartanburg County and who had married a young man of the Renwick family of Goshen Hill. She was later to marry Ben Hardy, son of William Dixon Hardy and grandson of William Eppes Hardy. The blacks of the place called her Boss; Ben Hardy they called Dick. John Renwick was the last child to be born at Orange Hall in August 1918, while his father lived there adjacent to his grandmother Mary McCarley Renwick (now Hardy), who had since purchased and moved to the nearby Chick plantation less than half a mile south down the State Road.

Renwick recalls that Orange Hall at that time had a "ten acre orchard of currants, pomegranates, plums (five or six varieties), apples, pears, peaches, and figs." The orchard had existed from as early as the 1820s and was similar to the extensive one at the Chick place. Primarily, however, it was still a cotton plantation. Renwick also reports that Orange Hall Great House was the site of the first Masonic Lodge in the state outside of Charleston. A room on the second floor, the formal second-floor drawing room, was used as "Solomon Lodge Number Two." "Solomon One" was in Charleston. The first Rogers was thus a Mason. During Reconstruction, the house was a rallying point for the Knights of the White Camellia and Hampton's Redshirts.

The Renwicks left Orange Hall in the early 1920s when a back wall collapsed. They moved in with Grandmother Mary McCarley Hardy and Ben. Renwick relates that Grandmother Hardy lost both Orange Hall and the Chick place about 1929 "to disastrously low cotton prices," the boll weevil, and finally to the land speculation of a small-time Spartanburg financier. This speculator had come through the farming area lending money to the hard-pressed owners during the Depression years. With low cotton prices and successive crop failures, the Renwicks could not repay their loan, and their land was taken from them through foreclosure. The speculator himself is said to have died in old age, a pauper in rags, selling pencils on the streets of Spartanburg.

In 1929 a tornado further damaged Orange Hall. The speculator sold the land into government ownership in the 1930s, and the mansion was allowed to fall into complete ruin under government management. In the 1960s a timber of its foundation could still be seen surrounded by high mounds of brick and broken columns. Some of the Renwick silver that graced the tables at Orange Hall is still in the family. These are fine colonial and antebellum examples of Charleston and Columbia silver, most engraved with the Renwick name.

In the era of prohibition there was a dispensary near Orange Hall and another at Goshen Hill. This first may have been in the old stone grogshop, tavern, and store. The tradition of the Orange Hall store was carried into this century in a new plank building across the road (called Crossroads Store) run by John Renwick's father. It too no longer stands.

In 1997 all that remains of the Great House at Orange Hall is a small mound of moss-covered bricks, one large granite monolith (probably a fence post), the inevitable ground cover of periwinkle that always marks an old house or cemetery site, and Jew's Harp Spring. The orange tree gateposts, as we have already noted, are preserved at Walnut Grove plantation; and the granite steps of the house are at the ruins of the Aughtrey home near Whitmire, whose conflagration in the 1980s left them fractured. Little else remains; but standing on the mound of crumbled bricks that was the Great House, one can imagine the spectacular view in all directions from this high place and still perhaps in the imagination, as did the Rogerses of old, climb to the cupola to witness engagements of Whigs and Tories on the distant Enoree.

As such a significant early house dating back to the earliest times of colonial settlement in the Upcountry, Orange Hall deserves an appropriate marker. The present sign of the U.S. Forestry Service at Jew's Harp Spring reads: "The deep gullies near the spring tell the story of poor farming practices common in the Piedmont that allowed the soil to erode and resulted in the farms being abandoned and returning to forest." This is not an accurate statement for Orange Hall and tells nothing of the story of both the house ruin nearby and of this once wealthy Tyger valley. Orange Hall, which still flowered in this century with large orchards and fruitful land despite the tremendous ruin and shadow of war, was not "abandoned" because of "poor farm practices," but instead was lost by its last farm family owing to the post-World War farm recession ushered in by dumping of government-stockpiled cotton onto the markets, thus making new cotton worthless, and capped by the industry-induced cataclysm called the Great Depression. In so many ways, several generations of the people of Orange Hall had been victims of forces beyond their control—the excesses, greed, and mismanagement of big business and big industry, too often aided by government. The Rogers and Renwick families were neither profligate "abandoners" of worn-out and eroded soil nor farmers practicing "poor" farming techniques. The Renwicks were forced to mortgage their land and could not repay the debt in hard money, and the land was taken from them. It was neither "abandoned" nor "allowed" to erode only to be saved by a wise Agency. If these particular farmers and their land were indeed in need of saving, government in its favoring of big business and industry had done much to create the situation in the first place; and buying family land at $2 and $3 per acre, thus uprooting its owners from family heritage and stability and the soil itself, was poor "salvation" indeed. Families, through such transactions, became the dispossessed—"wanderers" to towns and cities. "If this be salvation," said one wise old farmer of the area in 1930, "then let me be damned."

One might venture back sixty years earlier, and include the story of defeat in a war that made the agrarian South a virtual economic colony of an alien industrial region, and thus a war that did its own large share in impoverishing her rural areas. That these families were able to hold on for six decades after such a cataclysm, and with the cards of a nation frequently stacked against them, is testimony to their perseverance, energy, and endurance. It was at the point of the South's defeat that business and industry took control of the nation; and the entire country reaped the whirlwind in its own bitter, iron harvest of 1929. None of this long, sad story is even hinted at on the Forestry Service marker's explanation of why we see pine forest on these acres, and certainly the marker pays no proper homage to those early pioneers who shaped the land, helped achieve the new nation's independence, persevered through two devastating wars, and prevailed here for a century and a half. There is no mention even of these families' names; it is as if they never existed, their histories erased. Only one hero shines in the sign's wording, and that is today's owner of the land, whose monoculture tree-farming policy has created sterile rows of pines, where fruitful fields and orchards had stretched a century ago, or earlier, before Europeans came to this land, hardwood forests of rich and amazing diversity grew tall on its hills and in its fertile valleys.

Rose Cottage: The Chick Quarter Place Plantation

About three miles from the Hardy plantation was Rose Cottage, the Chick place, Orange Hall's nearest neighbor less than half a mile to the south. It sat on an elevation above the State Road about a hundred yards to the southwest of its intersection with the Crenshaw's Ford Road leading to the Hardys'. The precise date when the first house was built on this property is unknown, but tradition has it that, like Orange Hall, it was before the Revolution. As we have seen, bricks for Orange Hall were said to have been kilned here in the time of Burrell Chick. The Chick place was an early popular stage stop on the State Road from Charleston to Asheville.

In 1839 a grand new house was constructed under the ownership of Pettus W. and Sara Elizabeth Henderson Chick, a home which they named Rose Cottage. Here, travelers loved to stay the night, for there was ample accommodation for horses and coach, and the Chicks were celebrated for kindness, generosity, and hospitality. In fact, their hospitality went far beyond "Rose Cottage." Sarah Chick and her maid Liza operated the famous Buck Hotel in Maybinton before the war; and Chick Springs, between Greenville and Spartanburg, was an iron and sulphur spring owned and operated by Dr. Burrell Chick by 1840. Before 1842, Dr. Chick had built what a Greenville newspaper described as a "large and commodious hotel" at the springs, with "stables well-provided with horse-feed and attended by careful, attentive ostlers." When Dr. Chick died in 1847, his sons Reuben and Pettus bought the property, and Reuben and his wife continued to run the hotel. The Chicks were described as "courteous and liberal-minded men well-fitted for their occupation." Alice Dawkins Sims, born a slave before 1850, recalled that in the decade before the war, "Miss Sara Chick used to carry Liza up to dem Springs dat her husband owned whar he made all his money at, a-sellin' water to dem rich folks dat come dar from de Lowcountry." In 1857, the Chicks sold the springs to one of these Lowcountry entrepreneurs.

Just a few hundred yards up the road from Rose Cottage were the Orange Hall tavern and store for diversion, so this stopover on the State Road provided popular entertainments. If the traveler was headed to Chick Springs, he was thus able to partake of Chick hospitality at two stops on the road.

We are lucky to have both a photograph of the front entry of Rose Cottage and a detailed description of the house by John Renwick, one of the last to live there. Rose Cottage had two central chimneys eight feet square and a clapboarded upper main story over a brick first floor with a full-story garret topping these. It was thus a three-story dwelling with the look of a large raised cottage.

On the upstairs main floor, one room had elaborate plaster ornamentation, the excellent work of the plaster artist John Finger, who lived nearby. The other rooms were simply hard-plastered and without ceiling decorations. There were two rooms to each side of a very wide central hall with a single chamber attached to each side as wings. One of the two wings was not underpinned with the brick first floor. Under the north-side wing, carriages drove for convenience in mounting and dismounting. Renwick recalls that the central hall was used for reel or square dances, in which about fifty persons usually participated. This was also the case at the Ben Sims plantation Great House on Tyger.

The windows of the upstairs main story had louver shutters. In the brick downstairs, there were large fireplaces and concrete floors. A one-story portico, set on high piers, projected from the house and ran the length of the second story. It was supported by four large shadow-paneled square wooden columns. The front steps rose a story high so that one entered the main floor from the portico. The entrance on this level had a single door and precisely the same triple-segmented small-paned sidelights and transoms as those at the Hardy plantation and Pomaria—only here at Rose Cottage the transom was taller and surmounted by a flattened rectangular Greek revival lozenge exactly like that over the entrances at The Oaks and the Berry Richards plantation (c. 1845–1849), some six miles distant down Crenshaw's Ford Road. The downstairs brick story, as family tradition relates, was used to house the black house servants. There was no entrance from it to the upper floor, and it was thus self-contained. A detached kitchen lay to the rear off the upstairs floor.

One of Rose Cottage's most impressive features, as its name would suggest, was its beautiful formal garden of rare and exotic plants, probably the creation of its gentle mistress, Sara Elizabeth Chick. What may be one of the largest magnolias in the Upcountry still flourishes on these grounds. There are also old pink crape myrtles. A rare *Cryptomeria japonica* (Japan cedar), which the Chicks bought from Pomaria Nurseries in the 1840s or '50s, grew in the pine tangle until it was destroyed by the U.S. Forestry Service in 1994 to build a fire-break. Its mate, which was still alive as late as 1976, still stands as a dead shaft to the north of the bulldozed one. These historic *Cryptomeria* were among the first planted on the continent, for the tree's official date of introduction to America is given in error variously as 1859, 1860, and 1861.

Until recently there was a large banana shrub *(Michelia fuscata)* in the tangle of old garden. Now a small one struggles to survive. There was also a giant tea olive. The Chick formal garden was similar to the Hardy garden of the previous decade, for both were symmetrically laid out and patterned with boxwood edging. The Chick garden occupied the space from the front entrance of the house down to the State Road.

In 1937 Balaam Lyles gave his memories of the place:

Hit was called "Rose Cottage" kaise dey had de purtiest flower garden in all de country. Sometimes I'd stop by and play wid de other lil darkies. In de orchard, dey had ever kind of fruit you could think of. Dere was the mor'est grape-vines I's ever seed on one place. De orchard done all gone now, but some of dem purty flowers is still dar. The news is gwine 'round dat de government gwine tear de house down but dey gwine keep de magnolia trees and things. Every time us pass . . . at the well to git water . . . us'd git to eat peaches or whatever dey had in de orchard den.

John Renwick recalls that in the 1920s his grandmother oversaw patient black men in their weeding of the formal parterres. He remembers "boxwood and many different kinds of flowers everywhere." Neither boxwood nor flowers remain, having been choked out by pines.

The 1850 agricultural statistics show that the Chick plantation contained 700 acres, 500 of them "improved." In 1860 the improved acreage had doubled to 1,000, and the plantation total acreage had grown sharply to 1,521. Like Orange Hall and the Hardy plantation, the Chick plantation was also a fine and growing, productive agricultural venture. In 1850 its 500 improved acres, compared to the Hardys' 800, produced 75 bales of cotton compared to the Hardys' 110 bales, 50 pounds of wool to the Hardys' 25, 400 pounds of butter to the Hardys' 600, and 2,000 bushels of corn to the Hardys' 2,500. The barnyard in 1850 included 25 sheep and 50 hogs.

By 1860 Pettus Chick had 80 sheep and 200 hogs, more in both categories than the Hardys, made 82 bales of cotton (to the Hardys' 81), and raised more wheat and ten times as much corn! The latter perhaps fed the horses of travelers who stopped there. The plantation, which now numbered 1,000 improved acres to the Hardys' 600, also had fine orchards and extensive grazing lands. The year 1860 was its high point. Under Pettus and Sara Chick's capable hands, it had flowered and thus risen in the preceding decade to being one of the finest in the valley. Their extensive garden and finely ornamented Big House also reveal that they valued aesthetics. To them, money was a means and not an end. Here is additional evidence that the Hardy plantation was more typical in the community than not. And at both these plantations and Orange Hall, cotton was an emphasis but most certainly not an obsession.

In the hard times of the 1890s, Rose Cottage and its lands were purchased from the Chicks by the widow Mary McCarley Renwick and her second husband, Ben Hardy. This property and the remnant of Orange Hall became one tract; and the Chicks thus lost title to their homeplace. It was through this purchase that the Renwicks, in financial straits themselves, could relocate from their crumbling house at Orange Hall to take up residence at Rose Cottage. This period was a time of great struggle for all area families; and only through thrift and hard work did they survive from agriculture as long as they did. Many families like the Chicks and Renwicks had to leave the land for towns and mills.

One old magnolia, a few stray garden shrubs, some brick rubble, and an impressive deep stone-lined well are all that remain of this fine old homeplace. Like Orange Hall, it fell victim to war, the boll weevil, the Depression, a land speculator from the city, and finally a government agency. As Joseph Simpson recalled, "The Depression was the end of this area." After the speculator who bought it from the Renwicks in turn sold it to the U.S. Forestry Service, Rose Cottage became a tree farm of pines, and the Forestry Service tore the Great House down, just as Balaam Lyles had heard in 1937 that it was going to do. Lyles was wrong, however, in saying that the garden would be protected. As of 1997 nothing had been done either to mark or preserve the pitiful remnants of this place. Accordingly, it can be argued that its present owner has not been a good steward of the land's history and cultural resources.

At its sale in 1929, Renwick recalls that there was an extensive orchard of bearing English walnut trees, grown to be giants, and no doubt of antebellum origin. As Balaam Lyles remembered in 1937, the orchard "had every kind of fruit you could think of" and the most grapevines he had ever seen. Renwick recalls figs, pomegranates, cherries, peaches, apricots, pears, "all manner of fruit trees," and extensive productive fields in tillage. The soil was excellent. Renwick also sadly reflects upon the beauty of the garden's old boxwood parterres and flowers. Today both Chick and Renwick family descendants live in nearby towns, but none remain on the land.

EISON HOMEPLACE

About a mile below Rose Cottage toward Maybinton and on the opposite side of the road was the home of the Eison family. A child of the household was killed in Confederate service and is buried at nearby

Ebenezer Cemetery. Nothing more is known of this important seat of a family. No Eisons remain in the vicinity. No doubt, they, like the Renwicks, are scattered throughout upcountry towns.

THE OAKS OF GOSHEN HILL

The Oaks was first known as Oak Grove, perhaps a pairing to nearby Poplar Grove, the post office address of Orange Hall. It was located about a mile to the north of Orange Hall, facing and rising above the State Road and with its back to the Tyger. The house was said to "afford quite an impressive view," especially from the elliptical window of the upstairs portico. The house site was chosen for the large grove of red oaks that would become part of its formal landscaping.

The builder and first master of this Great House was George Douglass, born in 1804, in the same year as William Eppes Hardy. He was the son of James Thomas Douglass Sr., who came to Charleston from Aberdeen, Scotland, about 1790 as a ship's-carpenter on his brother's ship. When his brother died in a shipwreck, James settled in Charleston, but soon learned of the opportunities for construction work in the new capitol of Columbia, to which he relocated. There on 2 August 1794 he married Rebecca Calvert, daughter of John Calvert of Charleston, and had seven children. In Columbia he built a sawmill on Crane Creek, where he sawed and dressed timber for many structures in the town. He was the builder of the original First Presbyterian Church there and was engaged by the State legislature to make repairs on the state capitol building. He died in 1834, and the present church structure rests over his grave.

Son George studied medicine with Dr. James Davis, a friend of his father's and cosigner with him of the petition to incorporate the First Presbyterian Church in 1812. Young George's study with Davis enabled him to get "a permit to practice in the State" after taking an examination in 1823. It was Davis who wrote him a letter of introduction to the Glenn family (also staunch Presbyterians) of Fish Dam in southeastern Union County, a letter still preserved in the family:

Columbia May 5th 1824

Mr. Bernard Glenn
Dear Sir,

    I beg leave to introduce to you Doct. George Douglass. He has studied his profession with me and has sustained his

examination and has a permit to practice in this State—He
informs me he intends settleing himself in your vicinity: and
as young men always need the countenance and support of
the respectable members of society I beg leave to recommend
him to your notice. He is the son of an old and respectable
inhabitant of this town and is a steady young man.

> I am, Dr. Sir, your
> Mo. Ob. Sert.
> James Davis

Dr. Douglass thus began practice at Fish Dam in 1824 under the
guidance of Dr. Tom Glenn. His practice extended to Maybinton in
Newberry County. In 1830 he was considering building a house for
himself. His father wrote to him on the subject in a letter delivered by
Tom, one of his skilled slave artisans:

> Crayon [Crane] Creek Dec 29 1830

Doctar George Douglass
By Tom
Dear George

I receved yours by Tom with regard to a hous you was a
going to bild or rathar asable [assemble]—if you will bild a
house laik a hous that is 20 feet long and 16 brod, Tom can
with anothar hand . . . can hav the stuf in 2 weeks and can
fram it in 2 more and I will send you the withar bording and
flooring and doors will cost you onlay the haling from the
mill to River Mill. You by that may put a piaza to the front
and if evar you want more rum can ad a shed to the back and
2 rooms will mak a comfortable hous as Tom can dou all the
work whin you have nothing fore him to dou—nothing
more at presant but we are will [well] at presant and send our
bows to you

> Remains yours afectionatly
> James Douglass

Perhaps the reason Dr. Douglass was thinking of building was that
he had begun courting Miss Frances Jeter Hardy (1813–1895) of the
Hardy plantation some twelve miles distant. It has come down to us that
this courtship was the talk of the plantations because the seventeen-year-

old Frances was a beautiful and wealthy heiress and George was a dark-haired, dashing, and eligible young bachelor. It is also reported that the hand of Frances "was being sought far and wide" especially since her beauty and polish came with membership in a wealthy family that owned "many acres, many slaves, many sheep, and many fine horses." Frances' eighteen-year-old sister Catharine had just married her cousin William Eppes Hardy in November 1829 in one of the area's biggest social events. And three years later, George was also successful in his courting and married the other Hardy daughter. The wedding took place on 12 January 1832, when she was eighteen, just as her sister had been when she married. The couple established their first home either at Fish Dam or in Newberry County, and soon had two daughters: Laura (called Lucy), born in 1834, and Rebecca Calvert, born in 1836 and named for her paternal grandmother.

Douglass was a member of the Nullification Convention in Columbia and signed the Ordinance of Nullification on 24 November 1832. This document declared null and void the tariffs of 1828 and 1832 that so hurt the South economically. In his political philosophy, he was like his new brother-in-law William Eppes Hardy, who was also a strong States' Rights advocate. Around 1836 the good doctor and his young family moved to the old Selby place at Goshen Hill, about six miles from the Hardy estate, and near to the Rogerses of Orange Hall. At Goshen Hill, widow Anna Hardy, Frances's mother, owned land and slaves, and had her own plantation on the "old Anderson tract," which she managed without the help of an overseer. She was a successful planter there, and into her seventies was increasing her holdings and the number of cotton bales she sent to market. From about 1845 to her death in 1861, she lived adjacent to the couple; and it was likely through her auspices that the Douglasses acquired the Selby place. She, too, likely provided the experience when Douglass entered the ranks of planter. As a green-horn doctor from the town, he no doubt needed it, and his mother-in-law and her black bondsmen had come from a long line of farmers in Virginia and Carolina. The Selby house was a two-story log dwelling from the eighteenth century, plain and rugged, with wooden shutters for windows—a large, drafty pioneer structure. There the Douglasses' first son was born in 1838. They named him James Thomas, after his paternal grandfather, the first of their family to come to the new land, and who had died just four years earlier.

By 1838 the doctor had greatly increased his real estate holdings and the number of his slaves. Like his Hardy in-laws, he had himself by this time established a plantation of many cattle, horses, sheep, hogs, barns, and granaries. Each of his children had a "mammy" or personal servant; his wife had a cook, a maidservant, a gardener, and a coachman. His years in Columbia and his connection to Charleston through his mother set his ways and confirmed him in this style. His wife now had fine silver, some of which is said to have come down with the Douglasses from Scotland; and the rough old Selby house was said not to be a proper setting either for it or the lifestyle of the family. In 1838, therefore, in the year of his sons's birth, the thirty-four-year-old father began the supervision of the construction of their grand new mansion in the giant red oak grove a few hundred yards from their present dwelling.

Using his builder father's old connections and the help of his brother James Jr. (who had taken over the father's business in 1834), George Douglass had the heart-pine timber for the mansion cut from the woods of what is now the Taylor Street area in Columbia. It was processed in his father's old lumber yard and mill, then hauled and rafted upcountry to the house site where slaves had built a kiln to dry it. Tom, trained by his father at the Columbia yard, came to Goshen Hill to dress the lumber by hand on site, a feat that he could accomplish at the rapid rate of 500 feet a day. (The locals considered this sum miraculous.) Tom trained two other slaves to assist him and set them a "task" to do each day, thus apparently supervising a task system of labor. Tom is said also to have carved the house's woodwork, including mantels and window cornices, and helped with the construction of the outbuildings. The house was allowed to sit several years before it was painted "either inside or out" so that it would hold paint more effectively. All this work was accomplished by a painter named Scully, who came from North Carolina. The wainscoting, millwork, and doors are so similar to those at the Hardy plantation that I surmise some involvement by the brothers Shell, or at least shared craftsmen. The mantels are distinctly different, however, as they exhibit the new Greek revival style.

One visitor described "a most peculiar type" of painting done on the mantel, wainscoting, and doors of the downstairs "left" room: a decoration of dropped white paint "raised" pebbly above the surface to give the appearance of the way "a very coarse sandpaper would look under a microscope." The large parlor mantel in the "right downstairs room" was painted "to resemble black marble." The "north" guest bedroom on the second floor had a faux yellow-grained marble finish on the mantel. An extant color photograph shows that it was particularly well done. The panels of the wainscoting downstairs in the parlor and hall were grained in two-tone design to represent contrasting fine woods.

The Oaks had two floors and a full garret, which was reached by a staircase of broken flights. Unlike those of the Hardy staircase, its spindles were not turned; but its newel post resembled an elongated version of the one at the Hardy plantation. The handrail had a delicate vertical curve unlike the straight, heavier Hardy handrail. Its tread ornamentation is unique and was also likely the work of Tom.

The house had eight rooms, four to a floor. In 1840 its heart-pine flooring was covered "entirely" throughout with carpet purchased and transported from Columbia. In 1936 one of the upstairs guest rooms still had the original floor covering, whose design was of flowers and peacocks "in very beautiful colors," with blues predominating, to complement the pale yellow-grained marble mantel and dark faux-grained doors. In 1936 the carpet was said still to retain its bright hues. Throughout the house the paneled doors had iron Carpenter's brand locks imported from England through Charleston. Their brass discs bore the seal of Britain, as do those at the Hardy plantation. All the doorknobs were "very small," made of brass, and again identical to those still present at the Hardy dwelling. The rear double doors had an "oaken bar" that crossed them for security. This bar was held in place by a chain. The front door had a large brass key and lock, still owned by a descendant. In the center of the hall downstairs hung a crystal globe for a single candle. It also still survives in the home of a descendant. It is said to have been imported from England.

The downstairs rooms were paneled with wainscoting "three feet high" and feather-grained to resemble walnut and yellow chestnut (the former surrounding the latter and separated by narrow molding painted white). In the hall, the wainscoting stops before the staircase's first landing and does not follow it to the top, as it does in the Hardy house. All in all, the Hardy entrance hall seems to have been a finer, more detailed, finished job; but the entry at The Oaks was considered very impressive as well. The walls and ceilings throughout the house were plastered and still retained this plaster into the 1970s. The plaster crown molding was described in 1970 to be "of rare beauty" with "attractive beading." Its plasterer again was likely master craftsman John Finger, who boarded at the Hardy plantation off and on in 1841 and 1842 and perhaps earlier. As we have seen, a Hardy plantation blacksmith repaired Finger's trowel, chisel, and hammer several times, and Finger bought bushels of lime there, likely for making plaster, in 1845 and 1846. In 1862 Garrie Douglass mentioned his leaving Goshen Hill on a trip to Spartanburg, so he was still working in the area—for example, at the home of Dr. James M. Eppes, about ten miles from The Oaks. (This house, built in 1857, has his excellent ornamental plaster decoration.) It was Finger who also decorated the magnificent Ben Sims plantation on Tyger, of which more will be said later.

Some time before 1936, a descendant of Dr. Douglass gave a detailed description of the house's furnishings. Likely very little had changed from its flush antebellum days. She wrote, "The dining room is across the hall from the parlor. It has a lovely high mantel, wainscotting, and corner cabinet." The dining room chairs were balloon-backs of rosewood, and with roses carved on them. One of these survives and reveals the set to have been particularly fine. The 1936 account continues:

> The wide floor boards run towards a large fireplace, the brick of which were made at the kiln at "Orange Hall." The bedrooms have closets whose doors open seven feet from the floor! A step ladder has to be used to get up to them. This was done so that children could not get to the Doctor's physics. . . .The rooms were furnished with elegant mahogany beds, with trundles for the children. Upon the carpets were rag and hook rugs [and rugs] made of lamb, goat, and other skins of animals wild or domesticated. Each fire place had large back logs and fires were kept going day and night by servants. The parlor has gorgeous tapestry draperies drawn back with ties of brocaded ropes—and sconces of crystal. There, hung paintings of ancestors from Scotland dated 1750 and 1760. The furniture in the parlor is rosewood and mahogany upholstered in mohair. Shutters keep the strong light from fading the delicate colors. . . . The house is so completely furnished with works of art that the visitor never tires of looking.

The observer even ventures into the garret, "which is completely finished up and well-furnished with old books, spinning wheels, [cotton] carders, candle moulds, loom, vases, wine crocks, *Godey's Lady's Books,* bedspreads, demi-johns, . . . old trunks, pictures, an ancient sewing machine." The last was among the first purchased after Howe's patent. In her letters of the late 1850s, Garrie Douglass remarks on their having difficulty using it. The family's silver spoons, forks, and knives were engraved with the initials GFD. Dr. Douglass, having no middle initial, took that of his wife's first name. Only one serving spoon of this large set remains with the family.

Luckily, several pictures of the Palladian front of the house reveal the graceful design of the double projecting portico with its fluted columns and simple bannisters. The portico had a semicircular window in its pediment. There were Greek revival triglyphs on the stringer course between the stories of the portico. The oval fanlights upstairs and down were flattened in Greek revival style. They and the sidelights surrounded a double-doored entrance on both floors of the portico. The design of these doorways is very similar to plate 28 of Asher Benjamin's *The Practice of Architecture* (1833) and identical to that at the Thomas Badgett House (c. 1845) in nearby Laurens. At the rear of the house, Ionic columns supported a one-story veranda that ran the length of the building. The dwelling had exterior louver shutters on the windows, even at the third-story garret, noted earlier as being completely "finished up." The shutters were painted green to contrast with the white clapboards of the house. The exterior window treatments were simple and unadorned. In the small details, the Columbia builders were not as precise and attentive as the Shell brothers who built Pomaria and the Hardy plantation; but the most significant architectural departure from the two earlier plantation models was the imposition of Greek revival elements on the Palladian design, thus bringing the house into the latest fashion.

Douglass was still putting finishing touches on his new estate from 1842 to 1846. The Hardy plantation ledger and account books note his purchases from the Hardy blacksmith of door hinges, locks, and window hinges, probably for the outbuildings, because, as we have noted, the locks in the Big House were imported. An entry for 1842, in fact, specifies that the purchased irons were "for crib door."

At the rear of the house was the detached kitchen where the cook also lived. Here a fireplace whose opening measured 6 feet was the place that all the family's cooking was done. As at the Hardy house and Orange Hall, the food was brought from the kitchen building in covered platters and ironstone bowls to the master's dining table. Later in the century the kitchen was built into the house's north side through additions between it and the main structure, thus creating the typical upcountry plantation ell.

At its front and to the north side, the mansion had an extensive formal flower garden tended by a black gardener and the ladies of the house. In their straw hats and white spring dresses, the young Douglasses oversaw the planting of roses, bulbs, and blackberry lily. Crape myrtle, gardenia, tea olive, and banana shrub cuttings came from neighboring plantations. The garden to the north side of the house was entered from a small one-story porch. A white picket fence enclosed these private grounds around the Big House. In 1936 the front walk which led from the gate to the front steps was said to be "paved with brick and lined with a brick border." The walk was "edged with low growing plants and dwarf boxwood" and was "flanked with boxtrees"—that is, tree box, so common in the gardens of this area. "The old-fashioned diamond and heart shaped flower beds outlined with native rock" were "still to be seen in the yard." This heart and diamond pattern is also to be found in the early garden (c. 1820) still extant at Mountain Shoals plantation, twenty miles distant on the Enoree, and at Colonel Robert Beaty's plantation, nine miles up the Old State Road. Photographs of The Oaks made in the 1970s show large tree box at the house front among a tangle of cedar and pine. There is also a lone red oak, grown to be a giant, the last of the trees that gave the house its name. Just outside the garden gate on the dwelling's south side sat the doctor's office, built in 1840. The remains of its chimney still stand in 1997, engulfed in kudzu.

Dr. Douglass had an extensive medical practice and, at the same time, oversaw the work of the plantation. In 1860, on 735 improved acres, he kept 5 horses, 10 mules, 12 milk cows, 4 oxen, 52 "other" cattle, 76 sheep, and 100 hogs, and raised wheat, 150 bushels of oats, 1,000 bushels of corn, 405 gallons of molasses, and 64 bales of cotton. He had orchards and bees, did some home manufacturing, and sheared 75 pounds of wool. This he accomplished with the help of 32 slaves, who lived in 9 slave houses. In 1861 he also raised peas, rye, sweet potatoes, and peanuts. He doubled his corn production to 2,165 bushels and increased his wheat from 30 to 500 bushels. These figures prove that like the other plantations of the Tyger, The Oaks was striving for self-sufficiency and achieving it.

The Douglass family thus prospered at The Oaks, which was a happy place for them. To their three offspring, they added nine other children born at The Oaks: Cornelia and Cordelia, twin daughters born in 1839 who died two years later; Garraphelia Arabella (1841–1915), called Garrie; Sarah Belle (1843–1935), called Sallie; Anna Powell (1846–1879), called Annie, and named for her maternal grandmother Anna Hardy; Elmira (1847–1924), called Mira and named for her cousin Elmira Hardy; Jane Taylor (1848–1928), called Janie; George Jr. (1850–1907), called Dock; and William Joseph (1852–1930), called Willie. Both William and George became doctors; Garrie took over her brother James's school while he was at war. Sallie married a teacher at Union Academy who later became a lawyer and a judge in Union, and Mira wed David Moore of Columbia. Annie married James Daniel Epps, a

Hardy and Douglass kinsman born in 1844 who died in 1935. Some in our own time still recall him as an old-fashioned gentleman with white mustaches who into his nineties wore a white linen shirt, tie, and formal black coat all seasons of the year. It was he who was planting cotton in the 1890s; and it was his children who were the last to care for the house when the other descendants of George Douglass moved away to towns.

The Douglass children were all well educated. Girls of the family enrolled in Salem Academy in North Carolina and a school in Columbia. The young ladies, especially Garrie and Sallie, were accomplished musicians, thus explaining the pianoforte in the parlor during antebellum times. After the war, Garrie was sought upstate as a teacher of music, but she declined, to remain at home. James studied at William Renwick's Academy, under Professor J. W. Hudson at Mt. Zion in Winnsboro, at South Carolina College (1856–1858), and at the University of North Carolina (1859–1860), where he was a member of Chi Psi fraternity. He transferred to Chapel Hill on the urging of his friend Pierce Mason Butler of Edgefield (1838–1878), who was a student there. A letter from Professor Lucius Smith concerning this transfer is an important document for a number of reasons:

> Univ. of North Carolina
> Chapel Hill, Oct. 26th [1858]
>
> Dear Jim,
>
> Your letter came to hand yesterday—Butler's also. I would procure a catalogue and send you, but B—. informed me this evening that he had done it, and it is therefore unnecessary. You will find the requisitions for admittance into the Junior laid down there. I do not doubt your entering it in all the departments save Mathematics. I suppose you quit the Soph. at S.C. College. There the Soph. class is almost advanced in the Languages as far as the Junior here. In Mathematics it is not. I guess you will be almost a year behind in that branch. However you must not let this deter you from making an effort to get into the Junior. The examination, you will have to pass, will be almost nothing, and if you will devote your attention almost exclusively to Mathematics until January, I do not doubt but you will succeed. Familiarize yourself so as to answer some of the most general questions in Trigonometry, Analytical Geometry, and Calculus,

242

and the Faculty will let you in. Procure Loomis' series of the latter two, if you can; it is much easier than any other. It will only be necessary for you to study Differential Calculus. My class left out Integral Calculus. I had forgotten to mention Natural Philosophy. I would advise you to procure Olmsted's work and study as far as chapter 10th, headed "Projectiles," and stand an examination upon the balance of it here. Should you have time and see proper to study more of it, omit all between the 10th chapter and "Hydrostatics," then continuing it regularly. I suppose my class will not get further than "Electricity" this session, so you need not go beyond that. This I believe is about all the information, I can give, that you cannot find in the Catalogue. Pitch in, study hard, and come. I would be very glad to see you here. It would make me feel like old times were coming again.

The session will close in five weeks. The next will open 16th of Jan. I will remain in N.C. somewhere during the vacation; I don't know where. I will make this my headquarters, and if you need any further information, write me and I will take great pleasure in giving it. A letter from you will at all times be most cordially received.

Very truly, your friend
G. Lucius Smith

Apparently Jimmie had known Professor Smith some time in the past for Smith to speak of "old times" together and to call him "friend." Douglass did transfer successfully to the junior class.

After Chapel Hill, Jimmie returned home to Goshen Hill to teach at the local academy before volunteering in April 1861 with the South Carolina Fifth Regiment. During the war he was three times wounded but survived to lead his company as captain, the company that came to be known as Johnson's Rifles. Throughout his campaigns he was attended by his faithful menservants Uncle Peter and Phil. Before the war his life had held unlimited promise, and he strongly desired to follow the medical profession of his father; but even with the diminished possibilities of the postwar period, which prevented a medical education, he still persevered to take on the farm responsibilities and to become a state senator for two decades, a banker, industrialist, and civic leader in Union village, and an influential promoter of local business and industry. He officially took over the duties as master of The Oaks after his father's death in 1875. In 1907 he would give this advice to a young audience: "Dogged perseverance is a winning virtue. 'Be sure you are right, then go ahead,' and keep steadily at it." His quotation from frontiersman Davy Crockett points to the pioneering heritage of upcountry Carolina that was his birthright. The advice was much needed in a time when the young of the South had fallen into resignation that theirs was a ruined world for which little could be done. Their confidence had been taken from them by defeat. Douglass himself endeavored to keep the spirit of will and doing alive among his people in their darkest hour. More will be said of him and The Oaks in the following chapters.

In February 1865, when Sherman's legions were burning their way through South Carolina, the family feared for life and property. They buried their silver in the State Road in front of the house where hooves and wheels would obliterate the evidence of fresh digging, the telltale sign the invaders looked for in their relentless search for booty. They then drove their cattle into hiding places in the woods. Neither Sherman nor his bummers, however, paid them a visit, although pillaging was to occur a short few miles distant. They counted themselves lucky, as indeed they were.

Dr. Douglass's granddaughter recalls that when her grandfather was nearing death in the 1870s, he told his wife that "after he died, if he could, he would try to make contact with her in the garden at sunset." She was to sit on a garden seat and face the setting sun. The granddaughter continues, "She sat there alone many times from sunset to dusk."

Although Dr. Douglass died in 1875, Frances lived until 1895 to witness the gradual but certain dwindling of the family lands. From the 1861 acreage of 1,905, the figure fell to 1,565 in 1865; 1,150 in 1870; and 665 in 1880. Frances's daughter Garrie composed the epitaph on her headstone at Ebenezer: "A kind and affectionate Christian mother has left us." Garrie, who herself died in 1915, and Janie, who died in 1928, witnessed even further the story's last chapters. They both died unmarried, and after a life devoted to one another through hardship and loss, are buried side by side at Ebenezer beneath a common gravestone reading, "Precious in the sight of the Lord is the death of His Saints."

This simple inscription speaks eloquently as the epitaph of a generation of patient, suffering women, who witnessed in silence. It is through Garrie Douglass's letterbook that we have a good picture of her antebellum society. The world she left in 1915 was mightily changed from the strawberry feasts, picnics, evening carriage rides, portrait sittings, and Sunday gatherings on the Tyger. What changes she had witnessed!—of a civilization that had flourished and quickly passed within the span of her lifetime, almost it seemed within the blinking of an eye. It is difficult to understand how these people of her generation were able to deal with such cataclysmic change and dislocation. That they did, and with good grace, and a great capacity for endurance, reveals something about their mettle and the centrality of the deep faith that sustained them.

Janie did not die alone in the house in 1928. She had with her, her brother-in-law James Daniel Epps (1844–1935) and his two unmarried children: niece Frances Elizabeth Epps (1875–1959) and nephew Jim Eppes. Janie's sister, Sallie Belle Douglass Townsend (1843–1935), had moved to Union with her husband after the war. With the deaths of her husband and daughter in 1911 and her son Ben in 1912, she returned to the place of her birth to live out her last years. Ben, who was a lawyer like his father and a state legislator, was her last child, so she was now gathered in among the remnants of a shattered family. It was Miss Fannie Epps who cared largely for her Aunt Janie, her own father Daniel, and her Auntie Sallie. And Sallie was the last of these; she died on 6 December 1935 at the age of ninety-two, having lived longer than any of her brothers and sisters. She was the last of the family born before the great war. Fannie and her brother Jim, themselves now in their sixties, continued to live alone at The Oaks and to keep the house for the many relatives who came and went. The house remained the family's center, and thus there was never a lonely or dull moment. Some of the house's furnishings and family silver were sold at this time to help them "get by."

In 1936 cousins Nettie Moore of Columbia and Caldwell Sims of Union wrote of happy visits to The Oaks:

> The house is still in an excellent state of preservation and each summer the grandchildren and great grandchildren come to visit and spend a restful vacation. On summer evenings when visitors from Atlanta, Columbia, and Newberry sit on the porch and watch the moon rise over the tree-tops in the distance, the aroma of pine, cedar, and boxwood intermingles with summer flowers, and the visitor is taken by enchantment into a land of ease and plenty, and the atmosphere of peace and solitude prevails here as it does in few places today.

> The mind is carried back to the days when neighbors were
> like brothers and when peace and plenty were abounding
> throughout the land. . . . The home has always been noted
> for its atmosphere of Southern charm and warm hospitality
> for generations, and the present owners [Fannie and Jim
> Epps] have inherited a rich share of these traits.

Miss Fannie, who had taken over as the last mistress of the place in
1929, continued into her seventies to keep up the old flower garden "as
a garden of memories for the summer relatives." In 1936 she was said
also to have created a "new garden" where flowers bloomed "the year
round and where many pleasant and diverting hours are spent."

In 1940, the centennial of the house's completion, a great celebration was held which was attended by a large crowd of Douglass descendants and friends. This was to be the home's last hurrah, for the World
War came and Miss Fannie grew ever feebler. During the 1950s she
could no longer keep the place going and so had to leave. (She died in
1959 at a rest home.) The scattered family now lived in postwar progressive towns and cities where the old was not so well appreciated as before,
and where they had succumbed to the pressures of the modern world to
raise their own separate families as best they could and "get by." They
had gone about their individual lives. Cousins often no longer knew
who or where their cousins were, a thing unheard of in the old times.
The old family cohesiveness had loosened; and their love of the rural
and natural had weakened because they had not been born to it, but to
an urban world instead. And so The Oaks was sold out of the family. Its
lands had already gradually passed to foresty companies. By 1950 the
Great House was sadly unpainted and beginning to decay, its lush "garden of memories" overgrown and feebly tended.

In the 1950s the Big House was sold to B. F. Means, said to be "a
light-colored negro with fine manners," who "kept it meticulously
clean, in a good state of repair, and is most courteous to those visiting
the place." By this time it had been unpainted for so many years that no
paint could be seen on it. After Means's death around 1959, the house
was occupied for a time by Margaret Thomas Boyce. Then it became
empty; soon it was sought out by curiosity seekers, and vandals burned
it in 1977. Today its tall chimneys rise high in stark outline above the
overgrown bed of the Old State Road. It is an atmospheric ruin and a
sad relic of the past. Nothing is discernible of the extensive garden, and

the many red oaks that gave the place its name have themselves disappeared. Recent clearcutting of trees has left the environs scraped, desolate, and eroded. The plantation's fertile fields have been depleted of precious topsoil.

In reviewing the melancholy history of this place, one can take solace from the old saying that only the spirit of a people is immune to weather. Descendants of the Douglass family, gracious, cultured, and prosperous, live today in Whitmire, Columbia, Kingstree, Charleston, Raleigh, and Atlanta. The family meet each year for a reunion. The papers of Garrie Douglass survive at the South Caroliniana Library. Family members have other well-preserved and properly valued letters and documents from the nineteenth century. The portrait of Anna Hardy painted for Frances Douglass is still with a descendant, almost, as she says, her "oldest friend and best guardian," her companion since childhood. Some of the house's furnishings still survive in the homes of the family. The vanished house itself has passed into the folklore of the area and is the subject of two enduring folk tales, one of which appears as chapter 18.

THE GIST LANDS OF GOSHEN HILL

The governor of South Carolina during Secession, William H. Gist, owned an extensive tract in Goshen Hill as early as 1850. By 1865 the tract included 2,760 acres, thus making him one of the largest landholders in the Orange Hall-Oaks plantation area. By 1867 this tract had dwindled to 1,910; by 1870 it was around half its size at 1,350 acres. Little is known of this plot, although it was undoubtedly a cotton plantation. Gist himself lived at Rose Hill plantation twelve miles up the Tyger.

It has been accurately stated that the Goshen Hill community was one of the premier agricultural regions of the nation before the war. From the Douglass, Renwick, and Rogers families, for which extensive records exist, one finds corroboration for this claim. Whether or not Governor Gist had much social commerce with the community is unknown. At least he and Mrs. Gist did correspond with William Renwick of Orange Hall on domestic matters. Like the Hardy, Chick, and Douglass plantations, Gist's own Rose Hill was a model of order and refined society. It is likely that he was on good social terms with the Douglasses, whose paterfamilias had signed the Ordinance of Nullification in 1832 and whose political philosophy was the same as his own. The Gists, Renwicks, Hardys, and Douglasses were staunch Southern Nationalists and were prepared to sacrifice all for the Confederate cause. This commitment insured a common bond and made it likely that they moved in a common social circle.

THE McCRACKEN HOMEPLACE

This two-and-a-half-story upcountry plantation plain-style dwelling was located on the opposite side of the State Road about a half-mile north of Orange Hall and to the south of The Oaks. A large grove of trees marks its site. The McCrackens were educated people, recalls John Renwick. The Arthur McCracken who educated the Hardy orphans may have been from this family. There was also a lawyer James Mc-Cracken in this area during the antebellum era.

THE BEN SIMS PLANTATION

Diagonally across the lower Tyger from the Hardy plantation, a half mile from the river and high on its plateau, rose one of the great mansions of upcountry South Carolina. This was the Ben Sims plantation, constructed in 1850, the Great House closest to the Hardys, about a mile and a half distant. From where it sat on its hill, its lights could be seen from the Hardy plantation on a clear night across cotton, corn, wheat, and pasture lands—quite a beautiful sight, in the recollection of those who witnessed it even in this century. Like the Hardy mansion, its location was chosen for beauty, health, and practicality. With respect to beauty, Andrea Palladio had succinctly summed up the case: "if one may build upon a river . . . it will afford a beautiful prospect." A high breezy elevation brought good health because away from the mosquitoes that caused malaria. And for practicality, a river location could not be surpassed. In the early century, the Tyger and Broad Rivers were ideal routes for transportation of crops to market. So too could building materials like the giant pine timbers of The Oaks and the Irish ornamental tiling for Cross Keys and Orange Hall come up them. Thus the Great Houses were built by a river, but on high plateaus or hills looking down to it across fields and pastures. This was the case with all the great Tyger River plantations: Orange Hall, The Oaks, Rose Hill, and the Hardy and Sims plantations.

The Charles Sims family had come with their slaves from Hanover,

Virginia, around 1783 and had settled on Tyger among the Gordons, Lisleses, and Hardys. They had built typical early houses, but this new one of 1850 was the talk of the valley. Although no pictures of the dwelling survive, we have several descriptions of it. It was built on high X-scored and finished granite piers under which one could walk without stooping. This area was open. At the rear of the house, the piers were about 8 feet tall. (One of these piers may be seen in the yard of the Hardy plantation, where it was brought in the 1970s.) The house had four rooms over four and a central hall. The chimneys were interior, and the house had no gables. The porch was one story and wrapped around the front and sides. Its columns were square and bannistered with decorative iron railings like those to be seen today at Rose Hill. A high flight of steps led to the porches at front and rear.

The central hall was said to be the largest room in the area; and, as such, it was often used for its biggest reel dances. This hall was plastered and elaborately decorated with plaster coffering supported by plaster acanthus-leaf brackets and surrounded by plaster crown molding of egg-and-dart design. The chamber facing the drawing room was decorated with an 8-inch plaster molding of strawberries and strawberry leaves above egg-and-dart beading. In the room's center was an ornate medallion of acanthus leaves like the one still to be seen at Herndon Terrace in Union, built 1845–1848, and Dr. James M. Eppes's house near Whitmire, built in 1857. One who recalls the Sims medallions in the great hall says that it "was just like that in the parlor of the Eppes house." The strawberry and egg-and-dart design of the Sims plantation was precisely the same as the molding in Governor Thomas Jeter's home in Union, built in 1859. All these houses were constructed close enough in time to have been decorated by the same artisans, almost certainly the John Finger and his crew of white and slave workers referred to in the preceding chapters. Finger, we know for sure, worked and resided in the Tyger-Goshen Hill area from as early as 1842 to as late as 1863. In 1937 Miss Fannie Epps did, in fact, recall that he did the plaster decoration at the Eppes, Hardy, and Ben Sims plantations, as well as other homes in Union County, thus verifying our surmise. A study of the art of John Finger is much needed. The rooms upstairs in the Ben Sims plantation were also said to be plaster-decorated; but no description of them remains.

All rooms in the Great House were wainscoted. The downstairs mantels were large, but not particularly memorable. The most notable feature of the house, as recounted by all who saw it, was John Finger's magnificent hard-plaster ornamentation. The surviving pieces of medallions and moldings preserved at the Hardy plantation corroborate the fact. It vied with the best of plasterwork in America, and the house had the tall and spacious well-lit rooms needed for this artwork's proper display.

No doubt the Great Houses at the Hamilton and Thomas plantations a few miles to the north of the Sims place also bore Finger's excellent craftmanship. There are a large number of plantations in Union, Newberry, Fairfield, and Chester Counties from the period 1820–1861 that still exhibit first-rate plaster ornamentaion. The elaborateness of both neoclassical and innovative new designs will likely be a great surprise to those who are not familiar with the houses of the Upcountry.

All the Big Houses of the area were well constructed, but the Sims house was especially so. The 60-foot-long heart-pine flooring ran the length of the house without piecing and was clear of knots. It was held in place by twentypenny cut square nails. The Great House had a detached kitchen to its rear, like most of the homes of its time.

Another house, the close twin to the Ben Sims Great House, sat about nine miles north of it at the northeast corner of the crossroads of the Santuc and Carlisle-Whitmire Roads. It had the same design, floor plan, and architectural details down to the decorative iron bannisters between square columns.

There is a brief record from 1912 of one of the Ben Sims slaves, Aunt Ciller. As we have seen, her portrait was painted in the 1850s by her young mistress, Miss Addie Sims, who read the Bible and *Pilgrim's Progress* to her as Ciller sat outside under the oaks surrounded by her household goods and kitchen utensils. According to Ciller, her father was a king who was taken in battle by a rival king. Instead of beheading him, as was the usual custom, the victor sold him into bondage to a slave trader who brought him to the James River in Virginia. He died in Virginia, but his daughter came to settle on the Tyger with Charles Sims in 1783. She became a waiting maid to old "Marster," as she called him, and died at the age of ninety, after having lived her last years on the plantation of Major Starke Sims.

The Ben Sims plantation, besides being the Hardy estate's closest Great House neighbor after it was constructed in 1850, had even closer ties to the Hardy plantation after 1869, for on 16 December of that year, William Dixon Hardy, home after four years of war and soon to take over the Hardy lands after his father's death in 1870, married the seven-teen-year-old heiress of the Sims household, Frances Booker Sims. William was twenty-eight and a very eligible bachelor in a region where over a quarter of the male population of his age had been killed in the war. The event was one of the largest to be held at the Sims house after the war. The newlyweds kept their Christmas well that year despite the postwar gloom. This would be the last big season reflecting the antebellum elegance of the golden years of both plantations. Although subdued in deference to all those families who had lost loved ones, the old-time reel dance was the order of the day, complete with fiddle and banjo. Young Frances traveled the short mile and a half over the Tyger to take up residence with her Hardy in-laws as the young mistress of a diminished Hardy estate. She was to bear a son in 1871, Benjamin Sims Hardy, named for her father, and, in time, nine other children, the scions who would bring the now allied Sims-Hardy clan into the next century.

It was natural that in the plantation world of Tyger, the sons and daughters of neighboring plantations would marry. This was the case on the Sims, Hardy, and Douglass plantations, separated by only a few miles. Then too, all three of these families attended the same church, Ebenezer, which Bishop Asbury had founded with the help of the Hardys shortly after the Revolution. Ebenezer Cemetery tells the story. Buried here side by side are the members of these three families, neighbors in death as they were in life in a lively plantation era and the time of trial that followed it.

In the second quarter of this century, the Ben Sims plantation was sold into the hands of tree-farming interests, which allowed the house to deteriorate. It collapsed around 1980. Square column capitals and wooden cornices can still be seen among the tin, brick, and remains of floor joists. One such cornice is incorporated into William Carter's house near Newberry. Pieces of the elaborate plaster moldings (acanthus-leaf brackets, egg-and-dart molding, strawberry leaves, and acanthus-leaf medallions) are preserved at the Hardy plantation. As at the Chick place and Orange Hall, little else remains but a mound of crumbled brick and plaster to mark the site of an American architectural treasure, as well as the seat of a family and its connection to a civilization.

THE HAMILTON AND THOMAS PLANTATIONS

Several miles north of the Ben Sims Great House were two fine antebellum homes. The first was the Hamilton mansion, a clapboard plantation plain-style structure of two and a half storys and a one-story front porch. It collapsed in the 1950s.

The Thomas plantation, likely built between 1830 and 1840, was in the Tuckertown community, some four miles north of the Tyger. It was another two-and-a-half story plantation plain-style structure with a one-story front porch and shed rooms to the rear. The core had two rooms over two and exterior end chimneys. Extant photographs of its mantels and wainscoting reveal close similarities to the 1825 section of the Hardy mansion. Some of the wainscoting had white panels with blue chair rail; others had dark red panels with blue chair rail. The walls were smooth-plastered. Mantels were stained black as in the Hardy mansion. The windows had exterior louver shutters. The house's last owner details a full, delicate spiral staircase and a formal entry with semicircular fanlights over front and rear hall doors. It had a particularly beautiful setting off the road. Mrs. Sarah Stokes remembers the great crash, like an explosion, when the long-abandoned house collapsed around 1975.

THE COMER (TUCKER) HOUSE AND VICINITY

When many Quaker families left southeastern Union County between 1800 and 1810, the Comers remained. Their two-and-a-half story clapboard plantation plain-style home was built around 1830 "from trees sawn on the place," as the seat of a large cotton plantation. It still stands on its rise in the heart of what is left of the Tuckertown community, to the front of the Thomas plantation site. Its one-story porch, shed rooms, exterior end chimneys, and two-over-two floor plan are very close to the design of the Thomas home. Its notable interior consists of Federal sunburst mantels, an interesting narrow staircase, and trompe l'oeil grained doors. The mantels and baseboards have their original black stain, as in the Hardy home. The central second-story window in the staircase is positioned precisely as is the one in the Hardy house. Many similar features exist between the two houses. Were it not for the double portico at the Hardy house and some finer details in woodwork and staircase, the structures would be close indeed.

A very old hewn square-log building, perhaps a former one-room slave cabin, sits to the east (front) side of the house, and an interesting dairy building stands on the north (rear) side. This is the only such milk-keeping structure I have seen outside the adjacent Dutch Fork area of Newberry and Lexington Counties. A good example can be visited on the grounds of the Lexington County Museum.

In 1934 the Great House had an old well "inside the lot gate" that in the summer made it "the most popular place for men and beast after a hard day's work." Across the road was said to be "a small corn mill, where the old and young darkies gather, and where seated on long benches attached to the side of the buildings, they pass many an evening talking over their joys and sorrows. Always there is keen interest when a car happens to pass that way. There are fifteen or twenty homes within sight of the old mill, and one . . . marvels at the neatness of the outward appearance of the homes, scattered here and there in the hills." In 1934 the houses were said to be white with blue trim: "no one in that section is able to buy paint, when so many are in need of food and clothes, owing to the shortage of crops. They would soon tell you that 'God gave us the paint,' for most of them are religiously inclined. All they have to do is go to the ditches and get white clay, mix it to a paste and with a rag apply it, . . . [clothes] bluing being used as 'Trimming.' Most of the houses have only the front porches 'decorated.'" Tuckertown in 1934 had only "a few scattered white families," who were land owners, or were "employed by the sawmill near the river." Beside the old corn mill was a small wood structure used by the black community as church, school, and meeting house.

Also across the road from the Comer house was the John Richards home. The U.S. Forestry Service bought this plantation for timberland at $7 per acre and allowed the house to decay and collapse "a good while ago," recalls Mrs. Sarah Stokes. A few miles further up the road toward Santuc sat the Renwick mansion. Still further toward Santuc at the crossroads of the Whitmire–Carlisle Road was the twin to the Ben Sims Great House, as previously described.

A note on Santuc and Fish Dam (Carlisle) is in order here. Four large Great Houses still stand there: the Tucker house (1859); Seven Springs, a pleasing classical revival structure with Doric columns, and very similar in design to both the James M. Eppes house in Whitmire and the Colonel Robert Beaty mansion that was a near neighbor to Rose Hill eight miles distant from Seven Springs; Juxa (c. 1820), with one of the best-proportioned classical revival exteriors in Union County; and the large and welcoming Woodland Home (c. 1858), seat of the Jeter family. The last is a three-story mansion with a two-floor front portico, whose square first-floor columns are fitted on all four sides with glass panels, and in which lanterns were placed to welcome family and visitors on their drive up the lane to the home. To my knowledge, only the antebellum Clarkson house in Columbia, South Carolina, has such columns. At the Clarkson place they were designed to display exotic orchids to passersby even in the dead of winter, in what amounted to minigreenhouses. The elegance and ingenuity of Carolina upcountry designers never ceases to impress. Their imaginations were obviously free to create, and create they did. Woodland Home (which contains many of its original furnishings) also has about it many of its original log outbuildings, including a plantation commissary. The home is still occupied by descendants of the Jeter family who built it. They are now in the process of restoring house and grounds.

At Fish Dam, a graceful Federal structure called Hillside was constructed around 1820 as the plantation seat of the Hill family. This was the site of the Hill Quarry, from which the granite trim of Orange Hall was taken. Hillside's tall granite gateposts were the work of J. E. Sherman, who also did the gateposts and other carvings for Orange Hall. At Hillside the gatepost decoration consists of twisting grapevines complete with grape clusters. The scores of granite posts for the old picket fence provide an outline of the impressively large garden area spilling down the terraces from the Great House. The home itself is nicely preserved and features a grained marble mantel in the drawing room and an early two-story log barn. Descendants of the original owner still occupy the house.

Near Fish Dam on the Broad River, Amerindians built an impressive zigzag wall of rocks from bank to bank as a means of impounding fish for spearing. It is from this construction that the area gets its name. Chapman Milling, in his *Beneath So Kind a Sky* (1947), related that after such a harvest, these ancient fishermen and their families held communal feasts on the riverbanks. These same rocks were used as a ford by the first white settlers. On the Chester County side of the river occurred the significant Revolutionary War battle between General Gates and General Greene, the Battle of Fish Dam Ford. The fish dam can still be seen from the bridge on Highway 72 when the water level is low. It is without doubt the oldest man-made feature of the area.

THE BERRY RICHARDS PLANTATION

In what was called the Richards Quarter, near the confluence of the Tyger and Broad Rivers in Newberry County and two miles from the Hardy plantation, Berry Richards built a Greek revival cottage in the late 1840s on a rise above the two rivers. The house faced east with its back to the Broad. It sat on Shelton Ferry Road, which terminates at the Broad across from the old Shelton community in Fairfield County.

M. G. Berry Richards was born 15 April 1825. In July 1850 he married Elizabeth Kitchens of Unionville. The agricultural statistics of the census that year list his holdings as 574 acres, 220 unimproved and 354 improved. He had 11 horses, no mules, oxen, or sheep; 5 milk cows, 50 hogs, and 10 "other" cattle. He raised 700 bushels of corn, 200 bushels of oats, and 10 bushels of sweet potatoes, and made 200 pounds of butter. Cotton, his cash crop, yielded 60 bales of 400 pounds each.

By 1860 Richards had two daughters, Elizabeth and Leila, born in 1855 and 1857, and had hired an overseer, Caleb Gasaway. He now owned sixteen slaves, who lived in five dwellings. There were eight adults and eight children. One of these slave families included Lucy Richards Feaster, wife of Price Feaster (likely living on a neighboring plantation), and her children Gus (born in 1840), Albert, William, and Harriet. Richards now owned 4 horses, 5 mules, 2 cows, 30 hogs, and 11 "other" cattle. He raised 105 bushels of wheat, 110 of corn, 11 bushels of Irish potatoes, and 41 bales of cotton.

Richards's house, which stood until 1996, was a noteworthy Greek revival temple of a story and a half. It had two rooms over four, an oversized central hall, and fifteen-pane modified Palladian windows in the front pediment that projected over the porch. These same "Venetian" windows were also in the gables at either side of the structure. The house corners had wooden entasis column ornamentation similar to that at the Hardy mansion. The house sat on high brick piers and had external chimneys laid in American or "common" bond like the Hardy chimneys. The clay for these was dug on the place from a clay pit that can still be seen behind the house. The woodwork on the portico was classic triglyph and metope, as in many homes of the period in this area. Interior woodwork was simple. Mantels were dark-stained, as were the front doors. Interior doors in 1996 still bore blue and cream-colored paint. The walls were rough-sawn pine covered with linen, over which wallpaper was mounted. Strips of kelly-green flowered wallpaper were still to be seen in the hallway when the house was dismantled. The windows had wainscot panels beneath them that were similar to those in the Hardy house. Similar also was the double-doored entrance with trabiated sidelights and transom. But the lozenge over the entrance (to match the one in the porch pediment) was like the one in the 1849 Rose Cottage. These two structures were likely built around the same time and probably by the same artisans. All in all, the Richards cottage presented a beautifully pleasing design.

House rafters and floor joists were made of smoothed pine poles. This construction is often seen in the area, as for example at Seven Springs in Santuc. Blacks of the community took some pride in this dwelling because they relate that its building was overseen by an African-American builder-overseer.

The grounds were planted in a large cirque of oaks in front of the house. These were cut in 1995 to plant pines. Many daffodils and jonquils still reveal the outline of a small garden about the house. A story-and-a-half rusticated board-and-batten slave house with a central stone chimney still stands on the site, as does an old pegged well shed. The family cemetery is situated to the north of the house and looks from its high plateau to the Broad. The gravestones face due east. Here is buried Berry Richards, the plantation master, who died in March 1865 in battle near Goldsboro, North Carolina, in service of the Confederacy. At the time of his death he was lieutenant of the Fifth Regimental Cavalry, South Carolina Volunteers. The Fifth was the regiment that most of the neighborhood boys joined. Richards was also a Mason, as his tombstone, with the Masonic emblem encircled by a chaplet of carved roses, declares. What became of his widow and two young daughters is not known. The plantation, at any rate, passed from Richards family ownership after his death. Mary Summer Foster sold most of the lands to the U.S. Forestry Service in the 1930s; but the house itself was retained by the Kennedy family of Union County as a tenant property. The house at its dismantling was in excellent repair. Its wood is said to be destined for a reconstruction near Chapel Hill, North Carolina.

MAYBINTON

The flush times for this bustling little stagecoach village along the Charleston-Asheville road were the three decades from 1830 to 1860. In 1950 it was called a ghost town. Now it is not even that, having lost its last store building in the 1960s and the Benjamin Maybin house in 1980. Today the only evidences of the once busy town here at the intersection of the Maybinton and Tyger River roads are the old Whitney house (c. 1830), a solitary fieldstone chimney, and a deserted antebellum home hidden by oaks and tangle on a hill south of the road.

Irish pioneer William Maybin came through the port of Charleston from Bellamena, County Antrim, Ireland, and settled here in 1771 with his wife and child. He started a trading post in a log cabin on the State Road but soon died in the Patriot cause on a prison ship during the Revolution. His younger brother, Matthew, also died in the Revolution. William's widow, Jane Duncan Maybin, and their son, Colonel Benjamin Maybin (1775–1849), survived him. It was the latter who through his genius and energy established the village, and for whom it was named. Benjamin and his widowed mother continued to operate his ill-fated father's store. Living with them were her mother (the widow Duncan, as she was called) and Jane's sister. Being directly on the chief thoroughfare in the state, Colonel Ben's business thrived. Some time before 1826, he also built and operated the famous Buck Hotel, which became a favorite resort for tourists, travelers, and aristocratic sportsmen. Game had always been superabundant in the area owing to the rich land and the three rivers. Long before the white man came, the Cherokee had singled it out for a preferred hunting ground. Tradition is that the name Buck was given the hotel on account of the many large deer hunts originating from its doors in the antebellum era. These events were particularly popular with the Carolina plantation gentry. As we have seen, there was another Buck Hotel in Asheville, North Carolina, operated in the 1830s by an in-law of Dr. James Hardy, who had moved to Asheville by 1824. Whether or not there was any connection between the two hotels cannot be said, but the Hardy tie makes for interesting surmise.

In its heyday, as remembered by former slave Pick Gladdeny, the venerable old Buck "had large stables and a lots of folks" stopping there to rest "overnight on their way to the Springs . . . Glenn's, Chick's, and West Springs." By 1865, he continued, "Stages had done gone out, but that's where dey stopped when they come from Spring Hill" (further south toward Columbia on the Old State Road). When Gladdeny first recalled it (that is, in the early 1860s), it "was run fer a dwelling house by Mr. Jeff Stewart." Alice Dawkins Sims, born a slave around 1850, recalled in 1938 that it was operated at one time by Mrs. Sara Chick of Rose Cottage and her maid Liza. In 1970 some of the hotel's foundation stones could still be seen behind the country store operated by Mrs. Gertrude Henderson at the present intersection of Maybinton and Tyger River Roads.

By 1829 Maybinton had a post office. John Maybin served as its first postmaster from 1829 to 1841. A succession of postmasters (George Ashford in 1842, John Allen in 1843, Morris Maybin in 1845, James

Henderson in 1849, Joshua Bishop in 1852, W. F. Holmes in 1853, John Jeter in 1854, James Glenn in 1857, David Gross in 1858, and William Oxner in the 1860s) kept it running until it was discontinued some time after 1867, when the South's defeat pronounced the village's death sentence and boom and flush times turned to bust and hard times. In 1937 former slave Eison Lyles recalled Bill Oxner "who had the post office and live up in a big grove where the squirrels was real tame and loves to play."

But in 1829 the "big doings" had just begun. In this decade Colonel Maybin had just constructed an imposing two-and-a-half-story house for his family in the village center. It was of Palladian design similar in conception to the new front section of the Hardy mansion. Another two-and-a-half-story dwelling was built shortly thereafter (c. 1830) adjacent to the Maybins. This home later became known by the name of its subsequent owner William Brown Whitney (1851–1935), who came from Charleston, where his Bostonian father owned a candle and coach-lamp factory. As is readily discernible from the history of the Hardys, the decade of the 1830s in this area was a time of growing fortunes. Local historian Leland Summer accurately describes the village at this period as rapidly expanding in enterprise "as large quantities of cotton were shipped by flatboat down Broad River to Charleston." Summer reveals that some of the stores were brick buildings. In fact, a brickyard was established in the town to make use of the excellent clay in the vicinity. There was also a large tannery. The town had a Baptist church, and Ebenezer Methodist had been functioning since the 1780s a few miles away. A lot was set aside for a new Presbyterian church, which, however, was never built on account of limited membership. Summer also reports the existence in the village of a large and active Masonic lodge and hall. This was in addition to the Solomon Lodge at Orange Hall.

Colonel Benjamin Maybin, historian O'Neall reports, retired from his businesses in 1826; but the original Maybin store continued to sell its goods under new management, and the popular Buck Hotel simply got a new proprietor to serve a new generation.

In 1836 there were academies in the village for both males and females. The males' school was on an elevated site on the edge of the town; the one for females was at its center. Summer reveals that "they were both schools with high standards of study, teaching English, Higher Mathematics, Latin, and Greek." The female academy had a course in music. Each school had a board of trustees to govern it. One principal of the male academy was Professor Chancey Stone; while his daughter, Miss Sarah Stone, had charge of the female academy. The schools persevered as best they could into the 1880s under the direction of Miss Helen Hodges. There was a grade school in Maybinton as late as 1929.

In 1839 Maybinton was designated as one of eleven polling places in Newberry County. It still exists as such at the present time, though one of the smallest. Citizens voted at James Bond's store, the rival to the Maybin establishment. In the 1840s an important sawmill near the village was operated by Albert G. Maybin. It was at this mill that much of the boarding for the buildings in both the village and the surrounding area was cut and dressed during this decade.

By 1850 O'Neall could describe Maybinton as "a pretty little village." The census for that year provides a detailed picture of the town at what was close to its peak. One person doing business there was Thomas Murtishaw (1813–1873), a bootmaker and member of Ebenezer Church, where he is buried. He had a wife and three children in 1850. There was also Thomas Nance, a twenty-nine-year-old shoemaker, married and the father of three. By this time, Benjamin Maybin had died (in 1849); but his seventy-year-old widow Elizabeth (1780–1865), the only surviving child of Colonel James Lisles, was listed as head of the household that included an eight-year-old adopted daughter, Martha Smith, and widower James M. Henderson (1812–1860), likely Elizabeth's son by her first marriage to Captain John Henderson. In 1850 James was the new merchant operator of Maybin's Store. He was also postmaster of the village. There was at least one other store in the village besides Maybin & Co.; this was owned by one-time postmaster George Ashford, a forty-three-year-old bachelor who died in 1866 and left hs estate to his two sisters. Living in his household were a "ship carpenter," H. T. Gary (thirty-seven) and a store clerk, T. E. Tucker (eighteen). The village sported a tailor, Jesse Bishop, a forty-seven-year-old father of two daughters. It had two excellent blacksmiths: Thomas Wells, a fifty-one-year-old father of three; and Pierce Wright, a twenty-four-year-old father of two. There was also a wheelwright, Benjamin McJunkin, who died insolvent at age fifty-four, leaving a widow and four children. Also in the village were C. E. Sims, a thirty-three-year-old clerk and father of three, and Siney O'Neil, a fifty-seven-year-old native of Ireland, who resided with the Piercy Slattery family, who lived between the Maybin and the Whitney houses.

By 1865 there was a popular store on the periphery of the Whitney porperty. Gladdeny recalled it as being "a big store . . . kept by Mr. Pettus Chick and Mr. Bill Oxner . . . a good store. Didn't have to go to Newberry to git no candy and 'bacco."

There were at least three village physicians in 1850. One was Dr. Thomas Jefferson Lyles (1808–1879), originally from the Lisles plantation on Tyger, and close neighbor to the Hardys. He was forty-two, was recently widowed for a second time, and had a young daughter Sarah. The second was Dr. Charles W. Hodges. He had a wife and two children and boarded William Kelley, designated in the census as a "student physician." The third was Dr. Joseph Reid, twenty-two years old, who lived in the Buck Hotel in 1850 and moved west before the war. The village was soon also to acquire the service of a fourth physician, Dr. William F. Holmes, an ex-postmaster. Around 1865 Dr. James Ruff was the most popular physician.

In 1850 the Buck Hotel was being managed by J. A. Black, who was twenty-five. He had two younger relatives living with him. Also residing in the hotel were the previously mentioned Dr. Reid; Mr. A. Sims, a seventeen-year-old clerk; Mr. Thomas McConnor, a twenty-five-year-old Ohio-born stage driver; and Mr. Low Harvey, a twenty-five-year-old North Carolina-born stage driver.

The population of Maybinton village in 1850 thus numbered between 70 and 85 whites with an extensive plantation country surrounding it. Doubtless there were as many, or more, black retainers in the village who helped with the various duties and business of the day. The Maybins and others of the town also had adjacent farmland and made use of farm labor, thus necessitating a number of humble cabins in the environs. There was at least one free black in Maybinton in 1850. Her name was E. Koon. She was fifty years old, and the census reports that she lived alone. Her patronym was prominent in the German Dutch Fork area in lower Newberry County. In 1845 the Hardy ledgers report a free black by the name of Charles living in the household of Albert G. Maybin, who was paying his blacksmithing bills. Another free black was in the household of Bennet Hancock on nearby Enoree River in 1845.

The town was able to present a relatively high show of refinement and "society." Hunting and horse racing were the great entertainments. Because this was blooded horse country, Maybinton, like Goshen Hill and Santuc, had its own track. It was owned by the Maybins and located directly behind the Maybin house. The proximity of the Buck Hotel allowed for visiting horsemen to join in the festivities. These races had the reputation of being particularly spirited and well attended. They were much celebrated, and their fame spread throughout the Upcountry. Other than the big race days and academy graduations, perhaps one of the chief social events in the history of the town was the barbeque, speech, and celebration of 3 August 1848 in honor of the Palmetto Regiment in the Mexican War. Another was the send-off given to the gallant boys in gray in 1861. One of the town's most significant events was the 1840 convention that nominated P. C. Caldwell to run for Congress. The meeting was held at the Buck Hotel. Because Maybinton was a major polling place in the antebellum era, it was a center for political speeches and the barbeques that surrounded them.

Another favorite pastime of Maybintonians was dancing—both reel and "fancy." By 1859 the town had become sophisticated indeed, as indicated by this note sent to Mr. William Renwick of Orange Hall:

> Maybinton, S.C.
> May 7, 1859
>
> Mr. Renwick
> I shall commence my second session in Dancing—Thursday the 12th and I would be more than pleased to have you send your sons to me as Pupils. I will teach them any fancy dance you would wish them to learn.
> Yours truly,
> Rosannah Carncross

When a village gets a "fancy"-dancing mistress, it may be said to have arrived. On the eve of the war, the slaves enjoyed their dances too, but of a different nature: "Pats our feets and knocks tin pans was the music dat us dance to all night long. Put on my clean clothes dat was made right on de plantation and wear them to the dance. Gals wore their homespun stockings. Wore the dresses so long dat they kivered their shoes. My britches were copperas colored and I had on a home wove shirt with a pleated bosom. It was dyed red."

In 1937 this same former slave recalled a momentous day in Maybinton in the year 1865. It was called Emancipation Day. There was a big speech by Daniel White, telling the slaves of their freedom. There was a big brass band (of the occupation army). But let us listen to Gladdeny, who was about ten years old at the time:

Site of folks dar all day, settin' aroun'. Us clam trees, so us could see and hear. I sho did listen, but I don't 'member nothin' what de man say. I knows dis, dat I still hears dat band music ringing in my ears. At dat time, I was so young dat all I cared about on dat day, was the brass band which let out so much music. Niggers being free never meant nothing to us chaps. . . . Dat de first band dat I ever seed, and . . . I never seed no more til the World War fotch de soldiers all through here. Bands charms me so much dat dey just plumb tickles the tips of my toes on both feets.

In 1892 historian John Chapman wrote of Maybinton: "Since the war, great changes have taken place. . . . The parts of the country which were richest, when the old system of labor was destroyed, suffered most. Maybinton section did not entirely escape, though there is still a considerable degree of prosperity, and the people are slowly but surely recuperating. There, as well as everywhere else, we find that there is life in the old land yet." Chapman, however, had not foreseen the effects of rail travel that bypassed the town and diminished the importance of the Old State Road, or, still more seriously, of the double scourges of government insensitivity to cotton culture in the post–World War I era and the devastation wrought by the boll weevil. With no railroad and no strong crop, the town had no economic base on which to build and survive for a new era.

Maybinton struggled on as a placename into the 1950s until the store operated by Mrs. Gertrude Henderson finally closed its doors shortly after 1970. It was a white wooden country store, typical of those seen throughout the rural South. Now even this building has disappeared. The Maybin home burned in 1980; and today only its ruins, the deserted old Whitney House, and a stone chimney remain as melancholy vestiges of a lively bygone era.

12

A World Kicked to Pieces

They make for man a new Thermopylae
—W.G. Simms, "Morris Island" (1863)

Although a time of eager and great expectation, 1861 saw the Hardy Great House sad with loss. By its close, over half of its inhabitants were gone, and for the master and mistress it must have been a trying year indeed, and a prelude to even more difficult times ahead.

The first departure was a happy one. Their only daughter, Elmira Frances, whose closest friend at Salem Academy was Mary Frost, had spent much time with the Frosts at their Richland County plantation since they graduated. And Mary had as frequently stayed at the Hardys' and The Oaks, for she had also been a classmate of the Douglass cousins at Salem. Mary and Elmira were inseparable, and now Mary's older brother, John, who had been courting Mira for some time, had asked Squire Hardy for her hand in marriage. The Frosts were well-to-do planters with "vast tracts of land in Richland, Fairfield, and Newberry Counties" and a townhouse in Columbia. Their principal seat was their cotton plantation just north of the village. Mira would be well cared for and John had the reputation of being a bright and learned man of sterling character. The squire's answer was "Of course." She would be their first child to wed.

Mira, now twenty-five and her father's delight, married twenty-nine-year-old John Davis Frost III on the 26th of February in a great and festive celebration at the Hardy plantation. Printed cards announcing the event and reception had been hand-carried by servants or mailed to those distant:

Mr. & Mrs. W. E. Hardy,
At Home,
Tuesday Evening, Feb. 26th, 1861,
Half past 7 o'clock.

MIRA F. HARDY.   J. D. FROST, JR.

All this occurred during stirring times. The war fever and excitement were at their height. Carolina had declared its independence two months earlier, and the Hardys and Frosts were staunch Southerners. Their loyalty was to church, family, home, and the South as a nation. It was becoming increasingly clear that certain elements in the North were determined to rule the Union, to dictate policy for all the country. This push to make the rest of the republic conform to its pattern was destroying the careful old-time friendly balance between the regions, and the very nature of republican government itself, seen by the Hardys as a kind of gentleman's agreement whose bond was the Constitution, now being violated. It was time to resist. All said so in public and in private.

Neighbor Renwick at Orange Hall had just summed up their views in an articulate and succinct letter successfully volunteering his services to Colonel Wade Hampton:

Orange Hall May 25th 1860

Col. Hampton

Sir, not having any personal acquaintance with you, I should feel a hesitancy in writing to you, but for the character of the business. From the present indications, information to be had on the demonstrations on the part of the Administration of the Federal Government shows a determination to subjugate the South to their craven appetites for gain, and the unscrupulous legislation of a northern Majority. I have been a looker on in the course of events and manifestations on the part of the government in Washington and of parties for near thirty years, and have been anxious to see a position of safety taken by the South. The Government that [was] set on foot for mutual protection and mutual advancement has passed into an engine of sectional oppression for sectional aggrandizement. Everything else that surrounds the issues of the day are frothy and calculated for illusion. The position of the North is that she will govern herself *and govern the South also*. As to the governing herself, she is welcome; but as to her governing the South—then we join issue. The North is the aggressor and may or may not push her designs. The South will have no alternative to resistance but extermination. I have never been candidate for office in my life though have served appointments occasionally. In this Issue, I feel like life and fortune are unconditionally involved, the only question being, how they shall serve the cause most efficiently.

Will you please send me some information respecting your Legion's organization and the perquisites and requisites etc.

Very respectfully yours in the Cause of the South

W. W. Renwick

Renwick was present at the wedding party on that night in February 1861, and there were none attending who disagreed with his sentiments. But now events had been pushed even further than when he penned his letter to Hampton.

With the state's brave secession in December 1860, a new young flag of an infant nation had been unfurled in Charleston, the white single star and crescent on a scarlet field—the flag of secession. It flew in the Southern breeze over the customs house as the new year began. Now the big question in everyone's mind was whether Southerners would have war made on them to force them to remain in the Union or whether they would be allowed to go in peace. They hoped and prayed for the best but rightly judged the new president Lincoln to be a man who would wage war. The party that had elected him was too often controlled by extremists aggressively out for spoils and national domination. These were the heirs of Hamilton, who believed in a Federal bank, tariffs protective of industry, and internal improvements to benefit business and industry, and paid for by the public at large, most particularly the Southern planters. Lincoln's election (without any support from the Jeffersonian South) proved to these opportunists that there was no longer any need for them to compromise and that they could have their way. No one could stop them. As those at the wedding party saw it, the South was forced to defend itself and must not lose, for if it was defeated, this band of new politicians would make the South into a colony for conquest, easy pickings for economic exploitation. Yes, it was indeed a matter of rampant imperialism; and, as the old squire put it, "The South must resist domination with every ounce of her strength."

Carolina knew clearly what was riding on her actions. As neighbor Renwick phrased it, success or extinction; it was as simple as that. They were making a brave gamble but a necessary one, which they felt forced into. The Secessionists lamented, "If only independence could have come earlier when the South was more evenly matched with the North in population and could better defend herself." This was their chief regret; but the rest of the South, until now when it had been pushed to the wall, was not ready to follow Carolina's lead.

The young, too, were keeping a close eye on affairs. Neighbor and kinsman Ben Maybin, a student at Wofford College, and for whom Squire Hardy served as guardian, wrote to the plantation on 12 January 1861 that in Spartanburg,

> There is no local news worth writing except the drilling of the Volunteers, among whom is your humble servant. Alabama has seceded, and Hon. Robert Toombs of Georgia called Gen. Scott a Liar to his face, and he (Scott) got up to fight, but friends interfered. . . . It is reported that seven men are to be shot for trying to desert. This was found out by the Priest being sent for.

Dickie was there at Wofford with him and also working in the mercantile establishment of his uncle Hamlin Hardy's son, Cousin John Wesley

Hardy. He was drilling with Ben. At the time, as Ben reported, Dickie was "sick in bed with the measles, but in good spirits, I think." He would not be able to come home to the plantation on the railroad and be "sent for" at the station, as planned: "Dickie told me to tell you that he is better and that he will not be down Monday. You must not be uneasy about him." As for Ben himself, he was asking Squire Hardy to settle his accounts at school:

> asking you to please attend to them if it is in your power, as I have been dunned already, and it is very disagreeable indeed. The whole amount is about $250 inclusive of tuition for 4 sessions which is $108. These commenced about April 1859 and have continued up to the present time. I have complied with your request to be as economical as possible. 'Tis true I have bought things I did not need. . . . I will close by sending my Love to all and a due share to you.

As he had for his own sons at Lee's Academy, the good squire was once again cautioning his nephew against excess, and Ben was manfully admitting that he had not been all too Spartan in Spartanburg.

Though life was thus going on in its externals in its usual jog-trot way, these were tense and stirring times for young and old alike. The talk of freedom and the rights of a people to self-determination moved the spirits of Hardy men and women, who had the blood of Magna Carta, the Virginia House of Burgesses, and the first American Revolution in their veins. They and their neighbors were Jeffersonian to the core and knew quite well that separation now looked inevitable if they were to save an agrarian way of life, and, further, that Southern independence and Jeffersonian principles were truly worth dying for. The young Hardys faced the prospect bravely with faith and hope. If their homeland were attacked, they would defend it, for doing so was a matter of survival. All of this was much the subject of conversation in the three-day wedding festivities this February of 1861. As the candles in the drawing room burned high, Squire Hardy gave his daughter to young Frost with the usual happiness mingled with regret at her going. Catharine and he would miss their only daughter sorely, but they had faith that this would be a fruitful marriage, and so it was to be. Their first grandchild would be born the next year and was to be followed by eight others, all of whom lived to maturity. With the hurry and bustle of activity, of wedding and reception, and all the Frosts staying with them at the Great House, they had little time to be sad. The house was packed to over-flowing for days. Dickie and Ben were home from Wofford. Grand-mother Hardy was there, and all the Douglass kin. But then too quickly, as it seemed for William and Catharine, they were gone.

On the heels of Mira's departure, tragic losses struck the family in rapid succession. While the guns of Sumter boomed that April, the mas-ter's twenty-nine-year-old son Charles Wesley lay ill with typhoid fever, which was epidemic in the area that spring. His father called in both Dr. Douglass and Dr. Will Holmes of Maybinton. Holmes had a servant run the following note from the Hardys to The Oaks, where Douglass was himself attending the widow Anna Hardy, also sick with the fever:

Dear Dr Douglass

Dr Hardy's case presents a tout ensemble of *symptoms* far from promising. I do not know that there has been any de-cided change for the worse but the circulation remains abrupt and rapid notwithstanding, a free perspiration all day. There is some incoherence, some subsultus, some starting from sleep. If you can come down tonight we would be glad to see you.

Holmes

Uncle George did come, but Charles's condition grew worse, and he died on the 15th of April. Young Charles had graduated from the Medi-cal College in Charleston only six years before—his short and promising life was now cut off unexpectedly. This broke his father's heart. The parents had scarcely time to grieve before the widow Hardy, Catharine's seventy-eight-year-old mother and the grand matriarch of the family, died three days later at The Oaks. Although some consolation was taken from the fact that she "was fully prepared for death," as a granddaughter described her, the loss left both the Hardys and their Douglass kin "lonely" and "impossible to reconcile it . . . that we will never have her with us again." Aunt Anna was also a favorite of Squire Hardy, her orphan nephew and son-in-law, and like a mother to him. She had lived for a time in the Hardy house with the couple after their marriage before moving near her younger daughter at The Oaks. Here, as we have seen, she oversaw an estate of over 700 acres and 32 slaves right up until her death. In her last year, she was still an active lady, strong, vigorous, and effective as a plantation mistress. Just months ago, she had taken the cars to Spartanburg for a long visit with kin.

As for Catharine, the departure of her only daughter and the loss of son and mother, all of which had taken place in a matter of weeks, left her "desolate." Her sister's family at The Oaks feared that her loneliness was now serious enough for comment and importuned the new Mrs. Frost to come home from Columbia and visit her. For the young Douglass nieces, Garrie and Annie, it was "very lonely down there for one of us to sit" with Aunt Katie, "with no girl around." But Catharine had "been so lonely of late" that they made long and short visits to see her, family pulling together to sustain an individual in time of her need.

Meanwhile, the bombardment in Charleston continued. For a week now the giant guns of Sumter could be heard as far inland as the lower part of the county. Young Dickie, now twenty years old, enlisted on the 13th of April, the very day after the shelling began and two days before his brother Charles's death. Though slight of build, he had always been a lively, active young fellow at a hunt, on the race course, or with the ladies in the reel; and now, like his great-grandfather Hardy before him in the Revolution, he was one of the first to volunteer. He, like his father and brother Haywood, wore the crest of the family well: *Arme de foi Hardi*—armed with boldness. It would be a defensive struggle for freedom and independence, not a war of Southern aggression. As he professed, he was "protecting hearth, home, and Southern rights." Their new Southern president would soon express precisely the way they all felt: "All we want is to be let alone"—to be allowed to go in peace to control our own destiny. This, tragically for the Hardys, and for the agrarian tradition itself, was not to be.

Dickie and Ben Maybin volunteered from Spartanburg, where they signed their papers before Captain Joseph Walker. Dickie came home for a short stay before going into service with Company K, Fifth South Carolina Volunteers, the company known as The Spartan Rifles, and a part of General D. R. Jones's Brigade. He left the family on a fine spring day while his brother lay ill with the fever. As he rode out in his new gray private's uniform, the black men and women were busily preparing the fields for planting cotton on the near high terraces. They leaned on their hoes and wished him a safe return. He acknowledged their greeting with a bow of his head, then a flourish of his soldier's cap. "Excitement and the sadness of leaving," as he later put it, was having its own war inside him. He took one last look over his shoulder at the hands again bending to their work on the wide, rich fields, with the tall portico of home fading behind him. He saw there that "Mother and Pa still stood at the door, arm in arm," looking after him, "finding it hard to say goodbye." He himself looked long because he knew he would have to make this image last. Had he realized that he was seeing the end of an era, he would indeed have stopped to gaze in earnest.

Soon after his departure, Dickie was joined by a Hardy slave named Silas who served as his *valet de chambre*—his *chambre*, however, now being only a tent when he was "lucky enough to have one." In this way he was like his cousin Jimmie Douglass, who was attended throughout the war by one or another of his faithful menservants, three of whom were Uncle Peter, Phil, and Charlie Giles. These largely uncelebrated slaves cooked, washed, carried letters and provisions from home to the front (the "boxes" so often mentioned in soldiers' letters), nursed the sick and wounded, and in various other ways provided for the personal comfort of their young charges. In time of need, many shouldered arms, although unofficially. As Douglass's former slave and body servant Charlie Giles recalled of the Fifth Regiment: "Lots of de soldiers" had black "body guards wid dem." Giles, in battle, as we shall see, shielded Douglass from enemy shells in battle with his own body. After the war, it was left for a fellow soldier from the Hardys' home county to pay tribute to the black Confederate: "No mother could nurse a child with greater tenderness and devotion than the dark-skinned Son of the South to his Master. . . . His first solicitude after battle was his master's fate—if dead, he sought him upon the field; if wounded he was soon at his side." In the remembrance of former slave Richard Jones, his friend Uncle Wylie Smith, the "bodyguard" of Jim Gist of Union County, "come back wid his master's body" from Virginia "and told us dat Marse was kilt by a Yankee." He and Miss Sara "buried him in his uniform and wrapped a Confederate flag over de coffin." In matters of honor and right behavior, these men were also good influences, acting as surrogates for old master in counseling the young. The advice of one such wise old body servant was no doubt often repeated across the Southern lines: "You got to be brave young marster, but not *too* brave."

Dickie's twenty-one-year-old brother Haywood also enlisted in the Fifth South Carolina on the same day as Dickie, but from Union County's Company D, riding with his cousin Jimmie Douglass and their neighbor Tom Wilson the twelve miles to the muster grounds at Santuc to sign their papers before Captain Sartor. Here at Santuc, where the cousins had run some famous races before the war, they were committing themselves to a far more serious contest. The deadly magnitude of the venture was not lost upon them or their families despite enthusiasm and high spirits. The act was quick and decisive but not a thoughtless and rash one, as Jimmie's letters reveal. He knew very well the lion's mouth he was entering.

The Confederate soldiers of the Goshen Hill area were called "minute men," according to former slave Nellie Loyd: "They had wide hats with palmetto buttons in front." This was, no doubt, the hallmark of the Fifth's uniform; palmetto buttons were prominent on their jackets as well. Dickie's letter home in June 1861 reported that the ladies of North Carolina who greeted their regiment on its way to Virginia "all wanted Palmetto buttons" from their clothes.

Like Dickie, young Haywood said good-bye to his mother and father, and also left the great double doors of the Big House. The dwelling seemed empty indeed now, the suffering of the parents intense. Old Master was said to age rapidly during these months of waiting and now became subject to spells of sickness, swelling of the legs, and depression. He missed his friend and neighbor Renwick, off with Hampton's Legion in Virginia by June of '61. With the news of the invasion of the Carolina coast at Beaufort and the wholesale confiscation of civilian property there, Hardy went about the place "armed to the teeth," as Haywood described him.

The anguish and anxiety of both "Old Mistis" and her sister Frances at The Oaks, with their mother dead and their sons going off to war, was recorded by Frances's daughter as "heart-rending." Old Master at times tried to keep up his spirits with his accustomed "teasing," but it was clear to all that a shadow had fallen over him. Dickie realized the magnitude of his father's responsibilities at home without his sons to help manage plantation affairs. He wrote his father in December 1861 attempting to discourage brother Dolph from volunteering, "for you need some one to help you. You are not able to attend to all the business yourself. It will soon lay you up." Aware of his father's infirmities, Dickie was always solicitous of him. No father could have asked for a better son.

From the squire's brother James Hardy in Asheville, he and Catharine received news that James's son William Henry (the old master's little namesake, Willie, of whom he had been so fond as a child) had volunteered at Morris Island, outside Charleston. Like Dickie, Haywood, and Jimmie, he had been among the first to answer the call of his country after Sumter. Willie, a student in Charleston, living there with his sister Emma Hardy Tennent, had witnessed the initial bombardments from the rooftops of the city and wasted no time in coming to the defense of the beleaguered town. As a member of the Second South Carolina Volunteers stationed for coastal defense, he was soon often in the company of his first cousins Dickie, Haywood, and Jimmie in these early months of the war. Willie and Dickie, with only a year between them in age, were as close as brothers owing to the period in the 1850s when Dickie and Haywood were often in Willie's father's home while students at Lee's Academy in Asheville. Willie, in fact, was a pupil with them there for a time. Two other of Dr. Hardy's sons, Cousin Wash and Cousin Geddings, also enlisted early, but from North Carolina.

The scene must now shift a few miles from the Hardy plantation to The Oaks at Goshen Hill. Dickie's twenty-year-old first cousin, Miss Garrie Douglass, in her letters to him, to her brother Jimmie, and to other family members and childhood friends, provide us a graphic eye-witness account of the day. She and her family, like their Hardy kin, were staunch Southern nationalists. In early 1861 she wrote Cousin Dickie that she "prayed that before many months will pass, our Glorious Independence will be established" and that all the brave young volunteers would be "spared to enjoy the Peace and Independence" they "so richly deserve." As a school exercise the previous year, she had written an essay entitled "It Is Sweet to Die for Our Country," in which she showed that she understood well the price of Southern Independence and the nature of sacrifice. "When a person feels that he is living for the good of those around him," she declared, his unselfish devotion ennobles him and in turn endears him to those for whom he sacrifices. These, in turn, will never forget him, will keep him in close memory, and in this sense, will never let him die. This enshrinement in memory is the "role of sisters and wives, who cannot themselves take up arms." Her essay is the sign of a family and a society steeling themselves to meet adversity and death with dignity and fortitude and to give that suffering meaning, all in advance of the inevitable event.

Garrie's own father, Dr. George Douglass, at this time fifty-seven years old, also strongly favored the cause of a Southern homeland. As we have seen, he had signed the Nullification Ordinance in 1832 and was ready thirty years ago for Southern action in defense of Southern rights. When son Jimmie left The Oaks to join his cousin Haywood on their ride to Santuc, he gave him this advice, which carries the uncanny ring of prophecy: "Do your duty and stay strong, knowing that you are fighting to protect those you love here at home, for if you fail, we will be destroyed. We can expect no mercy at the hands of this enemy."

Cousins Jimmie and Haywood had always been close. Like their fathers, they were the same age; and, like Dickie, both loved their hounds and setters and participated in both hunt and horse race. On many a Christmas hunt together with brothers, cousins, and uncles, they had learned the depth of their friendship. The music of their horseback conversations blended with the echoes from their horses' hooves, binding all in family experiences that would never leave their memories. Now, from their ride to Santuc onward, there would be a bond between Jimmie and Haywood that in some ways would be even deeper than their blood kinship. At Chapel Hill, as a daguerreotype of him reveals, Jimmie had dressed elegantly, in almost dandyish fashion, but had not strutted the part. He was a serious student. Young Haywood, who loved the outdoors, was, like Jimmie, a thoughtful, practical-minded lad, strong of muscle and long on stamina. Both were bold lads, *arme de foi Hardi*. The family resemblance of jet-black hair and gray-blue eyes was noticeable to those around them. They were both considered handsome and had the same Hardy love of life and sense of humor. As their letters reveal, both had an eye for the pretty girls. Captain John Giles of the Fifth Regiment's Company D soon learned that he could depend on them both in equal measure. Well-liked, admired, and trusted by their comrades, they soon rose to positions of leadership after service as privates.

And the homefront waited. To a friend, Garrie described her feelings when Jimmie left The Oaks: "Since I last wrote you, you have been made to part with your dear brother. I can deeply sympathize with you, for I have parted with a dear and much loved one. But we should feel proud that we have them to fight for our Country's rights. It was indeed a hard struggle to part, but let us look to a higher power and pray to

Him for their safe return." To her absent brother, on 28 April 1861, she reported the deaths of their grandmother Hardy and their cousin Charles Wesley. "We have had a sad time since you left us," she summarized, "Everything around us looks so desolate . . . yet we should not murmur at the afflictions of Providence, but humbly submit to his dispensations." In this same letter, she told Jimmie, who was serving in coastal defense at Sullivan's Island near Charleston, that her sister had just received a letter from Cousin Dickie. He has had to be absent from family when both brother and grandmother died and were buried, and now this waiting outside Charleston, the old "hurry up and wait" of army life, was unsettling him. For a bold and lively lad of action to be kept like a "bear in chains" was daunting. "I don't think he is very much pleased with events," she wrote with her accustomed understatement. She then turned to more pleasant possibilities:

> Thinking you would like to have something good to eat we fixed you up a nice box and sent by [neighbor] Mr. R[euben] T. Chick. I suppose you have received it by this time. Did they let you have the brandied cherrys that Mother sent you in the box? Father sayed he did not think they would let you have them as they are all inspected before delivered. I have taken part of your school, and am trying to teach them, but I do not know how I will succeed. I have fourteen and expect three more next week. I wish you were back again to carry it on, for every one was so much pleased with you as a teacher.

James, who had just turned twenty-three this month, had studied at Renwick's Academy at Orange Hall until 1849, then at the excellent Mt. Zion Academy in Winnsboro, at Lee's Academy in Asheville, at South Carolina College where he was a sophomore in 1858, and then at the University of North Carolina from 1859 to 1860. As his sister related, he had himself become a teacher at one of the neighborhood schools until his enlistment, perhaps at Renwick Academy, where, as we have seen, she and all the other Douglass and Hardy children got their elementary education in the 1840s and '50s. She was herself soon replaced in Jimmie's school by George Cofield, much to her relief, for she regarded him "very highly" as a teacher. She and her family still missed Jimmie, Haywood, and Dickie, but continued to realize "that in defense of hearth and home, such sacrifices must be made."

274

While Jimmie was engaged in coastal defense in early 1861, he wrote his sister Garrie a humorous letter, which she then reported to her friend Sallie Maybin: "We received a letter from Jimmie on Tuesday. He was quite well and was cooking & washing. Uncle Peter was sick. Poor fellow. Don't you know Jimmie had a hard time. He said, 'Tell all the girls if I should ever get back, I will not have anyone for a wife,' for he was cooking and washing for himself." This letter provides the valuable information that attending young Private Douglass even this early in 1861 was his body servant Uncle Peter, who had always been particularly close to young Douglass, and who went to war with his young charge to look after his domestic concerns. It was this same Uncle Peter that Jimmie had reported missing while at Chapel Hill.

Garrie then reported to a kinsman that "everything up this way seems sad and desolate and reminds us of those who have been taken from us . . . such heart-rending scenes. . . . We have missed Jimmie so much." Still, she passed on to small and happier matters, thanking her correspondent for the "trimming" she had sent her for the chemise she had just completed. "It was a sufficient quantity," she wrote, and the dress was "very much admired. Mother thinks it is beautiful. I put it on as you advised." Her health, after a stay in the pine woods, had improved. (She and her era felt the antiseptic smell of pine boughs was good for malaria.) Of Jimmie, she wrote that he was still on Sullivan's Island with the coastal defense but planned to volunteer for Virginia when the next call was made. His doctor-father agreed with this decision "that it would be better to go [to Virginia] than to remain on Sullivan's Island all the summer." Dr. Douglass feared bullets less than fever. Brother "Jimmie writes very often," she reported, "and seems to be satisfied." On the homefront in 1861 she attended a "Pick Nick" at Gordon's Bridge down the road a short piece from the Hardys', but did not relish it for the thoughts of the war and those absent.

Later, in the early summer of 1861, she informed another kinswoman that Jimmie and

> the volunteers came home on a furlough preparatory to going to Virginia. Dickie and Jimmie have both improved much; Jimmie gained ten pounds. We were glad to see him but was saddened by the thought of his leaving for Virginia, perhaps never to return. Mother took his leaving very hard, but I think she ought to be proud that she has a son to defend

his Country. We received a letter from him on Monday. He was in Richmond but did not know how long he would remain. Dickie said in his letter to his father that they treated them as kings and not privates, at every depot [along the route]. The ladies met them with provisions. They gave them a dinner in Charlotte. Jimmie says Cousin Haywood looks better than we are use to see him.

Dickie's actual letter, in fact, survives and corroborates Garrie's commentary:

Richmond Va. June 11th, 1861

Dear Father

We arrived here yesterday morning about day, after one of the most unpleasant trips I ever had. We had to ride in box cars nearly all the way. Haywood is here. He got a transfer from William's Regiment and joined ours. There is no news about here at all. Everything is quiet now. There are some eight or ten thousand men in and around Richmond. I guess we will leave here shortly for Manassas Junction. I dont know what day yet. If you dont hear from me anymore before you write, you can direct your letter to this place. We had a great time coming here. We stayed at Charlotte nearly two days. When we got to Sal[i]sbury, they had dinner prepared for us there; and at Greensboro we had supper. The Ladies all wanted palmetto buttons. They gave us flowers by the handfulls. It is a bad chance about writing now. We are in tents and have nothing to write with. There are now five Regiments in this State from South Carolina, and more are expected very shortly. Col. Hampton's Legion will be here today or to-morrow. It came to Raleigh yesterday. You must write soon. I am anxious to hear from home. I will try and get Haywood to write occasionally. Give my love to all.

Your son
W. D. Hardy

This is the proper direction of a letter:
W. D. Hardy
Spartan Rifles
Col. [Micah] Jenkins' Regt., Richmond, Va.

The three young privates arrived in Virginia on 10 June and settled in, in time for the Battle of First Manassas on 21 July 1861. All three fought in this battle. Their Fifth Regiment commander was the gallant young Micah Jenkins (1835–1864), first honor graduate of the Citadel and founder of King's Mountain Military College in Yorkville in 1855. During Manassas, Jimmie served as Jenkins's orderly sergeant. Just after Manassas, Haywood contracted measles, which kept him in a Charlottesville hospital from 1 August until he returned to duty on 4 September 1861. Cousin Garrie wrote her childhood friend and neighbor James Oxner at Manassas Junction that many back home were also still sick of typhoid, that neighbor Tom Glenn was "in Virginia at Harper's Ferry," that the ladies were doing what they could on the home front to support the Cause. They were "praying and sewing," and wishing they could do more. The community had formed a "Society" that stayed busy making socks and "over shirts." They were spinning "stocking thread" and knitting socks.

With First Manassas came news of the family's first casualty. Cousin Willie Hardy, while serving as aide-de-camp on the staff of General Joseph Kershaw, was shot dead in the field "amidst the raging of the battle" on 21 July. He was the first son of Asheville to fall in the war. Garrie's sister Sallie had been young Will's sweetheart. Indeed, they had been so close that his mother when writing the Hardys of Tyger in 1864, would ask Sallie to visit her in Asheville, for Will's sake—poor Will, who "had loved her so much." In time, they no doubt would have married. Sallie shared her grief with Uncle William and Aunt Catharine. Old Master and Missis now began to fear fully for their own. They received news of Willie's funeral. His body was brought home to Asheville, where it was interred with full military honors. On his person was found a note: "Dear Mother, we are about to go into an engagement. I want you to know that if I should be killed, all is well—Willie." Known for his devoutness, Will was no doubt referring to his "wellness" with God. The death of his nineteen-year-old nephew and namesake greatly affected Squire Hardy. Those who saw him noted the deepening lines about his mouth and eyes. Nor did the fallen youth's finely phrased obituary praising the "nobility and sweetness of his character" do much to allay the sting of grief for any of them. The clipping from the *Asheville News* was sent to him bearing the penciled comment "Death loves a shining mark." But hear the words themselves, just as William and Catharine read them over a century ago:

> Departed this life on the Manassas Plains amidst the raging of
> battle Lieutenant William Henry Hardy, aged nineteen years
> and four months. . . . Thus early in the freshness of his years,
> he yielded up his life for his Country, and died at the post of
> duty. Fragrant is his name, associated as it is with many virtues
> and precious reminiscences. . . . He was a member of the
> First Presbyterian Church here, and from the time of his pro-
> fession of Christ's holy religion, was true to his trust. He fell
> at the head of Col. Preston's Virginia Regt, while leading it
> to its position in the line of battle, being dispatched for that
> duty. It was at the time when the tide turned toward the
> Confederate victory, a victory in which he, in his measure,
> contributed, that he fell, dying instaneously and without
> pain. . . . Both Gen. Kershaw and Col. Preston expressed the
> highest admiration for his conduct on the battlefield. Thus in
> life's morning, he died a hero's death—with his earthly and
> spiritual armor on—in defense of sacred rights. With his
> mind pure and heart unscarred by trouble and care, he has
> thus passed from the shadows of earth to the peace and joys
> of the Spirit land. We shall miss him on life's journey—sweet
> is the memory of his name.

Willie had been a "very popular and much admired" lad in Asheville.
His funeral was said to be attended by "the whole town, which continued to speak of him reverently for years" after his death. His grave soon
bore a marker with an inscription from Sir Walter Scott's *Lady of the
Lake* bidding him to rest, his "warfare o'er." William and Catharine did
their best to console James and Delia in heartfelt letters that have not
survived. Their eyes and prayers were now constantly directed north
toward the plains and hills of Virginia.

With the late summer of '61, the separation from family and friends
in Virginia and the war casualties that were mounting up in the community deepened to extremity the sadness of the family. In the first days of
September 1861, Garrie sent word to her friend Sallie Maybin that Tom
Wilson, their close friend and young neighbor at Maybinton, had just
died: "He received a wound in his left arm and had to have it amputated.
. . . He took the measles which terminated in typhoid fever." Her reporting of the details of his death is stark and realistic and reveals that
she was suffering under no romantic illusions. As we have seen, this had

been the case with the family from the start. Such scenes were to grow more numerous for her and the family into 1862.

Wilson, who had been wounded at Manassas in July, was discharged at Richmond on 14 August and died at home eleven days later. As Garrie said, "He arrived home in time to die among his friends." He had enrolled at Santuc on 13 April with her cousin Haywood and brother Jimmie and now was dead at the age of twenty-one. His father, a near neighbor down the State Road, was a small farmer; and he thus hailed from sturdy yeoman stock. The Wilsons attended Ebenezer Church with the Hardys and Douglasses.

At this same time, Henry Francis Jones, one of Jimmie's best friends at Chapel Hill, and now in a Georgia cavalry unit, was inquiring of his whereabouts. (Jimmie was in camp near Germantown in Fairfax County, Virginia.) Dashing young Jones of Greenwood plantation outside Thomasville, Georgia, had a gift with words and was particularly gallant with the ladies. The jaunty air and optimism of his letter served to cheer the Douglass homefront, at least for a while:

> Richmond, Virginia
> Sept 2nd 1861
>
> Dr George Douglass
> Dear Sir,
>
> I hope you will excuse my *audacity* in writing to you, but as I am anxious to know where Jim is at present, I know of no other way of informing myself than through you. The last letter I had from him was short after the "fall of Sumter," and since then I have been unable to hear from him. Probably he is at Manassas and probably home on furlough, but not knowing, and having a desire to write him, I will feel truly obliged if you will give me his address in full. I am at present located at Richmond—member of a cavalry company from Athens Geo.—Capt Deloney, Cobb's Legion: but when or where we will march I have not the most distant idea.
>
> I hope though, when we shall have taken Washington, to have the pleasure of meeting Jim there—armed & equipped for the Ball—similar to the one the "Grand Army" anticipated having in Richmond.
>
> I hope, Sir, you will excuse both pencil and paper, for it

is the best I can do, and have to, as you are aware, adapt myself to circumstances.

Accept my regards for yourself and family and believe me,

Yours truly,

H. F. Jones

The homefolks were not so high-spirited. Garrie wrote with her accustomed realism to a friend from Spartanburg to let her know that "I am still living notwithstanding the hard times." She invited her "to the country where everything is free." "Father is having hogs killed," she related, "so you had better come to see us while we have something to eat." "Please send me my shoes if they are finished," she importuned, "for I am needing them badly." She also asked, "What has become of Mira's shoes?" With the letter, Garrie sent her some cloth made there at The Oaks. The family had fallen back on pioneer skills, skills the family, in its resourcefulness, still had. Her mother, Frances Hardy Douglass, had been weaving gray flannel cloth "for Jimmie's over shirts." "It was impossible to get any, any other way," she reported. "The piece she wove was both pretty and substantial." Although Grandmother Anna Hardy had died, she had taught them well, and they were "carrying on." The plantation's sheep were now coming in handy as a source of wool; and with the steady abundance of cotton, the ladies of the family were kept constantly busy at wheel, loom, and sewing table providing raiment for the men of Giles' Company, Jimmie's Company D. Their "winter clothes" spun at The Oaks were delivered to Jimmie's camp in Virginia "in a box" carried by a neighbor, Schoolmaster William Renwick of Orange Hall. For the kin who received them, these clothes woven out of the literal and figurative fabric of home, bearing its smells and the impress of family and loved ones, became "the very emblem of the Cause for which we face Death." No machine-made uniform of fancier cloth or fit could inspire so well. In October 1861 Colonel Micah Jenkins, commander of the Fifth, also assisted Renwick in the important duty of "getting cloth for Capt. Giles' Company." It is likely on such a mission that Renwick went to New Orleans in December 1861. A Hardy relative was similarly involved. Dr. James Hardy's son-in-law, Gilbert B. Tennent of Charleston, had been dispatched to Paris and Liverpool to secure cloth.

Cousin Robert B. Lyons of the Fifth, who had been in Virginia since June, wrote young Rogers Renwick, son of William Renwick, an encouraging letter from Fairfax, Virginia:

> Camp near Germantown
> Sept. 3rd, 1861
>
> Our flag is now within five miles of the city of Washington. Our forces, Longstreet's Brigade, the advance, are on a line between Fall's Church & Alexandria in plain view of Washington, Arlington & Alexandria. Our pickets are in about three or four hundred yards of those of the enemy. They are firing on one another constantly. We expect to attack a hill in a few days, which some think commands Alexandria. We get about three of them to their getting one of us. Old Lowe came up in his baloon to reconoitre our positions, when our artillery fired at him and made him go down again. I am inclined to think we will have more stirring times in the course of a couple of weeks. I believe we will take Alexandria before three weeks from this date. I have not seen Old Beauregard since the big fight. I received a letter from Dawk [Dawkins] Rogers a few days ago; he says Uncle [James Rogers] and Aunt [Nancy Dawkins Rogers] are still about as I left them. Tell me, Rogers, how everybody, place, and thing is getting along. I wish I could be there for a week or so just to see all the folks. Give my love to Uncles Bill and James—also to the people of the neighborhood. Give all the *Girls* my best love.
>
> Your cousin as ever
> R. B. Lyons

Lyons's cousin Dawk Rogers had been a member of the First Company of South Carolina College Cadets in early 1861. He had, in fact, been elected their First Lieutenant, their second in command, when the entire student body enlisted en masse. In April Dawk was among the cadets who participated in coastal defense during the bombardment of Fort Sumter, and by September was in the thick of things.

On Christmas Eve 1861 young Dickie wrote his father from Warrenton, Virginia:

> My Dear Father
> I wrote you a few days ago, on receipt of your letter,

informing you how I was doing. I am going back to camp to-morrow. I know I am not fit for duty, but as I am a soldier, I think I ought to try and do all the duties of a soldier. I would stay here longer, but I have just enough money to pay my board, and as money is so scarce, I would not ask you to send me more, for I know you have use for it, everything is so awful high. I am sorry to hear Dolph has volunteered. I think he did wrong, for you need some one to help you. You are not able to attend to all the business yourself. It will soon lay you up. I would like very much to be at home with you all to-morrow. I know you will have a much more pleasant time than myself. I suppose Sister is up home now. She said in her last letter to me that she was going to spend Christmas with you all. Tell her I am looking for an answer to my letter. Our Right is now building winter quarters at Centreville. It is high time, for almost every night the tents blow down. I guess you will see full particulars of a little fight our troops had at Drainsville last Friday. The Yankees had such a great force that they got the best of it. Winder's Right (formerly Rion's) was engaged in the fight and had nineteen men killed and a good many wounded. Major Woodward of Fairfield was wounded in the thigh and had his horse killed. The 1st Kentucky Right, mistaking Winder's Right for Yankees, fired into them, and did a good deal of execution. The Adjutant of our Right died here this morning. His name was Clinton. He was from Yorkville, and as perfect a gentleman as I ever saw. He will be a great loss to the Right. Every man in the Right I think liked him. I am glad to hear that my mare is so well broken. I hope the day is not far distant when I can have the pleasure of riding her. How is old Polly's roan getting on? I reckon George Eppes [Dickie's young brother] has him broken by this time. When will Dolph leave for the coast? He will be the sickest man that ever you heard of, in about a month after he gets into service. Give my love to all. I hope to hear from you all again very soon.

Your affectionate son
W D Hardy

Direct your next letter to Manassas Junction.

From his letter, it is obvious that Dickie had been ill and despondent and boarding himself in town while convalescing. Sister Elmira was home from the Frost plantation to be with her parents for Christmas. Her husband was now also at war. The squire had broken in a mare for Dickie, who asked about his brother's success with a roan stallion belonging to Mary Hardy ("Polly") Eppes, mother of Dr. James M. Eppes, with whom she lived. Polly was Catharine Hardy's first cousin. The Hardys' habitual interest in good horses had not abated with war.

Three days after Christmas, young Dickie again wrote to tell of his return to camp and of how the lads longed for home:

Centreville, Va. Dec. 28th 1861

Dear Father

I arrived at camp day before yesterday. This is the coldest place I ever saw in my life. Our Regiment is camped on the top of a hill, where the wind has a fair sweep. I have not reported for duty. Some of my officers advise me not to, for some time. I have been out of my tent three times since I got here. I dont expect to do any duty for a month, if I do any while I stay here. I found Haywood, Jimmie and all the boys but Jack Henderson well. Jack is complaining a little, but I think he is better today. Jim Gross is sick. He was sent to a hospital the day I got here. I did not learn what was the matter with him. Wylie Holleyman left the day I got here, having been discharged by the Secretary of War. His brother wrote to the Secretary of War, and he discharged him. The proposition offered by Congress to the twelve months troops will be put to our Regiment next week. I am very confident it will not take, for all the men want to see home. It would amuse you very much to hear Haywood talk. He is the sickest man of the war, I ever saw. I see from the papers, that they are about to get everybody in South Carolina in the war. Gov. Pickens has called for twelve thousand more troops. I would like to see some young men that I know, drafted. I wrote to you the day before I left Warrenton, that I was coming to camp, so you must direct your letters to Manassas Junction. Ben Maybin says he will write to you in a day or two. I suppose Sister [Elmira] is still with you. I am looking for a letter from her. This has been the greatest Christmas I

ever saw. No one scarcely knows it is Christmas. Silas is very
well. Give my love to all. Write again soon to Your Son
W D Hardy

Silas was now the servant attending the Hardy sons at the front and, as
Dickie reported, was "very well," information no doubt to be relayed
to Silas's family.

Six weeks later, on 17 February 1862, Haywood wrote home from
Camp Centreville, Virginia:

Dear Father

Your letter by Mr Chick came to hand yesterday, & I
gladly embrace this opportunity of answering it. I was happy
to hear that all were well. This leaves us all well except Jack
Henderson and he is not any better yet. I am fearful he will
have a hard spell before he gets well. We were all delighted
to see Mr Chick. The Box came safely after so long a time
and we were glad to find something to eat besides beef. I
think it a good notion in clearing the Valentine bottom, because I am a great man for an abundance of Corn, and if the
War was ended I could raise Hogs and Corn in plentiful style,
as they are the foundation of a Plantation, but you are Hog
man and myself the Horse man. The ground is white with
snow and has been for a long while. Since I commenced this
letter, Tom Moorman came in from William's Regiment. He
is well and strongly in the spirit of volunteering for the War
before he comes home, but I dont think many of the neigh-
bourhood Boys will volunteer until they return. I think our
State expects us to do more than is in our power; we dont
expect to stay out. We are going to come again and see the
end of this struggle for independence. I wish you would
write me the opinion of our People about reenlisting for the
War before we come home. Our Generals appeal strongly to
us to volunteer again, but I am of the opinion that I shall
return when the 13th of April comes. I understand that some
of the Ladies were going to meet us at Alston. I think we will
be in a poor condition to receive female company, with our
Pants out in the seat, at least, a greater part are.

I wish you would send my red Slut to the Dog Dr

Thomson sent from Virginia. Whoever carries her, tell them to be sure and not get her lost. I think he is splendid stock. You can do so or let her be put up and go out of heat. I think the latter is the best conclusion. I am proud to hear of the success you have in raising Pigs. When you read this letter; be sure and burn it up, because I dont want the Ladies to see it. Well I must close for the want of news. Give my love to all and tell Dolphus he ought to have his musket, not be affraid of the Yankees. Also give my best wishes to all the Girls and believe me your affectionate Son,

Haywood

P.S. Have my Mare kept in good fix and attend to my Dogs. Also let me know how Pomp comes on in the Partridge line.

This letter reveals Haywood's continued interest in the land and his great love of the rural life. If ever a man was suited to farming, it was certainly he. To raise hogs and corn in plentiful style was his fond desire, and he knew he was fighting to be allowed the peace so to do. "Attend to my Dogs" and "my Mare" was his final request.

Several weeks later Dickie wrote his father that the lads were in good health, but still suffering from the cold. They were drilling and preparing to march:

Centreville, Va. March 4th, 1862

Dear Father

I will try and write a short letter this morning, so that you may know that we are well. We came in from picket yesterday. We had a very hard time. It snowed, rained, and did everything you could imagine. I would have written by Mr Chick, but he left before we came back to camp. There is some move on foot now, but what it is I am unable to say. We have sent back our heavy baggage etc. The general impression is that we are going to fall back. How true it is, I dont know. We hear so many rumors, that we never know what to believe. Everything looks gloomy for us now. We meet with defeat on almost every side. I am looking every day for Savannah to be taken. The Yankees have been so successful lately, that they may muster up courage to advance on the Army of the Potomac. If they do, I think they will get a worse whipping than they did, at the battle of Manassas. A large number of the twelve months troops have reenlisted for the war. About half of our company have reenlisted. Our term of service expires in a little over five weeks, which I am truly glad of, for I am wanting a little rest. Haywood, Jimmie Douglass, and in fact all the boys are very well. Silas is getting on very well. We have commenced drilling again, which is better for the health of the men, than lying in their quarters all day doing nothing. From what I hear, there is some prospect for a wedding, about the time we get home. I think both parties will do very well. We are expecting to march any time. I will write again soon. Give my love to all.

Your affectionate son
W D Hardy

Silas, as he said, was still attending his charges.

Then Silas was missing. Later from Richmond in April 1862 Dickie wrote his father that Silas was found, and that he himself had survived the fury of the fight at Williamsburg, where the "balls flew around me thicker than hail":

[I have wanted] to write to you for more than a week, but we have been on the march all the time. When I last wrote you, I said that Silas was missing, but he has come up. He heard that we were going to retreat from Williamsburg and struck out for Richmond. Having got lost from our wagons, he did not know where to go. We are looking for a fight here pretty soon. The Yankees can come within eight or ten miles of Richmond. Our attention is turned to Stone Wall Jackson. Now he seems to be doing more for the South than any of our Generals. I would not be surprised at any time to hear he was in Maryland. Jackson and Beauregard I think are the best Generals we have. I know of no news to write. We scarcely ever see a paper now, and it is folly to write what I hear, for we can hear everything but a man saying his prayers. I said in one of my letters not to send me a uniform, but I wish you would send it. I got one in Richmond, but it is so inferior that it wont last any length of time. We got nearly all of our clothing destroyed when we fell back from Centreville. I have not heard a word from home in nearly a month. It is very hard to get a mail now; we have not had one in more than a week. It is hardly worth while for me to say anything about the fight at Williamsburg. I suppose you have seen full accounts ere this in the papers. This much I will say: it was the hottest place I ever got into. The balls flew around me thicker than hail almost. I told you something of the officers of our Regiment some time ago. We were ordered to reorganize, and Jack Giles was elected Colonel, Jackson of York, Lt. Colonel, and Bill Foster of Spartanburg, Major. Jimmie Douglass is now Captain of Giles' old company [Company D]. He and Haywood are very well. You must write us as often as you can. Please send the clothes we wrote for as soon as you can. Direct your letters to the care Capt. Douglass, 5th S.C. Regt, Richmond. Give my love to all. What has become of [brothers] Thomas and George Eppes? Your affectionate son,

W D Hardy

On 23 April 1862, upon the reorganization that he mentioned in his letter, Dickie was made sergeant-major of Company D, with the rank of corporal. Haywood was elected sergeant. Cousin Jimmie now commanded the company, and the three lads were all together, all in positions of leadership.

Then Dickie wrote from "Camp near Richmond" on 4 June 1862, after the Battle of Seven Pines four days before:

Dear Father

I would have written to you all by Jimmie Douglass, but it was impossible. I knew that you would be uneasy about us, but knowing Jimmie would give you the particulars, I delayed writing longer than I would have done otherwise. I suppose you have seen full accounts of the fight [at Seven Pines] more than I could write. I went through unhurt by bullets, but in making a charge, I fell and came near breaking my leg. For several days I could scarcely walk. I am not well yet. Haywood was sick. Dr. Thomson has sent him to Richmond. I think he went to James Hardy's. He has been unwell for a good while. I have not heard from him in two or three days. Tints Jeter, poor fellow, died the other day from his wound. I am sorry for his family. I thought Mr Oxner would have been on long ago. I made sure he would come as soon as he heard that James [his son] was wounded. I hear that Jim is doing very well. Our wounded are dying very fast—so I hear. A great many persons believe the enemy poison their balls. If it be true, every Yankee in existence ought to be killed. I guess Old Jackson's second victory is having some effect on McClellan's movements. Gen. Lee is in command of the army. Gen. Johnston was wounded on Saturday last. I have a hat at Spartanburg that I wrote John Hardy to send me by Jimmie Douglass. I wish you would tell Mother to send me three or four collars by him. She did not send any with the shirts she sent to me. My clothes all fit me very well, except the coat, which is rather small, but does very well. Haywood has Silas with him in Richmond. I suppose he will be well attended to. I will write to you again as I hear how Haywood is getting. Give my love to all.

Your affectionate son,
W D Hardy

This letter reveals that like the Douglasses at The Oaks, the Hardys were weaving cloth to make shirts and uniforms for sons at the front. What Dickie did not say in his letter was that Jimmie had been shot through the arm and shoulder at Seven Pines on 31 May and was coming home on furlough to convalesce. Their colonel, Jack Giles, formerly the captain of their company, was killed in this battle. As Dickie wrote, Haywood was indeed sick at hospital in Richmond. Silas was nursing him.

James Oxner died from his wounds some nine days after Dickie wrote his letter. Oxner, whose new buggy Garrie Douglass had taken such pleasure in describing to Dickie two years earlier and to whom she had written faithfully during the war, died on 13 June 1862 at the age of twenty. He was the first from their community and church to volunteer—on 12 January 1861, three months before Sumter—and had volunteered for the defense of Virginia in May. His body was returned home, mourned, and buried at Ebenezer. His tombstone, erected the following year, tells the story:

James Algernon Sidney Oxner died June 13th 1862 aged 20 years 3 months & 18 days. Among the first to respond to the call of his country he became a volunteer as early as Jan. 12th 1861. He entered the service of his State in April of the same year and in May nobly volunteered his services in the defense of Virginia. A soldier, brave, obedient and faithful, he was always at his post. As a Patriot, it is enough to say he was at Manassas, Williamsburg, and Seven Pines. Here he lay his last & dearest offering upon the altar of his country; having received a wound in his leg, he was carried to Richmond where he soon died. Let him rest in peace undisturbed by martial sounds until the trump of God shall awake him to brighter honors and more lasting glories than those won upon the field of battle and to a better country & happier home than that for which he contended here. We mourn his death but not as those who have no hope, for we console our hearts with the hope of joining him in that happy land whose prospects were spread before him at the close of his life.

Dawkins Rogers of Orange Hall was also killed. He had gone to war with his bodyservant Hilliard. But hear Hilliard's sister, Aunt Alice Dawkins Sims, born a slave around 1850, tell the story:

> Dawkins Rogers took my brother Hilliard as his servant to dat 'Federate War. Marse Dawkins got shot down dead out dar somewhar, I does not know whar; anyway Hilliard fetched his body back to ole Mistis, and she laid him away in de Dawkins graveyard up on Pacolet. Dat wus Nancy [Dawkins Rogers], my mistis, dat cared for me so good.

The Fifth Regiment, to which Oxner, Dickie, Haywood, and Jimmie belonged, had been nearly annihilated by the fighting around Richmond. On 10 July 1862, after the Battle of Cold Harbor (27 June), and less than a month after Oxner's death, Haywood described the situation in this way: "Since the battle we have about eighty men left in our Regiment & but six or seven in our company"—a company that had numbered over a hundred at the outset. They were thus among the groups most severely affected. Because Company D was composed of young men from the Tyger, the home front now began to know a suffering never before imaginable. By March 1862 there were "scarcely any young men left" from the area between Tyger River and Glenn Springs.

They had volunteered en masse to fill the ranks of their fallen brothers and kinsmen. At home, the sound of weeping was common in the land, and the furrows absorbed many a tear.

On 1 July 1862, after Adjutant Meek's death at Gaines Mill on the 27th of June, Dickie was made adjutant of the Fifth Regiment. Soon thereafter, Haywood's letter home told the family that Dickie had been shot in the hand (an event that occurred on 30 June 1862) and that Jimmie Douglass was convalescing at home from a severe wounding "six weeks ago" (on 31 May) at Seven Pines. Haywood requested his father to "Tell Jimmy he must make haist & come back, that we have hard times coming." Haywood's letter was carried home to the plantation by the resourceful Hardy slave Jack. He had brought provisions and a new horse for Dickie, whose old one had been shot out from under him in battle. Jack brought home the news to Big House and Quarters alike. It had been a grand adventure for one who had never left his native state before. All the youngsters listened to his stories with wide-eyed amazement.

But let us hear Haywood:

Richmond Va., July 10th, 1862

Dear Father

As Jack will start back tomorrow I will drop you a few lines to let [you] know how we are. I am improving. Dick's hand is getting well but he has been suffering with the ear-ache. I expect Jack can give you more news than I can. Any-how the Yankees have met with an awful defeat in their attempt to capture Richmond. They were one time [with]in five miles of the City; now they are thirty five or forty from Richmond. Jack tells me that the hounds all have the mange. Let me beg you to try & have them cured & if you cant cure them, kill all that wont get entirely well, & take good care of my mare. Jack says she has fallen away. It may be that you ride her too much. Dont lend her out any more to no one under any consideration & be sure & not allow Dolfus to have any thing to do with her, in no shape manner or form. I would like the best in this world to be with you all but it is impossible unless I get wounded. I would be right willing to take a right severe wound to get two or three months furlow, but would hate to be killed, as I am not ready to leave this world yet. Jack tells me that you go armed to the teeth. You are not afraid of the Yankees coming up your way are you? Since the battle we only have about eighty men left in our Regiment & but six or seven in our company. Tell Jimmy he must make haist & come back, that we have hard times coming. I must come to a close. Jack will give you the news. Give my love to mother & George. I remain your affectionate son,

Haywood

Write soon. I have not got a letter from you in six weeks. I have not seen any thing of the Boots yet.

Jimmie, as Haywood had suggested in his letter, did "make haist" and returned to the front in time for Second Manassas on 30 August 1862. There he had his sword shot from his hand. All three boys survived this important battle, as well as Sharpsburg in September 1862 and Fredericksburg in December 1862. At Sharpsburg, when all Jimmie's senior officers were killed or disabled, he commanded the Fifth. Micah Jenkins, who had first held this position, had already been promoted to brigadier general on 22 July 1862. Jimmie's old position as captain of Company D was now taken by Captain Walker.

But let us hear Dickie's letter home soon after the great battle of Sharpsburg:

Camp near Martinsburg, Va.
Sept. 24th, 1862

Dear Father

I have not had an opportunity of writing to you since the fight at Sharpsburg [17 September] until now. I have been unwell for some time consequently. I was not in the fight, and know very little about it. From what I hear, I think it was a draw fight. The second day after the fight, our army fell back across the Potomac. The men have been marched so hard that a great many had broken down, which reduced our number very much. If all the men had been there, the enemy would have been whipped very easily. The Yankees say they lost thirteen Generals killed and wounded, and thirty thousand men. The capture of Harpers Ferry was a brilliant affair. Jackson took thirteen thousand prisoners and any quantity of arms, ammunition, cannon, commissary stores, clothing, etc. I guess you have heard that Jim Roebuck was dead. He died from wounds received in the Battle of Manassas. I dont know what will be the next move of the army. It is getting time to think of wintering I think. The fighting will cease for a while now. There is some talk of our Brigade being ordered to the coast. I hope it is true, for so much hard marching has almost broken me down. The news of Sallie Lyles's marriage produced a bad effect on Jim Douglass. It made him sick. I consoled him by telling him that Mag and Sallie Maybin were still single. I think Jimmie will have to marry both of them. I was sorry to learn that Dolphus had acted so badly. You did right in sending him to the Asylum. That is the place for him. I would keep him there by all means. John Richards is getting on very well, but grieving about Sallie. Tell Sallie his bowels dont worry him as much as they did, when she asked me what was the matter with him. You wanted Haywood and myself to write to Mag. I for my part do not want to write to her, for I dont choose to be called one of her admirers. What has become of Miss Mary Frost? I have not heard whether she has gone home or not. I wish you would have my mare broken to harness. I will write before long. Haywood and Jimmie are very well. Give my love to all.

Your Son
WDHardy

On the homefront, the mood of gloom deepened. Garrie wrote her cousin Dickie at Manassas Junction in late November 1862:

The day is very inclement and everything wears a dull and dreary aspect. We have had a great quantity of rain for the past four weeks. Most of our farmers have finished gathering their corn, and think they have made a very good crop. Your father has recovered from his attack and is looking very well. He had a very severe spell which lasted over a week. I was sorry to hear that Haywood had the misfortune to sprain his arm. I hope he is recovered in this.

The harvest was going along as usual despite the cataclysm of war. Then the soldiers went into winter quarters. In March 1863 Jimmie was at home on furlough, but returned in April. Dickie was likewise on furlough, from 27 February to 26 March. The two had come home together. Upon their return to camp in April, morale was good in the Fifth. Their friend Bob Lyons reported to his cousin Rogers Renwick at Orange Hall from the camp of the Fifth on 1 April 1863:

> We are all getting along finely. The men generally are healthy. . . . Our Regt is larger now than at any time since the "Seven Pines" fight. We have a very strict good colonel and I think he will make our Regt. as it was formerly. I think one more summer of hard fighting and the war will be near its end. I am compelled to think that if we can hold our lines intact this summer we will accomplish our end. . . . If you get this letter before Jim Douglass leaves for camp, tell Uncle Bill [Renwick] to send me a pair of boots or shoes. Tell Aunt Nancy to send me a pair of pants if she can get them before Jim leaves. . . .
>
> Your cousin affectly
> R. B. Lyons

In July 1863 Lyons again wrote his cousin at Orange Hall:

> Camp of the 5th S.C. Regt., Near Richmond, Va.
> July 19th, 1863
>
> Master J. R. Renwick
> Dear Rogers,
> . . . The main object of this letter is to inform you that Jim Douglass has given me his setter "Slut." She is a fine animal, a splendid "huntress"—His reasons for giving her away is that he cannot keep her at home—she will in spite of all the homefolks can do, go off on a hunting tour and remain absent for two or three days at a time. I do not like to act or speak as if I expected to see home for fear I may not—In this instance, however, I have acted otherwise. I have accepted the gift, thinking I would keep her until she had pups. . . . I want to get a fine puppy from her from a fine dog. . . . Jim Douglass says he would not give her away for nothing hardly had he not so many setters.

Then Lyons turned to military matters. His old resolution and optimism had not been shaken even with the shifting tide of war:

> Since writing you last, the aspect . . . is very much changed. Vicksburg has fallen and Gen. Lee has recrossed the Potomac. Don't think me disheartened however, for I have always said that for the North to subjugate us is an almost impossibility. They may whip us for five years successfully and then subjugation would be so far off as it was the morning of the 12th of April 1861. Our Western Army has never done what this Army has or we would have had peace long ere this. I think Gen. Lee will have to reinforce Johnston to prevent Grant from overrunning the entire west. I am still quite hopeful of having peace within the next eighteen months. We hear here that there has been a draft in So. Ca. I want you to write me in your answer who was drafted in our neighborhood. We are lying here in three miles of Richmond and having quite an easy time. There are no enemy in our front at all. When we came here, Dix, a Yankee general was near the city and urged on with the certainty of his being able to take it. It took Jenkins but a few days though to convince Dix that he could not get the much coveted prize. There are some rumors of our being sent to Charleston shortly—I do not credit them though. Rogers, take the Slut and take care of her, and I will do as much for you as soon as an opportunity presents itself. Tell Jimmie [Renwick] I will write to him soon. Give Uncles Billie and Aunt Nancy and Jimmie my best love—the neighbors generally my respects.
>
> Your cousin affectionately
R. B. Lyons

To his cousin Garrie Douglass, Haywood wrote his usual lively account on 2 July 1863, relating Ben Maybin's body servant's delivery of coffee and "eatables" from home, and how brother Dolphus has brought another horse. Dickie himself was at home. He was listed in the official records as having been sick at hospital in Richmond since 1 July. Haywood cautioned Dick to be sure to bring another of the Hardy slaves with him when he comes. But let us hear Haywood himself:

Camp around Richmond July the 2nd, 1863

My Dear Cousin

Your welcome letter came to hand in due time, and would have been answered sooner, but we had marching orders to go to Richmond. Consequently you must excuse my neglect. We came here three days since, and this is the only chance I have had to write since we came. This leaves us all well together with the balance of my friends. I imagine we are here to defend Richmond while Lee's army is in Maryland. I see all of his army has crossed the River, so you may hear exciting news from him soon. Garrie, our Brigade has been newly uniformed. We look like Yankees. I dislike the color; it is blue. We have not had much fighting this summer, but an innumerable quantity of marching, more than we had when we were with Lee's army. I am in hopes we will remain here until winter and then be sent to Charleston. I am partial to our Old State, and rather die there than anywhere else. The people of Richmond were very glad when we came. The streets were crowded with Ladies when we passed through. When Ben [Maybin]'s Boy came back from home, Aunt Mary [Maybin] sent us forty dollars worth of pure coffee besides other eatables. You have no idea how delighted we were. Coffee in Richmond sells at six and seven dollars a pound. Dolphus came safely to us with Dick's horse on the 28th of June. He remained only one day with us. I am astonished at Dick for sending such an animal out here. It will suffer for something to eat. Any cheap horse would have answered his purpose just as well. Tell him I could have bought a very good one the other day for $125 dollars. I would not have mine sent out if I were a Brigadier General. We have plenty of rain out here. It has been raining for a week, and continues cloudy. I am in hopes our Farmers will all make good crops this year. I hear favorable prospects from all parts of our Confederacy. I am fearful the Yankees will finally capture Vicksburg. Johnson is too slow in his movements; he has allowed Grant to fortify his army in front and rear. Forcing him from there will not be a Fox chase, but we will live in hope. I am not uneasy about Gen. Lee's army. He is all right. Hooker knows who he is fooling with when Lee commences one of [his] killings. You asked how long the war would last. I must confess that I do not see any prospect for peace whatever. I think it will continue during Lincoln's administration. Then if a change does not take place, it may continue a number of years. Garrie, I scarcely ever hear from home. Father has only written me two letters since I left. We do not know whether you all are dead or alive. Tell Dick he must be sure and bring one of the Negro Boys with him when he returns. I want someone to toat my knapsack while marching. The Yankee prisoners made an effort to rebell in Richmond just before we came. Our men planted some cannon in range of where they were staying; but soon silenced, they thought all of our troops had left Richmond, but were badly mistaken. Well! Cousin, I must finish this badly written and uninteresting letter. I know you are tired of my foolishness. We have nothing to write, only hard times. Give my love to Uncle, Aunt, and all the family, and with many kind wishes to you and all, I remain as ever your affectionate

Cousin Haywood

Write soon and give us all the news. Always burn my letters after reading.

Good bye

Three months later, in a letter to his father, he was the same jaunty Haywood, who despite the hard times, was speaking of the ladies, his love of home, and his now entrenched hatred of the aggressors upon his native land:

Camp at Petersburg, August the 7th, 1863

Dear Father

I intended writing by Jim Douglass, but he left so unexpectedly that I did not have the chance. He left in ten minutes after the order came detailing him to go home after some deserters from our Regiment, but I am in hopes this will reach you before he returns to Virginia. This leaves us all well, togather with the balance of the boys. We are camped in the edge of Petersburg, and we are having a glorious time. Hundreds of pretty girls visit our Regiments every evening to see the dress parades. I have formed the acquaintance of several, and find them to be nice people. The people about this place think there never was such a Brigade as ours, especially the Ladies; but I am fearful that we will not remain here very long. There has been a heavy cannonading going on down the River all day. It is the enemy's gun-boats shelling the banks of the River, but I dont think it will terminate in anything serious. One object I have in writing is for you to get Thomas to make a pair of high quartered shoes, number 8½ ts. Tell him to make them neatly and out of good material. Make them on the gater order, stout, strong & neatly, and send them by Jimmy. Also, dont fail to send me one of the Negro boys by him. I saw one of the prettyest young Ladies the other day I ever saw. This is a great place & I am willing to remain here until the War ends. When you write back to Dick, ask him how many pieces of music he sent to Mat Henderson. He sent his ambrotype also. I am of the opinion that he is considerably thunderstruck; and Ben [Maybin] and myself are wonderfully pleased with some of the Virginia girls. Jim Douglass has strong inclinations in the direction of Raleigh, No. Ca., and if the War ends soon, you need not be astonished if I bring a Virginia Lady home with me; but alas how many of us may be under the cold clods before another year. The Yankees seem to be determined to carry on the War. Lincoln is raising 300,000 more men to be immediately brought into the field. As soon as that is accomplished, they will make [a] desperate attempt for Richmond, but I am in hopes it will stand as firm as the rock of ages. The enemy seem to be slow in their undertakings at Charleston. I trust our little State will bid defiance to the abominable Yanks as long as the War lasts, and forever and eternally after it is over. They have more spite at South Carolina than any other in the Confederacy. I trust our people will freely meet any emergency that may be attempted at Charleston. Well! Father, I will have to conclude. I imagine you have heard enough of my foolishness this time. Give my love to Mother. Remember me to all relations and friends. Also give my kindest regards to all the pretty girls. Now with many kind wishes to yourself, I remain your affectionate son

Haywood

Let me beg you to send me some more money. I hate to ask for it, but I have some debts in the Regiment which I am anxious to pay, and will not be able to do so with what little I draw from the Confederacy. I want $50 dollars.

Good bye

Jimmie Douglass was thus briefly at home in August. Thomas, probably Haywood's eldest brother Thomas Powell Hardy, was making shoes on the plantation for the family at war. Ben Maybin, Jimmie, and Dickie all had "love interests," Jimmie for a lady in Raleigh (he had been a student at nearby Chapel Hill) and Dickie for a girl of the Maybinton community back home, Mat Henderson, to whom he had sent sheet music and ambrotypes of himself. Haywood himself favored the Virginia girls. His parting admonition was to "bid defiance to the abominable Yanks as long as the War lasts, and forever and eternally after it is over." It is a letter of spirit, conviction, and grit. Haywood, again *arme de foi Hardi,* shows himself to be the liveliest of the lads, the most high-spirited, a right worthy young squire of the old English stamp, who loved his hounds as much as life and, as he says, would not risk a fine horse's welfare in war were he even a brigadier general. As all accounted, he was wonderfully well liked and abounding in personality.

In the fall of 1863 Lyons and Jimmie Douglass, accompanied by their black body servants, went with Longstreet to Georgia and East Tennessee, where they fought in several engagements and rendered much "arduous campaigning." Whether or not Dickie went with them is uncertain. Returning to Virginia in early spring 1864, Jimmie was shot through the thigh on the second day of the Battle of the Wilderness, 6 May 1864—a severe wound that was to keep him in the hospital at Richmond and recuperating at home until September. All felt it miraculous that he did not die. On the same day of his wounding, General Micah Jenkins, who was leading his former old brigade into battle on 6 May, was shot through the head as he rode with General Longstreet, his commander. Both he and Longstreet were injured by friendly fire. Jenkins died at the age of twenty-eight.

Haywood did not go with Longstreet to Georgia and East Tennessee. Instead, in the fall of 1863, sick and exhausted, he stumbled home to his father's house on sick-leave furlough. There in his old bedroom in the Hardy Great House, "After a painful and protracted illness," he died in the spring of 1864 "amid the dear associations of home" and in the loving circle of family, his hounds and setters at his feet. His eulogist's words of 27 May, two days after his death, tell the story:

> This young man possessed, in a remarkable degree, all those qualities which ennobled their possessor and enshrined him in the hearts of the people. Modesty, sincerity, fearlessness, and an undeviating purity of life—these were the virtues which adorned his character, this the spotless record which he kept in these eventful times. When war's clarion notes first rung over the land, he promptly responded to the call, and, joining Company D, 5th Regiment SCV, went to Virginia and moved unharmed through all the tremendous scenes of 61, 62, and 63. To say that a young man had been, for three years, in Company D is no faint praise, indeed. This, itself, is epitaph sufficient; language can express no more, eulogy can go no further. For assuredly this company, whether led by Giles or Douglass, and this Regiment, whether commanded by Jenkins, or Giles, or Coward, have written their names in flaming and ineffaceable letters on the scroll of fame.
>
> In the autumn of 63, broken down in health, he returned home, sadly and wearily, to die. He suffered much and lingered long; nevertheless, he was happy—happy in the warm regard of his friends—happy in the patient and loving attention of his relatives—happy in the retrospection of a well-spent life—happy in the hope of a glorious immortality beyond the grave. I hold it to be a truth, whatever else may befall, that he who dies amid the dear associations of home, with the pleasant memories of childhood clinging about him, with a sister's hand to press his aching temples and a mother's voice to whisper words of comfort in his failing ear, is blest, indeed.—And thus Haywood Hardy passed away. With his hopes firmly stayed upon the precious promises of the Saviour, and the loved ones of home clustering around his bed, calmly, trustingly, courageously, he moved from the shores of Time and went forth into the vast ocean of Eternity. His relatives will see him no more until the grand resurrection morn, when Christ shall make His jewels up into His starry crown. Then they will recover their treasure. In the sweet

fields of Eden they will regain the companionship of him whom they have loved and lost. There he awaits their coming.

H.

"H." was no doubt the old squire himself. The piece is penned in his style, and in its emphasis on religious faith, family, and the importance of hearth and home, restates the values he had stood for throughout his life. He had taught his son well, who had grown into a worthy heir with the promise to be a fine steward of the family fields. This tattered newspaper clipping still rests in the family Bible, where the grieving father placed it that day in 1864.

Haywood died at twenty-four, and his prophecy of ten months before came true. "Alas," he had written, "how many of us may be under the cold clods before another year." He had also written how "partial to our Old State" he was and would rather die there than anywhere else. In that he got his wish.

The day before his death, his Aunt Delia Hardy, who had lost her eldest son Willie three years earlier, was inquiring after Haywood's health in a pathetic letter to his father showing the dire situation on the home front for the Asheville branch of the family:

> Belleview
> Near Asheville
> May 23ᵈ [1864]

My dear Brother

. . . I write you now to ask a great favour. I really feel morti-fied to ask it after all your kindness, but tis even so, *necessity has no law*. We can buye nothing with money, not even one dozen Eggs. So I write to beg you will try to send me a little cotton, no matter how little, to exchange for country produce. The country people will only sell for Raw Cotton or Factory yarn. Dr. Hardy bought a farm but cant probably stock it while this terrible war lasts. I was trying to raise chickens, but the soldiers stole all my poultry, Turkeys and all. You can form no idea how hard we find it to have at all every thing to buye. I sometimes get out of heart & think I might as well give up. I send out day after day & cant get a chicken or doz. Eggs. I make some butter. Our season is so dark now. We have no vegetables yet, but some Lettuce. We still have a little corn for Bread. Last Summer we lived on Irish potatoes, but I will not complain any more of hard times. Dr. Hardy & Kate have just got home from Wilmington. They took Mr. [Gilbert B.] Tennent's boys Sammy & Gilbert [the doctor's grandchildren] to send them to their parents in England. They left them to go with a gentleman in the first steamer that runs out. Emma [Hardy Tennent]'s health is very bad. Mr T said her life depended on having her boys with her. Dr Hardy wanted to have come by to see you, but travelling is such an expense and conveyance so hard to procure, he gave it up.

Dr. Hardy, upon his return to Asheville, wrote Mrs. Edward Tennent in Wilmington on 23 May 1864, expressing his great anxiety over the children he had left with her. "Tell me when they leave and in what Ship," he wrote, regretting his consent to let them go on this dangerous run through the blockade. "You know they are my only grandchildren and their Mother my only daughter." But the latter had missed them so desperately that it had imperilled her own safety. And Hardy was thus sending the two boys to their parents, who were variously in England, Scotland, and France, where Tennent was on a diplomatic mission for the Confederacy to acquire cloth and materials for the Southern Cause.
Delia Hardy continued her letter of 23 May:

I do hope Dick and Jimmy Douglass are spared to you. I feel very anxious to hear. My nephew Cal Ardis had his arm amputated & his thigh broken. I fear he will die. Another younger Brother severely wounded in the mouth. Do let us hear from you & how Haywood is & of Dick and Jimmie. Wash [her son in the sixtieth North Carolina] is at home so sick, for he, though looks very bad, is better for a few days. I do long to see you all my dear Brother. Since I lost my darling Mother, life is very sad to me. Give much love to Sister [Frances Douglass] & the boys, Dr. Douglass, Jimmey. Do pray come to see us this year.

Your afft & devoted Sister
Delia E[rwin] Hardy

Do come & see us. Tell Sallie Douglass I want to see her.

Will loved her so much. All send love. Do come & bring
Sister [Frances Hardy Douglass] with you.

In 1928 it was still remembered in Asheville that Delia Hardy "until her
death" in 1876 always kept her son Willie's grave "beautiful with the
flowers of each season."

On 1 June 1864 Jimmie Douglass's good friend and former classmate
Henry Jones reported from Ashland, near Richmond, to his sister in
Thomasville, Georgia, that indeed Douglass "was painfully wounded . . .
but was doing well when last heard from." Young Jones, who had
sought Jimmie's address from Dr. Douglass back in 1861, was himself
shot and killed in August 1864. It was another deep loss for Jimmie,
comparable to Haywood's.

By 17 July 1864 Dickie was hospitalized at Jackson Hospital with
lumbago, cephalgia, and cystitis. He recuperated there and at home and
returned to duty on 28 October 1864. In September Douglass had returned to Richmond, where, on the first day of his arrival, he was ordered to take his company out on the Darbytown Road. During the
battle next day, he was wounded in the other leg. After another thirty
days in the hospital, he resumed command of his tattered lines. He was
unable to attend his sister Sallie's wedding at The Oaks but was glad that
"somewhere at least, life is struggling to go along as usual." He did not
know, but likely guessed, that this was not to be the great event it would
have been in the old days. On a scrap of rough brown paper cut into a
small square and folded, Sallie wrote their nearest neighbor at Orange
Hall:

Home 1 Nov. 1864

Mr. Renwick
    I will be married on Thursday night—request the plea-
sure of your company about 6 o'clock or sooner if you like.
If you have any eggs and pullets, I would like to buy all you
can spare.

Your friend
Sallie Douglass

This is a far cry from the engraved announcements and invitations delivered by servants just three years earlier. Three years, as Sallie reflected,
was now become "a chasm of time." She and Jimmie had been so close,

and now he must miss this important event in her life. Life, however, as he wrote her, "must go on" without him. He would "be there in mind." Her new husband, D. A. Townsend of Union, was mustering in; the couple wanted to make their vows before he left for war, knowing that in the uncertainty of the times, this might be their only chance.

Virtually everyone had gone to war now, even the "children." Cousin Sallie Beard of nearby Glenn Springs wrote her Renwick kin at Goshen Hill in December 1864: "It seems so strange to see some of the little boys here going off to war, but I dare say some of them will make fine soldiers." The situation, as they knew, had become desperate. In late '64, Sallie's father, Clough S. Beard, also wrote to his Renwick kin, this time to report the death of his son James. Still, through his sadness, he closed his letter with the request to "Remember me kindly to Rogers, Jimmie & Blackfolks."

Throughout 1864 Douglass had had with him for his body guard Charlie Giles, a twenty-five-year-old slave who had been Captain Giles's body servant until his death in 1862. Giles himself recalled in 1937 that he went off to war

> wid Captain Douglass. . . . Our train went dat fast, dat it took my breaf away. . . . De Yankees act like dey was gwine to blow everything up. I crawl along de ground wid my Marster, and try to keep him kivered as best as I could. Us reached Chickahominy River and go over to Petersburg. Den dey blow up Richmond. De river turn to blood while I was looking at it. De cannons deafened me, and I has been hard of hearing ever since. Some of de blue-tails clumb de trees when us got atter dem.

Although Giles, in his old age, confused places and dates, he clearly remembered that he did his duty by protecting his master, and that the Yankee sharpshooters got after him one day, and his Confederate comrades "sent fer de cannon balls" to run the bluecoats off. The Confederate pickets had dogs cared for by the body servants that "lots of de soldiers had wid dem": "At night in de camp when de Yankees would come spying around, de dogs would bark. De niggers would holler. One Confederate officer had a speckledy dog that could smell dem Yankees fer off. When de Yankees got dare, everything was ready." For his interviewer, Giles had this advice: "Don't never go in no war, 'less you is

gwine to give orders like my marse Jack [Giles] . . . or act as bodyguard."
For Giles, the war was a great adventure and not all work. "I drunk as
much as I wanted," he remembered:

> De soldiers would drink by de barrels. . . . Old man Sammy
> Harmon had a state still. . . . Dem dat had wagons come and
> fotch it off, as many barrels as de mules could draw, fer de
> soldiers. I drunk as much as I wanted. De drum taps say,
> "Tram-lam-lam," following on de air. De spirits lift me into
> a dance, like dis [he danced some] except I was light on my
> foots den—atter I had done drunk, anyhow.

Apparently, at this point, as Giles observed, morale in the ranks was still
relatively good, surprisingly so, considering the circumstances.

On 3 January 1865 Jimmie Douglass sent his father a remarkable
letter from the Fifth Regiment encamped on the north side of the James:

> Dear Father
>   Yours of the 20th December (confirming the long and
> unpleasant rumour) has been received, it having been on the
> road ten days. As soon as I received it, I went to Bob and
> offered my sympathies, which he thankfully accepted, as he
> thought I could share them with him better than any one
> else. I was very sorry to hear that Savannah had fallen and
> more so to see what a depressing effect it had upon our troops
> here, a good many of whom are badly whipped on account
> of Sherman's uninterrupted march through Georgia and
> Hood's defeat before Nashville. I have lost confidence in
> Hood. He will do very well to command a Division, but he
> cant manage an army—I think his campaign into Tenn. one
> of the worst moves we ever made, particularly at this season.
> I suppose you have heard of the great New Year Dinner the
> people were getting up for Gen. Lee's Army. Well it came
> yesterday and there was about enough given to our Regt. for
> one good Company. . . . I am getting oneasy about some-
> thing to eat for the Army, for we are just getting enough to
> keep us alive, not enough to keep us warm this cold weather.
> Ben [Maybin] and Dick [Hardy] both have a box on the
> road, but it seems as if they will never get here. We are look-

ing for them with unusual anxiety in order that we may get a little fat on us to keep us warm. I suppose you received the money I sent you by [indecipherable]. I told him to take you some smoking tobacco. I dont know whether or not he carried it. Write and let me know. Say to Mrs. Gross that Mr. D[avid] Gross is doing finely. All he wants is plenty to eat. He is beginning to look like a soldier, plenty of dirt and I expect some lice on him. Tell Mother Phil is needing some soap to wash our clothes. I have to pay $8.00 per pound for it here. Where is Mr. Townsend and his Company? I suppose near Charleston or Branchville. He will have a chance to show off his boys to the Yankees if he dont mind. Well, I believe I have written all I can think of. The weather is very cold with plenty of snow. The boys are *all* well. Give much love to all the family. Tell them to write.

Your affect Son
J T Douglass

The severe cold on poorly fed and ill-clad men this winter of 1864–'65 was no less cruel than Valley Forge had been in the previous century. Phil was now suffering alongside his master, washing his clothes and taking care of him as Uncle Peter had done before. Peter, now up in years, could not withstand such hard campaigning. He had been with Jimmie in both South Carolina and Virginia in 1861; but when events heated up, resourceful Phil and Charlie Giles took his place. Jimmie was thus attended by faithful slaves into the last months of the war. "Love to all the family. Tell them to write," he concluded, sounding like so many soldiers across the centuries as they closed their letters home.

After his three serious woundings, Jimmie served without further injury on the Petersburg and Richmond lines until retreat, when he was in several engagements with the rear guard. Historian Clement Evans summed up his military career nicely by saying that Douglass was for the South "in her days of trial, one of the most devoted soldiers who defended her cause and maintained her honor. . . . Besides the wounds mentioned, he had testimony of hard fighting in sixteen bullet holes through his hat and clothing." Obviously it was the destiny of certain men to survive the war, no matter how squarely in harm's way they came.

Douglass himself always attributed his survival to "strong physical development" and a resilient constitution forged in hunting and agricultural labor; and he was no doubt at least partly correct. He thus balanced sound mind with strong body in the old classical ideal. He surrendered with Lee at Appomattox as captain of Company D, Bratton's Brigade, Field's Division, Longstreet's Corps, and came home with Phil to take over the plantation, which he did successfully. He had strongly wanted to follow in his father's footsteps and study medicine; but as the eldest son, he was "compelled by circumstances" to care for the family after his father's death. He enabled his younger brothers George and Will, however, to continue the family tradition in medical careers.

Cousin Dickie also survived the war. He had a similarly athletic upbringing on the land, being raised with the outdoor sports of riding and hunting; but although described as "a spunky lad," he was thin and his health was less robust than Jimmie's. Yet he made it through those same basic campaigns with his cousin to stack arms with him at Appomattox and make the long walk home. By the time of surrender, he had become the adjutant of Cousin Jimmie's own Company D. Although Dickie was often hospitalized, Evans deemed his war service "exemplary." At Appomattox he was not yet twenty-four, thus still a young man in years, but an old one in experience.

Many of the local boys were members of Dickie's and Jimmie's Fifth Regiment. In addition to Haywood and Ben Maybin, these included James C. Eison, Tints Jeter, T. W. (Jack) Henderson, James A. Oxner, Walker Glymph, T. S. Moorman, G. L. Evans, Thomas L. Wilson, Jenkins Smith, David Gross, and Robert Lyons. Neighbor Berry Richards was in the Fifth Cavalry. This was the typical way for Southerners in the war. Neighbors and family volunteered together and fought shoulder to shoulder. As fellow Newberrian Augustus Dickert phrased it so well, they went to war together and if they died, it was "the death of the happy warrior, fighting as our Anglo-Saxon forefathers fought, in the midst of kinsmen and friends." When in 1862, Jimmie was captain, Dickie sergeant-major, and Haywood sergeant of the same company, they did indeed create a family's united front against the foe. This was in no way a "civil war" for the men of Maybinton–Goshen Hill. It was instead, most emphatically, a family effort with brothers and cousins striving shoulder to shoulder in a wall of defense of a single home.

Of these sixteen neighbors, Oxner, Jeter, Henderson, Evans, Wilson, Smith, Richards, and Haywood Hardy lost their lives, exactly half the tally, and most of them in the terrible fighting around Richmond in the summer of '62 that Haywood reported in his letter to his father as having left only six or seven men in a company that had numbered a hundred. Neighbor Berry Richards died at Goldsboro, North Carolina, in the last battle of the war and left a widow and two young daughters. Their 50 percent casualty rate doubled the rate for Southerners in the war as a whole. The community and the Hardy family were thus directly touched by the war in the most poignant manner. The added burden of defeat and a land in political and economic chaos weighed heavily on the mourners in ways we today can only poorly imagine. The doubly high fatality rate in an area that had sent all her young men to battle— down to the "children"—perhaps explains why this once thriving region was doomed to virtual extinction in the decades to follow. There were simply too few left to pick up the pieces.

Appropriate for all these young dead of the Tyger is the inscription on the gravestone of one of their own, another lad of the Tyger valley, killed at the age of twenty-three in the western campaign near Knoxville on 18 February 1863 while commanding the Fifteenth South Carolina:

> In Memory of William M. Gist.
> He won an honored name,
> Girdling his young
> Brow forever,
> With the patriot
> Wreath of fame.
>
> Sleep! Thou art free!
> And dost not watch
> With tearful eye,
> The lingering death of
> Liberty.

This second stanza, chosen by the dead soldier's father after the end of the war, speaks graphically of the state of mind of the defeated civilian population. William Gist Sr., who was three years younger than William Eppes Hardy, was similarly ruined by circumstances, and died within four years of him. They both lost bright young sons of about the same age and understood that they themselves had to remain behind as silent witnesses to the "lingering death of Liberty"—the eclipse of the old fair Republic of their fathers, for them perhaps as hard a thing as death itself.

Haywood was laid to rest in Ebenezer churchyard, where his parents mourned him. Six years later, his father, the old master, was buried directly by his side at the age of sixty-five, largely a man broken by events and too many losses, his last years marked by a stoic struggle with hardship. Too old to go to war, he had been one of the civilians forced to stay home and be a more or less passive witness to events. He raised his crops, sent shoes, clothes, and comforts to his sons at war, and backed the Cause with his wealth. For a man of such conviction, energy, and devotion to duty, this inaction was a deeply frustrating ordeal. In the words of the upcountry Carolina diarist Mary Boykin Chesnut, he was forced to stand helpless while his world was "kicked to pieces" and much that he valued was destroyed before his eyes.

In February 1865, bummers following Sherman's army rode on horseback up the steps of the Hardy mansion and into the Great House, abused both the white and black families, particularly Catharine and the black female house servants, and fired pistols in the hall. During restoration of the house in 1989, following the guide of family tradition that said it would be there, I uncovered one of their large pistol balls embedded in the hall door to the right front sitting room. It had for many years been sealed with wood putty and painted over. Again according to family tradition, it is said that the women of the house saved the Hardy silver by placing it down the well on pianoforte wire. That this silver exists today with a family member in Virginia lends credence to the story. The inhabitants of the slave quarters were also robbed. All their portable valuables were stolen, and their food was either taken or ruined. The hams not hidden were burned; the flour was poured out of its barrels, trampled, or mixed with molasses to spoil it. The plantation was left without food for any of its members. The house, however, was spared a torching, though the family rightly lived in fear of the act. Toward Columbia, some forty miles distant, the red night sky of 17 and 18 February had told them that this army's element was fire. The majority of families in the paths of Sherman's Left Wing and Kilpatrick's Cavalry in lower Newberry County had not only been robbed and abused like the Hardys but then had had their homes burned as well. Many families were left to shiver in the unusually bitter February cold without so much as blankets to protect them. Some of the weak, old, and infirm died of exposure during these cruel days. Word had indeed spread before the army's path that as much as possible in Carolina would be put to the torch, and like conquered Carthage before her, her soil was to be "sowed with salt" so that "future crops of Secession would not grow there." Although the suggestion of salt-sowing was offered only half in jest by General Halleck, and not carried out literally, business- and industry-dominated Federal policy toward the defeated region was eventually to have the same long-term effect on Southern agriculture and the land itself. As for now in 1865, the scorched earth, smoking ashes from fires escaped into the forests for mile after mile, huddled and homeless old men, women, and children, and the desolate chimneys of homesteads in Sherman's path from the coast inland to the Hardys' own up-country home, proved the sad report of promised destruction only too true. "Sherman's toothpicks" was the name Southerners learned to call these solitary chimneys in the burned landscape. The surface of the earth was itself scorched for countless miles of barren waste. It was America's first major man-made environmental disaster—a holocaust indeed. "What manner of men are these," Southern civilians asked, "that would make war on women, children, and old men?" It now seemed certain that this was truly "a war of conquest," just as Dr. James Douglass and William Renwick and William Hardy had so clearly predicted it would be. These Southerners had correctly gauged their enemy. Northern soldiers were now out to line their pockets with Southern wealth and leave the landscape desolate and its citizenry prostrate. The mile-long wagon train of silver, jewelry, and other portable riches taken from South Carolina homes and now winding its way from the middle country of South Carolina to the North with the conquerors, made this point all too convincingly. For decades thereafter, even the engraved chalices, flagons, and patens from South Carolina churches would turn up from New York and Boston to Ohio and Iowa. For example, the colonial communion silver from St. Michael's Episcopal Church in Charleston, sent to Columbia for safekeeping during the three-year Federal bombardment, was stolen by the invaders. One of the two wine flagons surfaced at a New York pawn shop in 1867. A chalice paten was returned to the church from Ohio. The whereabouts of the communion chalice, large flagon, alms basin, and various other pieces of church silver are unknown. An inlaid panel from the church's pulpit with the symbol of Christ on it was stolen from the ruined church and presented to Mrs. Henry Ward Beecher, a Boston abolitionist, who in turn presented it to a church in Ohio as a "souvenir." Even the organ of the Huguenot Church was crated for shipping north from the Charleston wharves. Long after the war ended, there were large numbers of Northern tourists and souvenir hunters combing the ruins of the helpless state intent on taking "keep-sakes" back home from the conquered territory. Nearer home, in Columbia itself, during the burning in February 1865, drunken soldiers (including officers) drank whiskey from the Catholic church's communion chalice before "appropriating" it, and then setting fire to the Ursuline convent. These last events occurred under a flag of truce and over the loud protests of the Irish soldiers in the Federal army. In Cheraw, South Carolina, north of the Hardy plantation, a newly interred corpse was taken from the Episcopal graveyard and placed in jest at the church organ. Any freshly dug spot was investigated as a potential source of buried silver, even a grave. (As we recall, that is why the Douglasses buried their silver in the rutted roadway before their house.) Such was the thoroughness of the conquerors in their close search for booty. And they came in hordes, fifty-four thousand strong, in a path sometimes fifty miles wide. It was indeed *Vae Victis!*—woe to the conquered—as (in the words of Sherman) "Carolina howled" in pain. The military occupation to follow was simply more of the same: thieving, destruction, and subjugation disguised under the term Reconstruction. One Northern soldier made it clear to a family on the Santee. We don't care about your people black or white, he said to the lady of the house. "We want your country." Conquest was now made official by the extremist Republican-dominated government in which white Southerners were disenfranchised and had no voice whatsoever. It would take over a decade for these Carolinians merely to get back their right to vote. Disenfranchised and ruled by a military occupation government, they were at the complete mercy of the conquerors, and received none. Here there was no pity for the conquered, only abuse, scorn, mockery, and a continued policy of regional conquest—political, economic, and, finally, intellectual. For as Ralph Waldo Emerson, the sainted Sage of Concord, could write in his journals about the conquered Southern land near war's end: now New England will find a field of endeavor for her young minds who can sow her principles across the vanquished territories; and through the absolute and final "confiscation of rebel property . . . at once open the whole South to the enterprise & genius of new men of all nations, & extend New England from Canada to the Gulf, & to the Pacific." (He might have added "*into* the Pacific" with the Boston missionaries' soon sailing in force to Hawaii and shaming the natives from their traditional ways, in advance of U.S. usurpation of their land.) Such were the conquerors' openly expressed Nationalistic attitudes, and such was the brand of economic and intellectual imperialism that the Southerner of the postwar generation had to face. Such was life for the Hardys in a conquered territory. While blacks had gained the priceless blessing of freedom—economically, both white and black Hardys suffered alike.

Thus the family, in keeping a roof over its head, was indeed fortunate when compared to a vast number of fellow Carolinians. The encounter, however, took its toll on William Eppes Hardy, who had been in ill health throughout the decade and had worked himself too hard in the absence of his sons. The deaths of his nephew William and sons Charles Wesley and Haywood had added much to an already heavy burden. And perhaps an even greater tragedy was unfolding beneath his bootsoles, as he was witness to the decimation of plantation productivity, a decline that perfectly mirrored what was happening across the entire Southland. In 1869 the plantation's acreage remained intact at 2,100, the same as in 1860; but the improved acreage had fallen from 600 to 200, a reduction of 66 percent. The cash worth of the place had fallen from $40,700 to $6,300, or to only 15 percent of its former value, and this did not count the loss of his slaves, which had amounted to more than half of his personal property valued at $45,000 in 1860. Hardy was now paying wages to his workers: $1,200 for the year 1869, barely enough for them to live on. There were now more mules than horses—ten of the first but only four of the latter. The balance had gone to the war effort. The number of milk cows fell to six; but with that number, the Hardys were indeed blessed in comparison to their neighbors. The starkest change was in the number of swine; the tally fell from the hundreds to twenty in 1869, most of them too small to butcher. The total value of his livestock plummeted from $5,250 in 1850 to $1,000 in 1869. Even with all these reductions, however, the Hardys again fared far better than most Carolina planters.

In March and April 1865 Edwin Scott, on several desperate missions from the burned city of Columbia to secure boats, food, and supplies, was aided by William Renwick, Colonel Robert Beaty, and William Eppes Hardy. Scott could only marvel at the contrast between the relative fruitfulness of Tyger valley farms as opposed to the complete devastation of the burned midlands through which he traveled to get there—a place, as he wrote Renwick, "of only chimneys and ashes." Scott's own Columbia now bore the nickname "Chimneyville." The "fruitfulness" of the Tyger was, however, only a matter of degree, for the war was such a severe blow to the rich valley that it was never to recover even to a point approximating its prewar self-sufficiency. Instead, it and the South were to become a colonial producer of raw materials for Northern mills, which paid low prices for the cotton and received tariff-protected premium prices for their manufacturers from the very black and white men and women who grew the cotton fiber and were struggling merely to eat. The government, now in the hands of business interests, saw to it that this would continue to be the case. Such was the sad punishment for losing this war. As the South had no power to influence the government in a major way, that government would keep this unfair situation in place well into the twentieth century with discriminatory freight rates and like measures. Yes, indeed. Such was the harsh penalty of political domination. The gentleman's compact had been replaced by a tool for one region's exploitation of another, as the men and women of Tyger had so accurately predicted.

The old squire, after his cotton sales in winter 1867, had enough money to purchase from M. David & Co. in Columbia a bonnet ($5.00), 4 pairs of stockings (2.00), 3 shawls (12.00), a pair of pantaloons (4.50), 9 handkerchiefs (2.75), 2 bolts of homespun (14.00), a man's shawl (9.00), 3 shirts (6.00), and 2 pairs of socks (.75). He also bought, likely for his grandson and namesake William Hardy Frost, a pair of pants ($2.50) and 2 pairs of children's hose (.75). For the house, he purchased 4 towels ($2.50), 9 yards of sheeting (11.25), 3 pairs of blankets (20.00), 6 yards of table cloth (15.00), 6 spools of cotton (.50), a comforter (1.00), and a hook (1.50).

Squire Hardy made the trip to Columbia in December to make these purchases himself. He had recovered from the "bout with cholera mortuis" and edema of the legs reported by Dr. Douglass to his daughter Garrie on 30 July. The year 1867, in fact, saw much illness in the neighborhood. The subject takes up almost the entirety of Douglass's letter, worth quoting in full:

At Home July the 30th 1867

Dear Daughter

As we are expecting your return home on next Saturday, I enclose ten dollars, and wish you to purchaise and bring with you, 2 ounces of Quinine, and, one pound of sulph soda, or Glaubus salts.—the Quinine I expect will be $4. per ounce, and the salts 20 cts. Say to Dr. [Robert] Gibbes I will return the Oil Erigeron by the first favourable opportunity as I have a supply, but if he has received the oil of Male Fern, to send it. This leaves us all well at this time. I have no local news worth dividing. Mr. Gaillard and Bettis, is the gossip of the neighbourhood. He has been here nearly three weeks, and looks as contented as if he were at home. We have had a shower of chill & fever in the last week or two, principally among the Freedmen. John V. Lyles, his sons Tom, Willie, & Abe, also his little daughter Eliza, have been quite sick with fever. Willie [Douglass] is still sick. Your Uncle Billie [Hardy]'s family are well. He had a bout of cholera mortuis himself the other day. His legs are much better. Daniel was over yesterday and reports his father sick with dysentery. I hear of a Pick-Nick at the spring next Saturday. I close by tendering my love to all. Your father,

George Douglass

A month after Squire Hardy had made his purchases in Columbia in December 1867, Mary Frost, sister-in-law of his daughter Elmira Hardy Frost, sent the squire a cheering letter from Richland County, full of news of the family and local doings:

Home, Jan 28th, 1868

Thinking a letter from me would not be objectionable, dear Uncle Billy, I forthwith write you, though having little or nothing of interest to communicate. It has been a source of regret to me ever since you left, that I did not accompany you on your return home, so good an opportunity I lost. Strange that a person of tolerable good sense will act so injudiciously at times. Perhaps experience will teach me a lesson for the future. I hope to come up now about the first of March. Brother Uriah [Frost] left us for parts unknown some two weeks since. We presume he is making you a visit. If so, please hand him the enclosed note. If not staying with you, but in the vicinity perhaps with your son Adolphus, please be kind enough to convey the note to him, as it is on business, urging him to return speedily, his business being at a standstill, his cotton ginned and picked during his absence of two weeks now, and the hands all waiting for a settlement from him. It is important that he should be here. I leave the matter with you, knowing your good judgement. If brother Uriah has not been to your house, please write me immediately acquainting me of the fact, as I feel very anxious about him, always acting as he does from impulse, and rashly too. He left home rather with difficulty and embarrassment attending him, so did not say where he was going, designedly I presume, but thought he would have returned ere this, leaving his business in so unsettled a state. The trial of the man father had arrested for stealing a hog from his pen, came off the last District Court. He was convicted, sentenced to a year's imprisonment in the penitentiary with hard labor, as also three of the Guignards for hog stealing, a great institution that. It has tended greatly to the relief of the community. Our neighborhood generally are supplied with a complement of hands. They hired readily with little or no delay, made bargains at the commencement of the year. Brother John [Frost] has thirteen employed, will have no trouble in getting them as he gives more than any one. I hear of eight dollars a month; he could have hired them as easily at six or seven. Stands in his own light, I think. Wages are reduced, a great number of idle freedmen in Columbia searching for labor. I suppose your plans for the year are now fully matured. Dick, I presume, is installed in his new house. Tell him when I come up, I will pay him a call to see if he is a tidy housekeeper. As he has the cage, ought now to get the bird to put it in. Mr. Guignard and family are moving up this week, will live in close proximity, occupying the house that Mr. Walton formerly had. Our neighborhood is improving. Mr. and Mrs. Marshall will also live only a mile and a half distant. We still miss our little darling boy, his vivacity so much greater than that of other children. Kate's head is better, has been exceedingly sore. Has been taking Heinish's Queen's Delight, a powerful purifier of the blood. It has done her more good than anything else. So if your ankles still give you trouble, I would advise you to take a few bottles of it. Hope they are well however. The baby is still nameless. Is it not a shame? [Born on 18 April 1867, he was later named Charles Wesley Frost after his dead uncle.] He is growing very like his absent brother, is a sweet dear little fellow. Tell Aunt Katie [Catharine] it would do her good to see him; and as for Will [William Hardy Frost], he cannot be surpassed in beauty, is a perfect love, so very interesting withal. I spent last Sunday with them. Kate had a hearty cry for me to stay. The children are all greatly attached to me, and the feeling is mutual. I suppose you have read some of the proceedings of the Grand Convention. The Columbia papers are very meagre in their reports; but the Charleston journals teeming, particularly the *Mercury,* at the commencement of its sessions, the accounts very ludicrous, and description of many of the delegates, so sarcastic that many were opposed to their reporter having a seat on the floor. I will send you some of the papers, really amusing to read. Nash denounces Gov. Chamberlain. I consider it the greatest humbug of the nineteenth century. Mr. Robertson is quite an important personage also, reading his few commonplace remarks that some Yankee doubtless wrote for him. The *Mercury* says of him, he is the richest man in the Convention, worth $400,000 made during the war staying at home etc. The reputed wealth flatters his weak mind and vanity, I dare say. What a quantity of rain has fallen recently, which prevents necessary preparation of lands, for planting. The negroes in some of the lower districts hesitate in contracting, saying the Convention is going to give each a mule and forty acres of land. Deluded wretches they are. Kiss my little nephew for me. Tell him I want to see him very much, and I am coming up soon, and he must beg grandma to learn him to spell, or Kate and Willie will be smarter than he is. You must have a nice beau ready for me by the time I come up, no red flannel on his neck though. When does Annie [Douglass]'s marriage take place? Daniel [Epps] has a goodly stock of patience to wait on her so long. [They married 8 days later.] Love to all. Tell Mr. Thomas to write to me. Should be very glad to hear from him. Yours most affectionately,

Mary

Squire Hardy and Catharine now had four grandchildren by their daughter Elmira Frost, one of the few bright spots in their lives. They were Annie Catharine (the Kate of the letter, 1862–1904), named after her grandmother and great-grandmother Hardy; Campbell Walker (1864–1931); William Hardy (the Willie of the letter, 1865–1948); and Charles Wesley (1867–1941). The following year would see the birth of John Davis (1869–1930), then Eugene Herbert in 1871, and Agnes Walker in 1873. Two more children, Laura and Haywood, would eventually round out the Frost household. Haywood, of course, was named for Elmira's brother, dead in the war.

The Hardy fields in 1869 yielded 200 bushels of spring wheat (down from 350 in 1860), 400 bushels of corn from about 35 acres, no sweet potatoes, 50 pounds of butter, and 3 tons of hay. The cotton acreage was now about 50, down from a minimum of 220 acres in 1850 and 150 acres in 1860, a reduction of 75 and 66 percent. The number of cotton bales was now only 16, down from 110 in 1850 and 81 in 1860, figures that show the plight of the plantation and the havoc worked upon it. Even the old pioneer before his death in 1814 had raised as much cotton as William Eppes Hardy in 1869. And, once again, Hardy's neighbors suffered even more severely. The one exception was Maybinton's largest cotton crop in the year 1869: 33 bales, produced on the farm of R. S. Chick and John T. Bynum.

Then, too, there were back taxes for the war years and more inflated taxes to pay to tax assessors who were practiced in bureaucratic bullying. A note from one such assessor to William Renwick reveals the peremptory tone of the demands:

> 10 Feb. 1869
> W. W. Renwick
>
> Dear Sir.
>   I will be at Goshen Hill on tomorrow to assess Taxes. You will please attend at the time and place to make your return. Also the freedmen on your place above the age of 21 years, please inform them. All who fail to make their return will be liable to pay 50 percent of their tax.
> Assessor.

It seems that now both Southern blacks and whites were being picked cleaner than a cotton field.

These changes came upon the planters swiftly and brutally and they had no time to adjust to them. The Renwicks were utterly ruined so that with William's death in 1872, the sons could look only to their father's library as having any great value in the estate settlement. It was truly a world undermined and cut from its moorings. Demoralized and confused, whites and defenseless ex-slaves were at the mercy of the whims of government, weather, circumstances, and sometimes each other. Still too, like the Hardys, most families bore the burden of mourning young sons or husbands. Yet the Hardys and Douglasses did their best to keep up their spirits. They pulled closer and fell back on inner resources, and especially on their saving sense of humor, for even in the worst of times, if you looked at things with any distance at all, there was plenty to laugh at, if only the "greasy doings" of butcherings or a musical daughter who was congenitally given to singing (or playing) ahead of the music. A hurried letter from Dr. Douglass written 2 December 1867 to his wife visiting near Shelton (on the Broad near the Hardy plantation, and likely at the Hardy plantation itself), reveals the way the family was getting by through relying on its own resources, how it was feeding a large white and black plantation population, and still having some time for song, even in the shadowed face of illness:

At Home Dec. 2nd 1867

Dear Frances

As I will send to Shelton on tomorrow I embrace the opportunity of writing a few lines. Janie had a light chill and fever on Sunday morning, was up in the evening, took quinine today. Garrie had a chill last night, is as usual quite sick today. I gave her an emetic & hope with quinine tomorrow she will be better. A chill affects her more than any of us. I feel lik[e] I am fine, but Janie and Garrie was quite well on Saturday and very hopefull too.

I killed 15 hogs today and therefore have greasy doings at our house. [Daughter] Mira was the superintender, in the kitchen. Winney is here helping with the lard. I shall kill the balance in the course of five or six days if the weather continues favourable, as they are eating up all my corn. I expected Sally as usual was ahead of the musick. Give my love to her & accept the same for your self.

P. S. Mary Fair is dead.

Yours as ever
Geo. Douglass

317

Even if Douglass had to kill all his hogs, then he did at least have hogs to kill; and besides, they were eating up all the corn. As so many from these times soon knew, there is a silver lining to every storm cloud if you are prepared to find it.

And, too, both Hardy and Douglass families, like Margaret Mitchell's famous literary heroine Katie Scarlett O'Hara, still had their land—and a Tara in much better shape to boot. Squire Hardy looked to that truth for some measure of consolation, even though the monetary value of his Tara had decreased by 85 percent. And he was allowed to live to see one of his sons return home and marry a young lady from a neighboring plantation. Yes, as Cousin Jimmie Douglass had said during the war, "Life would and must go on."

In a letter to his daughter Garrie, who was on a visit to the Frosts in Richland County, Dr. Douglass sent news of "home, sweet home," where "Momus . . . the God of laughter" was again to be found:

> At Home May the 26th 1869
>
> Dear Daughter
>
> Having a private opportunity of writing a letter to Columbia, and having nothing of more importance to do, I concluded to address to you a something, as a momento, to remind you of home, "home, sweet home," knowing the solicitude which everyone feels, who can duely appreciate home, to hear in their absence, what has transpired or may be transpiring, during that absence; and to gratify that desire is the prompting motive to this effort.
>
> Well Garrie, your Aunt [Catharine Hardy] arrived home safely on the day she left you [at the Frosts], and visited us the next day, with the articles sent by you. I think her visit improved her health, as she was looking better than before she left.—The next item is, Sallie's visit. She spent two weeks with us, having both of her children with her, and her *Alum,* old Aunt Jinnie, to take care of them. Sallie is Sallie still, full of life and laughter, a perfect Momus, (Momus was the God of laughter—or the laughing God). The children are looking well. Mamie is a sweet little creature, and a very good child. She took a great fancy to me. Frank, on the contrary, is a bad boy, mischievous and obstinate. He is still with us; and I expect to improve him a little. Old Aunt Jinnie left disap-

pointed. She expected to catch Old Man Dick, but made a woefull failure. Annie went home with Sallie, to spend two weeks. Mirah is therefore solitary and alone. However, she and Nora is gone to spend the day with Miss Sue Carlisle, but I hardly think they will get sight of Jule. Ben & Etty spent a day with us during Sallie's visit. Etty was suddenly attacked on her return home with Erysipalus, which rapidly spread over her face, neck, and chest. She was promptly relieved, and is now doing well, but considerably disfigured from the caustic applications.—Well Garrie, this concludes my stock of news, and I conclude this brief Epistle, with business matters for Miss Frankey [Frances Hardy Douglass, his wife]— She desires you to get some buttons to suit the piece of calico I've enclosed, also some pins assorted. She received Elmira's message relative to your stay with her during the summer. She thinks that it is rather too long, and can't exactly consent to that arrangement. Give my love to Mira [Hardy Frost] and the children, and best respects to the Frosts in general, and kiss Mary [Frost] for me.—Remember me affectionately to all my relations, and believe me as ever, your affectionate Father—

Geo. Douglass

The young folks who had survived the great conflict were trying to pick up the ways of the old world of their childhood. With energy and light hearts, they put on a series of costume balls and medieval-style jousting tournaments, or "Tilts" as they called them, just as their parents had done in the days before the war. The "Queen of Love and Beauty" no doubt came straight from the pages of *Ivanhoe*. We are fortunate to have a description of one such season from Mary Beard to one of her Renwick cousins at Goshen Hill:

2 Jan 1873

Dear Cousin
    Your kind letter was duly received & highly appreciated . . . you have had a bad time of it since you left Florida. . . . You wish to know who the young lady was who expressed such a strong desire to see you. It was none other than your old friend Janie Douglass of "The Oaks." By the way, that brings to mind the fact that she was crowned "Queen of

Love and Beauty" by Mr. Jim Sims at a Tournament which they had on last Tuesday [31 December] at Goshen Hill. Frank Maybin got one of the prizes and Will Douglass took the fourth prize and crowned Miss Jessie Evans. None of us attended the Tilt, but Cousin Bob [Lyons] attended the costume ball and said he enjoyed it very much. I attended one they had a short time before this last at Goshen and had a pleasant time.

She continued about the dullness of the times:

Cousin, how did you spend your Christmas?—We had just the dullest time imaginable, for the ground was covered with snow so that we could not go anywhere and no one came to see us. I wish you could have been here to help us eat the fine Turkey dinner on Xmas day.

The young were putting on as bright a face as possible. There were Christmas gatherings when the weather permitted, and costume balls on New Year's Eve. Courtings continued, and the community was surviving with as much grace and joyfulness as was possible. The hospitable and gracious old ways had not been forgotten. The manners of the people of the old society at least remained, and so did the sense of style, even though the wherewithal to accomplish its material manifestations was lacking.

In January 1866 William Eppes Hardy signed articles of agreement with his former slave Eglan and her daughters Cornelia and Emma for their work on the place. They were to receive $35, their food, "a house to live in, and firewood to burn." Eglan was to "do all manner of work set for her, conduct herself in an orderly manner, to be respectful and obedient at all times, not to keep fire arms or intoxicating liquors, or introduce or invite visitors without consent of the employer." If Eglan were to fail "to do a fair day's work from any other cause other than sickness, or should become disobedient or impudent, or found guilty of any manner of theft," she was to "be discharged and paid for services rendered to the time of discharge." If Eglan voluntarily left service, she would forfeit such prorated pay. Similarly, on 19 January 1866 Hardy made agreement with his former slaves Pleasant and his wife Vilet. They were to receive $100, a "killing hog," a house, and firewood. The further terms of their contract were worded the same as Eglan's.

In 1868 Squire Hardy and his freedman Tom Suber entered into an agreement with Hardy & Agnew Co. of Spartanburg to borrow $200 for "provisions clothing etc. in accordance with the act of the General Assembly to secure advances for agricultural purposes" and thus gave "the first lien on our crop." In April 1869 Hardy & Agnew Co. was again urging the old squire to give "your joint note with [son] Dick for $1200 at 10% interest. This note you can make payable 12 months after date. . . . It will be giving you the chance to make another crop before the amount is due."

The year 1869 was to find Old Master trying desperately, and unsuccessfully, to purchase enough corn and bacon to feed the whites and the remaining large number of blacks on the plantation. Many of the latter were old and had no means to leave. Even more than he, they were at the mercy of circumstances. They could not do the hard work of the young, yet still must be fed. Conscience, humanity, and affection demanded it, and indeed, as Hardy knew and said, "they had earned it." If he could sell enough cotton to pay taxes and wages and keep all of them fed, the plantation would survive. If not . . . well then, he did not know what would happen to them all.

A letter dated 20 August 1869 from Robert Moorman & Co. of Newberry reported the sad intelligence that the company was unable to fill his order for food because of the "uncertainty" of the railroads. Moorman had been an old friend before the war, and this no doubt made the refusal hurt even more. Old Master's similar order four months earlier to Hardy & Agnew had pled for bacon, which the company said was "not in our power to accommodate you with." Hardy's poignant pleas show a breakdown in the ability of the plantation to meet the needs of its members for the first time in its long history. Before the war there had been 220 hogs even after extensive butcherings. In so short a time, Hardy was forced to order corn and bacon merely to sustain his people with the bare necessities. Such was the brutal reality of the old squire's last days. From all accounts, he met it with a quiet and uncomplaining dignity, and at rare moments, even flashes of his old wit.

On 25 August 1870, just over a year after receiving these letters from the merchants, he died in the violent and chaotic days of Reconstruction, leaving his strong wife Kate to help her son begin the process of starting life under new and less than auspicious circumstances. Two-thirds of his estate, he left to Catharine, one-third to Dickie. There were back taxes to pay, inflated out of reason by a hostile bureaucracy with greatly expanded powers, whose policies were now directed toward breaking up and, in effect, confiscating the planters' lands. There were many opportunists, official and unofficial alike, scavenging over what was left of the helpless countryside and eager to take the Hardy lands. But most of all, there were people to feed in a time of no food. There were psychological scars and wounds from the war to heal, and in direct parallel and as significantly, a ruined and scarred land to repair. Like the man, so the land.

All these tasks would fall largely to the lot of Dickie, now becoming "Captain Dick" to his people, the last "Young Marster," who at his father's death in 1870 was twenty-nine years old. Much was expected of him, and he met the challenge with fortitude and a strength of character that was tutored and forged by the old civilization. The war had toughened, not broken him. The land and the era thus had the substance to bear yet another giant. In February 1871 the new young master sold the cotton crop for the preceding year and realized $1,534 for it. Even though this was only a tiny fraction of the sales during the flush prewar years and promptly was absorbed by a bill of $1,629 from Moorman & Co. for "supplies," it was, however, a good beginning, and a moral victory besides, showing that the new generation of Hardys would not be pushed off the land, or at least not without a good fight. Like Jimmie Douglass, they were game for the battle. They would indeed, as Dickie phrased it, "struggle on the best way we can, though all the world seems to come down against us." The prophecy of Isaiah had special meaning for him: "They shall build up the ancient ruins; they shall raise up the former devastations." Yes, as Dickie phrased it, like their pioneer ancestors before them, "the Hardys would meet their hardships, not sit with idle hands." The family had survived hardships many times before, each generation in its own way and over its own special set of circumstances, and they would again give it their best try. The plantation fields would once more be covered in a bounty of corn, cane, and cotton; and there would once again be Meat, Meal, and Molasses for all. While the glory had departed, the will to do had not. The inner substance of their civilization still remained in the character of its people, even if many of its outward forms had been irrevocably lost. It was a civilization perhaps more strongly guarded and valued now precisely because so much *had* been lost; and a true Southern nation was formed out of the ashes, the

Southern nation without a government. For this family, the old culture had built a strong moral basis that still bred the will to "struggle on." In a way, as the new young squire saw it, "we are now privileged to show what we can endure by sheer will and determination." Although he did not say and perhaps truly did not realize it, no past generation in the long line of Hardys, in old country or new, had been dealt more difficulties to surmount than his own. It was indeed, as he said, their "brief hour upon the stage of history."

13

New Giants in the Land
The Last Young Master

With us of the younger generation in the South since the War, pretty much the whole of life has been merely not dying.
                                                    —Sidney Lanier (1875)

The plight of the veteran returning to a scorched and poverty-stricken South would seem almost incomprehensible to us today. The civilization had virtually been turned upside down. Chaos ruled. The state government in Columbia lay in shambles in the burned city and, for the most part, in the control of dishonest opportunists, masters of the art of lining their pockets and egged on by those intent on humiliating the people of the old society. The state itself had a Federally-appointed governor. Dickie Hardy's first and most natural duty, however, lay not in Columbia but at home—cleaning up and restoring his family's own plantation world. He must have allowed himself no time to pamper his battle scars or wallow in self-pity. He quickly put his shoulder to the wheel. Apparently Dickie was now becoming Captain Dick in earnest. Toughened by the war, he had the necessary grit to stave off the land confiscators and negotiate with the former slaves for the raising of crops. The Hardy family was truly lucky to have one member in each generation who could rise to the occasion when circumstances demanded it. This was a measure of both its resiliency and the good moral fiber of which it was made—as it was at the same time an indication of the solid strengths of the men and women of both races of the antebellum South.

As he returned to the welcoming great portico and walked the box-wood paths that led to it, he was impressed by the peaceful quiet of the scene. After the unspeakable scenes of death he had witnessed for four years, when rivers did indeed "turn to blood" before his eyes, the sight of home was truly welcome, even with the air of tragedy hanging about it. Despite its serenity, the old place had changed in a way that could never be restored. It was not so much a matter of the house's worn paint and its look of ill repair, but of a deadly sad silence everywhere, of the black children who looked at him with eyes that stood preternaturally round and large over cheeks hollowed from want. Their pitiful quietness hurt him. "How unlike the past," he wrote his sister. "Their freedom is yet an empty thing." Haywood lay in the sod at Ebenezer churchyard, one who had been close to him from his earliest recollections—then in the turmoil of battle for three long years that seemed longer than their entire childhood together, until his poor brother was worn out and sick to death. Dickie himself knew this exhaustion all too well, what it meant to be used up. It was good that Haywood could get home to die among family, to be nursed and comforted by sister, father, and mother, to die in the old room of his boyhood. He only wished he could have been there to say his good-byes and vow a brother's love. But Haywood knew, he consoled himself. Dickie's own childhood friends—Oxner, Wilson, Evans, Rogers, Henderson, his neighbor Richards—they too had perished in the conflict. Now the lined and haggard face of his father presented the visual image of all that had occurred. It was the very picture of loss, of a world lost. As they embraced in the mansion's hall, he could see past his father to their reflection in the hall mirror: he himself a gaunt, muddy, scarcely human-looking man in rags, his father the tragic figure of a broken man in a broken world, a civilization kicked to pieces before their gaze, and now his father's eyes blasted and filmed. Worse by far than all this, the dream of a life in the fruitful valley of an agrarian republic had been irretrievably lost. The wound was dynastic, and his grief was fittingly deep. "Haywood?" the old squire murmured. But it was Dickie who embraced him. All three were bound in that embrace, as they had all three witnessed a bright new country unfurling its banners with principles firmly based on Magna Carta and the old chivalric values, brought down to defeat, its shining pennons trampled in the dust by an enemy nation controlled by financiers and industrialists.

If, as Napoleon said, England was a nation of shopkeepers, so too was this country's destiny: a land of shopkeepers and factory workers in an endless string of smoke-polluted Cities on Hills. Flawed though it may have been, the society of the South had based its life on the land; and now her eclipse was truly a great global loss. From here on, the American utilitarians and materialists, not to mention self-serving politician-bureaucrats, would have their way unchecked and without opposition, to march their barren idea of Progress across the land. No more would his father's fields bloom as they had with the produce of the seasons. Soon he himself could no longer be the servant to those seasons. Yes, he foresaw it, past the glass in which he saw himself and father reflected. Beyond the embrace of their reunion, a new world order was dawning, and one he did not relish seeing. This world would too often be a world of waste, a sterile place of assembly-line sameness where one conned and savaged his fellowman in cold and impersonal ways under the sacred banner-excuse of business. *Loss, loss* . . . now he knew: these were the words that had seemed to echo from his worn bootsoles as he made his last weary steps home from Appomattox, that had sounded in the pregnant silence when he and Jimmie Douglass took their separate ways at the Tyger, that had echoed heavily through the box allées that led to the steps of the family mansion, his footsteps still tied with iron links to that distant Virginia place called Appomattox.

He had been with Lee there, had felt the bittersweet tragedy of the moment, had seen the gray leader's tired face, been close enough to touch Traveller. He relived his feelings in the march down the narrow street after surrender. They had set up a press on the edge of the village and printed up paroles. He was forced to take his, almost in a daze of sorrow and defeat. Then all there was left was the drying of eyes, the quiet stacking of arms, the final embraces, and the long, empty walk home to Carolina—the sleeping on his feet nothing new. He had done this often while marching. In his mind there blended in a rush the first flush of excitement in 1861, the ladies with their flowers and red-checked, cloth-covered baskets of food along the train tracks to Virginia, the fear, the agonies, the heroism, the friendships, the memories of great sacrifices, and tender mercies and confidings, the fatigue, then Lee and surrender, crushed hope, the numb walk home, the gaunt but friendly Southern faces who aided him on his way, passing in solemn blurred review in his memory. All this would forever remain a part of him, but now he would put it aside for a while. How could he patch his world together? He knew only that he would have no time for self-pity and little time for reflection, for he would have other battles to fight no less important for his family than the recent ones on bloody battlefields. He must keep battle-tough and "at the ready." No, the war for him was not over. He and his Southern comrades could have no such luxuries. The men returning North went home to celebrating crowds, to settled towns untouched by the torch, to a booming economy, and a stable government which they controlled. His was not that destiny.

As he crossed the Tyger and saw the distant fields of home, he felt encouragement in the mathematically ordered lines of the new cotton with its bright young iron-green leaves that surrounded the house, spilling down their same old terraces in the very patterns they had when he first opened his eyes on this land. Regularity after chaos. Quiet after unspeakable commotion. The noise of battle now seemed gratefully far behind him. A beautiful scene too, through its ruin. Perhaps for the first time, he was aware of the true tender loveliness of the place. As he was later to write (in much the same words his father had used three decades before), it was indeed a "timeless landscape." He appreciated it as fully as mortal could.

Despite the change and cataclysms of which both he and it had been a part, there was a familiar sameness to the land and the slow-whirling cycles that ordered it—and which he too could use as the pattern for order in his life. He might again, after all, at least for a time, become "servant to its seasons." "Home," he whispered to himself as he saw the Big House rise out of its geometric fields and tidy garden. Here his wounds would heal.

The rich soil did not disappoint him. Neither did the faithful black men and women who were bone and marrow of the place. What else were they to do? Like him, farming was what they knew. Liberation had as yet been a hollow thing when neither black nor white had a way of surviving. That the descendants of these loyal men and women would in the present century still revere the Hardy name and Hardy descendants shows both their kindly good nature and the fact that the Hardys also treated them decently, "like kings" as several ex-slaves told their children and children's children after them—the Hardys never letting their black bondsmen go lacking when they had the power to sustain and care for them, treating them, if not as equals, then honestly as fellow human beings, who must eat and have clothes and shelter just as they.

327

In winter, Dickie knew, "the fire felt just as good to black skins as to white," and "a hungry belly gnawed the same."

With the house coming back to order, he began to court a young lady from a neighboring plantation, Miss Frances Booker Sims. Her family, like his own, worshipped at Ebenezer, and he had known her since she was a child. In 1867, he was twenty-six; she was fifteen in a country depleted of whole-bodied men. They married two years later, 16 December 1869. Despite the economic privations of the times, it was a happy ceremony. His father lived to see it—this his first son to be married—and then was dead the following August before their first child was born. For Frances it was little more than a mile across Gordon's Bridge on the Tyger to her new home with the Hardys. Dickie was glad that she remained close to her mother and visited constantly. The Simses and Hardys continued to see each other every Sunday at church. Life was continuing in its old patterns of close neighborhood ties through marriage. These were the means by which the people of this era would keep a sane balance in the midst of the disruptive forces that swirled around them. These ties and their religious faith. There was also solace in the calm Southern nights, the slow healing power of nature, the mansion's quiet rooms and fragrant garden, the pure country air, the settling rural peace and solitude that repaired a shattered psyche.

Frances brought to the plantation as dowry about 200 acres of adjoining land in Newberry and Union Counties. (These included 127 acres in Newberry and a quarter-interest in three tracts: Sims Bottom of 147 acres in Newberry, and the Creek place of 45 acres and the Taggart place of 50 acres, both in Union.) Besides this fine farmland, her dowry included some of the household furniture that had graced the Sims plantation: three beds, "bed clothes," a bureau, three tables, three washstands, chairs, a handsome grandfather clock, a wardrobe, a clothes chest, four trunks, two safes, window curtains, crockery, spoons, knives, pots, and kettles. These furnishings were to come in good when William Eppes Hardy's personal estate was sold at auction in 1874. It was through her dowry that the plantation house kept its elegance despite the hardships of the times. The price of cotton also increased dramatically in this postwar period. By 1879 some of the worst financial times since the war were behind the young captain and his new bride. They had made it through a crucial decade, and now their world was settling down somewhat. With the birth of three healthy sons and a daughter by the end of the decade, they could put at least some of the tragic past behind them.

Dickie's cousin Jimmie Douglass had not waited as long as he to find a wife. In December 1866 he had married Mary Jane Jeter Giles, the twenty-nine-year-old daughter of Argulus Jeter of Santuc and the widow of the Colonel Giles who had led their company at the outset of the war and had been killed at the Battle of Seven Pines in 1862. Jimmie had promised him he would care for Mary Jane if he survived, and this he was doing. He returned to The Oaks with his new bride, where their first child was born a year later. He then began a fruitful life as farmer and master of his father's fields, and later, after the redemption of the state, as county commissioner for six years and a senator from Union from 1894 to 1906. From 1894 to 1896 he served in the legislature with Dickie, and the two were both members of the State Constitutional Convention of 1895. For these few years, their service to the state overlapped. They were once again "doing their duty" shoulder to shoulder as in the old times of the war.

In 1880 Jimmie had only one surviving child, Frances, named after her paternal grandmother, Frances Hardy Douglass. She was born in 1877 in her mother's fortieth year. At his death in 1911, Douglass would be a director and stockholder in several upcountry cotton mills and industrial enterprises and president of the Citizens Bank of Union. At the turn of the century, Clement Evans called him "one of the most extensive and prosperous planters in the State." Whereas he tended toward a New South philosophy, his cousin Dickie helped form granges, farm alliances, and agricultural societies and had a stronger Jeffersonian orientation to the soil. Hardy's deep devotion to this same land and a life upon it had been engrained by Hardy family tradition unbroken now for nearly a century, whereas Douglass was the son of a doctor-planter and grandson of a builder, and did not have the reinforcement of such continuity. Furthermore, The Oaks had been in their family for only a generation.

The process of state redemption replaced more than a decade of graft in state government—to be precise, ten years in which the people of the old order were effectively barred from citizenship and participation in the legislative process. Following the Reconstruction Acts of 1867, state officials were elected by a constituency in which most of the native whites were disenfranchised and voting occurred under harassment of occupation troops stationed throughout the State. During this time, the Douglasses and Hardys had a rough struggle to keep all of their family lands from being taken from them, and thus had little time for state politics. It was during this era that the Knights of the White Camellia was formed to protect citizens from the violence of unprincipled opportunists, some intent on open thieving and others on the legally sanctioned stealing of speculations and land grabs. William Dixon Hardy was an active Knight. For the Hardys, the era recalled the period of the Cherokee War in the 1760s and the 1780s, after the Revolution—times when the laws failed, chaos ruled, and decent citizens had to band together for their own protection. Only now the citizenry had the added burden of fighting a conquering bureaucracy that had sent an occupation government sanctioned by the courts of the land. As the Hardys saw it, they suffered the exploitation of a "tyranny more cruel than King George's." And Dickie reasoned that because it was coming from within their own land and was enforced by powers so close at hand, this tyranny touched every facet of their lives.

As Captain Dick recalled before his death in 1932, the decades following the war were a time when "if you found a body floating in Broad or Tyger River, and didn't know him, it was best to pass on and not ask questions." "Carpetbagger Justice," they called it. "We did not go after the Negroes, who were our friends, just the crooked opportunists and the thieving carpetbaggers who would just as soon rob a Negro as me." Innocent people of both races also suffered at the hands of these Knights, but many of their victims simply got their just deserts; and some manner of hard order finally prevailed from this brutal form of justice. The post-Reconstruction era was in no way a pleasant world for either black or white, but for the Hardys it was better than the chaotic and rawly avaricious one just eclipsed.

With some degree of local normality achieved, both Hardy and Douglass played significant roles in the ousting of Reconstruction governor David Chamberlain, a Massachusetts native whose administration was at least better than the incredibly corrupt one of his predecessor, Franklin Moses. By the end of the latter's regime, so little remained in this once wealthy state that Moses had to float bonds, for which future generations of both black and white Carolinians would have to pay and which would seriously hamper the recovery of the struggling state until the last ones were paid off in 1953, the year Reconstruction in South Carolina might be said to have ended. With the money from these public bonds, Moses and his crew grew rich, gambled, and held drunken parties in the legislative halls of the statehouse itself. Moses was finally sent to prison for graft and theft in three states. Such was the situation in 1876—the centennial year of America's freedom and independence, which found nearly half the nation in bondage to the other. The irony was not lost on Dickie and his fellow Carolinians. While the North was celebrating the Centennial, the conquered South was realizing the true meaning of American hypocrisy.

Wade Hampton defeated Chamberlain in the governor's race in November 1876. Hardy helped organize Hampton's Red Shirts, a group instrumental in achieving this victory, and was thus among the party that redeemed the State, practicing the dubious method of riding lickety-split on horseback across the county to vote for Hampton at as many polling places as he could reach. Hampton, however, was at first denied his seat by occupation troops under orders from Washington. With the withdrawal of Federal garrisons by the new President Hayes, he was finally inaugurated in March 1877. Beginning in 1882, Captain Dick was himself elected to the state legislature and was to go on to serve a total of five terms from 1882 to 1885 and 1890 to 1896. For two of these terms, he served the Newberry delegation with Cole Blease, a savvy, fiery politician who was himself later to become governor. Like his friend Jimmie Douglass and his own father before him, Hardy was a public-spirited man who felt it his duty to lead. His service to the state and county was to span five decades of stormy change.

But all this was still some years in the future. In 1870 he was faced with a life-and-death struggle simply to provide food and survive. Carpetbaggers swarmed over the community, draining the once wealthy area of what was left—a plague that existed all over the South. The region's carcasse was being picked clean, and especially the wealthier areas like this one. Hardy did lose over half the family holdings, but managed to hold onto the best acreage, fighting the attempted confiscation of his lands through the levy on them of back taxes from the war years and increased current ones. The policy's aim was obviously to wrest money and property from the once prosperous planters, to punish them, to take away their political power and leadership, and thus totally to restructure society, at the same time entrenching the dominance of the Republican Party, whose goals these were. This was the era of Restructuring, not Reconstruction, and of the old planter class's final Destruction. Republican Party policies had by now already led to the demise of America as an agrarian republic. Young Hardy was an able opponent, however, and the attempt to exploit and vanquish him was not completely successful.

As we have seen, in 1870 the plantation acreage remained intact at 2,100. In that same year, with the old squire's death, Dickie was made the executor of his father's estate, which, exclusive of land and dwelling, was valued at a pitiful $2,500. During the perilous span of years from his father's death in 1870 to the settlement of the estate in 1874, Dickie had an incredible tangle of problems; but he fought through them, taking each battle in stride as he had during the war. In the agonizing four-year process, he was finally forced to sell his father's personal effects, farm tools, machinery, and household furniture. This was done in 1873. Then there was the paying of lawyers' fees, the finding of wages for farm workers who could barely produce enough to cover these outlays, the providing for a new and growing family of his own, the paying of both old and new taxes, the battling of the efforts of speculators attempting to seize real estate and the surviving of bullying at the hands of the Reconstruction government that had a stranglehold on the state.

Indeed, as he knew, life was now no less a struggle than it had been in the previous decade. Today the struggle was of a different nature, yet a terrific conflict nonetheless, and just as desperately serious. He had soon learned, as he said, "that the normal state of life is not peace, but constant war, in the face of which I must be vigilant if my family is to survive." It was as chaotic a time as could be conceived. Still, through Captain Dick's perseverance and good guidance, the plantation came out relatively intact, even if vastly diminished in land and production. The decade of the 1870s had become the most trying and precarious era for the plantation, and crucial in determining whether it would survive in any form at all.

The times were indeed troubled for everyone in the South; her people were still attempting to get a footing, casting about to find ways of making it through. Theirs was not the blind and cheerful optimism of the "American dream of ultimate success," in which *failure* and *loss* were ugly words not to be spoken or faced directly. Life's constant and daily realities of failure, loss, suffering, and death enforced deeper truths on him and his family. They learned to accept these facts of existence and to grow from a knowledge of them, a fact expressed by the old Southern adage that "Minerva's owl only flies by night." The quality of endurance that was their pioneer heritage was thus reinforced and bred more deeply in them. It was now their turn to learn a truth taught to generation after generation of Southerners from the time that the first ship's keel touched the soil of the new continent and when wagons wound their way southward and westward carrying pioneering families like the Hardys: that the Southern genius was for surviving, not flourishing, and the strength to endure was indeed their birthright. In the face of loss and disaster, they rose to their highest and noblest. With material wealth gone, the more valuable lessons of the spirit taught them what truly mattered. In this way the family moved closer together. They, now more than ever, gently and generously protected each of its members. Family and character had always mattered more than mere wealth in their Southern land, and now the light of this truth was strongly magnified. Determined to make it as an intelligent farmer, as was his own father before him, Dickie became master of the local grange at Maybinton as early as 1875 and vice-president of the Newberry Agricultural Association in 1878, then president of the new Farmers' Alliance in 1888. He was showing leadership, just as his father had, and was becoming respected throughout the county.

Dickie, his family, and the widow Catharine thus continued on the land; but from 1860 to 1879 the plantation's total acreage shrank from 2,125 to 821, a reduction of 61.5 percent—thus to almost a third of its size before the war. (In 1897 it would fall further to 557 acres.) The old design of bringing the planters to their knees through taxation and other strategies was thus partially successful in Dickie's case. Still, as he knew, it was more land than could be farmed under the new order.

In 1879 the 821-acre Hardy plantation consisted of 117 tilled acres, 100 acres of meadows, pastures, and orchards, 410 of woodland, and 194 of "Other" that included "old fields." It was thus still large enough to continue many of this plantation's old prewar patterns of land use—so unlike the "average" postwar farm. By 1890 the average farm in South Carolina would consist of a total of only 143 acres, acreage on which the soil must be pushed to its limits for its owner to make a living—and all of which must be planted in the cash crop, cotton. On these monoculture farms, there would be preserved no more woodlands as there had been in the antebellum era. Instead, cotton would have to grow to the very doorsteps, and every inch of the soil be utilized for the family to survive. The new order dictated this. The Hardys of this era, however, were not forced to this extremity.

With its 217 improved acres in 1879, the Hardy plantation had fallen from the 300 of 1870, and the 600 of 1860, and the 1,000 of 1850. In

1879 the plantation's tillage had dwindled to one-fifth of its 1850 acreage. This decline over a thirty-year period was dramatic for those who lived through it. It is no wonder that the witnesses to the scene looked on with a disbelief that for lesser people would have cut deeply into the will to do. It was the aging widow Catharine who knew the story most completely, but her son had also seen much of this history with his own eyes. As he recalled as an old man, "It was one thing to maintain one's own, but to move downward, surely and constantly, was another thing altogether. . . . It was that which hurt most sharply." They had known high times, and now their lot was hard times. The sharp contrast no doubt made the hard harder. As Dante Alighieri, the great Italian master of human nature, expressed it so well: "There is no sadder time than when one remembers happiness in a period of unhappiness." Ironically, however, knowing both extremes also bred a feeling of serenity, assuring one that fate could not throw anything his way that he had not already experienced.

From 1869 to 1879 the value of the farm fell from $6,300 to $4,400, a far cry from the $40,700 of 1860, which in that year was also supplemented with a tally of $45,000 in personal property that included about $20,000 in slaves, now freed. The 1879 sum was merely 11 percent of the 1860 figure; and the Hardys had gone from millionaires in the top percentile of wealth in America to "just getting by," and all in the short space of ten years. Owing largely to the sale in 1873 of the plantation's farm machinery and tools, the value of the "farm implements" fell from $400 in 1869 to $140 in 1879. The decline since 1869 continued across the board in farm animals and crops. The value of livestock dropped from $1,000 in 1869 to $250 in 1879. Because Captain Dick's tenants probably supplied their own mules, he himself now had only 2 horses, a mule, a milk cow, and 9 hogs—these last to supply his own family, since there were no longer slaves to be fed. In 1879 his poultry yard contained 34 fowl and yielded 100 dozen eggs. The farm produced 290 bushels of corn on 26 acres—down from 400 bushels in 1869 and 2,500 in 1850; and 91 bushels of wheat on 10 acres—down from 200 bushels in 1869 and 500 in 1850. The new master raised 400 bushels of oats on 20 acres in 1869 and 12 bushels of rye on 3 acres. In 1879 he harvested 50 bushels of sweet potatoes on one half an acre, down from 200 bushels in 1860 and 500 in 1850, but better than the old squire had done in 1869, when none were produced. The son also managed to increase the number of his cotton bales by 2, to 18 450-pound bales in 1879—far short of the

110 bales of 1850. In this last figure, the plantation fared far worse than South Carolina as a whole. By 1880 the state was producing more cotton than in the antebellum era, but on far smaller monoculture operations, about half of which were in the Upcountry. These smaller farms, no longer stressing self-sufficiency as keenly as the Tyger plantations before the war, accelerated soil depletion and chemical dependency. The Hardy lands did not suffer this fate.

In the year 1879 Hardy paid out $550 in wages to an all-black labor force who worked a total of 300 weeks. This payment of wages was down over 50 percent from his father's total of $1,200 in 1869. It is clear that in general the plantation suffered as frightfully in this decade of the 1870s as it had in the decade of the war itself. The son was decreasing the rate of the collapse and disintegration, but what he had been given to work with had already been so drastically reduced in the first place, as to be only a shadow of the original farm. The value of all farm production in 1879 was $1,380, an all-time low; and what we have witnessed in all this was the ruin of a prosperous and fruitful farm owing to the destruction of the plantation system itself. The fate that was to lie in store for the plantation in the early years of the next decade was to be even worse: a period of droughts that made it virtually impossible to get a living from the soil during these already hard and unsettled times.

By the decade of the 1870s, Hardy had made a name for himself as a civic leader. In 1875 he was the master of the local grange. In 1878 he helped organize and became vice-president of the Newberry County Agricultural and Mechanical Society. These offices he held in an attempt to aid farmers and resurrect the farm economy. Ten years later, in 1888, he would for the same reason become the first president of the local Farmers' Alliance, an organization he had been instrumental in creating. Its object was to band farmers together for political action and to provide a cooperative for purchases and sales. This farmers' movement was important in nominating and electing state leaders, one of whom was the Populist Ben Tillman.

A letter by Hardy to the *Charleston News and Courier* at this time expressed his political beliefs:

> Is the *News & Courier* a Democratic paper? Let the records answer. During Radical days, it was mixed up with Joe Woodruff in the public printing business. In 1876 it advocated Chamberlain's nomination for Governor. Last year, it

opposed the will of the majority. Now it says if the Ocala demands are incorporated in the Democratic Platform, it will not support the Party. If this is Democracy, then I must admit I dont know what Democracy is. Do the businessmen of Charleston endorse what the *News & Courier* says? Do the businessmen of the towns throughout the State endorse? If they continue to subscribe for the paper, we will be forced to believe they do. Let us be fair and give credit where it is due. The *News & Courier,* in its fight against the Farmers Movement last year did more to secure Tillman's nomination than any paper in the State. Let us hope its opposition will accomplish as much for us next year.

A Democrat.

The farmers' movement mentioned in his letter was his great love and a cause on which he expended his greatest energies. William Eppes Hardy would no doubt have been very proud of his son, who was acting in predictable ways that did honor to the family's traditions and agrarian heritage.

In 1882 Hardy had been elected to his first of five terms in the South Carolina state legislature. By 1880 he and Frances had three sons and two daughters, who were being educated in the one-room schoolhouse in Maybinton, and "for short periods by a private teacher in the home whenever the extra dollars could be scraped up to afford it." The fact that despite economic hardships, the parents spent scarce money on educating their children, proves that the family continued to value education. Again, the pattern had been set in antebellum days.

From 1881 until 1885 there were four successive crop failures in South Carolina, and the family had difficulty weathering times that had gone from bad in the 1870s to worse in the '80s. in 1886 Dickie found his youngest brother George a job in Columbia as a guard at the state penitentiary. George was forty years old when he was forced to leave his father's fields, but there was little choice. In Columbia he performed his duties well. At his death in 1915, his obituary would state that he "was a man of fine parts and because of his humane treatment of the prisoners, had become their friend during his long service." He had inherited the legacy of his kind father and gentle mother in dealing fairly with those less privileged than he.

In the midst of this trying period of crop failure, loss of land, and dislocation, Hardy also lost the strong and steady support of his mother Catharine in 1884. No doubt for those around her, "Old Mistis" provided a last tangible link to a world that had disappeared. She had been born on the place in 1811, had been plantation-bred, had flourished during its golden age, and now had seen its terrible decline and eclipse. What a history of contrasts her tired eyes had witnessed. She died with her family's fortune completely ruined and its future uncertain. She had gone from being a millionaire squire's lady to the doorsteps of poverty. What would become of the grandchildren? They were, despite the family's reduced circumstances, being well-educated, sometimes by private tutors when they could manage it—an aim worth sacrificing for. The young ones were not sliding into the semi-ignorant state of the unfortunate children of some of her fellow ex-planter friends in Carolina, youngsters with good manners but no knowledge of the world beyond their fathers' fields. And they were all good children. She and her son and daughter-in-law had raised them to be respectful, religious, diligent, hard-working, modest in their needs, generous, gentle-natured. Events had made them an unselfish little brood, responsible and realistic and tolerant. They too would survive and possess a strong measure of the quality of endurance. Her son Dickie was well thought of. Yes, their father, now in the legislature, was going to see them through. Though the days had turned dark, and the years when as a young woman she rode in silks in her father's carriage to strawberry feasts, the springs, and picnics on the river were not to return, they would live in the memories of her grandchildren, for she had told them the way things had been "when I was a girl here on the old plantation." Family traditions and family solidarity had been passed on to them mingled with such an abiding sense of loyalty to that land which had given them life—the much-loved place itself that was the seat of family and to which its members always clung and returned as the stable, fixed point in an unsettled world—that while many other families had been forced to towns and cities, they were fortunate enough to hold on, even if only by the skin of their teeth. And even if they were required to take jobs as a prison guard, merchant, or legislator, they were always called back by the tug of the place, and she helped keep it waiting there for them, the boxwood avenues like arms reaching out to give them welcome, the Great House and its fields symbolizing family and all it stood for. Hearth, home, the lares and penates of the household—these had been in Catharine's keeping since the death of her own mother; and these she passed on undiminished in luster to her granddaughters, despite sleeves worn ragged at the cuffs. Granddaughter Helen, born in 1880, understood all this perhaps best of all. Catharine could not know it, but it was to be in Helen's character that the old strengths of self-sacrifice, patience, gentleness, honor, and family devotion were best to manifest themselves and to burn in as clear and clean a flame as ever in the new century.

"Old Mistis" died on the first day of the new year 1884 in the circle of family. Her daughter-in-law Frances held her hand as she lay in the four-poster bed where she had been born seventy-two years ago. Daughter Elmira Frost and her family had hurried up from Columbia. Her sons stood tall at her side. She had already bestowed her blessing on Dickie's children—each in their turn as they were brought before her, from the eldest who was twelve to the baby not yet a year old—and now the same for Elmira's large brood. The march of time and the pageant of continuity; she was merely playing her role in the broad give and take of things. The remaining old folks from what had been the Quarters had come up the Big House steps and filed by her bed with their respects. Now finally her loyal sister Frankie and her niece and nephew Douglasses from The Oaks gathered around her, and she passed peacefully, speaking of their play as children among the flower paths of the plantation yard, and with the name of William on her lips. Garrie Douglass was there to pass down her description to us. Three days later Catharine was laid to rest by the side of the old master and their son Haywood in the family plot at Ebenezer. With her death, another heavy chapter closed.

Five years later, daughter Elmira would also be dead in Columbia in the year 1889, and at the age of fifty-four.

William Dixon and the young ones of his family left the homeplace for a period of four years from 1890 to 1894 to live in the village of Prosperity twenty miles distant, while Hardy was again serving in the legislature. The farm remained in the hands of the eldest sons, Ben (who was nineteen in 1890) and Nathan Haywood (who was seventeen). While in Prosperity, William's young children attended school there. During these years, Hardy spent much energy on the Farmer's Alliance, as proved by documents still in the family's possession and at Duke University Library. In 1893 Hardy was supporting Wyche over Cole Blease, a choice that led Blease to write him the following pointed letter:

Newberry, S.C., May 1st 1893

Hon. W. D. Hardy,
Prosperity, S.C.
Dear Sir;

When but a little boy I remember making little speeches for Mr Hardy. As I grew older, I still talked for him, and when I reached the right period, I voted for him; and in 1892, when he said that he could not lose the time, I said "run Mr Hardy. I will do my speaking and yours too." During this entire period, my father's time, money, horses & buggies were at your command, and his stable and hotel was ever open to you & your friends. Even his pen was used for you in the newspapers in your behalf. When you could not leave home, he fought your fight and stood almost alone in town as the farmer's friend. Where was Dr. Wyche in 1884? Where was he in 1888 when the reform party made its first fight in this County with J. A. Sligh as its standard-bearer? Did he support Pope or Sligh? Did he ride over 9 & 10 townships working for Pope and giving Sligh "hail Columbia" on account of a certain Rail Road tax? Where was he in 1890; on which ride? When did he join the reform ranks? Did he have a brother-in-law in the race for clerk and one for sheriff? Who did he vote for in 1892? Did he vote for Riser or Halfacre in the second primary? I do not want you to write me an answer to these questions, for that would be too much trouble. I only want you to think over them for yourself, and then say which is most worthy of your support: one who has always been a reformer or one who has been in the party only a short time. I do not blame Dr. Pope for supporting Wyche, for he owes it to him for Wyche's service to T. J. Pope in 1888. But how you and Mr Sligh can support him as against me, I am totally at a loss to see, for I know all of us have done all that we could for you for every office for which you offered and will continue to do so as long as you fill them as well as you have in the past. Give us Dr. Werts, Dr. Lake, T. Conner, Capt Folk, or any old line reformer, but if a new-made (1 year old convert) is put up, then if it hurts our party, let the responsibility rest where it will. As for me,

I am for whoever the reformers put up in a fair, open caucus.
Respects

Cole L. Blease

Blease went on to become governor of South Carolina in 1910 and
1912.

The years 1895 and 1896 were hard for the struggling family. July
1895 saw the death of the last of the Hardys born in the old times. Uncle
George Douglass had died in 1875 and left Aunt Frankie in the care of
her children, who were struggling to make their way in the New South
as bankers, doctors, and merchants. Her daughter Laura was married to
her cousin John Wesley Hardy, a merchant in Spartanburg and Columbia. From Columbia he wrote his new mother-in-law, Frances Hardy
Douglass, at The Oaks on 26 July 1876:

1 Tub Lard	$9.45
1 Bacon	12.88
Frgt to LylesFord	1.00
	23.33

Dear Mother,

Above find bill of Bacon & Lard. Hope this will reach
you safe, and please. I have been quite unwell. Laura & Sallie
the same as usual. Our love to all, and the same for yourself.
As ever yours,

J. W. Hardy

A few months earlier, Hardy and his wife had written Frances Douglass
a much fuller account:

Columbia, Oct. 19, 1875

Dear Mother,

I have sent you today as per Dock's [George Douglass
Jr.'s] letter, one Bacon, 143 Dry Salt Sides, 55 Country Bacon
Sides. . . . I also send a Box containing Janie's cloak, and
some other articles which Laura sends. . . . I had no smoked
Bacon, and tried to purchase, but the price was so high I
thought I would send more white, and I had a small quantity
of the Country, so I put it in at the same as Smoked is worth,
16¢. The white is selling here at 15¢. I send to you at

14 3/4¢. Bacon is quite high in Balt[imore]. And also in the west. I am glad to say we are both well, only colds, and my hands are sore. Will you please tell Garrie to send me the 3 bottles of Corydale's by Dock, if he does not leave before this reaches you. If so, send by Express when you send for the Bacon. Since writing to send by Express, please do not send that way, as it will cost me 50¢ to get it that way, but send by first safe opportunity. Say to her I will send her the money or give it to her sister, as she may direct. We have had some cold mornings the past week, but not much frost. Cotton is selling very well in this market, but business is dull. Seems to be moreso than for some time past. But this is the general complaint from most every place. The circus is to be here tomorrow. Suppose it will take a large quantity of the spare change, but none from me. I have nothing like news to write about. Would like so much to see you all, and I wish much that we were keeping house so you all could pay us a long visit. I hope it will not be long before we will be able to do so. Since I have changed my business, I have a longer walk to my meals. Nothing more, but to send our love to all, and a double portion for yourself. As ever yours,

J. W. Hardy

Mother, I have nothing special to write about but will add a little to Mr Hardy's letter. In the small box sent with the bacon, you will find the calico for the quilts, also your undergarments I made for you. You will have to get some of the girls to mask them. Tell Janie she can cut and fix her cloak so it will be of service to her. They are short and tight. . . . Mother, I am so much obliged to you for your kind offer to lend me some things in the housekeeping line. As yet we have not decided about it. There are so many taking boarding that we would be unable to get any; and you cant get a house for less than 25 or 30 dollars a month, and then we have no furniture, so it would cost us a good deal to get ready for housekeeping, but are so anxious to be situated so I can have some of you with me all the time. The cold weather makes us feel like fires, though we have no wood as yet. You have no idea what an expense it is, and what small fires some have.

I dont like coal, though think it is cheaper than wood. . . . I hope Sallie is better. Tell her to put on flannel, and do take good care of herself. If she had some regular business to attend to, she would be much happier. If nothing else, it would do her good to read a good deal. I am looking forward to [her brother] Dock's coming with much pleasure, and expect to wear him out with questions. . . . This is a day of commotion among the darkies and children, as the Circus is here. About the blankets: thought I would wait until Annie sent for hers, and see about getting yours at the same time. I still have six dollars of yours, which will get you a pair if you wish. The coffee runs $5, calico for quilts $1, flannel $1.65. What are you going to do about finishing your log cabin [quilt]. Have you material enough for it. If so, would finish it for my bed. Tell Garrie to try and sell our alpacas. Mine is just like new. And ask what she thinks they are worth. I am in hopes I will get a letter by Dock from some of you. Give much love to all. Write soon to your affetionate daughter,

Laura

Laura and John Hardy survived the cold that winter in the burned-out city of Columbia to go on and raise a large family.

By the 1880s Jimmie Douglass was becoming affluent as a banker and industrialist while still helping to manage the plantation. Willie Douglass became a doctor in Spartanburg. In the 1890s George Douglass Jr. (the Dock of Laura's letter) was practicing medicine near Peak, in lower Newberry County. Passed down in his family is a letter from his mother, eighty-two years old at the time she wrote it. Its envelope bears his notation: "This is the last letter Mother ever wrote me." It is also the final letter by the Hardys of Catharine and William Eppes Hardy's generation and speaks well of the old values: of family closeness, of love of the simple rural life and growing things, of the continuing ritual of cotton planting, of a strong religious faith:

Ap[ril] the 23, 1895

Dear Dock

I received your letter. Was so glad to hear from you and how you we[re] get[t]ing on. Hope you were satisfyed and were pleased with your bo[a]rding house. You cannot imagine how I miss you and that quiet little home, there being so much noise here. I go in the garden and work a little. They will not let me do any thing. I do not take interes[t] in these chickens as I did mine. Have not heard from Santuck but once. Tekeah wrote to me. Did not give me much news. Dock, I hope you will be satisfyed and do better than you did up yonder. Do dont smoke so much because you are loansome. Hope you will get into business soon. We have measles in the neighborhood as near as Renwicks. I hope Janie and Annie will not take them. Garrie has been sick with sore throat like Mr Fleming, but is well now. She received a letter from Willie asking her to come up there and teach school, particular if she would teach musick. Have not seen Jimmie since I came down here. You do not know how nice my pear tree looks. One of the peach trees looks well. The other does not. I am very quiet today, all having gone to Church but Daniel, Sallie, and myself. I would have gone but fear I would cough so much. Dear Dock, failing to get my letter off Sunday, will have to wait until I can send it. Do write often and let me hear from you. Hope you will be satisfyed. Daniel and Bubber are planting cotton today. I hope Jimmie will make a good crop. Dock do excuse this letter. Hope when I write again, will be more interesting. Do go to Church when you can. I must close. All send much love to you. From your affectionate Mother

FJD

Dickie Hardy was at his Aunt Frankie's bedside when she died three months later on 25 July; and the Douglasses and Hardys were again drawn together. She was laid to rest at Ebenezer in the Douglass family plot adjacent to the Hardys, where she and her sister Catharine and the matriarch Anna Dixon Hardy lie in close proximity.

Dickie lost his wife Frances on 3 February 1896. She died of the measles that Aunt Frankie had mentioned in her letter as being epidemic in the neighborhood. Two days later, he lost his much-loved eldest daughter, twenty-year-old Anna, to the same malady. Three months after that, measles also took his infant son George. It was a cruel time for him; and with five deaths of loved ones in quick succession, against a backdrop of drought, crop failure, eroding and ravaged lands, his world was again shaken to its foundations as in the old wartimes. The red earth of Ebenezer churchyard, as he said, was too often seen in his dreams. He did not adapt well to all these losses. Then too, the Hardys did not take to "New South" ways as readily as the Douglasses, and the war had claimed a Hardy son, as it had not a Douglass. It was much harder for their family than their more fortunate kin. They merely wanted to stay on the land, a desire that was becoming more and more difficult to achieve. Yet, for the Hardys, as for Carolinians of the previous generation, they knew "We must touch earth perpetually, to renew our wholesome strength and energies, for the fable of Antaeus is figurative, of the first of human necessities"—strong Antaeus, he who could not be defeated until his feet were separated from the soil, the magic source of his strength.

In 1896, with the death of her eldest sister and her mother, sixteen-year-old Helen, now the oldest woman in the household, took over the duties of plantation mistress. She looked after her grieving father, now in his fifties, and her five younger brothers and sisters "for whom she had to be both mother and sister." One of these children was only a year old, another two, another twelve. As her brother John, whom she raised from the age of ten, recalled of her in a moving tribute, "When her mother died, she never knew any girlhood as she turned from child to woman. . . . Her life was one of unselfish service and sacrifice."

By the time of their mother's death, there were ten children—seven sons and three daughters. They were Benjamin Sims (17 July 1871–9 May 1949), named for his maternal grandfather, and who married the widow Mary Caroline (Carrie) McCarley Renwick on 21 November 1898 and lived at the nearby Chick plantation; William Eppes (19 February 1873–3 June 1927), named after his grandfather who had died three years before, and who married Cora Herring in June 1898, divorced her, and afterwards married Bessie Coggins; Annie Dixon (16 March 1875–4 February 1896), named after her great-grandmother Hardy; Nathan Haywood (21 November 1877–22 November 1949), named after his uncle who died in the war, and who moved to Spartanburg as a merchant and never married; Helen O'Neal (12 September 1880–11 March 1958), who married Hugh M. Henderson on 30 October 1912; Francis Booker, called Frank (11 May 1883–16 June 1949), who like his uncle George was a prison guard in Columbia before returning home as the bachelor keeper of the plantation after his father's death; John Frost Sr. (12 March 1886–8 June 1963), who married Alice

M. Dunn on 27 November 1912, moved to Spartanburg as a merchant, and who later would return to the plantation in 1950 after purchasing it following his brother Frank's death; Mary Catharine (born 24 February 1894), who first married John Austin Scott in 1914, then Paul Holbrook, and with her daughter Frances was living on the plantation with Captain Dick at the time of his death; Paul Hayne (25 September 1888–3 May 1954), who fought in World War I and moved to Spartanburg as bachelor merchant before returning home to the plantation in his last years; and George Douglass (27 June 1895–10 May 1896), named for his great-uncle of The Oaks and cared for in his brief span of life by the neighboring Lyles family after his mother's death of measles in February of 1896.

In 1897 William Dixon Hardy sold the Lyles tract adjoining the Tyger River to Benjamin Graham. This comprised the 267 acres given him by his mother the year before her death.

During the period 1898–1902, the several grown sons of the household managed the plantation while William Dixon served as master-in-equity of Newberry County. Captain Dick was also president of the local grange, a leader of the county agricultural association, a manager of the Farmers' Alliance Warehouse in Prosperity, and a county school trustee. This service, added to what we know of his war record and his five terms in the legislature, all prove him to have been a man of great energy who led a full and useful life. During his term as master-in-equity, he and the younger children moved to Helena, a depot town adjacent to the county seat. The children thus had the advantage of Newberry schools. Helen, as her brother John remembered, was popular there and "made many friends, among them young men who were very much in love with her, and whose offers of marriage she refused so that she would continue to look after her younger brothers and sisters, as well as her father. After residing at Helena for four years, the family moved again to the Hardy homeplace, where she continued as head of the house." The tug of the land always kept bringing the family home; and while the elder sons managed the fields, the land was always in the minds of those family members separated from it. Helen continued as the lady of the household until her marriage to Hugh Henderson in 1912 at the age of thirty-two. By this time, her sister Mary Catharine was eighteen and could take charge for the two years before her own marriage in 1914.

Helen would eventually have three sons and four daughters of her own. While the children were young, her husband took ill and became an invalid for the rest of his life, "so again she became the head of a family. . . . During the depression years, life was pretty hard for them, but Helen fought her own battles and usually won the victory." She lived with her daughter Mary Ella at the Hardy plantation from 1926 to 1932 in order to care for her aged father, now into his nineties. From 1942 to 1956 she lived in Arlington, Virginia, with one of her daughters. For her last two years she went to Germany with her daughter, whose husband had been sent there for government service. She returned to Virginia a month before her death, but failed to see the hills of Tyger which she had longed to view one last time. She died at the age of seventy-eight after suffering the loss of her second son Hugh two years earlier. She is said to have grieved his sudden death "very deeply." She is buried in Arlington far from her home, but near where her first ancestor to the new world debarked on the continent. But these last events, although pertinent here, have rushed us over a half-century into the future. We must now follow our steps back to the previous century to pick up the thread of our story.

After his wife's death in 1896, Dickie did not remarry. He was fifty-nine years old when the new century began and with the help of his daughter and sons had "held things together" for the new generation of Hardys growing up about him. His first grandson was born in the first year of the new century, once again an auspicious sign of continuity.

14

Captain Dick

Misrule and oppression were my birthright, and poverty the inheritance of the land in which I dwelt. But it was poverty so nobly met by our elders, it was life so gallantly, so cheerfully lived . . . that I have always been grateful that it was given to me to grow up even in the shade of the civilization that had produced the generations of the past.
—Alice Ravenel Huger Smith, *Reminiscences* (1950)

Soon there were so many grandchildren that Captain Dick had some of the overgrown boxwood borders in the side yards removed to avoid the danger of snakes while they played among them.

Captain Dick was a much respected man. As he is still remembered today, he is spoken of with awe and reverence, as one from a time when there were indeed giants in the land, and whose likes would not be seen again. For the new century, he now provided a living link to the golden days of the flush times before the war. He had lived through and participated in the Southern *Iliad,* had been an actor in the drama of Manassas, Seven Pines, Sharpsburg, Gettysburg, Fredericksburg, The Wilderness—names that were themselves now grown legendary and gilded with the aura of heroism in a land itself of monuments and long memories. He had survived intact both battle and defeat, had pulled things together when he got home, had lived through the violent and stirring days of Reconstruction and the Redemption, had seen the carpetbaggers and scalawags at their drunken parties in the statehouse, had helped oust them from the temple of government, and had himself served in their place. He was more than a living history lesson; he was the legend itself. For those who remember him, this modern era, by comparison, is filled with the little, the ordinary, the pale, and the petty. As his obituary in a Spartanburg newspaper concluded unequivocally: "Those were days that showed who men were!"

Mrs. Sarah Stokes of the nearby Comer plantation of Tuckertown, now in her eighties, recalls him well: "He was a dapper little man, who always wore a white shirt, black bow tie, tall hat, and black coat even in the heat of summer." In his last years, he always used a cane and was attended by a very old black servant by the name of Tom Hardy, a descendant of the old slave families. "Captain Dick would walk in the swept dirt yard and point to the sprigs of grass with his cane and say to one of his sons, 'Dig that up.' When commanded, they hopped." As with his father before him, such forcefulness and ease of command had been bred in him by his plantation culture, and such was necessary for the management of so large a family and estate as his, with so many depending on him.

Like most Southerners of his day, the Old Captain was a gifted story-teller, and he had lived through so much history that his tales, having the punch of authority, were even more effective than the usual. As for most Southern families, the "porch" yarns furthered the family's understanding of itself, and bolstered their pride because through them, the listener became aware of belonging to a people who had survived wars, typhoid, the Depression, drought, poverty and prosperity, and cat-aclysms great and small. One learned that he could lose everything and still have the strength to start over, that one could even lose a great war and still not be defeated. Through the tales, one saw the bigger picture—that through some generations we had been poor, in others prosperous; but "always we were survivors." Like our neighbors, we knew how to live off the good land. As one recent Carolina author has described it, "there was renewal in the oft-repeated stories" that family told from this porch, tales that bound them to this porch, and which spoke eloquently "of a family heritage spreading back over generations even older than the porch itself."

The venerable Captain would usually hold forth on the front ve-randa from his high rocker. Haywood Hardy Henderson, a grandson, recalls that "in his last years at age ninety-one, he was blind and would sit on the big porch attended by Uncle Thomas, an ancient black re-tainer who would cut his tobacco for him and fetch him the cheroots he loved to smoke." Here on the porch every twilight and evening, with smoke from his cheroot curling over his snow-white head, he told his stories to hushed audiences. The youngsters in particular would sit spellbound in the dark at his feet. On one such evening, Henderson remembers his blind grandfather placing his hand on their heads as the grandchildren were brought by one at a time to receive his blessing. In retrospect, the grandson surmises that the Old Captain was sensing his death and was paying a last tribute. These stories and this ritual sign of patriarchal devotion have made a deep impression on the grandson that has lasted now for over half a century, as well they should.

Mrs. Bertice Teague of Maybinton recalls Captain Dick from her earliest childhood. She was born in 1914 and lived in the Hardy house from 1918 to 1920. In the 1920s she was the messenger who carried conversation back and forth between Captain Dick and her grandfather, John Robert McCollum, as they sat on the veranda. "One would sit on the right of the porch and one on the left," remembers Mrs. Teague, "and neither could hear thunder." She had to run back and forth from chair to chair with the conversation. Although of somewhat different circumstances, her father and Hardy were good friends who had been in the war together. To this ten-year-old, Captain Dick was merely a "crabbit old man." She didn't think too much of either one of them or the stories they told. To her, it was all boring. She was more interested in playing. Both the Captain and her grandpa, however, "thought well of themselves." She concludes today that Captain Dick was a man of substance.

Like Sarah Stokes, John Renwick recalls that Captain Dick had a formal bearing. Renwick further recollects that he and the family in general were "high-toned." This did not preclude enjoyments such as grand outdoor feasts and singings. Henderson remembers that in the late 1920s the entire family feasted outside in the summer under the big hemlock tree in the front garden. At one of these dinners, his uncle and namesake Haywood Hardy paid him a quarter to curse Haywood's brother John. This the child did (from under the table) to the astonishment of all and the laughter of some, but his mother Helen whipped him and took away his quarter. The family often put tables under this big tree and had many hours together there. For those three brothers who had moved to Spartanburg and for the married sisters, these were very important homecomings.

On one such occasion, Henderson remembers that Frank, when his brother John was saying grace and taking a long time doing so, told him to break off, that this was a *prayer* not a *prayer meeting*. John rode back to Spartanburg in a huff. Haywood, Frank, and Ben were indeed the closer ones. All three had a great sense of humor and enjoyed practical jokes and a lively time, while John was the more serious one. Frank, particularly, was known for being a character and full of "devilment." John Renwick admired him and Ben most of all. Like his grandfather before him, Frank was said to be quick of wit, always "jolly and teasing" in his wry sort of way, "ready for a lark or a joke, and good for a laugh." As the family remembers him, their handsome brother Paul was the "sporty" one of the sons. After returning from World War I, he would always have a flashy new car, and a different lovely lady on his arm each time he returned to visit the old homeplace. He always dressed fashionably and never married. While Paul was the man about town, Frank, as we shall see in the next chapters, was the most individualistic and the most original.

It is clear that by the time his children were grown, Captain Dick had evolved a philosophy of life to which he now adhered without deviation. Family, home, and land were at the center of his world. He had little desire to "get ahead" in the manner popular in the new century. Although not wealthy, he considered himself successful in the most significant way: success to him was the *how* not *how much* of achievement, of being quietly contented with his lot and being allowed to enjoy life itself. In this, he was so like his own father William, who, as we have witnessed (and no doubt as his son also remembered), after seeing his plantation prosper, chose to stop short of pushing the soil and its people to their limits merely in order to amass more wealth. Modesty, forbearance, the golden mean, consideration for others, respect for the land— these were attributes of the successful. The "bank account," acreage, or number of cotton bales did not figure into it beyond providing for one's own. In this, the wise Old Master had set the proper example for the Young. This was, in fact, no doubt his greatest legacy to him.

Here, then, on the same soil for four generations, had been evolving the tradition of a gentle, healthy, finished sort of living, where there was no excess of hustle, bustle, and grabbing after material wealth, no jostle and grasping for power and fame. In this philosophy, avarice and success were opposites and mutually exclusive. Captain Dick's definition of the word "success" precluded a great material goal; its meaning rested squarely, as he phrased it, "in what manner of person one had finally learned to be." Success was finally thus a matter of high character, what the old patricians knew so well lay at the foundation of their concept of aristocracy. The cruel experiences of war, loss, and adversity had made the Old Captain gentle rather than harsh and grasping, compassionate rather than cynical and bitter. Was it not that his early introduction to passionate suffering and death had given him the power to see life whole, and deeply to discern the springs of human nature and human destiny? Throughout the "conflict" of life, he learned successfully to maintain "a quiet grace of heart" that afforded the happy symmetry that redeems human nature.

No doubt he subscribed to that traditional Southern valuation of a man's worth given by a wise Carolina author fifty years ago: "What a man's true worth is in this world, depends upon the kind of wake he leaves behind him as he passes through life." As for power and the fame that it brings, if he had the power to make others happy, then this power was enough, for it made all others appear insignificant. As a man who lived his life according to this wisdom, Captain Dick exhibited an abiding strength of the Southern heritage and way of life. It might be said of him that his life was a product of the Southern soil from which he grew, her fragrant woodlands where he roamed, rode, and hunted, of a quiet and nature-guided existence on the land. Thus, he grew from the Southern civilization of old, and, like his father before him, successfully passed many of his values to his children.

Captain Dick, after he left the legislature of the State and the administrative service of the county, retired home for good to his fathers' fields to enjoy his family and the rural life. Although he never was really very adept at farming, and though others of his acquaintance and even three of his own sons moved to town to pursue "New South" dreams, he was content to dwell in the midst of his family fields with the nature that came to his doorsteps. There was no regret at the loss of "excitement" and other signs of so-called progress. He drove no car, and used none of the new paved highways. (There was no paved road near the Hardys until the 1950s.) As he put it, a young pear tree coming into spring bloom was excitement enough, and the "progress of the seasons was more satisfying than man's new idea of the term." As did all old-fashioned and true Southerners, he walked slowly rather than sped down the thoroughfare of life, not because he was indolent or backward, but because he knew that in his hurry he would be certain "to miss the wonder by its wayside." He "walked at his leisure" rather than ride. On all counts, his was a long, happy, and successful life.

In 1937 ex-slave Charlie Giles, who was Cousin Jimmie Douglass's body servant during the war and a friend of Captain Dick's, summed up their attitude toward the car most succinctly with this memorable comment: "Ain't nobody got no business in automobiles 'cept lawyers, doctors, and fools." Ex-slave Bob Young of Santuc agreed: "De chilluns travels fast in automobiles, but I just as lieve walk to Union as to ride in dem things. Wrecks kills you off so quick dat you doesn't have time to repent. Walking never has hurt nobody, and I buys leather and tacks it on my shoes, and in dat way it don't cost me nothing much. Folks goes so fast in dem automobiles, and half de time dey ain't gwine *to* nothing no way. . . . My chilluns says dat I is 'old timey' and don't know nothing 'bout living. Jes' de same, I likes slow moving, and takes mine out in walking. . . . Dese fast ways don't bother me. Dey makes sassy chilluns. Sassy chilluns dat can't serve deir pa, need not think dat dey can ride to de Promise Land in narry automobile dat dey ever seed. Gwine round in fast circles and never getting nowhere seems to satisfy dem, so I don't know what is gwine to become of dem." Similarly, on the subject of airplanes, ex-slave Cordelia Jackson of Tuckertown, near the Hardys, in the year 1937, said: "Airplanes jest tickles. . . . I went out dar and see'd 'em light. Dressed-up white folks hopped down out'n it from a little do' . . . Right dar I 'lowed, when I goes up like dat, I sho ain't gwine up wid no man—I'se gwine up wid Jesus." From Lang Syne plantation, Julia Peterkin had a character say, "Old Miss was a wise woman. She was right not to like railroads. What good did trains do? Trains take people away, and often never bring them back." Maum Lou had lost too many children to the wanderlust of modernity not to know this truth. Thus, black and white alike who were born in the plantation era resisted nobly the siren song of technology and the new and wasteful machine culture that would destroy ties and concrete and human bonds to the earth, in an abstraction symbolized perfectly by mechanized motion. How wise of them to recognize the dangers and resist. Their instincts were solid and their philosophy profound in its utter simplicity.

By 1900, about sixty percent of the farmers of South Carolina had become tenants, but the Hardys held on to their land through the guidance of Captain Dick. On his property, however, lived many that made up that sixty percent, for by the 1920s many blacks still lived in small houses on both sides of the plantation house—some of them in adapted slave cabins. In 1930 two of these structures were occupied by the Rooks and Hodges families and sometime later by the Beards. This is how the farming continued after the fall of slavery and until it ceased altogether in 1973. The Hodges family, who lived close to the Big House, were descendants of Hardy slaves. Wade Jr. (nicknamed Fella) told John Renwick that his father and mother (Wade Sr. and Vinie, called Aunt Vinie) told him that "their folks born in slavery times said never to let the Hardys down because they were good to them during those days and after. They said they felt lucky to belong to the Hardys rather than to others. And Wade Jr. related that he'd indeed always listened to his daddy's request." There was obviously cordial feeling between these descendants of former slaves and their master's family, a closeness that continued throughout the next generation. The bond seems to have been roughly analogous to that between the English country squire and his various retainers living around him (from groundsmen to groomsmen), who usually held their positions through inheritance, that is, as long as those on both sides of the agreement so wished it.

Captain Dick relished life to the last. John Renwick recalls moonlight sings on the back porch in summer. On one occasion, the good captain, from his upstairs bedroom, kept demanding that the sons and daughters continue their singing. When they would flag, he would tap on the porch roof outside his window with his cane and admonish them to go on. That night they sang nearly til daybreak, Renwick recalls. The Hardys, since fiddle and banjo times on the frontier, had always loved their music and the dance. When "Cap'n" got too old to climb the steps to his bedroom, he slept downstairs in the drawing room. Here, he had a slant-front desk, four-poster bed, and his bookcase, but was too blind to read and write.

In 1932 an interviewer noted that the captain "has always been fond of gardening, and despite his advanced age, takes a keen interest in men and affairs." In his last months he tended his peacocks, which were abundant in the plantation yard, and often talked of his distinct remembrance "of his feelings as he marched down the street after the surrender" at Appomattox. He had been witness to and part of the history that had so changed his world.

In one of his last visits with "Cap'n Dick" before his death in October 1932, Renwick recalls that the blind old patriarch sat on the porch one late summer evening in the early dark and looked up at the blur of new crescent moon and said, "You know, one day men will walk on that moon up there." "You see those planets up there," he continued; "They'll get up there too." His polite listeners, recalled Renwick, "said nothing but knew he was full of baloney." "Now," concludes Renwick, "It is all coming true. The old man was right." Though he often spoke of the old days and of the "Lost Cause," he was "a forward looking, young-minded man even in old age," Renwick concludes. "He was bright and alert to the last, not whipped by events, not even the Great Depression that was humbling many around him. He still had hopes and vision and could dream big dreams." Though he tempered his hope with realism bred of experience of loss, he kept the spark of promise alive, in an imagination younger people did not have. He was truly "a giant of the old times" made from the grand mold. Obvious in Renwick's fine assessment of the man is the assurance that "Ole Marster" came out of and belonged to an epic, heroic age, which those of his own new generation could never hope to know fully or yet equal with their own lives. The young were themselves of a lesser time of little people in which there were no more giants in the land. They could know this past epic age only through venerable elders like Captain Dick whom they were privileged to know and revere. Renwick's humble regard for the "heroic" age is so reverential as to be typically Southern in its attitudes toward the past, and a very attractive trait of character when contrasted to the raw and ugly vanity exhibited by those typical of the modern era who feel that the present time is the apex of all civilization.

The captain's personal remembrances of the old times were reinforced for his hearers by the physical presence of stark chimneys, decaying mansions, and overgrown gardens, the physical presence of a world that had been ruined, and a civilization that had passed. They must ride to and fro through this land of monuments on the daily commonplace business of their lives. And so the ruins, as well as the echo of Captain Dick's voice, worked themselves into their bone and marrow, linking them to a Southern experience that had become well-nigh universal in the region. Both Haywood Hardy Henderson and John Rogers Renwick touched those halcyon and heroic days of the past sitting by the Old Captain on his veranda; and now, in turn, these two elderly gentlemen are able and deserving rememberers and keepers of these traditions that still have important meanings for them and for us all. Such is the legacy of the Norman knight le Hardi, of the old pioneer, of William

Eppes and Catharine Hardy, of the faithfully enduring black Hardys, of William Dixon and Frances Sims Hardy, and of the civilization that both they produced and were shaped by. A measure of that civilization, as in every culture worthy of the name, is that it not only keeps and reveres the Past and its traditions, custom, and precedent, but also preserves ways of life and of thought and even of motives dictating behavior. All these live on in the memory and tradition of the Southern family.

In the year that cotton prices fell to their lowest in the recollection of the living, William Dixon Hardy died on 15 October 1932 with his children around him. His mind was clear to the last. He knew that the recent collapse of Big Business, Finance, and Industry had vindicated another loss in which he and his family had spilled their blood seventy years ago on the soil of Virginia. The victorious ones had accomplished their own destruction; it was a pity his beloved rural Southern homeland had been dragged into the great vortex with the guilty. His final gaze out over the blur of green boxwood at his window and into a splendid and golden fall sunshine, wandered to and rested like a blessing upon the year's bountiful harvest of white, the scene so familiar, serene, and beautiful to him, but one "of little market value" in this bad season—indeed, veritably worthless to the financiers, factors, and factories. "The Profit Motive," interests over values, consumerism, these were the gods of the new age—a time of technology, speculation, industry, and all manner of "New Dealings" to come—a machine culture's impersonal and amoral age in which each would be out for himself, where ruthlessness would reward rather than censure, and the old gods would depart from the scene out of very shame. His eyelids were tired and heavy; it would be good to close them at last. His eyes that had seen so much dark history in their ninety-one years, in shutting for good now this fine October Sunday, revealed the light and image of the hope of a glorious resurrection. He was buried by the side of his wife and adjacent to his father and mother in the family plot in Ebenezer Cemetery, the last of the masters born during halcyon years. What would remain of these old times would now exist only in the memory, manners, and values of the living, or come down palely to us through books.

15

Holding on in a World We Did Not Make

After the Boll Weevil and the Great Depression

I was born to a world that had been ruined, and to a civilization that had passed. Over my childhood slanted the long shadows of the end of plantation life . . . the resignation and pathos of its atmosphere were with me from the day of my birth. . . . Even as a child I had a dim sense of knowing that it is far more difficult to retrieve family fame than it is originally to establish it. A Confederate child had a heritage of heroism, but it was as weak in a practical way as it was powerful spiritually.
—Archibald Rutledge, Hampton Plantation, South Carolina (1937)

Already by the 1850s (as shown in chronicles like John Belton O'Neall's), some planters of the Tyger valley had to varying degrees depleted their soil. Some erosion of topsoil occurred; but among the wisest planters like the Hardys, the Rogerses, the Renwicks, and the Douglasses, the soil was properly valued, manured, terraced, rotated, and protected as the plantation's life blood—for indeed it was. They knew well the Carolina adage (written down by one of her planters in 1843) that "the proper cultivation of a soil enriches it."

Pushed to extremities, and with the resurgence of cotton prices in

356

the period after the War Between the States and during World War I (when cotton soared from 6 to 40 cents a pound), the farmer of the upcountry South moved more and more to cotton as a single crop. The diversity of the antebellum era was thus greatly diminished. It was sometimes necessary to abandon exhausted cotton rows to "old-field" pines; and doing so invited erosion before the pines could get established. By 1932 nearly eight million acres of farmland in South Carolina had been turned out of cultivation. South Carolina farmers had to purchase more fertilizer than those in the rest of the country, a good indication of the soil's condition in the '30s.

After World War I, cotton farmers reeled from the one-two-three punch of governmental dumping of unneeded cotton stores on a market that had been encouraged to produce quantities of it before the war for the war effort; the boll weevil in the early 1920s; and the economic recession for farmers during the entire decade culminating in the Great Depression. As a result, many farmers and sons of ex-planters abandoned their fields altogether, moving to towns and cities to make a living as merchants, cotton mill workers, supervisors, clerks, and teachers. The luckier of them became doctors and lawyers. Photographs of child laborers in the cotton mills of this area of upcountry South Carolina provide dramatic evidence of the magnitude of their problem. The gaunt faces, thin limbs, and frail bodies of these children are haunting records of malnourishment and overwork—the new heritage of an industrial takeover in the forced American Union.

It was during the post–World War I era that many old families like the Renwicks, Douglasses, and Simses, unable to pay loans and mortgages necessitated by the economic situation in America, sold their family lands at two or three dollars an acre or lost them through foreclosure or failure to pay taxes, eventually to be made into Federal forest lands. It was at this time that most of the great plantation houses were abandoned in these forests, and their abstract new absentee owners assigned them to their death through decay. Such was the lot, for example, of Orange Hall, the Chick plantation, the Ben Sims plantation, and the Colonel Beaty mansion. A photograph of the ragged little Renwick children on the decayed steps of the Chick plantation Great House is another obvious record of deprivation.

In 1950 Leland Summer would describe the Tyger valley from Maybinton to Whitmire as containing plots of "large soil erosion wastes," with "large gullies and small ravines . . . especially near rivers and creek."

The growth of forest lands slowed the erosion process for a time, but through the methods of harvest (particularly of clear-cutting and the bulldozing of roads for access), the land suffered as much as before. Modern popular "forest management" techniques whose aims are to maximize profits in the short term are even more guilty of causing precious topsoil loss and soil depletion than any of the most improvident of uninformed farm techniques in the past. Sometimes the unlawful practice of cutting the river and creek banks for old and valuable hardwoods has accelerated the progress and clogged the streams with eroded soil. Few planters of the old day would have been so unwise, improvident, or greedy. Aided by the machine culture's tools of rapid destruction, even one man's error, or one government's choice and policy, can do a magnified damage. The modern practice of replanting these old hardwood forests with only the fast-growing pine has created as barren and sterile a woodland environment as is possible. The pine tree farm is the area's new crop monoculture.

The Hardy family maintained a better hold on most of its land than did the great majority of ex-planter aristocracy. By 1930 a third of all farms in the state were mortgaged, and of the other two-thirds, almost three-quarters of them made it by on borrowed money—that is, if they did survive at all. The Hardys did not mortgage. While the average farm in South Carolina in 1930 was about twenty acres, and six out of ten farmers who remained true to the land were tenants, the Hardy family lived on its own land and tilled an acreage in the hundreds. They had held on. They had resisted better than others the necessity to convert all crop acreage to cotton in order to feed the devouring monster mills of industry. With soaring cotton prices during World War I, many upcountry farmers planted cotton right up to their doorsteps, in taking every inch of soil possible for the lucrative cash crop. In 1910 only twenty percent of South Carolina farm acreage was in cotton; by 1920 it was fifty percent, and this out of encouragement to supply the war effort. The Hardys, however, still planted a diversity of crops and gardens, a practice made possible by their large acreage. Captain Dick passed his wisdom of antebellum Hardy self-sufficiency on to his sons, and the plantation remained somewhat in its antebellum mold. Unfortunately, there were few Captain Dicks left on the land whose understanding had its roots in antebellum days.

The war boom was short-lived. After the war, government no longer needing cotton, dumped its huge stockpiled holdings on the market, causing the price per pound to plummet. The farmer suffered tremendously, while industry benefited from cheap raw material for its mills. With such roller-coaster boom and bust in the space of a few years, farmers were confused and at a loss as to what to do. Cotton farming was their life, and they had an affection for the staple, an implicit and innocent faith in it, for it was neither cotton that had failed them, after all, nor the good land itself, but the crash of prices.

They were direct victims of the kind of big distant tampering and regulation that would subordinate one interest for another more favored, without any just regard for those who had no power and influence. This tampering had cataclysmic effects for the Southern farmer, and to the benefit of industry. It is yet another example of governmental insensitivity to Southern agriculture, and of how Southern agriculture had absolutely no good way to defend itself. No better proof exists of the correctness of the antebellum planter's theory that if business and industrial interests were ever to get control, then the agricultural South would be bled dry, and the financiers and industrialists would grow fat at her expense. And so it came to pass throughout the century following Appomattox.

Republican Party goals in 1861 were to ram through tariffs protecting industry, create a national banking system, and embark on a program of internal improvements that would facilitate industrial growth—all paid for by the public at large for the advancement of the few. With the election of Lincoln, who supported these ideals, Captain Dick's old Jeffersonian South saw the proverbial handwriting on the wall. Yes, he had much to tell his children and grandchildren about who owned the Union, and how, and why. Nor did the shrewd Northern financiers and industrialists in 1861 lose any time pushing through their programs. Without the checks of the agricultural South, now out of the Union, it was smooth sailing; and it was from this time on that the nation's course was changed and agriculture, in essence, was doomed—except in the case of large, monocultural, chemically dependent, "agri-industries"—not the same thing at all as farming.

In late 1920 the value of cotton had fallen from 40 cents to 13.5, marking the beginning of relentless farm decline climaxed by the Depression. Three years earlier, to make matters worse, the Mexican boll weevil had first made its appearance among the tender bolls of Sea Island cotton along the coast. It rapidly worked its way inland; and by 1920 and '21, the Hardys, like their Newberry and Union County neighbors, felt its curse. Luckily, they had the capital to invest in the arsenic and molasses necessary to kill the pest, and the shorter-staple cotton they grew responded to such treatment. They thus continued to make bales. This was no small achievement. As a result of the glutted postwar market and the boll weevil, cotton production in the state dropped precipitately—from 1.6 million bales in 1920 to half a million in 1922, a reduction of about seventy percent in a two-year period. According to scholars who have studied the culture of cotton in this country, of the two curses, the governmental, man-made one was far worse than the natural, although both were curses indeed. Because of the collapsed cotton prices, the bales that the Hardys produced and sent to market brought little compensation. They certainly did not make the family rich, just let them and the black people around them barely scrape by. At least, however, the Hardys did not lose their land through mortgages and loans as so many were doing.

Then, as if matters were not bad enough already, a series of devastating droughts came in the 1920s on the heels of the boll weevil and low cotton prices. The Hardys were tremendously affected, but persevered in silence. They and their Southern farm brethren were forgotten by "progressive" America; and at moments, when their plight was recognized, the solution offered them was to leave the farm or industrialize (that is, "Americanize") the area. How little "progressive" America understood the soul of the man of the soil. The crops, cotton prices, government, the weather, the bad times for farmers—these were the topics of many a quiet summer evening on the great veranda. And the worst was yet to come. They could not foresee the effects of the Depression, which, besides the other evils it brought, would cause cotton prices to plummet from the 1920 low of 13.5 cents to 4.6 cents in 1932, its lowest since 1874.

With Captain Dick's old age (he was eighty in 1921), his sons Frank and William Eppes took an ever increasing role in the management of the farm. They had been forced to sell some land but still retained over five hundred acres of their antebellum holdings—thus roughly a quarter of it. The high price of cotton during World War I had been a temporary godsend and kept them going. When William Eppes died in 1927 at the age of fifty-four in a year of great drought and collapsed cotton prices, most of the burden of managing the farm devolved onto Frank. Then came the Depression. With the death of Captain Dick in 1932, it fell almost solely to him—in the hardest of times since the great war between the states.

These dark Depression years, with the destruction wrought by drought, governmental interference, boll weevil, and soil depletion, were dire days for the plantation. It is almost miraculous that the family could hold on; and doing so came only through tenacity, old-fashioned grit, and strength of will. To make matters worse, heavier cotton production in the vast Southwest had now increased cotton volume in America at the same time that many overseas markets for cotton had been lost owing to cotton production in India. The price of cotton continued to plummet until the Depression crash, when there was no money to borrow and some farmers were in actual danger of starvation. Farm children of black and white families alike suffered in varying degrees from malnutrition. This was more the rule than the exception. The Hardys did their duty in helping less fortunate friends and neighbors, but many farmers simply had to give up. Their children had to be fed and clothed. As they were forced off the land, they often sought refuge in the cotton mill villages of Newberry, Union, Goldville, Whitmire, Laurens, Clinton, Chester, and Lockhart. Other farmers, of better advantage and schooling, were able to take a limited number of jobs as clerks, merchants, lawyers, supervisors, and teachers.

Many South Carolinians thus left the country for the town. As one former slave from a Maybinton plantation put it in 1937: "We lives in the towns now and does odd jobs and little jobs here and there where us can." In the 1920s some 30,000 of the state's 188,000 farms were left behind. More seriously, many South Carolinians, black and white, had to expatriate to the large cities outside the region, for there was little money or opportunity in the small cities of the state, towns that had been stunted by unfair national practices created to favor and enrich interests of every kind outside the region. For example, the Hardys' own cotton from upcountry South Carolina cost 46 cents to ship to New York and $1.50 to ship to Charleston—more than three times as much for less than a fourth the distance. The result was that Northern factories got it, Northern rails hauled it, Northern factors factored it, and Northern governments taxed it. Many Northern nonagricultural jobs were thus created by it, and if shipped overseas, Northern ships hauled it out of the port of New York, where Northern duties were levied on it. Each Northern interest took a part of the boll raised with Southern sweat. Or if a Southerner did manage to manufacture industrial goods, a similar rail-rate discrimination cost him more to send his produced goods from South to North than for Northern factories to send those same goods from North to South. With this manner of government-sanctioned discouragement to Southern incentive and its protection of Northern interests across the board, what wonder the South was poor—farm, town, and city—black and white—and could not support its own population. As we have seen, it was obviously the cost of defeat in war, a conflict many Southerners like the Hardys, Douglasses, and Renwicks of the antebellum era saw as being waged to enrich one region at the expense of another. As Captain Dick understood it, the hypocrisy of "Saving the Union" meant only saving it for one's own exploitation. He labelled this a "pious sham" and resented the official national version that he felt "sought increasingly to sentimentalize and disguise the issue." In 1937, former slave Frances Andrews of Newberry came remarkably close to Captain Dick's assessment when she observed that the Yankee promise of help to the black man during and after the War Between the States was a hypocritical trick: "I think this was put out by the Yankees who didn't care about much 'cept getting money for themselves." Thus a war of domination, cold economic exploitation, and imperialism had accomplished its goals. As a direct result, despite its lack of natural resources, the North had become vastly wealthy, the once wealthy South, full of rich resources (in coal, oil, lumber, soil, and climate) had become vastly poor. Where there had been no hunger, now it was widespread, particularly among the blacks; and now the decent and hardworking Southern people were having to say good-bye to familiar homeplaces, to families, and to communities, breaking ties that had the greatest meanings to them and traditions that were vitally important in an almost spiritual way. To the victor belonged the spoils. For the conquered, it meant dispossession, the virtual extinction of an agrarian way of life— and of much else that one held dear.

In 1922, after the disastrous harvest of that year, over 500,000 black farmers left the state. This trend continued for blacks and whites alike throughout the 1920s and '30s. By 1939 approximately eighty percent of the state's male high school and college graduates of both races moved elsewhere to seek "better opportunities." It is said that in 1930 more South Carolinians lived in Buffalo or Chicago, Cleveland, Detroit or Pittsburgh, than there were in whole counties of the state. In 1941, twenty-five percent of native-born South Carolinians lived in other states.

Some took to their new lives. After all, what real choice did they have? But the great majority of them went unwillingly to town and city, or out of desperation. Even though they usually prospered in a small way, they became the displaced, the dispossessed, often living among strangers in a new and less congenial place, where there was little warmth in climate or in the faces of the people met in the cold streets. Their sickness for home sometimes drove them to return when they were able; or if they toughed it out, they often carried that longing with them to the grave. Yes, the Southern loss in '65 had set the stage for the disruption of the lives of countless decent farm families. This was another of the great American tragedies for South and North alike, but primarily for the South, whose genius and preference had always been rural—the pleasant valley, not the cold, shining Puritan City on a Hill. With the evils of industry and technology unchecked since 1865 and now unleashed on the world, the twin forces finally wrought chaos on the land in 1929, a destructiveness that had the monster turn on itself and devour its own vitals. In the words of the wise poet,

> Then appetite, an universal wolf,
> So doubly seconded by will and power,
> Must make, perforce, an universal prey,
> And last, eat up himself.

The Great Depression was indeed the final blow to life on the Southern land and to the farm way of life. Those wise agrarians who had predicted such an outcome of man's greed and hedonism with its excesses of power and domination of government policy, took no pleasure in saying "We told you so." Yes, as they had warned, the mighty serpent was now swallowing its own monstrous self and taking all into its gorge with it.

In human terms at the Hardy plantation, the result of the domination of America by the industrial way of life meant that not all the many young Hardys of the new generation and their families could be sustained by their soil under such economic conditions. A few could remain; but many must join their fellow dispossessed Carolinians and wander from home. The best of farm practices, the richest soil, the best weather, the wisest management, the soberest living, the hardest work, the best discipline, could not shield the family from the outside influences of a nation's unwise choices, its unchecked greed, profligacy, waste, and excess—the consumer society triumphant.

Luckily, the three brothers who left the land did not have to wander far. This indeed was a blessing and a large and important difference between white and black, the latter individuals having their traditional moorings to the land they knew cut loose from beneath them by a separation of many hundreds of miles, while a larger percentage of whites often could move to within traveling distance of the old homeplace and the old community, the family church, the burial place of their ancestors, and all the old associations of family and childhood. In the push and shove for a severely limited number of jobs, the whites took first choice in the manner of the day. Except for a short time in Columbia, Frank Hardy stayed on the land, as we have seen; but his younger brothers Haywood, Paul, and John moved forty miles north to the mildly prosperous cotton mill town of Spartanburg. This, in the first decade of the new century. There in 1919, they became grocers, modest and respectable, at the Hardy Grocery on East Main. As Bertice Teague recalls, Frank spoke about his "city brothers": "They are up there in Spartanburg raking in the money, and don't give a damn, and I don't give a damn either." Brother Paul would come to the plantation and bring his town friends from Spartanburg "to be entertained, to see the place." Once on the veranda, when his guests lacked chairs, Paul asked Frank why he didn't buy him some more rockers, and Frank, with his usual quick and wry wit, replied that he didn't need any more chairs—just fewer guests.

The eldest brother, Ben, must have been a great pillar and prop for Frank. Ben, who married the widow Renwick, remained a fellow farmer and lived at the nearby Chick plantation, that is until he lost it in the 1930s after the Depression. He then moved to the old Reuben Sims Rice house near Whitmire, where he lived until his death in 1949. Sisters Mary and Helen had married and moved away with husbands who no longer farmed.

After his father's death in 1932, Frank was therefore the sole white Hardy on the place, surrounded by as many as five black tenant families. These were the Hodges, Hardy, Sanders, Rooks, Renwick, and Ruff families, many descended from former Hardy slaves. They had also managed to make their stand rather than go north for the dishwashing, janitorial, or other menial jobs that sometimes bought cars but little satisfaction. Often the cars bringing their "Northern" relatives from the city were rented to make a big display before the country kin; and this became a source of quiet but genuine amusement for those who remained at home in Carolina. Frank's chief and most dependable associates were the Hodges family, who lived across the little creek to the north of the house. Fella (Wade Jr.) and his wife Wren must have done more than their share of the farm work. Wren's daughter Ellen cooked for Frank during this time. Wade and Wren's son Clarence also remained on the land and took over from his father. He and his wife Thad were loyal friends to the last Hardys, remaining until 1973. They and the Sanderses were, in fact, the final family members to go from the land in that year.

Some time in the 1940s, Frank's brother Paul returned from Spartanburg to the homeplace. He had been the flashiest and boldest of the lads. He went off to war against the Germans, then during the roaring twenties always had a sporty new car and beautiful lady friends. He had never married and now was beginning to suffer from Parkinson's disease, his sporting days spent. He slept in an iron bedstead in what had been the large drawing room, which still retained most of its antebellum furniture. Paul was company for Frank, who slept just across the hall in what had been the small parlor. The two bachelor brothers spent their last days together in the old house.

Despite the boll weevil and all the other disasters, Frank continued to grow cotton throughout the period until his death in 1949 with the solid help of Wade and Clarence Hodges and the other black tenants. The cotton lands extended from the front of the house eastward to and across Tyger River Road and to the south of the house toward Maybinton. Cane for molasses was also grown on the south side of Peters Creek Road; and corn was planted in the moist, rich bottomlands along Peters Creek.

Cotton brought some money and helped the place survive as a farm until 1949; but it would never have been able to do so without the aid of the corn harvest and, more importantly, with what was made from it. For it was corn liquor that provided the margin for survival; and remnants of two stills are yet to be seen in the overgrown woods along the creek. Frank and company were in charge of this facet of the plantation economy; and from the testimony of several today, they made a superior product. The endeavor was a natural one that could draw on rich corn land and family tradition as well, for one of the first inventories of the plantation, taken in 1814, included a still. It was only now that the produce of the still was to bring in money or that the process was deemed "illegal" by a government determined to protect its citizens, while at the same time getting revenue and guarding the interests of the big liquor industry.

At one time during the late 1930s and early '40s, when Frank lived in the house only with his widowed sister Mary Hardy Scott and her daughter Frances, the "traveler's room" where Bishop Asbury had once slept was completely filled with Ball jars full of the clear white gold. Like the Hardys, several other local families also kept body and soul together by distilling "shine." One of Frank's friends across the Tyger served time in the penitentiary for it. It was virtually the only way some of the families had of resisting "moving to town" and of holding on to the farm life and family traditions, for in this valley in 1940, the plantation culture was a thing of the past.

From all accounts, the Hardy family, now largely in Spartanburg, appreciated Frank's efforts to keep the place going, for they returned home as a source of strength and ties to the past. Too, they owned a part-interest in it, for Captain Dick wisely had willed it equally to all of his children as a place of family. The old homeplace and its still productive fields continued to have the obvious symbolic importance for them. They visited it for family gatherings beneath the hemlock tree of a Sunday summer noon. This occurred less and less after the passing of Captain Dick in 1932, but it still occurred.

16

High Times with the High Sheriff

N'used to be dar was money in farmin'; but t'ain't no mo' since dat 'press-
ion done fell on us like a plague. . . . It gittin' so dat a man wid no trade
is sho' burnt up wet!
> —Alice Sims, former slave, Union County (1938)

With Frank Hardy's advanced age in the 1940s, he became more
and more of a character. As neighbor Margaret Thomas and nephew
Haywood Henderson recall him, he was an old bachelor, who slept in
the enormous family bed under a canopy and behind tapestried bed
curtains, with a gun always ready at his pillow. He was, after all, practicing an illegal trade. This he continued to do under the benign eyes of
certain lawmen, some of whom were his chief drinking buddies. It is
said that these men would come on their obligatory monthly raids and
take the official number of jars back to town, leaving the great majority
behind. Frank would pay the usual fine, and the raids would customarily
end with the confiscators returning to drink up some of the "shine"
with their buddy. I expect that the officers felt it was nobody's business,
certainly not a distant government's, that Frank and cohorts were selling
"shine." Carolinians were always rather independently tolerant in these
matters. They reasoned quite correctly that this was the only way some
had of toughing it out on the land. If the government did not get its
taxed percent, then hadn't it already taken enough from these people?
Had it not, in fact, virtually taken many of the other old families' land,
pushing them into other corridors and away from the family traditions

that were rightly theirs and that had sustained them? No, indeed, why arrest Frank and company? They were just trying to get by like everybody else during these ragged, starve-acre days—"raven days," as the Southern people had learned to call them. It was nobody's business but theirs, certainly not the business of rich and well fed, comfortable bureaucrats in some abstract place called Washington. Yes, the Carolinian of their day still maintained a healthy unreconstructed disdain for centrally located Power and, to their credit, a strong streak of Southern independence and self-assertiveness.

So the gun at the pillow. And the story goes that one night Frank nearly shot one of his lawmen friends who was in the yard making noises like a prowler as a practical joke. "Who's there!" Frank had shouted. "None of your damned business," had come the lawman's reply. And then as rapidly, "For God's sake stop shooting! It's Mott! It's Mott!" as bullets lodged in the old elm by Mott's head. The drinking buddies no doubt cussed and laughed this incident off over the head of their communal "shine"—Fella's best. The era was thus not an altogether sad one for the plantation. Its circumstances were reduced, the lace had yellowed, the silver tarnished, the house grew gray from no paint, its bannisters rotted and fell, its porch sagged. The glory days had given way to activity that did not always bear the decorous scrutiny of daylight; but life went on and Frank Hardy apparently "remained full of life" to the end.

John Renwick recalls him clearly. "He got a real rise out of folks; he was devilish and lively, full of pranks." Bertice Teague, who knew him well throughout his life, remembers that he was "quite a character, an individualist, good in his own way." He loved "going on all the outings with us younger folks, to fish fries, and the like. He, like all the Hardys, had a good sense of humor, and he entertained everyone." She sums up his character with the conclusion that "He said and did exactly what he wanted; he was as independent as a man could be and as devilish as he was independent. Devilishness ran in the family." Above all, he was a man who "enjoyed living."

She recalls that as a young girl, on a butchering day one late fall afternoon, Frank's niece Frances Scott, who was staying there at the time, went into Frank's room and got some five-year-old scuppernong wine, and the two girls drank several big tumblers of it on the sly. On the way down the staircase, the steps came up to meet them. Frank called his wine and choice moonshine "the good stuff." When he realized how tipsy they were, Frank said: "I know. You've been in my good stuff. I'm going to take a stick to you girls." Of course, he never did. But Bertice's mother did just that when she found her daughter giggly drunk. "Yes, devilishness ran in our family too," Bertice concludes.

Renwick remembers that Frank's sense of humor included buying a "five dollar box of candy, like nobody in these parts had ever seen, to use in courting. Later, after witnessing another beau eating from it, he took it back from the lady fair and carried it to and fro with him every time he went to see her, but not leaving it with her." Perhaps, too, behavior such as this is why he remained unmarried. Not that he didn't have an eye for the ladies. Bertice Teague recalls that "he tried to date every new teacher in the vicinity." Joe Simpson remembers that he stayed an incorrigible bachelor to the end of his days, befriended by his brother Paul, his black tenants, and such drinking buddies as the confiscating lawmen in what was thus largely a man's world. He may never have recognized it or planned it that way, but he was allowing the plantation to hold on by the skin of its teeth. Otherwise, it would likely have become (like neighboring Orange Hall, The Oaks, Rose Cottage, and the Sims, Richards, and Beaty plantations) a solitary pinewood, clear-cut by loggers every few decades, and with Great House and garden fallen into ruin.

Another tale that Simpson tells is that "when certain ladies from the county seat and the school board wanted to bus the black children into town and away from their community in the 1940s, Frank said he didn't see any need of that, and why should they care more than he? for most of the children were his." Bertice Teague recollects that when Ben Maybin chastised him for having opinions on a particular school issue when he had no children, Frank replied that he didn't care because the issue involved white schools and that all his children went to colored schools anyway. He did indeed like "to get a rise out of folks." Whether or not he was accurate about his offspring, he was certainly not discreet; he cared not a whit for decorum. Mrs. Doris Douglass recalls that he wore only "outdoorsman's clothes," that he "would not go to things that required a lot of dressing up." When he "dated a teacher at the Normal School" who was a friend of hers, he always appeared in "countryman's attire, plain, down to earth." He "never put on airs, was simple and plain spoken . . . an individualist." He "did things his own simple way." "All the Hardy brothers were characters," Mrs. Teague remembers. "The others were just more polished than Frank."

Frank was also a good storyteller, like his father before him, and enjoyed telling ghost tales, one of which is remembered today by Mrs. Sarah Stokes. This tale involved Frank's encounter on a road at night with a black washerwoman with her tied-up bundle of clothes balanced on her head. He recognized her immediately as Auntie Jemimy Hodges, who lived in a cabin between the plantation and Maybinton. When he addressed her with "Why, Auntie, what are you doing walking out here so late at night?" she disappeared. It was only then that it struck him that she had died a year ago.

He apparently got spooked rather easily (perhaps because he was bootlegging and stayed nervous), for Renwick recalls what was to him the funniest story of all in which Frank was involved: that of the cat that jumped him in the old kitchen building and scared him so much that he ran completely through a closed screen door, taking the screen with him pressed against his face.

These high times with the high sheriff ended with Frank Hardy's death on 16 June 1949, when he was sixty-six. He was buried at Ebenezer Cemetery with his family in a ceremony as devoid of pomp as had been his countryman's life. His demise left Paul alone in the Big House. In 1950 William Dixon Hardy's youngest son, John Frost Hardy Sr., and his wife Alice sold their house and their share in the grocery business in Spartanburg and came home to the plantation. As Captain Dick had left the land to all his children, John now bought out their interests. In 1949 the plantation contained 405 acres, a fifth of its 1860 acreage.

John and Alice Hardy had always had a great affection for the family home. As we have seen, he was serious and religious; she was meticulous, gracious, and an excellent homemaker. They thus brought with them a renewed air of respectability. (As we recall, it was John whom Frank had miffed by telling him to cut his table grace short.) And John did not approve of whiskey, much less illegally made whiskey. Still, he tolerated Clarence's little weakness, and when the latter was nabbed by the county for selling, John never failed to go his bail and pay his fine.

Their return occurred around 1951 and was followed by modernization of the house to make it more "comfortable." They added oil heaters downstairs in front of the old fireplace. Electricity had come to the Big House with the house renovation in 1950, after reaching the Peters Creek neighbors, the Thomases, in 1949. The privy was superseded by an indoor bathroom in 1950. One of the 1804 rooms became the present-day kitchen. The detached kitchen was pulled down. Ceilings were lowered and "Celotexed"; original ceiling medallions and plaster crown moldings were thus destroyed at this time. The plastered walls were themselves replaced by wallboard in all rooms but one. The rear two rooms of the 1804 structure were torn away. These city Hardys brought the first television to the area. Ellen Thomas Boyd remembers two evenings a week watching TV with the Hardys, for they had none. *The Jetsons* on Saturday morning was the treat the young Thomases remember most of all. The space age was making its first brush with Maybinton; and with electric lights and indoor plumbing, luxuries Frank Hardy had lived and died without, the Hardy house began to partake of "modernity."

Life however still kept its slow rural cast. Until he was seventy-seven, John kept turkeys, chickens, guineas, cows, mules, and horses and continued to grow corn, cane, and cotton with the help of his black tenants. Grandson John Frost Hardy III recalls that cane was cultivated in the field in front of the house and cotton to the south. He remembers going into the town of Whitmire about ten miles away to buy arsenic and molasses to "mop" the cotton for boll weevils. It was thus still very much the working farm under Hardy's ownership, though on a scale greatly reduced from the last century. The family continued to do all they could to be self-sufficient. This was their upcountry heritage. Miss Alice was, as she described herself, "a tough old bird." She and Clarence's wife Thad made soap at the spring, raised, killed, and dressed chickens and turkeys, and butchered hogs, cured hams, and made sausage. She had a large vegetable garden on the slope behind the old kitchen site, and still had time for her flower garden. Her grandson recalls she was "very good with growing things . . . had the greenest of thumbs." She preserved figs from the giant sugar-fig trees that still grow on the grounds and made hawthorne, scuppernong, and blackberry jelly. She sold boxwood prunings to the Whitmire florist shops at Christmas time. She and Thad were resourceful and made a penny go a long way. They *had* to; in 1950 neither blacks nor whites in this part of the rural South had yet recovered from last century's war, not to mention the Depression.

Paul continued to live at the Big House with John and Alice until he died in May 1954. John Hardy III recalls him as a kindly old man who shook from Parkinson's disease, a gentleman generous and warm. On their trips into Whitmire every Saturday to buy farm provisions and groceries, Paul would give the lad a shiny silver dollar to spend on whatever he wanted. This made quite an impression. Clarence's mother Wren still lived with her son and his wife Thad. One of the few little enjoyments left to her was taking snuff, so Grandfather Hardy, as John recalls, would always remember to bring a tin of it home for her from the Saturday trip.

There was mutual affection between the whites and blacks who lived on the place. The tenant families, both Hodges and Sanders, were these same descendants of Hardy retainers who had remained with Frank and Paul. Both Clarence and James lived in renovated slave cabins near the Big House. The farming operation was not a large one, but it continued to provide the tenants with a place to stay and a means to get by and raise large families. Hardy himself realized no monetary profit. As his grandson remembers, "Grandpa was a good grocer, but a poor farmer." Notwithstanding this fact, "he loved trying," and he knew he was keeping the old Hardy homestead from going the way of most of the old places in the area.

No, it was hardly a large operation, with its two mules, but it was a notable one for existing at all in a vast territory which had long since yielded to forestry as its only economic base, if one could glorify the condition by the term, for the land was usually "tree farmed" from a great distance by absentee landlords—either timber interests whose owners never saw or cared to see the land, or the U.S. Forestry Service itself. In either case, little of the profits remained in the land from which the trees were cut; it was a classic case of environmental exploitation. And John himself did his share to diminish the number of acres in the plantation. By the time of his death he had sold off about three-quarters of the land he had acquired in 1949—these acres going to timber companies that would henceforth clear-cut and erode the soil. By 1963 only 127 acres of the old patrimony of 2,035 acres remained. The rest was largely in the hands of "big business," mostly controlled outside the region. All but a few of his fathers' fields had passed to the control of others.

In 1963 Hardy was seventy-seven years old. In that year he, Hodges, and Sanders raised eight bales of cotton with their two mules and a lot of sweat. These bales yielded a total of $1,381. It is a remarkable testament to the land's richness, to the fidelity, skill, and endurance of the black tenants, and to the tenacity of Hardy family tradition, that these meager eight bales made their way to market. Their journey from the gin faintly recalled the glory days of the 1850s when a hundred bales yearly made the same trip. The year 1963 marked the end of the Hardys' agrarian legacy. For these were the last bales raised under the management of the last Hardy to live on the land; and with them, an epoch now clearly had come to an end.

After the death of her husband in 1963, Alice invited her sister to come live with her, and they stayed in the Big House alone until about 1973, at which time Miss Alice sold the plantation and moved to an apartment in Union, where she lived by herself. Her love of growing things continuing to the last, she dug the pink Hardy rose and her favorite ginger lilies to take with her. She wept as she left the place but did not turn to look back. Later, one of her last requests was for her grandson's wife to dig the rose from Union and take it to their home in Spartanburg to care for it. Such was her love for that last tie to the land.

Her two living sons continued to reside in the city of Spartanburg with families of their own. Here they were prominent businessmen with modern pressures and modern concerns. From 1963 to 1973 the black tenants continued to farm as best they could and provided great support for Miss Alice. In 1973, with Alice's departure, the last of the black families moved from the land when it was purchased by buyers from New Jersey, thus snapping the very last human ties with the old days.

Until her departure in 1973, Alice Hardy was well-loved in the neighborhood and presided over a gracious and cheerful board. Margaret Thomas King especially recalls one Thanksgiving dinner at which she served jelly made from the fruit of the flowering hawthorne on the place, as accompaniment to a baked turkey fresh from the plantation poultry yard. Miss Alice and her sister continued to keep guinea fowl and turkeys and a vegetable garden after John's death and well into their seventies. She continued to sell boxwood clippings at Christmas, making every penny count in her resourceful way—a true daughter of the Great Depression.

Margaret Thomas King's daughter Ellen Thomas Boyd recalls Alice as being almost a second mother, who would serve her pimiento cheese sandwiches while she watched TV on Saturday mornings and let her and her brother slide down the slick hill behind the house. Doris Douglass remembers her petiteness and kindness, her sweet nature and hospitality. Her grandson recollects: "She was the only person I have ever known who never uttered an unkind word about anyone." He particularly relished his summers with her and his grandfather. Each June from the 1950s into the '60s, he would travel from Spartanburg to spend the season. Often he would take the train to Carlisle, where his grandfather would meet him. They would make their trek back across Gordon's Bridge, then only a high, trestle-like affair with two wooden boards for tracks to place the car-wheels on. He remembers, "As Grandfather at his age was not a very good driver, this was always an adventure." The grandson cherished life in the country, and even his weeding and grass-cutting were not chores. His wife Sally also recalls Miss Alice: "When she was eighty, she fell from the porch on her back, an accident which only put her in bed for several days; it did not daunt her or slow her down. With the help of Thad and Clarence, she kept the place going as long as she could; and it nearly broke her heart to leave."

From all accounts, Alice Hardy was a worthy last plantation mistress, a true lady of grace, "great femininity, and charm." Without much material wealth, these last Hardys managed to show a hospitality that was effective owing to their warmth and sincerity. After all, the spirit of the thing was more important than the surface trappings in the first place, as well they knew, being good Southerners born, bred, and true.

As Margaret King remembers, Miss Alice kept the house spotless to the point of cleaning the sashes of the window panes in the great door sidelights with a toothbrush. She is recalled by Haywood Hardy Henderson, her nephew, as being able to create warmth and hospitality from "very little" and "with grace and ease." Juanita Hitt described her similarly as one who possessed true "warm Southern hospitality." In 1970 Miss Hitt spoke of the house and grounds as being "beautifully kept" even as Miss Alice approached the age of eighty. She died in the town of Union in 1985 at the age of ninety-four.

17

The Ruined Land

*Things are as they are,
and end as they must.*
—Aeschylus

The decade and a half following the last Hardy's departure was the low ebb of the grand home's history. When a single family has resided on a piece of land for two centuries—with their passing, so much of the unbroken substance of the place goes with them. Even if the house can be kept properly, it is always haunted by a grief and loss.

In 1973 the new generation of Hardy children was the first to be city-born, the first not raised on the land. Like their Douglass kin who left The Oaks, the scattered family now lived in post-world-war progressive towns and cities where the old, including the values associated with it, was not so well appreciated as before, and where they had to deal with the pressures of the modern world, raising decent and respectable families as best they could and "getting by," as one of them put it. They had gone about their individual lives. Cousins lost track of cousins. Their love of the rural had weakened in not having been born to it. One of John and Alice's two sons had helped establish Spartan Foods in Spartanburg—a forerunner of one of today's large corporations. The other went successfully into textiles with Spartan Mills. None of the new generation desired to return to the family plantation some fifty miles distant, so it was sold out of the family by Alice Hardy in 1973 with the stipulation that the old house "be cared for and kept up." At the time of the sale, the land, as we have seen, had dwindled to 127 acres, the balance in the hands of timber concerns that clear-cut it, absentee owners who did not have to live with the results of their policies.

Then began a sad deterioration of the Big House itself that mirrored the ruined and untilled acres. Alice's grandson recalled that its decay sickened him so on the two times he visited that he couldn't go back. As if in poetic justice for his family's sale of the place, one of the new owners' dogs "bit him in the butt" on his last visit. Miss Alice, in Union, felt dismay and "hurt" at what was happening and tried to put it out of her mind. In 1980 the second-floor porch of the decayed portico fell. Luckily, the porch pediment was so well-constructed that its giant timbers only bent and did not break. They were then supported by thirty-foot telephone poles. These props remained in place until restoration began in the summer of 1989. The rear porch floor also collapsed in the 1980s. By 1987 a hole three feet in diameter in the roof of the 1825 section allowed water to wash through the upstairs ceiling, and down into the drawing room on the first floor. Both ceilings fell. The superior construction of the house held, however, and no major structural damage occurred. With all the water, termites had begun to eat lightly into the downstairs heart-pine baseboards. No major damage resulted; heart-pine, unless it is thoroughly watersoaked, has the effect of dulling termites' teeth. Their tunnels were injected with epoxy; so it was not necessary to replace any of the original wood. Several parcels of the remaining land were sold after 1973, including all the land on Peters Creek and across Tyger River Road. In May 1989 all that remained of the Hardy parcel was 47½ acres when the author of this story bought it in the two parcels into which the owners were subdividing it for separate sale.

The structure was reroofed in June 1989. Later in the summer, the sagging portico was lifted eight degrees without any damage to the timbers, and the porches on both levels were inserted. The columns, which had been stored in the attic, were repaired and rose to their old place in August. As I remarked, it appeared the South was rising again. In other moods, I entitled the scene *Gone with the Bank Account*. During the fall of 1989, baseboards, mantels, and doors were stripped to reveal the original black-and-walnut opaque stains. The staircase and stained woodwork were treated with tung oil. The heart-pine floors of the rooms were cleaned, oiled, and waxed.

During the summer of 1990, the back porch was restored by local craftsman Jerry McCullough. I designed the rear porch entrance of double doors, using old doors that had been in the 1804 structure before it was torn away in the 1950s. The flooring salvaged from the rotted porch was tied into the partially decayed floor anterior to the double doors in the main rear hall in order to provide foyer flooring original to the house. The exterior wall of the porch partition in which doors and transom are set came from the rotted porch ceiling. The rear porch columns were constructed to the design and size of the one remaining engaged column on the back porch wall.

In the fall of 1989 the log mule pen was stabilized. In 1990 the collapsed antebellum harness and tack house was dismantled, its logs numbered, and the rotten logs pulled out and replaced with hewn logs from the fallen tack shed at the James M. Eppes plantation in Whitmire (c. 1857). The rafters, flooring, and doorway, complete with hand-wrought spikes, are original to the Hardy structure. So are the door and its fine strap hinges. It bears the initials P. H. H. of Paul Hayne Hardy (1888–1954) and the numeral 11. Some time before the initials were placed on it, the door had been turned upside down and rehung so that its hardware is upside down. This likely indicates that the door was rehung either before 1911 or when Paul Hardy was eleven years old— hence 1899.

It was this Paul Hardy and especially his brother Frank who are responsible for the existence of the plantation Great House today. Had the dwelling fallen to either Federal or private timber concerns during the bad years when almost all the last of the planter families gave up their land, it and its venerable boxwood gardens would now most certainly be rubble, honeysuckle-choked stumps, and a memory—another part of our shared heritage lost forever.

On a personal note—throughout the first five years of restoration, I had the unfaltering support and physical aid of my father and mother, both brought up on farms, and now, in a manner of speaking, my neighbors once again in the county of my birth. As for myself, after a twenty-year absence, I was establishing closer ties with the place and people who had given me birth, ties to my pioneering forebears on both father's and mother's sides, who took up the land in this same county over two and a half centuries ago. My father's people and my mother's people originally settled in the eighteenth century about six miles from each other in Newberry County, and my parents dwelled approximately halfway between these points—a rather remarkable thing for the American at large in our nomadic country, but still rather much the case in New-berry County. This, I have come to learn, is a birthright not to be tossed away lightly.

Into his seventies, my father climbed high ladders to paint, removed tree stumps with mattocks, and axed down trees and scrub to clear the overgrown grounds. Even with the debilitation from radium treatments for cancer, he continued to mow and chop. What a lesson in strength and spirit. The glint of the sun on his newly-sharpened ax spanned two centuries. My seventy-year-old mother was also known to wield a shovel and push a heavy wheelbarrow. Otherwise, with curtains and flowers she added the feminine touch that made life finer and easier and that brought back memories of Alice and Helen Hardy. Then, in a casual moment, without realizing its import, she also gave me a priceless trea-sure by way of an offhand story of how her father and his two brothers left the farm during the Depression to work in the cotton mills of New-berry. After a stay of two unhappy weeks in which he felt "thrown away," he returned to the soil to take up the hard life of the tenant farmer, but one that satisfied him and his own far better than the brief one he had just left. He never owned any of the soil he farmed, and the family worked hard merely to get by. Life meant moving and often building up another man's holdings; but there was never any bitterness or "class struggle" involved. Such was the measure of the man. He al-ways left a place and its soil better than he found it, even though it would never be his. His brothers remained in town on the "mill-hill"; but as my mother put it so succinctly well, "He always liked to walk behind a mule," and he died on the land, among fields not his own, still true to his middle name, Tiller, given him by his own farming father, and the name by which he went in his rural community. There, as I witnessed it, he held the respect of a prince. There, a lifetime of decency and genuineness would not go unnoticed and gave him a status which the brothers, who earned more of the things of the world, did not have. This bit of family history, of my grandfather's two weeks in the "city," and speaking to me of his wisdom, I had never heard before. I had known him merely as a quiet old gentleman in faded bib overalls, a man with a kind smile and tender, hard-calloused hands. How important to me, this scrap of the past out of a time long gone, and to lie dormant in my mother's memory for four decades, until at supper table unexpected, it stepped forth gleaming, fully revealed among the fried chicken, corn-bread, and cabbage. Sometimes it happens this way—these revelations that burn away the fogs of self, making us understand ourselves more clearly. Indeed, the closeness of family, drawn together by the land, now allowed this moment of revelation to take place. Without it, and from the abstraction of distance, the story, in our separate worlds, would have gone to the grave unexpressed and uncommunicated. The strong old blood reasserts itself in the ritual of continuity. This was clearly its teaching; and the lesson came by way of a treasured bit of family knowledge that helped explain me to myself.

Or yet again, more recently, after I had engaged myself in a very minor way in raising eggs and poultry, she spoke of the love she and her own mother had for the poultry yard, as a thing of family necessity but also for the pleasure in the fowl themselves. They loved birds of all kinds, songbirds especially. Grandfather, too, always gave some of his rather precious cracked corn to redbirds. She would see him there on his split-cane-bottom chair with a living carpet of red about him. And it was her memory now that summoned forth the image of a teenage country girl walking the dusty farm road to the crossroad's general store with a white pullet under her arm to exchange for the quarter that would allow her to buy ten printed high school invitations. Or of another time, with her father again having no money to spend on such, to exchange another hen for the money for her to go on the school trip to Charleston—after her uncle Monroe had added a quarter to round out the necessary sum of fifty cents. And this was the trip that gave her her first sight of the ocean, and in fact of a county other than her own. Indeed, the local store kept wire pens of such traded countrymen's chickens that were then picked up and sent to the towns for townsmen's tables. A life for a "luxury." The warmth of the hen in the arm's crook so tactile still over the distance of decades, and the knowledge of the living thing traded in such a concrete way, a creature tense and tight with life, exchanged for the cold shine of metal. My father and I listened hushed, and through the mastery of her simple telling, we walked on the same dusty road with her, feeling the same tense warmth beneath our arms.

As the work of reclamation became more and more a family enterprise, this most recent part of the plantation's history became tied closely with its origins as a venture—perhaps better, an adventure—of family. Being such, it taught—and I learned once again in my own personal experience—the lesson of the South's great strength through family. This important truth became impressed upon me clearer than ever and made me think back to the original pioneering venture on the land that began it all—described earlier herein as "truly a family enterprise like most of these Virginian ventures; the Hardys of the Old Dominion had equipped, supplied, and given moral support and encouragement." Satisfyingly complete, then, our story had come full circle in its pattern and rhythm of continuity. More than standing witness to the past repeating itself or of abstractly, vicariously feeling it, I was taking it upon myself to play my own active part in the pattern. Doing so, one enters into history oneself, not solely as intellectual exercise, or even as emotional response, but as integral, visceral part of place and the magic process that yokes past to present, bringing the one into the other, merging them through the chain of memory and action and being.

18

Interlude: Ghosts
(January 1990)

. . . faces out of a past that still is present,
Though crusted with time . . .
. . . faces of men that passed into mine.
—Donald Davidson, "The Faring"

"If you could paint a howl, this one was chalk-white, the color of bleached bone stumbled on in the woods." In her big drafty house, I sat by the New Year's blaze from old Mrs. Deans's fireplace. To this comment, she said simply, "Indeed," ill concealing the interest that had a shade of the startled in it.

"That dark stretch of the Old State Road is a gloomy enough one for sure," came her measured comment after a long quiet in which the fire popped and spewed and the air hung heavy.

I had heard the strange sound twice this sleety late afternoon, first a dismal, God-forsaken distillation of grief barely discernible, then louder the second time, having all the sound of being lost and alone after knowing closeness, the wail ending as if the breath for wailing were choked off by a hangman's rope.

"A hangman's rope!" Mrs. Deans shot at me, her eyes round, and this time not masking her surprise.

"Just a manner of speaking. But the sounds shook me like death. I can't explain it."

"Nor should you."

After our usual long pause, one of the many that punctuated all our fireside conversations like unsung refrains to ancient ballads, the talk moved purposely to the Christmas greens that lay dried and brittle on the old pine mantel.

It was not until the next evening by the fire that Mrs. Deans returned to the subject, looking nervously like a criminal coming back to the scene of a crime. "Did you say this was near The Oaks?"

"I didn't say, but yes it was in fact. I was standing by one of the old chimneys of the gutted house when I heard it come from the woods to the west, out over the ruined gardens of the old Chick place toward Ebenezer Church. I had gone there to take photographs."

Then began her narrative, which I remember clearly to this day. Nelly Deans, past eighty, and recalling more of this once rich but now ruined valley than anyone in the sparsely settled countryside, was a gifted storyteller.

"I will explain a little of what you heard," she said, settling herself comfortably into her storytelling pose, grown so familiar to me by now. "It was back in the old days long before the War," she began, "that a man whose name hasn't come down to us was hanged for murder. This was from a tree right off the Old State Road near Ebenezer Meeting House. All this would have been forgotten soon enough because hangings happened and people wanted to forget them soon enough. But this hanged man had a large white dog, and dogs don't have the same sense of law and order that us humans do, so he loved his master, who treated him well. I can see our murderer, probably a misfit in the country, not having much to say to folks but in a scowl, and a loner, no family, no friends. So he could show his feelings to old whitey. And like these little apples that fall to the ground after the frosts are on them, he had built up a sweetness under his twisted shape. And the dog, knowing like my old horse, Mannie, when a body shows attention, gave back a kind of blind love that lasts sometimes even past deserving, or even the normal.

"This is the way it must have been with the white dog, who sat whimpering on his haunches as his master fell at the end of the hangman's rope. Picture if you can the disarray in the dog's small brain, and now what to do! They carried his master's body away, but he stayed. This after several days sitting on the hanging site, maybe waiting for him to return as he had always done before. The big mastiff anticipating his outline in the store's door, or out from the old hotel in Maybinton. What else could he do but wait!

"Then on the third day he began to howl; and the mournfullest sounds ever heard came from his throat. This went on both day and night and the dog would not move from the place. So the hangman's duty was to return and resolve the issue. This he did by ending, as he thought, the dog's misery with a ball in the brain. The howling stopped and life around these parts returned to normal. The living went on their way as the living are wont to do.

"It was three years to the day of the hanged man's death that old whitey made his presence known once again, this time to the considerable great fear of the countryside. The hangman who had adjusted the noose was passing in his buggy by old Ebenezer when he was attacked and run from the road by a great white dog. He said it came like a moonlight mist out of the old graveyard, passing right through the heavy cast-iron fencing. He got between and among the horse's feet and wrecked the buggy. Our hangman's story the next day, from badly cut and swollen lips, was to the effect that the dog was most surely a ghost dog, because he had passed his whip through him, but more, his eyes were red like fire-coals and they spun like pin-wheels. To add the finishing touch, the dog had a grin on its jagged lips! This last was too much to abide, so the hangman was never quite the same afterwards, in the eyes of the villagers of Maybinton, or to himself. He killed himself some few years hence. The story goes, by hanging.

"Twenty years went by, and the great white mastiff was seen again, and this time by an innocent unconnected to the story. The year was 1855 and it was in the month of October. William Hardy, who lived at your plantation on Peters Creek, had a slave who became ill, so he sent Ben, a young black lad, to fetch Dr. Douglass, a Hardy kinsman by marriage and master of The Oaks some three miles away.

"Ben was told to ride fast but not overheat the mule. In the middle of the night the whole Douglass plantation was startled from sleep by the boy's shrieks as he came down the deep-cut valley road. When the good doctor opened the great double doors of the plantation, candle in hand, in he burst falling at his feet trembling and sobbing, 'Please marster, keep dat white varmint from gettin me!'

"Beads of cold sweat sparkled like stars on his black brow in the candlelight: 'Marse Doc, I is most scared to death. I would hab died if you hadn't got to dat door when you did. Please suh, let me come in the house.'

"Douglass, man of science as he was, treated Ben with some disdain, making light of the event and threatening him with a sound thrashing if he didn't get on back to Marse Hardy; but it soon became obvious that Ben was in a terrible state and might indeed die of fright if pushed out into the night. So in he came, cared for by the kind Miss Frances, 'Ole Missis' of the plantation. It was during this ministration that the whole story of poor Ben's fright unfolded, made doubly forceful by the Doctor's inspection of Ben's mule, lathered white with sweat, the bit making his mouth scarlet with blood, and the animal trembling far worse than poor Ben.

"From Ben, the tale unfolded:

" 'I was doin what Ole Marstuh bid, and was making time but not so as to sweat the mule, when down in de deep part of the ole road, I hears a noise behind me of a low growl right close up in them darkest woods. I then see the white thing come out of the ole grabeyard. I stuck my heels into de mule. De mule, he seed it too and broke into the fastest run, and we thought we was beating dat dog, when there he was coming out of the woods in front of us! I most died of skeer. De mule reared up when he seed de dog in front of him and I most fell off. When I looked again, dat varmint was grinnin at me like a skull grins and his eyes were a-spinning. Me and dat mule was a-shaking and a-running.

" 'Dat varmint never lef us till I started hollering down here at de Oaks and I seed de candle. I don't likes to tell you, but dat thing, he got up on de mule wid me and rid behind me and I couldn't jump off. Its hot breff was on my neck. De mule then reared and the spook, he got down.

" 'Ole Missis, I is bout dead of fright. Please have mercy on poor Ben and don't send me out no more dis night. I will die of skeer.'

"Miss Frances sheltered little Ben that night in the plantation kitchen with a bright fire and with kind old Uncle Peter to nod by it and keep him company; and in the morning Dr. Douglass, Ben, and the mule started their trek back to the Hardy plantation to attend the sick slave. Along the tree-shaded roadbed, Ben pointed with excitement to the places where the white dog joined or momentarily left them, the spot where he got up on the mule, the exact place where he appeared from the graveyard at Ebenezer—the same site he'd first appeared to the hangman, it was later learned.

"After the coming of the great War and the death of the Doctor, things around here fell apart. The old houses one by one were deserted and a kind of gloom fell over the land. The old cottonlands grew weed-choked and overgrown with briars, pines, and honeysuckle. Careful terraces eroded into dark gullies. Great dead trees fell across the roads and were left to rot themselves out of the way. Few people passed these lanes. Catbriars and blackberry thickets sealed off the old footpaths. It was like the white dog itself was sole inhabitant, melting his gray, ghostly self all over and through the land. You see how few of us are left, and we are all oldtimers—soon to be gone as well.

"In my own time I heard those speak who had also seen the white dog. After the death of Dr. Douglass, his practice was taken over by Dr. Cofield, and I have heard from his own lips as an old man, stories told casually of the times he'd confronted Happy Dog, as he called him because of the same strange smile that would always seem to show on his jagged lips. Sometimes Cofield would be riding quickly to or from a patient along the old road when all at once his horse would whinney and jump out of the lane, almost throwing him off. When he'd get back onto the path, he could see the great mastiff going all around and in between his horse's feet. When he would cut at the creature with his riding crop, it would pass entirely through his body. Several times the dog, as he had with little Ben, would get up on the horse with him, sometimes behind and sometimes before. The horse too would see the dog, sometimes before he did. Often they would think the creature was gone, but after they had traveled several miles, he would accompany them again, materializing out of the dark woods along the Old State Road where he had been following.

"The stories about Happy Dog are many among the blacks of this valley. And one of the most recent sightings was by one of them. Berry Sanders, when he was about seventeen years old, saw the ghost dog on an April night back in 1936. He worked for Mr. Watt Henderson and every Saturday night had to travel on this four-mile stretch on his way home. On this particular spring night, the dogwoods shone ghostly white as he passed through the ruined gardens of The Oaks. When he paused to close the side gate, he caught a glance of the white dog trotting after him. Sanders says he ran every foot of the mile to his house, screaming all the way. The neighbors verify the shrieks. When he reached the lit safety of his parents' home, he and the great white dog exchanged a long glance before it turned back and melted into the deep woods.

"Exactly thirty years later, another countryman was singled out to play his part in this singular history. Jim-Epps Oxner, from behind his counter in the hardware store where he now clerked in the market town, looked with heavy and downcast eyes beneath his green visor. The glow of the shade gave an unhealthy and unnatural look to his sallow skin as he told me about the big argument he had had with his father that fateful day in 1966. I had not seen Jim-Epps since then, and because his father had died later that year and the old Oxner homeplace had been boarded up and deserted when Jim-Epps moved to town, I had lost touch and had never known the story til now.

"It seems the argument was about whether Jim-Epps would stay on the red land and continue to farm as his ancestors had for the last two centuries. The father took pride in the soil and would hear of no other future for his son. Jim-Epps, however, was determined to follow the lights and easier life of the town. 'An old man could, but a young man shouldn't waste his sweat out here,' he said heatedly. The interview had ended with harsh and hurtful words that both men had regretted as soon as they had said them, but that neither would take back.

"Jim-Epps was on his way to share his predicament with and receive sympathy from his best friend Darby. They were plotters in crime together, both vowing to leave their families and their fathers' fields and make their way on the pavements of the market town. It was with mingled anger and excitement that Jim-Epps strode toward Darby's house. The cold of the bright winter night added energy to his step. As his mind ran over the preceding scene with his father in disjointed flashes, his anger rekindled; and it was precisely then that he saw the great white mastiff.

"Whitey stalked him as Jim-Epps slowed, chased him close as he fled, kept his very pace for two terrifying miles until in exasperation, Jim-Epps cursed him, using the same words he'd hurled at his father. It was then the dog jumped him. He felt a terrific weight on his chest, far beyond what even such a large dog should be; and as he passed out from fear and the suffocating pressure, he sensed a sharp pain from teeth at his throat.

"In the bright moonlight of the predawn, Jim-Epps bestirred himself and rose from the frozen ground. The cold of the night had nearly taken his life. He felt the wet of clotted blood all down his shirtfront. There were raw marks on his throat. Were they from teeth or from briars? Three weeks later his father died of pneumonia; and Jim-Epps was not there, as I was, when his breath came more and more labored, and was finally strangled off as he died with a choking sound.

"This settled the matter, and Jim-Epps moved to town, leaving the starved acres of his father's land for the joys and comforts of town life. The sad old house is still boarded up, not even sought out by young pranksters from the city out on larks and wanting the thrill of trespassing.

"For Jim-Epps himself, the dog's appearance was an omen of his father's death, and he never attached any more significance to it. A relative, it seems, reported to him that he'd also seen the dog some few years ago, but he hardly gave such any thought now from behind the barrier of his polished stainless steel store counter, gleaming with its antiseptic nickle and plate-glass shine, surrounded by the tools of male trade, and shielded by an unmistakably masculine scent. Quite the thorough city modern, protected behind his fortress wall of progress! His seat now the metal revolving stool throne of Village Hardware Store, his highest goal one day to own it, and with no thought of his boarded house and his own quietly eroding acres, or of the old deep wagon-wheel-cut trace where old Happy presides as the resident genius of the place in the dark woods into which he always melts so successfully after his manifestations to us startled mortals.

"In my eighty-four years, I have seen no place more desolate than this old stretch of road, a lane that was once the major thoroughfare of a great and wealthy state; and the road here passed directly through what had been one of the finest and grandest areas of all. Lord, child, even in my own girlhood, things were different." Mrs. Deans looked somewhat dreamily into the fire's coals as she foresaw her own future in the yard at Ebenezer, when she too would be gathered to her family and another chapter of this sad and grieving land's history would be written.

But the mingled odor of dried pine and cedar boughs from the Christmas greens came suddenly to me (in one of those unexplainable drafts in an old house) as I sat before her dying fire and recalled a passage I had once read describing this Southland not as a geographic place but as a lingering fragrance, here made palpable by lives and details that could wrench the heart. As the fire burned still lower and our good gentlelady fell to dozing, I silently took my leave, letting myself out through the big double doors of the old house, and made my solitary way over the deserted lane across hills already with the white of frost upon them, to another silent, dark, and cold house, half hoping to hear that dismal howl of two days prior. But I did not, and I soon settled myself into the heavy high-piled quilts in an unquiet sleep, again recalling snatches of something read many years ago: "Here, it is a realm of the lost and grieving, of tender beauty eclipsed, of emptiness and longing, truly the dark ruined Helen of the blood," then to dream fitfully through a long winter's night of a hanged man, gutted mansions, vanished families, weed-rank gardens, and frozen briar-choked fields silvered by frost and moonlight, of these lands lying helpless under a black winter sky in which the bright stars wheeled in some inexplicable pageant over which the velvet curtain has yet to be rung down. Suffused through all these blurred, jumbled, and broken images were both the distant howl and skull lear of the ghost dog, like a message the seal of whose truth was about to break into knowing.

19

Choices: A Rare and Bearing Vine

The farmer is tied to his country, wedded by the most lasting bonds. . . . While we have land to labour, let us never wish to see our citizens occupied at a work-bench.

— Thomas Jefferson

Without a complex knowledge of one's place, and without the faithfulness to one's place on which such knowledge depends, it is inevitable that the place will be used carelessly and eventually destroyed. . . . If the land is made fit for human habitation by memory and old association, it is also true that by memory and association men are made fit to inhabit the land.

— Wendell Berry

I need to see the earth under my feet. Our people live in the houses in which they were born. We love the land which feeds us and to which, when we die, our bodies will return. The land owns its people. Let the land feed you long enough and it possesses you and has the power to hold you fast. . . . I find the old place has played a trick on me: it has made me merely one of its creatures whose destiny is bound up with everything else here. Not only with the trees and beasts and men, but with this silent red earth that feeds us all, and that will some day, certainly, take back all that is mortal of us, and turn it again into its dust.

— Julia Peterkin, Lang Syne Plantation, South Carolina

With the privilege of ownership and the choices it makes possible, I face the future with hope, steeled by the truths taught by this story.

Now after a short eight years, the plantation has rewarded me with the satisfaction of knowing that I am keeping in trust, at least for a time, a place and its traditions. Besides good memories, the dramatic joy of surprise, and what has blossomed quite slowly and unexpectedly to be the quiet persistent joy of familiarity, the place has also given an undefinable something at the same time both humbling and ennobling, that comes only from constant and intimate communion with a long, bittersweet story and a closely felt association with the generations that preceded and survived for their time through triumph and failure. Reinforced as it is by the physical presence of a region of stark chimneys, decayed mansions, and overgrown gardens—in a phrase, of a world that has been ruined—it is a melancholy, even tragic place, with a melancholy and tragic history. Riding through ruins daily in the performance of the commonplace errands of life breeds a familiarity with that story, and acts as constant reminder of the slow dance of time, carried to the bone and marrow. There are truths to be learned here far deeper than the usual. They rest near each pile of moss-grown chimney brick and ruined hearthstone; they come to greet one out of each old roadbed in the forest cut deep from the passage of many wheels. For this, I am thankful to the genius loci of this Southern land of monuments and memories, and gladly will continue to reside where, as said the famous novelist of Wessex, "the two of us keep house, the past and I."

And in this house itself, the past is most literally close at hand. I am keenly aware when I find support from the stair rail, that my hand and body repeat a motion performed now for almost two centuries by all the people in that story. The hand rail's polish, glass-slick from wear, is tactile evidence of them. Rhythm, pattern, continuity. These are no small things, I learn, as my hand uses this rail, to climb toward a sleep in which those participants in this drama sometimes become palpable. It is as though, in the words of the Greek poet, "From deep in their graves in the soil of the land, the dead have embraced us. As deeply-rooted as they, then as high grow our branches to the sky." It is then we realize that though the particulars of this place remind us of the procession of time, they speak even more strongly of cycles and timelessness—the paradox and balance of complementary and returning opposites, in which this place abounds. And although diminished by the modern death of a machine-dominated era of empiricists, through the rhythms of healing nature, the land still sings of beginnings.

A measure of both its stature in the eyes of the community and the

pull of place across the miles is the large number of visitors who appear
at the house gate. Hardly a week goes by but that some stranger from
Tokyo, Scotland, British Columbia, Texas, or California will stop here,
or old neighbors from sixty years ago will come by to pay their respects
and to walk around the old grounds once again. What are they looking
for? Is it their own individual past or something broader, more inclusive?
They who feel the importance of place and the pleasures of place know
very well. Or perhaps a Hardy descendant will come to smell the bitter
fragrance of the boxwood that will instantly bring back so tangibly and
in a rush all the rich memories of childhood. Or another will recall his
ninety-one-year-old grandfather, seated in a rocking chair in 1932 and
attended by his ancient manservant, as the little grandchildren, he among
them, are brought for the kind old man, conscious of death's nearness,
to place his hands on their heads, and each, in turn, receive the patriarchal blessing in the manner of fathers from time immemorial. Many are
the tales of old times now remembered to me on this same veranda as a
distillation of our shared Southern past. These voices offer up sacraments
of remembrance that have a truth and wisdom surpassing the lore of
books. Such are some of the unforeseen intrinsic worths and pleasures
of the place; and these visitors who are instinctively drawn to it should
know that they will always be welcome while I keep its doors. I realize
that the roof of "my" house, in figurative manner, shelters more than
me and mine.

Southerners who are attuned to this story of the land are likely to
be unique among Euro-Americans in possessing the common bond of
the culturally shared experience of grief. As Ben Robertson, one of Carolina's very best writers, put it so correctly fifty years ago, we natives of
this place have known the heights and the depths, both within the short
span of a decade. We are a people who experienced the sadness of defeat
and loss to the point of utter desolation, of the total destruction of a way
of life—and also the ennoblement occasioned by the triumph over this
destruction—while not forgetting the grief. The memory of this last is
one of the traits that have given the unique edge and true import to
the Southern personality—that which separates Southerners from the
country at large and which binds us so closely to our kin and kind. The
awareness that grief is a necessary and elemental fact of life is thus a part
of a Southern cultural wisdom; Southerners accept grief, death, and loss
as integral parts of existence better than most Americans and face them
more realistically, at the same time retaining both a love of the tangible

and a sense of awe at an inscrutable design and destiny, perhaps summed up in the single phrase "the sense of wonder." Maybe it is a Celtic thing with us, after all, the mythic and archetypal knowledge that sees us through. A very wise Southern poet, himself of Scots-Irish descent, perhaps said it best in our own century:

> *Where are no griefs, can be no joys!*
> *Happy the land where men hold dear*
> *Myth that is truest memory,*
> *Prophecy that is poetry.*

As a people, we are not likely to have the superficial response resting on an exclusively material present, or the easy glib answer, or the blind, giddy, and smiling optimism that Europeans recognize as so typically American—a superficiality and glibness that denies fundamental realities and ends up, at best, fooling only itself. The occasional Southerner, remembering grief too deeply, may even go so far as to be wholly resigned to defeat, and then it becomes close to a fatal gift. But most of us fortunately achieve the balance of the old symmetry and wholeness, of the Horatian mean, whose wisdom of the Middle Ground had been inscribed on the great temple at Delphi—those traits of "moderation in all things" which William and Catharine Hardy so well exemplified in this family chronicle.

The other motto at Delphi, γνῶθι σαυτόν, "Know thyself"—that is, "Know your place before God," "Know that you are merely mortal"—also remains at the center of Southern thinking. There are bounds to man's achieving just as there should be to his desiring. No real faith is thus to be placed in the machine as savior or in technology as panacea. Above all, through acceptance of sorrow and defeat, the Southerner has learned from his cultural and historical experience that a man cannot do anything he sets his mind to, simply because he wills it and works hard enough for it—cannot, in other words, play the role of God, preempting the throne of the Creator. Such "innocence" is not his. The agrarian experiences of droughts and crop failures in their humble (and humbling) ways have taught such basic truths. As farming people, we have been well prepared for this revelation, for a life on the land usually leads eventually to this part of primary wisdom; and on the Southern land of memories, it is doubly certain.

At times the ruined land itself wears the aspect of grief to reinforce this truth, to which, in these moments and in these places, the only proper response is tears. In a more settled state, the viewer must vow understanding, involvement, and responsible action even in the face of what may very well be sure and certain defeat. He must take his comfort and hope from the smallest triumphs in the humblest details of the day-to-day.

Each Southerner learns the story of these pages in his own vocabulary. Though the family name changes, and the place, it is still essentially the same chronicle. Whether early or late, its truths are more often than not inevitable for him, and often they are felt before they are known. Such are the revelatory springs of place. At birth, by virtue of an inheritance in the soil, a great and priceless gift spreads both behind and before him, demonstrating the significance of such particular narratives as this, for the story of this family, echoing countless others, is a chronicle of his civilization, and the story of us all.

That is perhaps, after all, then, what our far-flung visitors seek, albeit unknowingly.

When Demeter gave mankind the art of agriculture on the fertile plains of Eleusis, she also taught that in the dead husk of the seed is the kernel of life, that life and death are but parts of a whole, and inextricably yoked. In a sense, the living feed the dead and are in turn fed by them in the cycle of existence. And so too, as the ancient Greek rites for the dead so realistically and bluntly express it, "The earth which fed you, now will eat you." If the earth is abused and neglected to the point of exhaustion, it will no longer feed and sustain, will eat but not feed, and the cycle be broken. So too will our spirit and humanity be shriveled and lost.

Just as true today as it was in the South Carolina of 1937, where and when it was written, is this wise conclusion about choices: "The modern boasted progress of the South is valiant, but it is not especially interesting; for no material greatness can ever satisfy the heart, which will keep on yearning over romance. It cannot live by material bread alone." Although the word "bread" has too positive a connotation in light of destructive and sterile technology and the life-denying abstraction to which it inevitably leads, this quotation, in its simplicity, does serve to sum up the whole matter. Nearly a hundred years before this particular statement was being made in Carolina, another native son had declared in the face of burgeoning industrialization and the new worship of technology: "The powers of steam—railroads—the capacity to overcome time and space, are wonderful things,—but they are not virtues, nor duties, nor laws, nor affections. I do not believe that all the steam power in the world can bring happiness to one poor human heart. Still less can I believe that all the railroads in the world can carry one poor soul to heaven. . . . The nation whose sons shrink from the culture of its fields will wither for long ages under the imperial sway of iron." Both these authors' assessments, spanning two centuries, stem from the traditional agrarian wisdom of the South, the birthright of all true children of this Southern soil.

In 1843 this same Carolinian of the last century also offered a wise alternative to the mechanizing of life: "We must concentrate our energies upon the little spot in which we take up our abodes, and, in making that lovely to the mind, we shall discover in it abundant resources to satisfy all the mind's desires." This is the essential wisdom of what he called "our home desires" and the key to preventing the hardening of man and his world into Iron.

The great Southern Nobel laureate William Faulkner understood this concept well and drew his strength from his native soil, never deserting it for more "glamorous" locales. His final comments on the modern American machine culture are pertinent here: "Maybe a group of Dismal Swamp or Florida Everglades Abolitionists will decide to free the country from machines." As he well knew, slavery comes in a variety of forms, and the worst of all is to bear shackles and not know it.

In Greece itself, Demeter's once-generous fields of Eleusis have themselves become a profane monument to the machine; an alien jumble of American-style commerce, oil companies, congested traffic, and old-car graveyards. Pomegranate and pine, grain, cypress, grape, and olive have all given way to asphalt and concrete. The haze of pollution from the nearby city of Athens hangs heavy over the land, eats away at its marble temples, and obscures the bright heavens where once resided a people's gods. "Home desires" have given way to foreign notions. The blue-green hills and valley of Tyger, while no longer crowned by the agricultural glory of fertile farms, still bear no such curse as that, for such sterility and violation of nature are the true modern curse of an industrial disorder—a world crazily out of balance.

For the Tyger, there is hope to move resolutely against the current of the times, in that its old gods are not yet totally departed. Its genius loci is still strong and broodingly discernible. Being half forgotten by the machine culture of the twentieth century and its version of barren consumerism and progress, the spirit of this quiet land has been spared. It has been blessed in its way by modern neglect, and thus half preserved, its potential for flourishing in proper manner in the new century dawning, thus protected in fragile balance. The realization of such a happy future rests in the inspired understanding of the living, nourished by the strong presence of all the deep-rooted dead who came in procession before us, and whose chronicle and romance can in the final analysis work better to satisfy the heart and give truer wisdom and more meaningful life than the false promise of a strictly material wealth.

While good in their own proscribed right, the machine culture's empirical fact and scientific knowledge can never bring satisfaction beyond the animal comforts. Modern man must relearn the limitations of the strictly empirical—and, more importantly, of himself. Sometimes his true progress should be measured not by what he does, but by what he chooses not to do, not by indulging but denying, not by striving to find all the answers but by tolerating the questions. Forbearance and denial of self, sadly, have become forgotten virtues. So has modesty. To realize the tragic gulf between cultures, we have only to recall William Eppes Hardy's wise letter to his son on the subject in 1854 and then measure the values of our own day against his. Such a comparison reveals that our time has not progressed but seems to have slid into relative barbarism. The real choice then, in a sense, still rests between the traditional Southern genius of a farming people, possessed from colonial times onward—a genius that through sweat and diligence creates the pleasant and familiar farm landscape of a fertile valley set passively in nature and within its rhythms, and not in violation of them—and the starkly contrasting modern urban nightmare of colonial governor Winthrop's coldly gleaming, impersonal, sterile, aggressive City on a Hill, a city that is always, after all, most attractive from a safe and shimmering distance. The latter is in essence but a man-willed and artificial landscape, where nature and her rhythms are at best irrelevant to man's constant *doing* in the holy name of progress, and at worst made war upon and violated.

The choice finally rests between the laying of hands directly and personally upon life (that is, the familiar and personal response to the particular) and the diminished possibilities of modern intellectual detachment (either of the clinically empirical or the scientifically abstract) that will always put a premium upon price rather than place and will find its home casually wherever monetary wealth, ease of position, or power exist most conveniently.

The wise chooser would strongly resist the abstraction that would further transform the Puritan City on a Hill into the even more impersonal World City of America, or Global Village—the nightmare at its most intense—and adhere instead to the regional, the local, the familiar, the personal, and the natural, where long associations exist that are local, familiar, personal, and natural.

Of our century, the wise Southern poet Donald Davidson wrote so truthfully:

> Few now are left who know the ancient rule
> That tame abstract must wed the wild particular.

Indeed, as Carolinians of the last century knew so much better than those of our own day, to live a life of completeness, a mortal must fully concentrate his being upon one finite place on earth and know it both tactilely and spiritually in all the fullness of the seasons, know all the creatures of that place who move there in the night world as well as the day. He must know its story and the interwoven chronicles of the human hearts and hands that have touched land and made impress on that place. He must hear the truths of its past. Only then will he approach understanding, and only this will ensure against abuse.

Such a full life on the land is a complicated dance with its own satisfying rhythms, in motions that circle and do not move relentlessly in single linear progressive thrust like the arrow. Dancers do not have to get somewhere, but instead turn and circle, never concerning themselves to go further than they began. It is the pleasure in the thing, in the dance itself, of how one gets back to where one started, that matters. And this is most surely a perfect echo of the traditional old Southern definition of success itself, as expressed in our chronicle: "the *how* not the *how much* or *how far* of achievement." From the start, as we have seen, the Hardys, indeed most of our Southern family, have taken joy in the literal dance. Our Southern home has been from its beginning, and still remains, a land of music. The visitors from the furthest distances seem to recognize this fact the most readily. In a broader, more significant way, our rhythmical existence on the land has itself been a kind of music, woven in harmony with natural rhythms played out under the mirrored wheeling of constellations. Cultures that forbid dancing should be immediately suspect; there is something at their base that is misshapen and terribly wrong. Unlike another early culture formed to the thoughts of Winthrop and Mather, our Southern valley ideal never forbade or foreswore the strains of lively fiddle and banjo, always welcomed the rhythmical sweep and shuffle of feet in both reel and buck-and-wing. Indeed, as the old phrase tells us, "There is music in our shuffling feet." The music of the South, long may it be played! May it sing loud the joys of familiarity and the pleasures of place; may it long celebrate memories and old associations, linked inextricably with new life and love. Let it sound loud even above the noise of city crowds of sour and long-faced Puritan achievers who have neither time, patience, nor desire for such impracticality in their hurry for linear "progress" and false achievement. I make my stand on Southern soil, and with feet at least capable of keeping time.

I leave you now with the voices of these shadow people out of the past to echo in the living flesh, and with the abiding memory of those who loved this soil and played their parts in this story—the fire of their blood rekindled in our own living blood, and the salt of their sweat in the salt taste of August from the living brows of honest labor in the fields of harvest. I leave you with the night air smelling of rich new-turned loam and alive with the music of yet another Southern spring—the liquid, close notes of the whippoorwill, the steady concentrated buzz-and-hum monotone of humble cricket and rain frog, the far-off sounds of beagles on a chase, and above them all the crowning joyous night-song of the Southern nightingale from her high home in the sheltering, flower-heavy branches of the Great Southern Laurel as it comes into bloom in May. As long as these have attractions for us, there still remains hope for the right choices, for as surely as this book is, so is the future in our hands.

We can take certain comfort in the fact that our hands will not have to turn the further, new pages of this chronicle-adventure alone, and without guidance. All the truths of this story suffuse our shared world and serve as guides in uncharted personal landscapes, for there have been many who have walked these same pathways before us, formed these same stories into other words—written or spoken or felt in the blood—and danced to these very same rhythms.

Perhaps the poet of the Mincio, in his great celebration of the virtues of good and proper work on the good land, and of a good life based thereon, has bequeathed us our most hopeful vision of a future of right choices and higher understanding. It is he who walks so firmly and joyfully in that path before us, saying quietly and assuringly: "When once thou shalt be able now to read the glories of heroes and thy father's deeds, and to know virtue as she is, slowly the plain shall grow golden with the soft corn-spike, and the reddening grape trail from the wild briar, and hard oaks drip dew of honey."

Or in simpler, less poetic frame of mind, and with the practical faith of pioneer mothers and fathers of nations, may we recall Marcus Cato's solemn admonition to keep our ploughs and ploughstocks always ready and in good condition for better days:

Aratra vomeresque facito uti bono habeas.

NOTES AND SOURCES

CHAPTER 1: A LAND CALLED AMOY-ÉS-CHEK

Pp. 4–5: Early descriptions of the Tyger valley are based on John Logan, *A History of the Upper Country of South Carolina* (Charleston, S.C., 1859), pp. 22–25; David Ramsay, *History of South Carolina* (Newberry, S.C., 1858); and Robert Mills, *Statistics of South Carolina* (Charleston, S.C., 1826). The description of the eagle derives from Mills (p. 647); that of the last tiger, from Leland Summer, *Newberry County, S.C., Historical and Genealogical* (Newberry, S.C., 1950), p. 6. See also Robert L. Meriwether, *The Expansion of South Carolina, 1729–1765* (Kingsport, Tenn., 1940). The "panther" referred to in the opening section is *Felis concolor.*

P. 6: The Hardy plat description comes from deeds owned by Haywood Hardy Henderson and William Dixon Hardy Jr.

P. 6: *"Pick-Nick":* As recorded in Garrie Douglass's letterbook, 1859–1862, South Caroliniana Library, University of South Carolina.

P. 7: *O'Neall:* John Belton O'Neall, *The Annals of Newberry* (Charleston, S.C., 1859), p. 163. The sections of the *Annals* used in this chapter were written in 1850.

P. 7: Information from William Dixon Hardy (1841–1932) comes from a typescript interview made by Eva Thurston Clark Justice, spring 1932, and in the possession of Haywood Hardy Henderson, with a copy in the Hardy Plantation Archives.

P. 7: *sidesaddle:* This continued to be the way the womenfolk of the family traveled into the new century. Nancy Hardy Shell, the old pioneer's daughter-in-law, left a "woman's saddle" in her estate when she died in 1818. Her own horse, Jack, she provided for carefully, stipulating that it should go to her eldest son. See the Will and Estate Settlement of Nancy Shell, Newberry County Probate Court Records, Newberry, S.C.

P. 7: *knoll:* The site of the original cabin was to the southeast of the present house, as remembered by Mr. and Mrs. John Frost Hardy Sr. in 1959 and in turn recalled by their grandson John Hardy III in an interview with the author on 14 June 1992, in the Hardy Plantation Archives.

Pp. 8–9: The leHardi-deHardie-DeHardie and other early European genealogy comes from Adelle Bartlett Harper, *Family Lines* (Atlanta, 1973) pp. 307–29. Later European lines and records of the family in Virginia come from Harper, Hardy family manuscript records (photocopies of which are owned by the author), and Landon Bell's three books: *Sunlight on the Southside: Lunenburg County, Virginia, 1748–1783* (Richmond, 1930); *Cumberland Parish, Lunenburg County, Virginia, 1746–1816* (Baltimore, 1974); and *The Old Free State: A Contribution to the History of Lunenburg County* (Richmond, 1927), vol. 2, pp. 216–80. For the record of the family in Isle of Wight, Virginia, see Gary Parks, *Virginia Land Records* (Baltimore, 1932), pp. 167, 169, 175. Bell was himself a Hardy descendant and was thus privy to much important Hardy family material; however, he includes nothing on the Hardys of the Tyger valley, about whom he was likely uninformed. For their history in South Carolina, I have used the William Eppes Hardy family Bible; an unpublished genealogy compiled by Gertrude K. Sims, c. 1930; and newspaper clippings c. 1920–1980 in a scrapbook kept by Alice Hardy (Mrs. John Frost Hardy) and now in the possession of her grandson. The South Carolina materials date back as far as the 1600s and corroborate the Bell records. I have found no major discrepancies among the various accounts. Recent significant genealogical help has been kindly provided me by Carol Hardy Bryan, Edgefield, S.C., and Anne Hardy Tennent Cecil of Spartanburg, S.C. The William Eppes Hardy Bible (signed by him 8 December 1843) states that the family moved to South Carolina around 1783 or 1784. I have settled on 1785, considering the hard evidence of land purchase in 1786.

P. 8: *French Hardys:* M. Hippolyte Leon Hardy, as quoted in H. Claude Hardy, *Hardy and Hardie: Past and Present* (Candia, N.H., 1935), pp. 3–4.

P. 8: *Dorset and Westmorland:* See Claude Hardy, *Hardy and Hardie,* p. 12. There were Hardys in these counties in the census records of the 1400s and 1500s. There are many Hardys listed on the parish registers dating to 1500.

P. 8: For the English line of descent, see Browning's *Magna Carta Barons,* pp. 163, 92, 100, 114, 186, 215, 160; Browning's *Americans of Royal Descent,* p. 35; and Burke's *Peerage and Baronetage* (1904), p. 463.

P. 9: Thomas and Phoebe Hardy, said to be "of Nottoway Parish Amelia County," sold a 200-acre "plantation" tract "in Nottoway Parish and Amelia, and bounded by the Woody Creek," to Francis Drinkard of Dinwiddie County for a sum of £155 on 24 March 1768. Information provided by Carol Hardy Bryan.

P. 10: Information on the Dixon family of Virginia and North Carolina is from Mrs. Darlene Bolton of Overland Park, Kansas, and Dr. George Douglass of Charleston, S.C. These records are now in the Hardy Plantation Archives.

CHAPTER 2: THE SWEET FIELDS OF EDEN

Pp. 12–13: Both Robert Mills in his *Statistics of South Carolina* (Charleston, S.C., 1826) and John Logan in his *History of the Upper Country of South Carolina* (Charleston, S.C., 1859) list some of the trees of the Tyger valley in the county.

P. 13: The description of the Hardys' journey to South Carolina comes from William Dixon Hardy, as recalled to Eva Justice in spring 1932. The William Eppes Hardy family Bible corroborates the names and ages of the travelers as he gave them in 1932.

Pp. 13–14: The Lisles-Lyles and Maybin family histories come from John Belton O'Neall, *The Annals of Newberry* (Charleston, S.C., 1859), and Leland Summer's *Newberry County S.C., Historical and Genealogical* (Newberry, S.C., 1950).

P. 15: For the Eppes family in Lunenburg, see Landon Bell, *The Old Free State: A Contribution to the History of Lunenburg County* (Richmond, 1927), vol. 2.

P. 16: Description of the Hardy cabin is from William Dixon Hardy's interview with Justice.

P. 16: *Tyger was navigable:* O'Neall reported that the Tyger was one of the rivers used extensively for commerce out of the mountains, so it was an artery above the falls as well: "The Enoree and Tyger furnishes a navigation for mountain boats, whereby most of the produce raised sought, and still [in 1850] seeks, a market" (p. 150). The Hardys launched their batteau from near Gordon's Bridge. In the Hardy plantation ledger for 1842–1846, it is noted that hauling by wagon is done to and from Gordon's Bridge for receiving or sending goods via the river. Original plantation ledger is owned by William Dixon Hardy Jr., with a copy in the Hardy Plantation Archives.

Pp. 17–21: These inventories are in the Newberry County Probate Court Records. Copies are in the Hardy Plantation Archives.

P. 18: For Rutherford's gin, see Thomas H. Pope, *History of Newberry County, 1749–1860* (Columbia, S.C., 1973), vol. 1, p. 73.

P. 18: *Mills's estimate:* From Robert Mills, *Statistics of South Carolina* (Charleston, S.C., 1826).

P. 20: The sales ledger for Orange Hall store (1821–1838) is in the South Caroliniana Library, University of South Carolina.

P. 20: *Edgefield pottery:* The pieces found at the plantation are green with dark brown looped decorations, rather typical of the Edgefield ware of the 1840s. Other alkaline-glaze shards come in a variety of clays, colors, and types that cannot be attributed at present. Some bear affinities with Union County pottery, only now being studied.

Pp. 21–22: These plantation statistics come from the U.S. census and slave schedules for 1850 and 1860.

Chapter 3: A Brave New Century

P. 23: *flatboats:* They could carry as many as sixty 400-pound bales of cotton. A smaller vessel for crossing at shoals was called a batteau, a word still used in the area by Sarah Stokes, Bert Kennedy, and others. Former slave Richard Jones described using the batteau with oars on Broad River in the antebellum era.

P. 24: *the Dixons:* The Dixons and Hardys were members of the same Episcopal church in Lunenburg. William Hardy and Robert Dixon were, in fact, fellow vestrymen in 1781. See Landon Bell, *Cumberland Parish, Lunenburg County, Virginia, 1746–1816* (Baltimore, 1974) pp. 28, 30, 241, 250, 436.

P. 25: *recalled in 1932:* Typescript interview in possession of Haywood Hardy Henderson; copy in the Hardy Plantation Archives.

P. 25: *central walkway:* From my interview with John Hardy III, 14 June 1992; copy in Hardy Plantation Archives.

P. 26: *stairwell:* From my interview with Haywood Hardy Henderson, 6 August 1989; copy in Hardy Plantation Archives.

P. 26: *remaining upstairs room:* As recalled in my interview with John Hardy III, 14 June 1992. In the 1950s and '60s John Frost Hardy Sr. used this room for curing hams. Earlier in the century Frank Hardy was said to have stored his homemade scuppernong wine and moonshine in it. Ball jars of the latter reached nearly to the ceiling. A diagram of a still worm still exists, penciled on the plaster walls, no doubt the handiwork of Squire Frank.

P. 27: *Asbury:* Asbury refers to his sojourn with the Hardys in his *Journal and Letters,* ed. Elmer T. Clark (London, n.d.), vol. 2, pp. 272, 311. His earliest and most important connections appear to have been Edward Finch and Rev. James Foster, both of whom helped him found Mt. Bethel Academy.

P. 27: *Family tradition:* Author's interview with William Hardy Sr., 5 August 1991; copy in Hardy Plantation Archives.

P. 27: *Covington Hardy's dwelling:* Described in Evelyn Arvin, *Ante-Bellum Homes of Lunenburg* (Richmond, 1969), 160. Covington Hardy was Thomas Hardy Sr.'s brother's son, thus Thomas's nephew. Lunenburg's Methodism is said to "have had its birth here." Asbury held his first meeting in the home's granary; then Covington donated the land on which the members built their church.

CHAPTER 4: MORE GOLD THAN GRACE

P. 30: *Waddel:* Contrary to the current widespread spelling and pronunciation of his name, Moses himself spelled it with one *l* and accented the first syllable.

P. 30: *Mt. Bethel:* David Ramsay, *History of South Carolina* (Newberry, S.C., 1858), vol. 2, p. 205; Phoebe Schumpert Singley, "A Survey of Education in Newberry County, S.C., Prior to 1870." Master's Thesis, University of South Carolina, 1934, pp. 33–40.

P. 30: *Charleston City Gazette* of 4 December 1812.

P. 30: The list of appraisement for Lemmon Shell's estate is dated 5 November 1814. The sale occurred on 21 December 1814. It is in the list of sales that his books are enumerated. Newberry County Probate Records, and a copy in the Hardy Plantation Archives.

P. 31: *Mills:* In his *Statistics of South Carolina* (Charleston, S.C., 1826), p. 653.

P. 31: *Stephen Shell Sr.:* Shell was an important supporter of Mt. Bethel. Francis Asbury's *Journal and Letters,* ed. Elmer T. Clark (London, n.d.), vol. 2, frequently shows his home to be a stop on Asbury's travels in conjunction with the bishop's work with Mt. Bethel. In Shell's estate appraisement of December 1822, an extensive library is listed by title. Newberry County Probate Court Records, box 52, folder 10.

P. 31: *"proper English Education":* As quoted in his will dated September 1814, Newberry County Probate Court Records.

P. 31: *Thomas Shell Sr.:* For more about Thomas, see Thomas H. Pope, *History of Newberry County, 1749–1860* (Columbia, S.C., 1973), vol. 1, pp. 93, 238, 262.

P. 31: *Precious Shell's estate:* The appraisement lists of 1828 and 1836 are in Newberry County Probate Records, box 53, folder 5; box 69, folder 14. They list the titles.

P. 32: These bills for the children's schooling are listed by year in "Settlement on the Estate of John Wesley Hardy," 1806–1821. Newberry County Probate Court Records; copy in the Hardy Plantation Archives.

Pp. 32–33: For the transfer of slaves from Nancy Shell to her son, see "Settlement on the Estate" by Dr. Curtis Atwood, 7 April 1826. Nancy Shell's will left settlement of her estate until William Eppes Hardy "came of age," hence 1825. Until this time (that is from 1818 to 1825), the slaves were "hired" at various times to neighbors and family: to William Beard, James E. Shell, David Lavender, John Hatton, Robert McCullough, Isham Shell, Asbury Shell, Isaac King, Dr. Curtis Atwood, Hugh Wilson, Dr. James Shell, and Dr. Thomas Shell. In this way, they were not sold and could remain in the family. All documents are from Newberry County Probate Court Records; copies in the Hardy Plantation Archives.

P. 32: *a slave named Ben:* William Eppes Hardy's Ben must have been a highly valued man. In 1818 he was appraised at $1,000 (around $20,000 in today's currency). The other values given are Delphy, $600, Fanny, $300; James, $300; and Guinea, $550. Newberry County Probate Court Records; copy in the Hardy Plantation Archives.

P. 32: *maidservant, named Guinea:* Even in sketchiest outline, Guinea's story is an interesting one. She chose eight-year-old Charles Wesley Shell, who was under the guardianship of his half brother Thomas Shell. Thomas Shell was studying medicine with Dr. Burr Johnstone of Newberry. The three all probably went to the Johnstone household, for it was Job Johnstone who purchased Guinea in 1818 for $636; the sum went to Charles Wesley Shell. This transaction was likely a step up for both the Shells and Guinea, for Chancellor Johnstone was among the wealthiest and most important citizens in the county seat at the time, and the style of life in his household was impressive. For Guinea's sale to Johnstone, see "Sale Bill of Estate of Nancy Shell," 10 November 1818, Newberry County Probate Court Records.

Pp. 32–34: The list of purchases for 1806 through 1821 for the sons of John Wesley Hardy are recorded in "Settlement on the Estate of John W. Hardy," 1806–1821, Newberry County Probate Court Records. The details of purchases in this section all come from these documents, copies of which are in the Hardy Plantation Archives. For John Wesley Hardy's will, dated 12 July 1806, see these records.

P. 34: *Shell & Hatton:* A Maj. John Hatton (1794–1847), listed earlier as a hirer of William Eppes Hardy's Ben, lived near the Shells and Eppeses near present-day Whitmire, Newberry County.

P. 34: *higher aspirations:* As reported by James Hardy's grandson, Gaillard Tennent, in his pamphlet *Medicine in Buncombe County* (Charlotte, N.C., 1906), p. 8.

P. 34: *purchasing from Orange Hall:* Orange Hall ledger 1821–1838, South Caroliniana Library, University of South Carolina. This ledger records purchases from the store and gives occasional facts from the plantation's farming and blacksmithing operations. The details of purchases from Orange Hall in this section are all from this source.

P. 34: *Grief:* This peculiar name was common enough among both blacks and whites of this particular community. See, for example, Grief Crenshaw in "Settlement on the Estate of John W. Hardy," 1806–1821, Newberry County Probate Court Records.

P. 35: *Rev. George Clarke:* In the minutes of the Methodist Synod of 1874, Clarke was described as having been made a Methodist preacher in 1792. He traveled some years in the Conference but located on the Enoree River in Newberry County. He was noted as having "respectable preaching talents, and was esteemed by neighbors and the public generally. Social and pleasant in his manners, all were at ease in his company. He was plain in his dress, though a man of considerable wealth." He gave the land for the second Ebenezer Church building in Maybinton in 1848. The 1874 minutes record that "the cause of Methodism in the County was much aided by his influence and talents. He lived to an advanced age."

P. 35: Information on Hardy at Asheville Academy comes from Lillian A. Kibler, *Benjamin F. Perry, South Carolina Unionist* (Durham, 1946), pp. 34–37. Perry refers to Hardy in his manuscript autobiography of 1874 (pp. 129, 221). In the Perry Papers at Alabama Archives in Montgomery, there are two letters from Hardy to Perry, dated 25 June and 2 July 1835. Three letters of Montraville Patton to Perry (15 October 1824; 17 February, 27 May 1825) were in the possession of Mrs. Sam Rice Baker in 1946 and are unlocated. These no doubt have references to Hardy's marriage to Jane Patton on 23 December 1824.

P. 35: The reasons for James Hardy's move to Asheville are given in Ella R. Matthews, "William Henry Hardy," unpublished typescript dated September 1935, Pack Memorial Library, Asheville, N.C.; and a copy in the Hardy Plantation Archives. The Phillips connection is reported in Gaillard Tennent, *Medicine in Buncombe County,* p. 8.

P. 36: *"finest residence":* Located at the southwest corner of Eagle and Main. Described by John Preston Arthur, *History of Western North Carolina* (n.p., 1914), pp. 504, 149. The house was demolished in 1905.

P. 36: Letter from Dr. James Hardy to William Eppes Hardy, Asheville, 19 February 1832. Original owned by William Hardy Jr.; copy in the Hardy Plantation Archives.

P. 36: *Ashevillians in the early century:* Guion Johnson, *Ante-bellum North Carolina* (Chapel Hill, N.C., 1937), pp. 749, 751; Foster Alexander Sondley, *A History of Buncombe County, North Carolina* (Asheville, N.C., 1930), vol. 2, p. 713; Ella Matthews, "William Henry Hardy"; and Gaillard Tennent, *Medicine in Buncombe County,* p. 8.

P. 36: *upper South Carolina:* Manuscript letter of Dr. James Hardy to William Eppes Hardy, 19 February 1832. Original in the Hardy Plantation Archives.

P. 37: Hardy's finances and purchases are given in a manuscript letter of Dr. James Hardy to William Eppes Hardy, Asheville, 19 January 1833. Original owned by William Hardy Jr.; copy in Hardy Plantation Archives.

P. 37: Hardy's comments on nullification are in a manuscript letter of Dr. James Hardy to William Eppes Hardy, Asheville, 16 September 1832. Original owned by William Hardy Jr.; copy in the Hardy Plantation Archives.

P. 38: Manuscript letter of William Eppes Hardy to James Hardy, Maybinton, 25 September 1832. Original in the Hardy Plantation Archives.

P. 38: *business trip West:* See letter of Dr. James Hardy to William Eppes Hardy, Asheville, 19 February 1832. Original owned by William Hardy Jr.; copy in the Hardy Plantation Archives.

P. 38: *Dickson:* It was Dr. Hardy who likely brought Dickson to the banks of the Swannanoa. Dickson (1798–1872), like Hardy, suffered from poor lungs and soon celebrated the area as the healthiest spot in America. Samuel's brother, Dr. John Dickson (born in Charleston in 1795, a graduate of Yale in 1814, and pastor of the Asheville Presbyterian Church from 1843 to 1845) also came to Asheville for his health around 1836. He died in 1847 after building "Middleton," and opening a school there. See Gaillard Tennent, pp. 10–11. The letter quoted here is from Dr. Hardy to William Eppes Hardy, Asheville, 3 March 1836. He also refers to Dickson in a letter to his brother dated 13 October [1833]. Both letters are owned by William Hardy Jr., with copies in the Hardy Plantation Archives. Dr. Hardy also sold 20 acres to Charlestonian Elizabeth C. Trescott on 18 July 1844.

P. 39: *March 1836:* Two letters of Dr. Hardy to William Eppes Hardy from

Washington on 3 and 17 March 1836, both owned by William Hardy Jr., with copies in the Hardy Plantation Archives. Dr. Hardy was back in Asheville by late September 1836. He wrote his brother from Asheville on 3 October 1836.

P. 40: For some of Dr. Hardy's many services, see Sondley, *History of Buncombe County,* vol. 2, pp. 639, 658, 707, 713, 721, 738, 748, 790.

P. 40: *Asheville Temperance Society:* Hardy's address on 4 July 1832 before the Society was printed in pamphlet form at Rutherfordton, N.C., in 1832. The title page lists Hardy as president of the society. In his speech he said, "The continuation of our liberty, must depend on the purity of our elective franchise," and thus temperance is a means to "perpetuate this inheritance of liberty."

P. 40: On Jane Patton Hardy's death, see *The Biography of James Patton,* a pamphlet in the Pack Memorial Library, Asheville, N.C., p. xiv. Patton's autobiography, incorporated in the Patton biography, and the source of my facts on the Pattons, was written in 1840. Copy in the Hardy Plantation Archives. Birth, death, and marriage dates are from Dr. J. F. E. Hardy's Bible, recorded there in his hand. Bible owned by descendant Charles H. Tennent, Simpsonville, S.C.

P. 40: For Hardy's new house, see Arthur, *History of Western North Carolina,* pp. 504, 149.

P. 41: *Hardy boxwood gardens:* Referred to in William Dixon Hardy's interview with Eva Justice in 1932. Manuscript interview in possession of Haywood Hardy Henderson, copy in the Hardy Plantation Archives.

P. 41: *Pomaria Nurseries:* See Linda Weathers, "Digging Into Gardens Past . . . an Antebellum Nursery Called Pomaria," *Southern Accents,* 15, no. 7 (September 1992) 88–92; and James Kibler, "On Reclaiming a Southern Antebellum Garden Heritage: An Introduction to Pomaria Nurseries, 1840–1879," *Magnolia: Bulletin of the Southern Garden History Society,* 10 (Fall 1993), pp. 1–12. The three nursery ledgers are housed at Pomaria plantation, Pomaria, S.C., the South Caroliniana Library, and the Hardy Plantation Archives.

P. 41: For Hardy's legendary hospitality, see Arthur, *History of Western North Carolina,* pp, 504–505, and Ella Matthews' 1935 reminiscence at Pack Memorial Library (p. 2). An *Asheville News* article of 1860 by Hon. J. L. Clingman thanks Dr. Hardy for "many kind services" (Reprinted in Sondley, *History of Buncombe County,* vol. 2, p. 790.)

P. 41: *"manner of a lord":* Arthur, *History of Western North Carolina,* p. 504.

P. 42: For the Charles Edward Tennent family, see *Asheville Citizen* (30 October 1953). Charles Tennent was born in 1812, his wife in 1828. They moved to Asheville in the early 1850s. Capt. James Albert Tennent (1842–1916) moved to Buncombe County in 1871. Gilbert B. Tennent married James's daughter Emma. See Gaillard Tennent, pp. 8–9. The brick house was demolished around 1904.

P. 43: *walking cane:* This relic is displayed on the second floor of the Confederate Relic Room and Museum, Columbia, S.C. Young Hardy's name appears on the Palmetto Monument erected on the statehouse grounds in Columbia during the antebellum era.

P. 44: For Dixon family history, including birth and date dates, I am indebted to Mrs. Darlene Bolton, Overland Park, Kans., and Dr. George Douglass, Charleston, S.C.

P. 44: Letter of 17 November 1832 in the possession of William Hardy Jr.; copy in the Hardy Plantation Archives.

P. 47: For the original transcript of Anna Hardy's will, see the Renwick papers, South Caroliniana Library, University of South Carolina. For more information on the two extant Scarborough portraits, see p. 76 of this work and note.

P. 48: *Family tradition . . . 1825:* This date was given by William Dixon Hardy (1841–1932) in his 1932 interview with Eva Justice.

P. 48: *Pomaria:* The date was given by Marie Summer Huggins in an interview with the author on 21 December 1970. Complete interview in the Hardy Plantation Archives.

P. 49: *John Jennings:* As reported in the Hardy-Douglass family Bible.

P. 51: Letter of William Eppes Hardy to Dr. James Hardy, Maybinton, 8 October 1829. Original in the Hardy Plantation Archives.

Pp. 53–55: Originals of the Willey and Gordon letters are in the Hardy Plantation Archives.

P. 55: *Sims Estate:* The land bought bounded on lands of Mrs. Lavinia Stewart, Samuel Kenner, a parcel of 613 acres sold at the same time to Dr. James B. Davis of Union District, the lands of Wm. E. Hardy, and lands formerly belonging to the estate of Reuben Sims, but now owned by John Lyles.

P. 57: *As one Carolinian noted:* W. G. Simms in *The Golden Christmas* (Charleston, 1851).

P. 57: *Singin' Billy Walker:* William Walker, born on 6 May 1809, was a close contemporary of William Eppes Hardy and his wife. Walker published his famous *Southern Harmony* in Spartanburg in 1834. This was to become the classic of the old-time Southern church music in the "shape note" tradition. It was likely the form of music used at the Hardys' own Ebenezer Methodist Church. Walker died in Spartanburg in 1875 at the same age as William Eppes Hardy.

P. 58: *saying their 'howdies':* The popular mode of address for blacks and whites alike. See Sallie Beard's letters to her Rogers cousins at Orange Hall, Renwick papers, South Caroliniana Library, University of South Carolina.

Pp. 57–58: The description of the courtship and marriage is from the descendants of George and Frances Douglass before 1936 and recorded by Caldwell Sims for WPA Project #1885 in April 1936. The preliminary informants were Ben Hardy and Fannie and J. D. Epps.

P. 60: *conscious link to . . . Classicism:* A local agriculturist from nearby Pomaria wrote in 1852 that the common architecture "which lines our public roads" in upcountry Carolina is of "white, be-porticoed attempts at Villas." His statement lends credence to the assertion that the link to Classicism was conscious and clearly understood and intended. In his essay he also attacks the related study of Virgil's *Bucolics* and *Georgics* at the expense of a practical agricultural education, thus rightly tying this villa architecture to classical ideals. A. G. Summer, *Anniversary Address Delivered before the Southern Central Agricultural Society* (Augusta, Ga., 1853), p. 11.

P. 60: *"snow of Southern summers"*: The phrase is from South Carolina poet Henry Timrod in his poem "The Cotton Bowl," written in 1861.

CHAPTER 5: PATERFAMILIAS

P. 62: *black bondsmen:* Hardy's former slave Pick Gladdeny called him all four in George P. Rawick, ed. *The American Slave* (Westport, Conn., 1972), vol. 2, pt. 2, pp. 124–28.

P. 62: One of Hardy's young nieces was Miss Garrie Douglass, daughter of George and Frances Hardy Douglass. She made this comment in a letter to her sister Sallie, then at Salem Academy, in February 1859. Taken from Garrie Douglass's letterbook at South Caroliniana Library, University of South Carolina; copy in the Hardy Plantation Archives.

P. 62: The family member (descended from Frances Hardy Douglass) who recalled the book was Robert B. Pasley Jr. of Spartanburg. In a letter to Mrs. G. B. Dyar Jr., 15 April 1965, he wrote: "Mr. Wm. Eppes Hardy wrote a book published in New York on the Hardy Family more than a hundred years ago. John Frost Hardy did have it." (Letter owned by Nelle Hardy Dyar, with a copy in the Hardy Plantation Archives.) Recent information has given the book's date of publication as 8 December 1843 and its New York publisher as Robinson & Franklin. This, however, is the publisher of William Eppes Hardy's Bible and the date he signed it. Hardy penned records in the Bible, and Pasley may be confusing Bible with book.

P. 63: Letter from James Monroe C. Eppes to William Eppes Hardy, in the William Eppes Hardy Collection, Perkins Library, Duke University.

P. 65: Letter from William Eppes Hardy to James Hardy in the collection of William Hardy Sr., with a copy in the Hardy Plantation Archives.

P. 65: *names like Lady Albion, Black Knight:* As recorded in the Hardy Plantation ledger of 1842–1846, in the possession of William Hardy Jr.; and in the plantation ledger of 1836 to 1846, William Eppes Hardy Collection, Perkins Library, Duke University. Copies in the Hardy Plantation Archives.

P. 66: *chairman of the committee:* See *Southern Agriculturist,* 1 (September 1853), pp. 275–76. The meeting was held on 27–28 July and was followed by a great picnic provided by the citizens of the town. John Belton O'Neall presided at the business meeting. In 1966 the silver cup awarded Hardy was still in the family of great-grandson John Hardy of Spartanburg and inscribed "For the Best Sucking Mule, N[ewberry] A[gricultural] S[ociety]." See *Names in South Carolina,* 13 (November 1966), p. 56.

P. 66: The two mule quotations come from Hardy neighbor A. G. Summer in his *Anniversary Address* (Augusta, Ga., 1853) and William Faulkner's *The Reivers* (New York, 1962).

P. 66: The Olmsted quotation is from *A Journey in the Seaboard Slave States* (New York, 1856).

P. 66: *closet . . . well-stocked with wine:* The Great House at Cross Keys also has a very similar room, called a wine–closet.

P. 67: *Jeter's track:* Family tradition as recalled to the author by Margie Young Leaman in an interview of 4 September 1991. Copy in the Hardy Plantation Archives.

P. 67: The apt description of the soil of Goshen Hill comes from *Names in South Carolina,* 13 (November 1966), p. 56.

P. 67: *whiskey:* As recalled by former slave Gus Feaster in Rawick, *The American Slave,* vol. 2, pt. 2, p. 57; and in *Names in South Carolina,* 13 (November 1966), p. 56.

P. 67: *Caldwell descendant:* Family traditions as recalled to the author by Elsie Caldwell Fields, 10 August 1991. Her ancestor John Caldwell hailed from County Antrim, Ireland, and came to the county with the families Renwick and Reid.

P. 67: The Irish author is J. P. Donleavy.

P. 67: *Hardy neighbor:* A. G. Summer, in his *Anniversary Address,* pp. 16–17.

P. 68: George Briggs is quoted from Rawick, *The American Slave,* vol. 2, pt. 1, p. 82.

P. 68: The two jousting lances (called tournament poles) and the stirrups used in "riding tournaments in the olden days" by participant Eldridge Davis of Cross Keys plantation are described in William Rice Feaster, ed. *A History of Union County* (Greenville, S.C., 1977), p. 104. The jousting ground is here said to have been a half-mile south of the Great House.

P. 69: *bill of 1829:* Original in the Hardy Plantation Archives.

P. 70: The quotation from Summer is in his *Anniversary Address,* p. 13.

P. 70: The quotation on pork comes from Summer's *Anniversary Address,* p. 13.

P. 70: *One Carolina planter:* William Gilmore Simms.

P. 71: The purchases from Orange Hall comes from Orange Hall daybook for 1821–1838, South Caroliniana Library, University of South Carolina.

P. 71: Auntie Rachael is listed as a cook for the plantation by William Eppes Hardy. See chapter 9.

P. 71: *stories of the day.* Like most Southerners born and bred in the country, the Hardys were and are still excellent raconteurs.

P. 72: Robert Stokes is quoted from the Columbia, S.C. *Farmer and Planter,* N.S. 2 (December 1860), p. 365.

P. 73: The Gracey receipt is in the possession of Haywood Hardy Henderson, with a copy in the Hardy Plantation Archives. By the 1850s the firm, now called Gracey & Hart, was located at No. 8, Brick Range, Columbia, S.C. It advertised itself as "Dealers in Staple and Fancy Dry Goods." The Gracey firm from the 1830s to the 1850s was one of the favored clothing establishments of several of the families of the Maybinton–Santuc–Goshen Hill area. There are many receipts from Gracey in the William Renwick papers; and Garrie Douglass of The Oaks wrote Gracey for drygoods. The complete Gracey receipt for William Eppes Hardy follows:

Columbia   5 December   1831
John I Gracey & Co.

2 Ladys cloaks		$21.00			
2 ps furniture calico					
56½ yds. @.25		14.12½	1 pc White Silk Hon	3.00	$3.00
1 Bleached shirting			1 Ridicule [Reticule]	1.50	1.50
30¾ yds @.17		5.23	1 yd white Ribleand		.12½
3 yds Blu Cerasham @ .50		1.50	1 bunch Black Cord		.31¼
4 yds White Flannel	.87½	3.50	1 Hooks and Eyes		.25
2 yds Drapen	.50	1.00	1 pr Side Combs		1.25
4 yds Barred Muslin	.50	2.00	1 gr Letter Paper		.31¼
1 yd Mull Muslin	.62½	.62½	1 Bottle Snuff		.37½
2⅞ Linen	1.00	2.87½	1.4 yds White Figured Sattan		
10 yd Silk	1.00	10.00	1.06¼		14.87½
6 yds Black Grosinap	1.50	9.00	1 yd Cambric		.31¼
3 yds Bobinet	.50	1.50	1 yd Milinet		.25
3 yds Cap Riblean	.25	.75	1 Bunch cord		.06¼
1 Black Bobinet Vail		5.00	1 Doz Hooks & Eyes		.06¼
1 linen Cambric					
Handkerchief		1.00	1 pr Buck[skin] Gloves		1.00
2 [?] Handkerchief	.87½	1.75	1 pr Kid Gloves		.75
2 Belt Ribleands	.87½	1.75			

	107.04
By Cash	75.
Balance	32.04

The Hardys also patronized the establishment of William Birge in Columbia. A note of payment dated 23 June 1830 for William Eppes Hardy is marked paid in full and lists the following items purchased:

6 yds of homespun	$1.20
2 cotton handkerchiefs	.50
4 yds of Brde	.25
3 pairs cotton stockings	2.07
a muslin cravat	.31

This note is also in the possession of Haywood Hardy Henderson, with a copy in the Hardy Plantation Archives.

P. 73: To convert dollars to the current values, the formula I have used is 1 to 20. According to *Standard and Poor's Trade and Securities Statistics* (New York, 1994), p. 76, the equivalent of a dollar in 1842 equalled at least $10 in 1982. A fairer equation of 1840 to 1998 would be 1 to 20, according to other sources for comparison.

P. 73: For gray cloth, see letter from Garrie Douglass written in 1862, quoted in chapter 12.

P. 74: The R. C. Anderson receipt is in the William Eppes Hardy Collection, Perkins Library, Duke University.

P. 75: *Four-poster:* The description of this bed comes from an interview with Hardy neighbor Mrs. Margaret King on 14 January 1991. Frank Hardy was still sleeping in this bed in the 1940s. When Mrs. King visited him while sick, "Frank came crawling out from behind the bed curtains."

P. 76: *great-grandchild:* Mrs. Mary Ella Henderson Finlay, in an interview on 21 June 1991.

P. 76: *portrait . . . 1858:* Scarborough's account book is published in Helen Kohn Hennig, *William Harrison Scarborough* (Columbia, S.C., 1937). See page 101 for the Hardy portrait. Hennig mistakenly lists Mrs. Hardy's name as Mary Ann but correctly surmises that there was "probably another portrait" besides the one located with Mrs. Heyward Frost of Columbia (whose husband descended from Catharine Hardy's daughter Elmira Hardy Frost.) This portrait is now owned by Mrs. Beverly Fulmer Kennedy of Columbia, S.C. The Douglass-descended portrait has now been located in the home of a descendant in Raleigh, N.C. A comparison shows the portraits to be exactly the same, even to the frames in which they are hung. These last were made in New York and supplied by Scarborough. A 1934 typescript of Scarborough's unedited and complete account book provides information that the subject was indeed Anna Hardy and notes cash payments.

P. 76: *pianoforte:* Author's interview with Mrs. Haywood Hardy Henderson, 28 August 1989. The story was told to her by Mrs. John Frost Hardy Sr. (Alice Hardy). Interview in the Hardy Plantation Archives.

P. 76: *inventory:* "Appraise Bill of the Goods & Chattels of Wm. E. Hardy," September 1870, and "Sale Bill of the Personal Estate of William E. Hardy," 27 April 1874. Newberry County Probate Court Records, with copies in the Hardy Plantation Archives.

P. 77: According to Haywood Hardy Henderson, the loom and traveler's rooms were used in our century for the cook and servants to take their afternoon naps in.

P. 78: *Villa Cornara:* Pictured as Plate XXXVI and described at p. 50 of the Second Book of the London 1738 edition. The complete work was first published in Venice as *I Quattro Libri dell'Architettura.*

P. 79: *Drayton Hall:* For some brief observations on Palladio's influence in

South Carolina, see Desmond Guinness and Julius Sadler, *Palladio: A Western Progress* (New York, 1976). Interestingly, the Draytons were descended from the DeVere family, Normans who came to England with the le Hardes.

P. 79: *one observer:* A. G. Summer, in 1852 in his *Anniversary Address* (Augusta, Ga., 1853), p. 11. Summer was himself raised at Pomaria, the twin house to the Hardy Great House.

P. 79: *Pomaria:* For the date of the building of Pomaria, I rely on my interview with Mrs. Marie Summer Huggins (1892–1974) on 21 December 1970. She remembered it from her great-aunt Catharine Summer, who, as a girl, was a witness to the construction of the Great House. She dated the construction at 1826–1827. Complete interview in the Hardy Plantation Archives.

P. 79: The quotation from Palladio is from the 1738 English edition of the Second Book, p. 46.

P. 80: *quarrelled . . . notes:* From my interview with Marie Huggins.

P. 81: For the estate sales of John and Amy Shell, see Newberry County Probate Court Records, box 54, folders 11 and 12.

P. 82: *Chick Place:* See chapter 11 for a description of this plantation.

P. 83: *family tradition:* As recalled to the author by Nelle Hardy Dyar, 21 December 1992, and Haywood Hardy Henderson, 25 August 1990. Interviews are in the Hardy Plantation Archives.

P. 83: *bud-and-scroll:* This is the same decoration used at Pomaria. It should be noted that a design somewhat similar to the doorways of both Hardy and Pomaria plantations is depicted in a pattern book by Asher Benjamin, *The Practice of Architecture* (1833); but the documentation of both South Carolina houses points to the fact that the structures predate the pattern book that so popularized the design and thus were not copied from it. The doorway at The Oaks, built in 1840, is, in fact, much closer to the pattern book, having a similar flattened elliptical fanlight. There is no evidence that either Hardy or Pomaria plantation was structurally altered after 1833; and further, it is unlikely they would have been updated in precisely the same way throughout.

P. 84: *circular ceiling medallions:* Interview with Mary Ella Henderson Finlay, 21 June 1991. Mrs. Finlay is the great-granddaughter of William and Catharine Hardy. She was educated in the 1930s at Winthrop College and William and Mary; she received a master's degree at Howard University, Washington, D.C. She returned to South Carolina in 1965 and now lives in Mountville, near Cross Hill. The medallions were also recalled by Haywood Hardy Henderson in an interview with the author, 6 August 1989.

P. 85: *1937 interview with Fannie Epps:* Interview conducted by Caldwell Sims on 2 September 1937, WPA Project #1885–1.

P. 85: For Hollywood plantation, see Leland Summer, *Newberry County, S.C., Historical and Genealogical* (Newberry, S.C.), p. 169. The Great House was built around 1770 "just off the Buncombe Road near Broad River" for Walter

Goodman, a pioneer from Dublin, Ireland, but was enlarged and renovated by later owners in the nineteenth century. It was said to have "beadings and mouldings of plaster" made by William Heffernan. The most comprehensive description of the Great House and its extensive gardens is in Juanita Hitt, *Newton Thomas Hogg* (Newberry, S.C., 1970), pp. 14–15. Its giant fluted chimneys still stand among the house ruins.

P. 86: *J. Murphy:* The Newberry County census for 1850 lists a John Murphy (born 1824) living near Maybinton. He had a wife and three-year-old daughter and a sister, E. Murphy, living in his household. John Finger was listed as an elder in Ebenezer Methodist Church in an undated newspaper article (c. 1960) written by Mrs. Arthur Maybin and entitled "History of Ebenezer." (Copy in the Hardy Plantation Archives.) A slave family, Sally Murphy and her son Pick Gladdeny, came to live with the Hardys in the 1850s. They had belonged to Dave and Betsey Murphy, overseers for Tom Henderson of Lyles Ford in Fairfield County.

P. 86: *Jeter House:* The Thomas Jeter house in Union, built in 1859, has the same strawberry leaf and egg-and-dart moldings as the Sims plantation Great House on the Tyger. The author has pieces from the Sims decoration salvaged by Haywood Henderson in the 1970s and comparisons of these with the Jeter plasterwork show them to be cast from the same molds. Therefore, it can be assumed that Finger did both of these houses in the 1850s.

P. 88: Facts on the building of The Oaks come from remembrances of J. D. and Frances Epps (descendants of George Douglass, their grandfather) and their cousin Ben Hardy, as compiled by Caldwell Sims, 30 April 1936, WPA Project #1885.

CHAPTER 6: IN TUNE WITH THE MUSIC OF THE UNIVERSE

P. 89: *Hardy in 1932:* From William Dixon Hardy's interview with Eva Justice.

P. 90: *granddaughter:* Mary Ella Henderson Finlay, in an interview with the author, 21 July 1992. Complete interview in the Hardy Plantation Archives.

P. 90: *common in the gardens of this area:* For example, those surrounding the Great Houses at Hollywood, Rosemont, The Oaks, Rose Cottage, the Hunter plantation, the Rice plantation, and the Colonel Robert Beaty plantation in Newberry, Union, and Laurens Counties. They all had parterres edged with boxwood. At both the Hunter and Rice plantations the parterres are still intact.

P. 90: *family tradition:* As told to me by Mr. and Mrs. Haywood Hardy Henderson, 24 August 1989, and by William Hardy Jr., 25 May 1990. The complete texts of these interviews are in the Hardy Plantation Archives.

P. 90: The record South Carolina Eastern hemlock, located in Oconee County, S.C., measures 10 feet 4 inches in circumference.

P. 91: *said to be $1,000:* This price made a lasting impression on the community, some of whose residents still recall the high monetary value placed on them. This figure is derived from my interview with Mrs. L. N. Huff of Whitmire, S.C., 20 June 1992. Mrs. Huff was a friend of the Hardy family and visited the home often while Captain Dick was still alive and at the time the offer was made. The price she remembers is likely correct. Boxwood from another sale to Historic Williamsburg (from a garden in lower Spartanburg County) brought $1,500, as recorded by Ann Leighton, *American Gardens of the Nineteenth Century* (Amherst, Mass., 1987), p. 215.

P. 91: *one descendant . . . mother:* Mary Ella Henderson Finlay recalls this of her mother, Helen O'Neal Hardy Henderson, who was born in 1880.

P. 91: *Colonel Robert Beaty's garden:* As described in William Rice Feaster, ed. *A History of Union County* (Greenville, S.C., 1977), p. 105. Like Dr. James Hardy, Colonel Beaty was a patron of Pomaria Nurseries, as revealed in extant nursery order ledgers.

P. 91: *fear . . . snakebite:* As related in my interviews with Haywood Hardy Henderson, 24 August 1992, and Nelle Hardy Dyar, 10 September 1989.

P. 94: *Two . . . palings:* One of these palings still has the large head of a wrought nail, identical to those on the clapboarding of the Great House. The palings measure $2^5/8$ inches wide and $3/4$ thick. They are 3 feet tall. Some flecks of white paint adhere. Even though they are of heart-pine, they are badly weathered.

P. 94: The quotation from Leighton is in her *American Gardens,* p. 211.

P. 94: *Several . . . grandchildren:* William Dixon Henderson, William Dixon Hardy Sr., Mary Ella Henderson Finlay, and Haywood Hardy Henderson, in various interviews with the author, 1989–1992. Complete texts of these interviews are in the Hardy Plantation Archives.

P. 95: Leighton, *American Gardens,* pp. 214–15.

P. 97: *snowdrops: Leucojum vernum,* sometimes called snowflakes in standard garden literature but always called snowdrops in Carolina from the nineteenth century to the present.

P. 98: *shrub rose:* Information provided in my interview with Mr. and Mrs. John Frost Hardy III, 14 June 1992. Copy in the Hardy Plantation Archives.

P. 99: *not to impress those outside:* Leighton notes that the finished side of the fences at Mountain Shoals was placed *inward,* to be seen to best effect from within. The beautiful carving on the gateposts at Hillside at Carlisle is also on the inside, whereas the outside is plain. This philosophy must therefore have been the common one in the area during the 1820s, when all three of these upcountry homes were built.

P. 99: *gardenias:* For example, at the T. A. Carlisle plantation, a few miles from The Oaks at Goshen Hill, former slave Gus Feaster, born in 1840, remembered hiding in the "Cape jessamine" bushes when about ten years old, hence

1850. These plants, he recalled, were "big bushes 'long de front walk." Since they were "big bushes," they must have been planted before 1840. They grow more slowly in upcountry Carolina than in the Lowcountry. Feaster is quoted in George P. Rawick, ed., *The American Slave,* vol. 2, pt. 2, p. 64.

P. 100: *Covington Hardy house:* Described in Evelyn Arvin, *Ante-Bellum Homes of Lunenburg* (Richmond, 1969), p. 37: "One of the tallest and most beautiful holly trees known stands as a towering, living memorial to the first Mrs. Vincent Hardy who planted it there."

P. 100: *Miss Alice . . . also enjoyed gardening:* As remembered by her grandson, John Frost Hardy III, in an interview with the author, 14 June 1992. Copy in the Hardy Plantation Archives.

P. 101: *Joseph Simpson recalls:* In my interview with Mr. and Mrs. Joseph Simpson, 28 July 1990. Copy in the Hardy Plantation Archives. My plantings of Brazil pine and twisted cypress have not survived the winters, thus perhaps explaining why no large specimens of them are to be found in upcountry gardens.

P. 103: *Pomaria Nursery ledgers:* The originals of three extant ledgers exist at the South Caroliniana Library, Pomaria plantation, and the Hardy Plantation Archives. Copies of the catalogues for Pomaria Nurseries are extant for most years between 1852 and 1862. See James Kibler, "On Reclaiming a Southern Antebellum Garden Heritage: An Introduction to Pomaria Nurseries, 1840–1879," *Magnolia: Bulletin of the Southern Garden History Society,* 10 (Fall 1993), pp. 1–12; and Linda Weathers, "Digging into Gardens Past," *Southern Accents,* 15, no. 7 (September 1992), pp. 88–92.

CHAPTER 7: THE FOREST

P. 106: The epigraph is from the Columbia, S.C. *Southern Agriculturist* (June 1853), p. 162.

P. 107: For his list of trees, see Robert Mills, *Statistics of South Carolina* (Charleston, S.C., 1826), p. 656. Mills also interviewed a pioneer settler on the Enoree who had been an amateur botanist. His list of the wildflowers native to this area has been the basis for my wildflower plantings.

P. 108: *Sabal minor:* Sometimes called scrub palmetto. This plant is noted as growing along the Broad River near the boundary between Richland and Fairfield Counties, in Chapman Milling, *Beneath So Kind a Sky* (Columbia, S.C., 1947), p. 15.

P. 108: *one Carolina planter:* W. G. Simms of Woodlands plantation, in his "Maize in Milk," *Godey's,* 34 (February–May 1847).

Pp. 109–11: The quotations on land use and stewardship are from William Eppes Hardy, in letters and notes dated 15 October 1838, 22 May 1846, 2 February 1847, and 6 August 1853. He no doubt made other such statements that have not survived. In the records of his land use and management, we find him putting his philosophy into practice, as our chronicle reveals.

P. 110: Hugh Johnson, *International Book of Trees* (London, 1973), p. 71.

CHAPTER 8: THEIR FATHERS' FIELDS

P. 112: The epigraph by Summer is from his "Monthly Talk with our Readers," Columbia, S.C. *Farmer and Planter,* 11 (December 1860), p. 372. Summer was horticultural editor for this periodical; his essays there are of some significance for both their environmental philosophy and their literary quality. The epigraph from Peterkin is from Frank Durham's edition of her *Collected Stories* (Columbia, S.C., 1970).

P. 112: *memory of those still living:* The quote is from the author's interview with Joseph Simpson 28 July 1992. Copy in the Hardy Plantation Archives.

P. 113: *Gus Feaster:* Quoted in George P. Rawick, ed., *The American Slave* (Westport, Conn., 1972), vol. 2, pt. 2, p. 61.

P. 113: *members of the family:* Haywood Hardy Henderson, in interviews in the Hardy Plantation Archives.

P. 113: William Eppes Hardy's plantation ledger for 1836–1846 is in the William Eppes Hardy Collection, Perkins Library, Duke University; the ledger for 1842–1846 is owned by William Hardy Jr. The 1848–1865 ledger is in the Hardy Plantation Archives. Family letters, business letters, and receipts are held by William Hardy Jr., Duke University Library, and the Hardy Plantation Archives.

P. 114: *Celtic traditions:* See Grady McWhiney, *Cracker Culture: Celtic Ways in the Old South* (Tuscaloosa, Ala., 1988).

P. 115: *Gus Feaster:* Quoted in Rawick, *The American Slave,* vol. 2, pt. 2, p. 57.

P. 116: *iron trough:* Both Haywood Hardy Henderson and John Frost Hardy III recall this trough as being "most impressive." Interviews with the author, 6 August 1989 and 14 June 1992, in the Hardy Plantation Archives.

P. 116: *detached kitchen:* Interviews with William Dixon Henderson, 21 June 1991, and John Frost Hardy III, 14 June 1992. Information on the other outbuildings and dependencies comes from my interviews with William Dixon Henderson (21 June 1991), Margaret Thomas King (14 January 1991), Haywood Hardy Henderson (6 and 24 August 1989), and Bertice McCollum Teague (13 December 1992). Interviews in the Hardy Plantation Archives.

P. 117: *blacksmith shop:* As noted in the Hardy Plantation ledgers.

P. 117: *bell and conch:* Remembered by Hardy neighbor Margaret Thomas King in the 14 January 1991 interview cited above. Bertice Teague, whose grandfather John Robert McCollum was a good friend of William Dixon Hardy and served in the Confederacy with him, often visited the plantation with her grandfather and recalls the plantation bell. It sat to the north of the dwelling and in the close yard itself. Interview 13 December 1992, copy in the Hardy Plantation Archives.

P. 119: Haywood Hardy letter to his father, 17 February 1862, in Perkins Library, Duke University.

P. 120: *slave shackles or irons:* Rawick, *The American Slave,* vols. 1, 2, 3, 11.

P. 120: *"spike nails":* Family tradition as passed down to John Frost Hardy III relates that the plantation had a "nailery" for the making and sale of nails. (Interview with the author, 14 June 1992.) These large hand-forged spikes are still to be seen in the construction of the log harness and tack barn; and I have found others buried on the grounds around the house. John Frost Hardy III was given some as a memento by his grandfather in the 1950s. They range from 5 to 6 inches long and are hammered square.

P. 121: *Charles Harvey:* Rawick, *The American Slave,* vol. 2, pt. 2, p. 249.

P. 122: *bill of purchase:* In Perkins Library, Duke University.

P. 124: *Gus Feaster:* Quoted in Rawick, *The American Slave,* vol. 2, pt. 2, p. 56.

P. 126: *wrote a son in 1849:* William Eppes Hardy to Charles Wesley Hardy, November 1849. This letter exists only in fragments in the Hardy Plantation Archives.

P. 127: The table showing relative wealth was compiled by the author from the U.S. census for Newberry County in 1850.

P. 128: *sale for a horse:* Document in Perkins Library, Duke University.

P. 129: *William Dixon Hardy Sr.:* In interviews with the author, 5 and 9 August 1992. Interviews in the Hardy Plantation Archives.

P. 129: *All the former slaves:* See, for example, Rawick, *The American Slave,* vol. 2, pt. 2, p. 275.

P. 130: *Zack Herndon:* Quoted in Rawick, *The American Slave,* vol. 2, pt. 2, p. 275.

Pp. 131–33: All notes and bills of payment on these pages are in the William Eppes Hardy Collection, Perkins Library, Duke University.

P. 133: Letter of Haywood Hardy to his father, 17 February 1862, Perkins Library, Duke University.

CHAPTER 9: WORKS AND DAYS IN THE QUARTERS

P. 136: Epigraph is from George P. Rawick, ed., *The American Slave* (Westport, Conn., 1971), vol. 1, pt. 2, pp. 124–25. Except where noted, all the narratives of former slaves in this chapter are from this source. Volume and page numbers of references are given in parentheses after each citation.

P. 136: See slave statistics, 1850 census, for the number of slaves and slave houses.

P. 137: *"to keep the hearth"*: Quoted in Rawick, *The American Slave,* vol. 1, p. 379.

Pp. 138–39: *Former slaves of Maybinton-Goshen Hill:* Narrations from Rawick, vol. 3, pt. 2, p. 180; vol. 2, pt. 2, p. 272; vol. 3, pt. 3, p. 64; vol. 2, pt. 1, p. 85. For rope beds, see Gus Feaster in Rawick, *The American Slave,* vol. 2, pt. 2, p. 43.

P. 140: *Aunt Ciller:* Quoted in Caldwell Sims, *Voices from the Past* (Union, S.C., 1979), 29, as taken from the Union, S.C., *Progress* around 1912. The 1937 comment is from Elias Dawkins in Rawick, *The American Slave* (vol. 2, pt. 1, p. 317).

P. 142: *differed from region to region:* Some selected volumes that may provide useful general context for slave life are William Dusinberre, *Them Dark Days: Slavery in the American Rice Swamps* (New York, 1996), a work that utilizes the WPA Slave Narratives to paint a different picture of the institution in the rice culture of Savannah and Beaufort. Other books that employ the slave narratives as primary sources include Randall Miller, ed., *Dear Master: Letters of a Slave Family* (Athens, Ga., 1990); Charles Joyner, *Down by the Riverside: A South Carolina Slave Community* (Urbana, Ill., 1985); Susan Dabney Smedes, *Memorials of a Southern Planter* (New York, 1965); Elizabeth Fox-Genovese, *Within the Plantation Household* (Chapel Hill, N.C., 1988); Herbert G. Gutman, *The Black Family in Slavery and Freedom* (New York, 1976); Willie Lee Rose, *Rehearsal for Reconstruction* (Indianapolis, 1964) and Robert W. Fogel and Stanley L. Engerman, *Time on the Cross* (Boston, 1974). From a strictly Marxist viewpoint, there is, of course, Eugene Genovese's *Roll Jordan Roll: The World the Slaves Made* (New York, 1975), a book that espouses theories that Dr. Genovese seems to have recanted of late. For the archaeological dimensions of slavery and slave buildings see Theresa Singleton, *Archaeology of Slavery and Plantation Life* (Orlando, Fl., 1985) and Charles Orser, *The Material Basis for the Postbellum Tenant Plantation: Historical Archaeology in the South Carolina Piedmont* (Athens, Ga., 1988). In addition to George Rawick's collections there have been other editions of slave narrative texts. Among these are Belinda Hurmence, ed., *Before Freedom: 48 Oral Histories of Former North and South Carolina Slaves* (New York, 1990), Charles S. Johnson, *Shadows of the Plantation* (Chicago, 1934), Paul Escott, *Slavery Remembered: A Record of Twentieth-Century Slave Narratives* (Chapel Hill, 1979), and B. A. Botkin, ed., *Lay My Burden Down* (Chicago, 1945).

P. 144: In Robert Stokes's "Hints for the Month" in the South Carolina *Farmer and Planter* (November 1859), the author gave this advice to plantation masters: "Guard against late hours and excessive possum hunting" as a way of helping prevent pneumonia, which he considered the most common cause of death among blacks.

P. 145: *Lyles was a skilled hunter:* As quoted in Caldwell Sims, *Voices from the Past* (Union, S.C., 1979), pp. 60–61.

P. 155: *Feaster . . . twenty years old in 1860:* Feaster notes here that his particular Fourth occurred on a Friday. The years that the Fourth of July came on Friday were 1856 and 1862, hence when Feaster was either sixteen or twenty-two years old. Our description may be from either year, but likely from 1856.

P. 165: *two slaves:* Thomas Hardy Sr. conveyed these slaves and land to his son in a document now owned by Haywood Hardy Henderson, with a copy in the Hardy Plantation Archives.

P. 166: *Later in 1806:* In the appraisement list of the estate of John Wesley Hardy, Newberry County Probate Court Records.

P. 166: *Seven men:* These names are derived from Thomas Hardy Sr.'s will and the appraisal of his estate.

P. 167: *In 1818:* The names of the slaves of Nancy Eppes Hardy Shell are given in her will, the appraisal list of her estate, and the settlement of that estate in 1825–1826. All these documents are in the Newberry County Probate Court Records.

P. 167: For Guinea's story, see chapter 4. For the value of Ben and Guinea, see appraisal lists of the estate of Nancy Shell. The sale document is also in Newberry County Probate Court Records.

P. 168: *plantation in 1844:* William Eppes Hardy made several partial lists on John Wesley Hardy's letter to him, dated 2 February 1844. Letter in possession of William Hardy Jr., with a copy in the Hardy Plantation Archives.

P. 168: *Dr. J. L. Reid:* Bill to William Eppes Hardy, Perkins Library, Duke University. The 1850 census lists a Dr. Joseph Reid living in the Buck Hotel, Maybinton. He had moved west by 1860.

P. 169: The inclusion of Jack comes as a result of a mention in a letter from Haywood Hardy to his father, Richmond, 10 July 1862. This letter is published in full in chapter 12 and is in the possession of William Hardy Jr., with a copy in the Hardy Plantation Archives.

P. 169: *"cook Sundays":* This cook list was penned in the front of his plantation ledger, 1842–1846; in possession of William Hardy Jr., with a copy in the Hardy Plantation Archives. The 1839–1844 ledger is at Perkins Library, Duke University.

Pp. 169–70: The second, third, and fourth documents are at the Perkins Library, Duke University.

P. 171: *"Happy Dog":* For this story, see chapter 18 and notes.

P. 174: *notes hiring:* In his plantation ledger, 1842–1846, and in loose-leaf records in the possession of William Hardy Jr., with copies in the Hardy Plantation Archives.

P. 175: All quotations from Gladdeny are in Rawick, *The American Slave,* vol. 2, pt. 2, pp. 124–25. Gladdeny's testimony is given credence by the appearance of the name Sally Murphy as the recipient of a bolt of homespun in December 1867 on a bill of payment by William Eppes Hardy to M. David & Co. Document at Perkins Library, Duke University.

Pp. 175–76: *Anna Hardy's will:* Original draft of 1859 is in the papers of W. W. Renwick, her neighbor in Goshen Hill. Renwick papers, South Caroliniana Library, University of South Carolina; with a copy in the Hardy Plantation Archives.

P. 176: *Cousin Sallie:* Cousin Sallie Beard of Glenn Springs, 21 March 1862. Renwick papers, South Caroliniana Library, University of South Carolina, with a copy in the Hardy Plantation Archives.

Pp. 176–77: *white Hardy descendant:* Richard Wesley Hardy, in an interview with the author, 14 June 1992. He is the great-great-grandson of William Eppes Hardy.

P. 177: *Suber family:* The Thomas Suber plantation, built in the 1850s, was a very extensive concern on Broad River, some eight miles south of the Hardys. The Suber family at one time also owned Hollywood plantation near the Broad. After the war, planter Tom Suber sold his home to Augustus Dickert, a Confederate captain and another strong supporter of the Cause. The "Tom Suber, Freedman" of the agreement with Hardy might thus have been one of the ex-slaves Suber left behind.

P. 177: *Tom Hardy:* As remembered to the author by John Tucker, 5 September 1992. Detail of his war service is from my interview with a resident of Tuckertown, 16 February 1992. Interviews in the Hardy Plantation Archives.

P. 178: *grandson. . . recalls:* Information about the plantation in the 1950s and '60s comes from Alice Hardy's grandson John Frost Hardy III in my interview of 14 June 1992. For the five tenant families and information from the 1930s, sources are my interviews with Nelle Hardy Dyar (10 September 1989), Sarah Cromer Stokes (12 September 1989), John Renwick (9 August 1990), Margaret Thomas King and her daughter Ellen Boyd (14 January 1991), William Dixon Henderson (21 June 1991), and John Tucker (5 September 1991).

P. 178: *slave cemetery:* Remembered by John Tucker in my interview, 5 September 1992.

P. 179: *buried . . . Comer plantation:* Thomas Hardy Jr. (1767–1823) and his daughter Elmira Hardy (1814–1830) are buried north of the Tyger in Union County. Interview with a resident of Tuckertown, 16 February 1992. The Hardys no doubt owned land in Union County in the early century and perhaps before. There are Hardys listed in the 1800 census for Union County. The ages given in this census would rule out Thomas Hardy Jr., however. These adjacent Hardys were likely close Virginia relatives who also moved to South Carolina in the late eighteenth century, probably before the Hardys of our chronicle.

P. 179: The Maggie Perkins reminiscence is published in B. A. Botkin, ed. *Lay My Burden Down* (Chicago, 1945), p. 35. I have not located it in Rawick's *The American Slave*.

Chapter 10: In the Way o' Finery and Style

P. 183: *Renwick's Academy:* A list of pupils at Renwick Academy, Orange Hall, is given in the hand of W. W. Renwick, its headmaster, and dated 9 April 1849. Renwick papers, South Caroliniana Library, University of South Carolina.

G. Boone	T. Dowdy
J. L. Caldwell	L. K. Glasgow
C. T. S. Carlisle	W. L. Glenn
R. C. Carlisle	Jas. Gross
J. N[ewt] Carlisle	T[homas] P. Hardy
M. A[nderson] Carlisle	C[harles] W. Hardy
W. Homes Carlisle	J. Huey
Geo[rge] Cofield	J. [Jack?] Henderson
J[oseph] E. Cofield	W. Henderson
L. R. Cofield	W. E. Lyons
J[ames] T. Douglass	T[homas] Moorman
G[arraphelia] A. Douglass	J. W. Renwick
Sally Douglass	Leander Rogers
A[nna P.] Douglass	E. D. [Dawkins?] Rogers
Ellen Douglass	

P. 183: Letter of Charles Wesley Hardy to William Eppes Hardy, in the possession of William Hardy Jr., with a copy in the Hardy Plantation Archives.

P. 184: Letter of Charles Wesley Hardy to William Eppes Hardy, 15 March 1852, at Perkins Library, Duke University.

Pp. 185–86: Letters of Elmira Hardy to William Eppes Hardy at Perkins Library, Duke University.

P. 187: The two deSchweinetz letters to William Eppes Hardy are at the Perkins Library, Duke University.

P. 188: *J. & H. Richards Co.:* The bills of payment from which these lists were compiled are at Perkins Library, Duke University.

P. 189: Letter of Haywood Hardy to his father, 17 February 1862 at Perkins Library, Duke University.

Pp. 189–90: Purchases from Gross and Anderson are documented by two bills paid by Haywood's father. Perkins Library, Duke University.

P. 190: Letter of Stephen Lee at Perkins Library, Duke University.

Pp. 191–92: *Stephen Lee:* Information on Lee comes from T. C. Read, *Descendants of Thomas Lee of Charleston, 1710–1769* (Columbia, S.C., 1964); and George Digges, *Historical Facts Concerning Buncombe County* (Asheville, N.C., 1935), p. 220. Lee opened his boys' school in 1846 and continued it until his death in 1879. On William Dixon Hardy's matriculation at Lee's Academy, see Hardy's information supplied to Clement Evans in *Confederate Military History,* 5 (Atlanta, Ga., 1899), p. 631. His obituary in an unidentified Spartanburg newspaper of October 1932 also gives the specifics of his education. Newspaper clipping in Alice Hardy's scrapbook, in the possession of her son William Hardy Sr., with a copy in the Hardy Plantation Archives.

P. 192: Letter of Stephen Lee in the Hardy Plantation Archives.

P. 193: *Renwick:* William W. Renwick was born c. 1812 and died in 1872. He was the son of the Reverend John S. Renwick Jr. (1770–1836) of the Kings Creek A.R.P Church area of Newberry County and the grandson of the Irish pioneer to this country (1735–1775). Renwick married Rosannah P. Rogers (19 January 1812–4 January 1850), daughter of John A. Rogers Jr. (1764–1847) and Rosey M. Rogers (1778–1841) of Orange Hall plantation. They were all members of Kings Creek Church and, like the local Reids and Caldwells, all descended from Scots-Irish dissenting Presbyterian emigrés from County Antrim, Ireland.

P. 193: Letter from Rivers to Renwick is in the Renwick papers, South Caroliniana Library, University of South Carolina. Copy in the Hardy Plantation Archives.

Pp. 194–95: For these charts of comparative land values and per capita wealth standings, compiled from census records, I am indebted to Mr. William Lamar Cawthon Jr. of Eufaula, Alabama.

P. 197: Letter from William Eppes Hardy to Charles Wesley Hardy, in the Hardy Plantation Archives.

P. 199: From William Gilmore Simms's *The Social Principle,* an address at the University of Alabama on 13 December 1842 (Tuscaloosa, Ala., 1843), p. 50.

P. 200: *Scilla:* Sometimes also written "Cilla," this was a common name for both animals and people (both black and white) in the Maybinton-Goshen-Fish Dam area, as shown by its frequency in documents, particularly those naming slaves.

P. 200: Robert Moorman's letter is in the Renwick papers, South Caroliniana Library, University of South Carolina.

Pp. 201–205: The brief quotations from the Hardys and Douglasses are all taken from Garrie Douglass's letterbook (1859–1865), South Caroliniana Library, University of South Carolina; and the cousins' letters to the family, in the possession of William Hardy Sr. and Jr.; copies in the Hardy Plantation Archives.

Pp. 201–202: Milton Marshall is quoted in George P. Rawick, ed., *The American Slave* (Westport, Conn., 1972), vol. 3, pt. 3, p. 174; Gus Feaster, vol. 2, pt. 2, p. 65; and George Briggs, vol. 2, pt. 1, p. 84.

CHAPTER 11: THE PLANTATION NEIGHBORHOOD

P. 206: *Historic American Building Survey:* Conducted 25 April 1977 by William Douglass Smyth of Charleston, S.C., with copies in the Hardy Plantation Archives. Smyth's survey contains an excellent plat search and family tree, both of which have been used herein. The papers of John Lyles and the Lyles family (1767–1842) are at the South Caroliniana Library, University of South Carolina.

P. 207: *The story is told:* In John Belton O'Neall's *The Annals of Newberry* (Charleston, S.C., 1859), pp. 186–90. See also Leland Summer's *Newberry County, S.C.: Historical and Genealogical* (Newberry, S.C., 1950), pp. 19, 23, 37, 190, and Thomas H. Pope's *History of Newberry County, 1749–1860* (Columbia, S.C., 1973), vol. 1, pp. 40, 63, 89, 123, 129.

P. 207: Eison Lyles is quoted in Caldwell Sims, *Voices from the Past* (Union, S.C., 1979), p. 62.

P. 209: *date . . . subject to debate:* Vera Spears in "Some Early Homes and Churches in Union County," *Names in South Carolina,* 12 (Winter 1965), p. 220, gives 1774 as the date of construction, as well as the information that its cupola was used as a lookout during the Revolution. The post–1796 date is given in William Rice Feaster, ed. *History of Union County* (Greenville, S.C., 1977). Because the Rogers family did not come to Charleston until 1773, it is unlikely that the house was built as early as 1774. It may have been there by 1780 or 1781, however, in time for dwellers to watch skirmishes during the last phase of the war.

P. 209: *1818 . . . plat map:* Union County Plat Book A & B, pp. 306–7. See also Allen Charles, *The Narrative History of Union County, S.C.* (Spartanburg, S.C., 1987), and Feaster, ed. *History of Union County,* p. 9.

P. 209: The description of the house's interior comes from *History of Union County,* chapter 8, p. 9, and my interviews with John Renwick on 9 August and 28 December 1990. Renwick was the last child born at Orange Hall (in 1918). The *History's* description was apparently taken directly from an interview of Caldwell Sims with J. D. Epps in April 1936 for WPA Project #1885.

P. 209: *record of a detached kitchen:* In a letter written by James Lyons to Rosannah Rogers from Orange Hall, 3 August 1824. In Renwick papers, South Caroliniana Library, University of South Carolina. Copy in the Hardy Plantation Archives.

Pp. 210–12: For the Rogerses' connection to Ireland, I have used the interview with John Rogers Renwick, 27 May 1936, WPA Project #1885-1, "The Pattan Watch."

P. 211: The Orange Hall plantation ledger is at the South Caroliniana Library, University of South Carolina.

P. 214: Letter of John and Rosey M. Rogers in possession of Mrs. John Renwick, with copy in the Hardy Plantation Archives.

P. 216: *Another letter:* In Renwick papers, South Caroliniana Library, University of South Carolina, with a copy in the Hardy Plantation Archives. The Lyons family hailed from Charleston. Former slave Eison Lyles recalled that he lived on the Bob Lyons place and Master Bob's "family refugeed from Charleston to Maybinton during the War, and stayed there until he died. Then his folks went back to Charleston." See Caldwell Sims, *Voices from the Past,* p. 62.

Pp. 217–18: The statistics for 1860 derive from the 1860 census for Union County.

P. 218: *"coal kiln":* As recorded in Orange Hall plantation daybook, South Caroliniana Library, University of South Carolina.

P. 218: *"Stone House":* Listed on an 1818 plat in Union County Plat Book A & B, pp. 306–7. See also Robert Mills's *Atlas* for Union County (1825).

P. 218: *Tavern sold its grog:* As recorded in the sales of Orange Hall, Orange Hall daybook, South Caroliniana Library, University of South Carolina. The long list of items sold at this store is compiled from this same source.

P. 221: *Gus Feaster:* Quoted in George P. Rawick, ed., *The American Slave* (Westport, Conn.: 1972), vol. 2, pt. 2, p. 57.

P. 222: Robert Mills's *Statistics* (Charleston, S.C.: 1826), p. 652.

P. 222: *poplars:* These may have been the native tulip poplar; but Mills does state that the Lombardy poplar is now found growing in Newberry County alongside the pride of India (Chinaberry tree), another import now naturalized. See Mills, *Statistics,* p. 644.

P. 223: Renwick's purchase in 1848 is recorded in documents in the Renwick papers, South Caroliniana Library, University of South Carolina.

P. 223: *J. E. Sherman:* Sherman was a member of Etoyle Comer Grissom's family. He made his living in the area doing ornamental carving of mantels, gateposts, and tombstones. His grapevine and grape cluster gateposts and carved scroll-ended granite steps at Hillside plantation at Carlisle are good examples of his work. He married a Union County woman and today has descendants in North Carolina. The stonework at the Hill family spring, like Jew's Harp Spring at Goshen Hill, is his work.

P. 223: *removed in 1929:* As recorded by Caldwell Sims in 1936 in an interview with J. D. Epps, WPA Project #1885.

P. 224: Alice Sims's story is from Caldwell Sims, *Voices from the Past,* pp. 44–45.

P. 225: *blockade runner:* See interview with Ida Baker, 10 November 1937, in Sims, *Voices from the Past,* p. 133. Here it is said that because of Rogers's activity, citizens of Union had luxuries not to be had elsewhere during the war.

P. 225: The statistics for 1863–1864 are derived from Confederate Assessment for Taxes, Renwick papers, South Caroliniana Library, University of South Carolina.

P. 225: *Library sold:* As demonstrated in letters in the Renwick papers, South Caroliniana Library, University of South Carolina.

P. 226: Information on Orange Hall after 1890 comes from interviews by the author with John Renwick, 9 August and 28 December 1990 and 6 July 1991. Interviews are in the Hardy Plantation Archives.

P. 226: *"Solomon Lodge"*: As recorded by Caldwell Sims in 1936 in an interview with J. D. Epps, WPA Project #1885.

P. 226: The story of the speculator is from an interview with John Renwick, 9 August 1990. Renwick remembered his name and that he was from Spartanburg.

P. 229: *travelers loved to stay:* See Juanita Hitt, *Newton Thomas Hogg* (Newberry, S.C., 1970), p. 16.

P. 229: For Chick Springs, see *Sandlapper*, July 1969, pp. 20–23. A photograph of the hotel appears there at pp. 20–21. Alice Sims's account of 1936 is recorded in Caldwell Sims, *Voices from the Past*, pp. 41–42.

Pp. 229–31: The details of the design of the house and grounds are based on the recollection of John Renwick (1918–1992), as given the author in a series of interviews from 1990 to 1992, particularly that of 9 August 1990. Renwick lived in the house in the 1920s and watched its slow ruin for decades thereafter. The size of the chimneys comes from my interview with Bill Carter, 2 September 1990. Carter visited the house several times before it collapsed.

P. 230: *Cryptomeria:* See Linda Weathers, "Digging into Gardens Past," *Southern Accents*, 15 (September 1992), pp. 88–92.

Pp. 230–31: *Balaam Lyles:* Quoted in Sims, *Voices from the Past*, p. 60.

P. 232: *1890s . . . purchased:* From my interviews with John Renwick, 1990–1992. Copies in the Hardy Plantation Archives.

P. 232: *Joseph Simpson:* From my interview with Simpson, 28 July 1990. Copy at the Hardy Plantation Archives.

P. 233: *The Oaks:* Facts on James Thomas Douglass Sr. are derived from family documents in the possession of Dr. George Douglass, Charleston, S.C.; Edwin Green, *History of Richland County* (Columbia, S.C., 1932), 189–90; "Original Petitition for Charter of First Presbyterian Church Found," *Columbia State* (13 August 1933), p. 12–B; and Edward L. Wright's essay on James Douglass in the *State* (22 February 1952).

P. 234: *"a permit to practice"*: As quoted in the following letter from James Davis to Bernard Glenn, dated Columbia, 5 May 1824. Copy owned by Dr. George Douglass. The addressee here is Captain Barnard Glenn (1757–1831), a Revolutionary War veteran of Fish Dam in Union County.

P. 234: Douglass letter to Glenn in the possession of Dr. George Douglass. Copy in the Hardy Plantation Archives.

P. 235: *moved . . . Selby place:* As recorded by Caldwell Sims for WPA Project #1885 on 30 April 1936. The information was gleaned from interviews with J. D. and Frances Epps and Ben Hardy in 1936. The description of the Selby place itself and a record of the years 1838–1840 also come from these same sources.

P. 236: That James Jr. had taken over the mill comes from Edward L. Wright.

Pp. 236–38: All details of the house construction come from Caldwell Sims (1936) and from color photographs made in 1970 by Dr. George Douglass, copies of which are now in the Hardy Plantation Archives. There are photographs of the exterior at pp. 68 and 116 of Nancy Roberts's *South Carolina Ghosts* (Columbia, S.C., 1983). The latter is a particularly good photograph of the entrance with sidelights and flattened elliptical fanlight surmounted by a lozenge.

P. 238: The description of the faux graining is based on existing color photographs made by Dr. George Douglass in 1973, copies of which are in the Hardy Plantation Archives.

P. 238: *John Finger:* Repairs for Finger are recorded in the Hardy Plantation ledger, 1845–1846. Ledger in possession of William Hardy Sr., with a copy at the Hardy Plantation Archives.

P. 239: The 1936 descriptions come from Caldwell Sims's interviews with Frances Epps.

P. 239: *Garrie Douglass remarks:* In her letterbook, 1859–1862, South Caroliniana Library, University of South Carolina.

P. 239: Information about the doctor's initials are recollected by descendant Mrs. Mary Ritchie Taylor of Raleigh, N.C., as remembered by her mother, Mrs. J. S. Ritchie. My interview with Mrs. Taylor, 7 September 1992. Copy in the Hardy Plantation Archives.

P. 240: The rear of the house is described by Caldwell Sims and depicted in photographs made 1970–1973 by Dr. George Douglass.

Pp. 240–41: *garden:* As described in the Caldwell Sims interviews of April 1936 with the Eppses and Ben Hardy.

P. 241: *Robert Beaty's plantation:* Colonel Beaty's house was located nine miles south of Governor Gist's Rose Hill in Union County.

P. 241: *In 1860:* Statistics are from the 1860 census for Union County.

P. 241: *In 1861:* Statistics are from the Confederate States Tax Assessment for that year; document in possession of Dr. George Douglass; copy in the Hardy Plantation Archives.

P. 242: *some in our own time:* Specifically, John Renwick (1918–1992), as expressed in an interview with the author in August 1989. Copy in the Hardy Plantation Archives.

P. 242: *planting cotton in the 1890s:* As described in a letter from Frances Hardy Douglass to her son Dock, in the possession of Dr. George Douglass, with a copy in the Hardy Plantation Archives.

P. 242: For the schooling of James T. Douglass under Hudson, see James Calvin Hemphill, *Men of Mark* (Washington, D.C., 1907), vol. 2, p. 111. Mentor James Hudson was born in 1802 and died in 1857.

Pp. 242–43: Lucius Smith letter is in the possession of Dr. George Douglass, with a copy in the Hardy Plantation Archives.

P. 244: The quotation from Douglass is in Hemphill, *Men of Mark,* vol. 2, p. 113.

P. 244: The source of the family's war experience is Roberta Moore Frost, a granddaughter of George and Frances Douglass, supplied in a letter from Darlene Bolton, Overland Park, Kansas, 24 August 1992.

P. 244: *1861 acreage:* These figures come from the Confederate Tax Assessments of 1861 and 1865 and from the U.S. census for Union County.

P. 245: Information on Sallie Douglass Townsend is provided by Dr. George Douglass from undated obituaries of Mrs. Townsend.

Pp. 245–46: Moore's and Sims's accounts are in Caldwell Sims's interview, April 1936, WPA Project #1885–1, "The Oaks." Copy at the South Caroliniana Library, University of South Carolina.

P. 247: The other folktale is "The Singing Portrait," published in Nancy Roberts, *South Carolina Ghosts,* 114–18.

P. 247: Figures are from the U.S. census for Union County.

P. 247: Renwick correspondence is in Renwick papers, South Caroliniana Library, University of South Carolina.

P. 248: *recalls John Renwick:* Author's interview with Renwick on 28 August 1989. Copy in the Hardy Plantation Archives.

P. 249: *columns were square:* A decayed section of one of these square columns was seen among the rubble in 1990 by the author.

P. 249: *used for . . . reel dances:* Local tradition recalled in my interviews with Joseph Simpson (28 July 1990), Sarah Cromer Stokes (12 September 1989), William Carter (2 September 1990), and Mannie Kennedy (23 June 1990). Copies of all interviews are in Hardy Plantation Archives.

P. 249: Description of the house interiors comes from interviews with William Carter (2 and 4 September 1990) and Sarah Stokes (12 September 1990).

P. 249: *One who recalls:* Joseph Simpson, in an interview with the author, 28 July 1990. Copy in the Hardy Plantation Archives.

P. 249: *Fannie Epps:* WPA interview by Caldwell Sims, 2 September 1937. See p. 85 for her comments on the matter.

P. 250: *pieces of medallions:* Pieces of these designs were given to the author by Haywood Hardy Henderson in 1989 and are on display in the hall of the Hardy plantation.

P. 250: The house was in fact so well constructed that William Carter, who tried to remove the 60-foot-long flooring, was unable to do it. Interview with Carter, 4 September 1990. Copy in the Hardy Plantation Archives.

P. 250: *Another house:* Author's interview with Mannie Kennedy, 23 June 1990. Copy in the Hardy Plantation Archives.

P. 250: *brief record from 1912:* In an article from the *Union Progress* collected in Sims, *Voices from the Past,* p. 29.

Pp. 251–52: For information on the Hamilton and Thomas houses, I have used my interview with Sarah Stokes, their owner, 12 September 1989. Copy in the Hardy Plantation Archives. Information also supplied by Michael Bedenbaugh.

P. 252: Tuckertown in 1934 is described in Sims, *Voices from the Past,* pp. 165–67.

P. 255: *Lucy Richards Feaster:* As recalled by Gus Feaster in Rawick, *The American Slave,* vol. 2, pt. 2, p. 43.

P. 256: *ghost town:* As described by Summer in *Newberry County,* p. 94.

P. 257: The Maybin family data come from O'Neall's *Annals.* O'Neall wrote them in 1850 from interviews with Colonel Benjamin Maybin, whose father was the original pioneer settler, William Maybin.

P. 257: Information on the Buck comes from Hitt, *Newton Thomas Hogg,* p. 17, and Summer, *Newberry County,* p. 94.

P. 257: *Gladdeny:* Quoted in Rawick, *The American Slave,* vol. 2, pt. 2, p. 127.

P. 257: *Sara Chick:* In Sims, *Voices from the Past,* p. 41.

P. 258: *William Oxner:* Gladdeny recalled that Oxner ran the post office out of his dwelling, where his daughter Miss Bessie Oxner was living in 1937. Of the building he said, "It looked better then than it does now." For Eison Lyles, see Sims, *Voices from the Past,* p. 62.

P. 258: *William Brown Whitney:* Whitney family history in Maybinton begins with Frederick Henry Whitney. He was born between 1805 and 1810 in Boston, the son of John (born 1779) and Silence Miller Whitney (born 1783) of Boston. Frederick moved to Charleston and married Sarah Church Anthony, who had also been born in Boston. They are both buried in Charleston. Frederick had a candle factory in Charleston that made all types of candles, but especially those for carriage headlamps. They had eight children: Frederick Jr., Henry, Sarah, William Brown, Edward, Irene, George, and Arthur. The Whitneys moved from Charleston to Maybinton but continued their interests in the city and kept up a home there as well. Son William Brown Whitney (born 4 December 1851) married Eliza Henderson, daughter of James Madison and Sallie Glenn Henderson of Henderson's Island in the Broad River, adjacent to Maybinton. After the war, William and Eliza Whitney moved to the house at the fork of the Buncombe Road and Tyger River Road. This house was built around 1830 and still stands. The Whitney family became members of Ebenezer Methodist Church, where they are buried. See Hitt, *Newton Thomas Hogg,* p. 58, for the children of William Brown Whitney. For business and personal correspondence between Frederick Whitney and William Renwick, see Renwick papers, South Caroliniana Library, University of South Carolina. Correspondence for the period 1850–1870 shows the Whitneys acquiring goods in Charleston as agents for Renwick and sending them upcountry.

P. 258: *Male and female academies:* Summer, *Newberry County,* p. 94.

P. 259: *important sawmill:* As evidenced by the Hardy plantation ledger, 1842–1846.

Pp. 259–61: The makeup of the village is reconstructed from the 1850 census for Newberry County, in which the individuals of Maybinton village are grouped together and the village thus kept intact.

P. 259: *Slattery:* As remembered by Pick Gladdeny in 1937 in Rawick, *The American Slave,* vol. 2, pt. 2, p. 127.

P. 260: *Gladdeny:* Quoted in Rawick, *The American Slave,* vol. 2, pt. 2, p. 127. Gladdeny is also the source for Ruff's being the most popular physician, quoted later.

P. 260: *free black . . . bills:* Recorded in the Hardy plantation ledger, 1842–1846.

P. 261: *celebration . . . 1848:* Dr. Will Holmes of Maybinton was the speaker for the day at this big event.

P. 261: The Carncross letter is in the Renwick papers, South Caroliniana Library, University of South Carolina.

P. 261: *slaves . . . dances:* As remembered by Pick Gladdeny of Maybinton in Rawick, *The American Slave,* vol. 2, pt. 2, pp. 127–28.

P. 262: *Chapman:* In his *Annals of Newberry, Volume 2* (Newberry, S.C., 1892).

P. 262: *Maybin home:* Surveyed and pictured in the South Carolina Historic Building Survey, housed at the South Carolina State Archives.

Chapter 12: A World Kicked to Pieces

P. 263: *Frosts . . . well-to-do:* They were, in fact, very well-to-do. John's father, Col. John Davis Frost II, owned 7,000 acres and 250 slaves, thus making him among the largest slaveholders in the state. (From an undated obituary of John Davis Frost II in the *Charleston News and Courier* in the possession of Mrs. Beverly Fulmer Kennedy, Columbia, S.C.)

P. 264: Rough draft copy of letter to Hampton is in the Renwick papers, South Caroliniana Library, University of South Carolina, with a copy in the Hardy Plantation Archives.

P. 266: Letter of Ben Maybin at Perkins Library, Duke University.

Pp. 267–68: Letter of William Holmes in the possession of Dr. George Douglass, with a copy in the Hardy Plantation Archives.

P. 268: *granddaughter described her:* Garrie Douglass in her letterbook, South Caroliniana Library, University of South Carolina.

Pp. 269–71: For the enlistments and war service of the Hardy and Douglass sons, see the official Confederate Military Records, South Carolina State Archives, Columbia.

P. 270: *Charlie Giles:* Quoted in Rawick, *The American Slave* (Westport, Conn: 1971), vol. 2, pt. 2, p. 116.

P. 270: *fellow soldier:* Augustus Dickert in his *History of Kershaw's Brigade* (Newberry, S.C., 1899), pp. 427–28.

P. 270: *Richard Jones:* Quoted in Rawick, vol. 3, pt. 3, p. 66.

P. 270: *Santuc:* Santuc had a large muster and parade ground for militia training. As Charlie Harvey recalled in 1938, the Confederates "drilled near the village of Santuc in what was then called Mulligan's Old Field, now owned by Rion Jeter. This was the only mustering ground in our part of the country. The soldiers drilled once a week, and for the general muster, all of the companies from Sedalia and Cross Keys came there once a month. During the summer time, they had what they called general drill for a week or ten days. Of course, on this occasion, the soldiers camped over the field in covered wagons. Some came in buggies. Slaves, called 'wait-men' cared for the stock and did the cooking. . . . The general store at Santuc and the store at Fish Dam did good business during the summer while the soldiers were in camp." Rawick, vol. 2, pt. 2, p. 247.

P. 271: *Nellie Loyd:* Quoted in Rawick, vol. 3, pt. 3, p. 126.

P. 271: *Renwick:* See Renwick's letters of 20 and 25 June, 15 October, and 17 December 1861. In Renwick papers, South Caroliniana Library. The letter of 25 June relates that Renwick has recently seen battle action. Renwick's order for his uniform and coat was made to G. M. Johnson, Merchant Tailor, Main St., Columbia, on 22 October 1861, at a cost of $28. Renwick paid the bill himself.

P. 271: *"armed to the teeth":* As quoted from Haywood Hardy's letter, printed in its entirety in this chapter.

P. 271: *Frances's daughter:* Garrie Douglass, in her letterbook, South Caroliniana Library, University of South Carolina.

P. 272: Garrie's essay is in her letterbook. The quotations from her throughout the chapter are from this letterbook.

P. 274: *George Cofield:* Cofield had also served as headmaster at Renwick Academy in 1859. There is a bill from Cofield to William Renwick for the tuition and schoolbooks for Renwick's sons James and Rogers. It is signed by Cofield from Renwick Academy. Tuition in 1859 was $24.50 per student. The texts used for the Renwick sons that session were Willson's *History,* a Latin lexicon, a Caesar, a *Compty's Reader,* and a *Parley's History.* Renwick papers, South Caroliniana Library.

P. 276: Dickie Hardy's letter is in Perkins Library, Duke University.

P. 277: William's note to his mother is recorded in Ella R. Matthews, "William Henry Hardy," an unpublished typescript dated September 1935, Pack Memorial Library, Asheville, N.C., with a copy in the Hardy Plantation Archives.

P. 277: *Asheville News:* Undated obituary included in Matthews, "William Henry Hardy."

Pp. 279–80: The Henry Jones letter is in the possession of Dr. George Douglass, with a copy in the Hardy Plantation Archives.

P. 280: For the Micah Jenkins letter of 15 October 1861, see the Renwick papers, South Caroliniana Library, University of South Carolina.

Pp. 280–81: The Lyons letter is in the Renwick papers, South Caroliniana Library, University of South Carolina.

Pp. 281–83; 286–88: Dickie Hardy's letters of 24 and 25 December 1861 and 4 March, April, and 4 June 1862 are in the Perkins Library, Duke University.

Pp. 284–85: Haywood Hardy's Letter is in the Perkins Library, Duke University

Pp. 288–89: The account of Dawkins Rogers's death is in Sims, *Voices from the Past* (Union, S.C., 1979), p. 41.

P. 289: *"scarcely any young men left":* This quotation is taken from a letter of Clough S. Beard, Glenn Springs, S.C., to William Renwick, 21 March 1862. Renwick papers, South Caroliniana Library, University of South Carolina.

P. 290: Haywood Hardy's letter of 10 July 1862 is in the possession of William Hardy Jr., with a copy in the Hardy Plantation Archives.

Pp. 291–92: Dickie Hardy's letter of 24 September 1862 is in the Perkins Library, Duke University.

Pp. 293–94: The two Lyons letters are in the Renwick papers, South Caroliniana Library, with copies in the Hardy Plantation Archives.

Pp. 294–97: The Haywood Hardy letters are in the Perkins Library, Duke University.

P. 297: An ambrotype labeled "Mr W D Hardy / Mat Henderson / Aug. 1860" descended to William Hardy Jr. and has now been given to the Hardy Plantation.

P. 298: *"arduous campaigning":* As described by James T. Douglass in Clement Evans, ed., *Confederate Military History* (Atlanta, Ga., 1899), vol. 5, p. 551.

Pp. 299–300: The Haywood Hardy obituary is an unidentified newspaper clipping placed in the William Eppes Hardy family Bible in the possession of John Frost Hardy III, with a copy in the Hardy Plantation Archives.

P. 300: Delia Hardy's letter is in the possession of William Hardy Jr., with a copy in the Hardy Plantation Archives.

P. 300: The Gilbert Tennent of Delia's letter (Dr. Hardy's son-in-law) was sent to Paris by the Confederacy to purchase supplies. Cartes-de-visite of both Gilbert and Emma Hardy Tennent and their two sons are in the possession of Anne Hardy Tennent Cecil of Spartanburg. They were made in Paris and Edinburgh. Tennent lived at Antler Hall in Asheville in the summers after the war.

P. 301: Hardy's letter to Mrs. Tennent is in the Tennent family papers, South Caroliniana Library, University of South Carolina.

P. 301: As remembered in 1928 by Ella Matthews in a typescript of 5 April 1928 in the collection of Anne Hardy Tennent Cecil, and with a copy in the Hardy Plantation Archives.

P. 301: Jones's letter is in Special Collections, University of Georgia Library, Athens, with a copy in the Hardy Plantation Archives.

P. 302: Sallie Douglass note is in the Renwick papers, South Caroliniana Library, University of South Carolina, with a copy in the Hardy Plantation Archives.

P. 302: C. S. Beard letter to W. W. Renwick, dated 29 September 1864, is in the Renwick papers, South Caroliniana Library, University of South Carolina.

P. 303: *Charlie Giles:* Quoted in Rawick, vol. 2, pt. 2, pp. 115–16.

Pp. 304–305: Douglass letter is in the possession of Dr. George Douglass, with a copy in the Hardy Plantation Archives.

p. 305: *Clement Evans:* In *Confederate Military History,* vol. 5, p. 551.

P. 305: The description of Douglass's stamina and situation after the war comes from James Hemphill, *Men of Mark* (Washington, D.C., 1907), vol. 2, p. 111.

P. 306: For Evans on Hardy, see his *Confederate Military History,* vol. 5, p. 631.

P. 306: This list of local soldiers comes from William Dixon Hardy himself, as supplied to John Chapman in his *Annals of Newberry, Volume 2,* p. 436.

P. 306: *James C. Eison:* Eison was corporal of Company D, Fifth S.C. Volunteers, and is buried at Ebenezer. His brother Thomas C. Eison was in the Seventh Cavalry and is also buried at Ebenezer.

P. 306: *G. L. Evans:* Evans, of Company D, Fifth S.C. Volunteers, was the son of G. W. and Margaret Evans. He fell in battle on 27 June 1862 in Richmond at the age of twenty. He is buried at the Sims family cemetery near Carlisle.

P. 306: *Augustus Dickert:* In his *History of Kershaw's Brigade,* p. 442.

P. 307: The tombstone of William Gist is at the Gist family cemetery, Rose Hill plantation, Union County, S.C. A miniature of this young man is in the Confederate Relic Room and Museum, Columbia, S.C.

P. 308: *1865 . . . Sherman:* Author's interview with Mr. and Mrs. Haywood Hardy Henderson, 28 August 1989, as remembered from the accounts of Haywood's mother, Helen Hardy Henderson (1880–1958), and John Frost Hardy Sr. (1886–1963), both the children of William Dixon Hardy.

P. 309: *"sowed with salt":* From General Halleck's words to Sherman after the fall of Savannah and before they entered South Carolina. See *Official Records of the Rebellion.*

P. 309: *St. Michael's:* Recorded in a history of the church, *A Guide to St. Michael's Church, Charleston* (Charleston, S.C., 1979), pp. 21–22, 26.

Pp. 309–10: *Columbia:* The best eye-witness account of the burning of Columbia is W. G. Simms's *The Sack and Destruction of the City of Columbia, South Carolina* (Columbia, S.C., 1865).

P. 309: *Santee:* In Louis P. Towles, ed., *A World Turned Upside Down: The Palmers of South Santee* (Columbia, S.C., 1996), p. 444.

P. 310: *Ralph Waldo Emerson:* In his *Journals,* ed. Ralph Orth, vol. 15 (1860–1866), (Cambridge, Mass., 1982), p. 445. The journal entry is for 9 October 1864.

P. 311: The figures are from the 1870 U.S. census for Newberry County.

P. 311: *Edwin Scott:* In his *Recollections of a Long Life* (Columbia, S.C., 1884), p 196; and letters from Scott to W. W. Renwick dated 25 March, 15 May, and 28 April 1865, in the Renwick papers, South Caroliniana Library, University of South Carolina. One letter notes that "Col. Beaty has been so good as to give me half a dozen hams if I can get them home to Columbia." This detail was used in Scott's account in *Recollections,* worth quoting here in full: "Wednesday, 22d. [March 1865]—A batteau took me from the boat across the river to Henderson's Island, which is two and a half miles long by three-quarters wide at the broadest point. Walked across the island to Mrs. Henderson's, on the West side, and thence was directed and helped by way of Reuben Lyles's and Wm. E. Hardy's to W. W. Renwick's, who went with me to George B. Tucker's, on Enoree, in search for boats, but the latter was not at home. From there we proceeded to Wm. Glenn's, an old boatman, who gave me the desired information as to the cost and building of such boats as we needed. At Robert Beaty's and ex-Governor Gist's I had a kind and welcome reception, with conveyance to Union . . . till I met with R. V. Gist, manager of the Iron Works, on Broad River, and he agreed to build two boats. . . . I returned to Pacolet and by railroad to Santuc, whence I went on foot to Gordon's Mills, on Tyger River, where, with several soldiers, each was charged 50 cents for crossing in a batteau and the same for riding in a wagon 3 miles to Wm. E. Hardy's. Mr. Hardy sent a boy and horse with me to Mr. Renwick's, and he conveyed me back to Mrs. Henderson's, on the island. From there Dr. Hancock brought me to the head of the canal . . . April 9th, and I walked to town on the railroad track. . . . Robert Beaty gave me half a dozen fine hams and made a present of the same number to Messrs. R. O'Neale and John A. Crawford. The abundance of provisions in that fertile region, which the Yankees failed to reach, was in striking contrast with our utterly destitute condition in and around Columbia, and the kindness and liberality of the people, except at Gordon's Mills, was unbounded. The light from the burning of our city had been seen 80 miles distant and our calamity excited their sincerest commiseration and sympathy" (pp. 196–97).

P. 312: *M. David & Co.:* Receipt in Perkins Library, Duke University.

P. 312: Letter of Dr. Douglass in Perkins Library, Duke University.

Pp. 313–15: Letter of Mary Frost in Perkins Library, Duke University.

P. 316: *tax assessors:* Document in Renwick papers, South Caroliniana Library, University of South Carolina.

P. 316: *value . . . estate settlement:* As documented very dramatically by letters in the Renwick papers, South Caroliniana Library, University of South Carolina.

P. 317: Douglass letter in the possession of Dr. George Douglass, with a copy in the Hardy Plantation Archives.

Pp. 318–19: Douglass letter at Perkins Library, Duke University.

P. 319: Letter from Mary Beard, Forest Home plantation, Glenn Springs, S.C.; in the Renwick papers, South Caroliniana Library, University of South Carolina.

P. 320: Hardy letters of agreement are in Perkins Library, Duke University.

P. 321: Moorman letter is in the possession of William Hardy Sr.

P. 322: Data for February 1871 derived from "Settlement of the Estate of W. E. Hardy," Newberry County Probate Court Records, with a copy in the Hardy Plantation Archives.

P. 322: Hardy quotation from undated fragment, c. 1867, in the Hardy Plantation Archives.

CHAPTER 13: NEW GIANTS IN THE LAND

Pp. 324–26: William Dixon Hardy's impressions of coming home are recorded in an undated manuscript fragment. The feelings expressed here paralleled Hardy's recollection to John Renwick around 1930 and were passed on to the author in interviews with Renwick in August 1990.

P. 328: The acreage of Frances Sims Hardy is listed in her will and the settlement of her estate, Newberry County Probate Court Records.

P. 329: *Clement Evans:* In his *Confederate Military History,* vol. 5, p. 551.

P. 330: *Knights of the White Camellia:* As recollected by William Dixon Hardy to John Renwick and in turn to the author in interviews with Renwick in August 1990. Other details of the era come from these same sources. Complete texts of these interviews are in the Hardy Plantation Archives.

P. 333: For Hardy's grange membership, see Renwick papers, South Caroliniana Library, University of South Carolina. A certificate for J. R. Renwick lists Hardy as "Master" of the Maybinton Grange.

Pp. 333–35: The figures for 1879 come from the U.S. census for Newberry County, 1880.

P. 334: Quotation from Hardy as told to John Renwick and in turn to the author in an interview of August 1990.

P. 335: *local grange:* On 26–27 July 1881 Hardy was a delegate from New-berry County to the state grange convention in Greenville, S.C. See *Proceedings of the Joint Summer Meeting* (Charleston, S.C., 1881), p. 5.

Pp. 335–36: *Charleston News and Courier:* This letter is in manuscript in Hardy's hand, in Perkins Library, Duke University.

P. 336: *private teacher:* Remembered by John Frost Hardy Sr. (1886–1963) in his tribute to his sister Helen Hardy Henderson (1880–1958) in a typescript dated 14 March 1958. In the possession of Haywood Henderson, with a copy in the Hardy Plantation Archives. Details of the whereabouts of Captain Dick's family from 1896 to 1910 come from this typescript. John Hardy wrote this tribute three days after Helen's death.

P. 338: *Prosperity:* Hardy is listed as a life member (from Prosperity, S.C.) of the State Agricultural and Mechanical Society in 1890. See *Transactions of the State Agricultural and Mechanical Society* (Charleston, S.C., 1890), p. 162.

P. 339: Letter of Cole Blease in Perkins Library, Duke University.

Pp. 340–41: J. W. Hardy's and Laura Hardy's letters are in Perkins Library, Duke University.

Pp. 342–43: Frances Douglass letter is in the possession of George Douglass, with a copy in the Hardy Plantation Archives.

Pp. 343–46: The details of the lives, careers, and accomplishments of the children and grandchildren of William Dixon Hardy come from a scrapbook of newspaper clippings kept by Mrs. John Frost Hardy from about 1920 to 1975 (in possession of her grandson William Hardy Jr.) and from scrapbook clippings in the possession of Mrs. Beverley Fulmer Kennedy. These sources also include numerous obituaries of the family from roughly 1910 to 1973, among them G. E. Hardy, Elmira Moore, John D. Frost, William Dixon Hardy, J. Frost Walker, Helen Hardy Henderson, Frank Hardy, Paul Hardy, John Frost Hardy Sr., N. H. Hardy, and N. G. Walker.

P. 344: *"fable of Antaeus":* From W. G. Simms, *Letters* (Columbia, S.C., 1952–56), vol. 3, p. 254.

P. 345: *sold the Lyles tract:* Plat Book 7, p. 778, Newberry County Court-house.

Chapter 14: Captain Dick

P. 347: One of those who remembered Captain Dick was John Renwick in interviews with the author, 1990–1991. Complete texts of these interviews are in the Hardy Plantation Archives.

P. 348: *obituary:* Written by "One who knew him 61 years." Undated clipping in scrapbook kept by Mrs. John Frost Hardy Sr., in the possession of William Hardy Jr.

P. 348: Henderson interview with the author, 6 August 1989, in the Hardy Plantation Archives.

P. 349: Sarah Stokes interview with the author, 12 September 1989, in the Hardy Plantation Archives.

P. 349: Teague interview with the author, 13 December 1992, in the Hardy Plantation Archives.

P. 349: Renwick interviews with the author, 1990–1992, in the Hardy Plantation Archives.

P. 350: Hardy's definition of success as remembered by John Renwick and told to the author.

P. 351: *wise Carolina author:* Archibald Rutledge, *My Colonel and His Lady* (Indianapolis, 1937), pp. 50–53.

P. 351: Captain Dick's words as recollected by John Renwick to the author in an interview in August 1990. Interview in the Hardy Plantation Archives.

P. 352: *Charlie Giles:* Quoted in George Rawick, *The American Slave* (Westport, Conn., 1971), vol. 2, pt. 2, p. 116.

P. 352: *Bob Young:* Quoted in Rawick, *The American Slave,* vol. 3, pt. 4, pp. 274–75.

P. 352: *Cordelia Jackson:* Quoted in Rawick, *The American Slave,* vol. 3, pt. 3, p. 6.

P. 352: Julia Peterkin, quoting Maum Lou in "Maum Lou" (1925), in *Collected Stories of Julia Peterkin,* ed. Frank Durham (Columbia, S.C., 1970), p. 278.

Pp. 352–53: Information on the tenants comes from interviews with John Tucker (5 September 1991), John Renwick (9 August 1990), Haywood Henderson (10 September 1990), William Hardy Sr. (5 August 1991), John Hardy III (14 June 1992), and Margaret Thomas King and Ellen Boyd (14 January 1991).

P. 353: 1932 interview with William Dixon Hardy by Eva Justice. Copy in the Hardy Plantation Archives.

Pp. 353–54: Renwick interview with the author, 9 August 1990, in the Hardy Plantation Archives.

P. 355: There are several undated obituaries from Columbia, Spartanburg, and Newberry newspapers in Mrs. John Hardy's scrapbook.

Chapter 15: Holding On in a World We Did Not Make

P. 356: Epigraph is from Archibald Rutledge, *My Colonel and His Lady* (Indianapolis, 1937), p. 47.

P. 356: *Carolina adage:* from W. G. Simms, *The Social Principle* (Tuscaloosa, Ala., 1843), p. 42.

P. 357: Leland Summer, *Newberry County, S.C.* (Newberry, S.C., 1950).

P. 358: These farm statistics are derived from Walter B. Edgar's *South Carolina in the Modern Age* (Columbia, S.C., 1992).

P. 361: Former slave Granny Cain is quoted in George Rawick, *The American Slave* (Westport, Conn., 1971), vol. 2, pt. 1, p. 168.

P. 362: *Frances Andrews:* As quoted in Rawick, vol. 2, pt. 1, p. 18.

P. 363: *Southern loss in '65:* William Faulkner perhaps said it best in 1946: "the machine which defeated his [the Northerner's] enemy was a Frankenstein which, once the Southern armies were consumed, turned on him and enslaved him and, removing him from a middle class fixed upon the land, translated him into a baronage based upon a slavery . . . of machines." Malcolm Cowley, *The Faulkner-Cowley File* (New York, 1966), p. 80.

P. 364: *Teague recalls:* Interview with Bertice Teague, 13 December 1992, in the Hardy Plantation Archives. Frank's comments about guests and chairs have now become a part of the area's fund of oral history. This story was again recounted to me in December 1996 by Sarah Bess McCollum Smith of Carlisle.

P. 364: Helen's husband Hugh operated a small store in Blair in Fairfield County, S.C., some thirteen miles from the Hardy homeplace.

P. 364: Reminiscences of Paul H. Hardy are from Haywood Henderson and John Frost Hardy III in interviews with the author, 6 August 1990 and 14 June 1992. Copies are in the Hardy Plantation Archives.

P. 365: *corn liquor . . . survival:* Joseph Simpson interview, 28 July 1990; John Renwick interview, 28 December 1990; and John Hardy III interview, 14 June 1992; all in the Hardy Plantation Archives.

P. 366: *"traveler's room":* Simpson interview, 28 July 1990. On this wall there is a pencil drawing of a still worm.

CHAPTER 16: HIGH TIMES WITH THE HIGH SHERIFF

P. 367: Epigraph is from Alice Sims in Caldwell Sims, *Voices from the Past* (Union, S.C., 1979), p. 43.

P. 367: From the author's interviews with Margaret Thomas King (14 January 1991) and Haywood Henderson (6 August 1989). Information on the raids comes from my interviews with John Renwick (9 August 1990). The Mott anecdote comes from the Renwick interview. My interview with Mrs. Stokes took place 12 September 1989. The Teague interview occurred on 13 December 1992. Copies of all interviews are in the Hardy Plantation Archives. Information on John and Alice Hardy comes from my interview with their grandson John Hardy III (14 June 1992) and one with Margaret Thomas King and Ellen Boyd (14 January 1991). Copies in the Hardy Plantation Archives.

P. 372: *These bales:* From records of the estate settlement, Newberry Probate Court.

P. 373: *grandson's wife:* Sally Strom Hardy (Mrs. John Hardy III), in an interview with the author, 14 June 1992. Copy in the Hardy Plantation Archives.

P. 374: Juanita Hitt, *Newton Thomas Hogg* (Newberry, S.C., 1970), p. 59.

CHAPTER 17: THE RUINED LAND

P. 000: *Alice. . . "hurt":* In the words of her grandson, John Hardy III, in an interview with the author, 14 June 1992. Copy in the Hardy Plantation Archives.

CHAPTER 18: INTERLUDE: GHOSTS

P. 381: The first written record of this folk tale that I have located is in *South Carolina Folk Tales,* compiled by the WPA and published at Columbia, S.C., in 1941. Its recorder was Caldwell Sims of Union County. The version in William Rice Feaster, *A History of Union County* (Greenville, S.C., 1977) follows this Sims telling very closely. Here it is said to have been "adapted from notes" made by J. Daniel Epps of The Oaks, Goshen Hill, and to be "the traditional ghost story told by all descendants of Goshen Hill families." Epps was the grandson of the Dr. George Douglass who appears in the story, and lived at The Oaks. A typescript account (undated) by Annie Cofield Jeter, in the possession of the author, is very similar. The most widely circulated accounts appear in Nancy Roberts's two volumes, *South Carolina Ghosts* (Columbia, S.C., 1983), pp. 93–97; and *Ghosts of the Carolinas* (Charlotte, N.C., 1962), pp. 18–22. The first Roberts account is very close to the Sims version. In a recent telling of the story to me in July 1989, a local black workman on the restoration of the Hardy house added several new twists to the tale. His grandfather lived at Maybinton in the early century and recalled from the lore of the area circulated during his childhood that the dog smiled and his glowing red eyes spun like pin-wheels.

CHAPTER 19: CHOICES: A RARE AND BEARING VINE

P. 392: *Southern poet:* Donald Davidson, in "Meditation on Literary Fame."

P. 393: The 1937 quotation is from Archibald Rutledge, *My Colonel and His Lady* (Indianapolis, 1937), p. 47.

Pp. 393–94: Quotation on steam power is from W. G. Simms, *The Social Principle* (Tuscaloosa, Ala., 1843), p. 53, that on iron is from his "The Ages of Gold and Iron," *Ladies' Companion* (May 1841), p. 14. William Faulkner's quotation comes from Malcolm Cowley, *The Faulkner-Cowley File* (New York, 1966), p. 80.

INDEX